THE
JERUSALEM
FILES

This edition first published in the UK and USA in 2024 by
Watkins, an imprint of Watkins Media Limited
Unit 11, Shepperton House,
89-93 Shepperton Road,
London,
N1 3DF

enquiries@watkinspublishing.com

2 3 4 5 6 7 8 9 10

Designed and Typeset by JCS Publishing Ltd

Printed and bound in the UK by TJ Books Ltd

ISBN: 978-1-78678-836-8 (Paperback)
ISBN: 978-1-78678-838-2 (eBook)

www.watkinspublishing.com

THE
JERUSALEM
FILES

The Secret Journey of the Menorah to Oak Island

CORJAN MOL & CHRISTOPHER MORFORD

WATKINS
1893

CONTENTS

CONTENTS

FOREWORD

History's greatest puzzles are often solved through cooperation and collaboration. The Oak Island puzzle has become more interesting as the complexity of the story has increased.

Corjan and Chris started their journey separately, but it was soon apparent that their theories, personalities, and research styles were complementary. At that point, I suggested they should combine their efforts to have greater success. They have taken on difficult subject matter and approached it from a variety of perspectives, stripping it down to the micro and then stepping back to look at the macro. That is the approach they have also taken in writing this thought-provoking book.

Corjan and Chris, my heartfelt gratitude for your investment of time and effort in helping to unravel Oak Island's wonderful, almost magical, story. I appreciate so much who you both are as people and, more importantly, your friendship.

I will forever "treasure" you both for being a part of this ongoing search for answers.

Congratulations on the book. It is indeed a journey worth taking.

Rick Lagina

ABOUT THE AUTHORS

Corjan Mol is an entrepreneur and recording artist from the Netherlands with more than a casual interest in history. He had a classical education, learning Greek and Latin, but is also fluent in Dutch, English, and French.

Corjan studied in the Netherlands and France and has spent his professional career working in Europe, Asia, and North America. Along with his business partners, he turned their company into a multi-million-dollar operation, with offices all over Europe.

In his spare time, Corjan amassed some 20 years' experience researching another historical mystery set in Europe. Like Oak Island, the mystery of Rennes-le-Château has captivated audiences for a long time. If you have not encountered this tale before, it's the story of a young 19th-century parish priest called Bérenger Saunière, who found himself appointed to a dilapidated church in the foothills of the French Pyrenees. During the renovations of this church, Saunière discovered a set of ancient documents, and from that moment on his lifestyle changed spectacularly. The poor, humble, rural existence he had known previously was gone forever and Saunière suddenly became wealthy. It is this swift, and dramatic, unexplained change of fortune that is at the heart of the Rennes-le-Château mystery. What followed was a century of theories, some more conspiratorial than others, and the mystery even inspired Dan Brown's book *The Da Vinci Code* (Corgi, 2009), one of the bestselling novels of all time at 80 million copies.

In a sealed crypt under the church in Rennes-le-Château, the priest is alleged to have discovered proof that Jesus had been married to Mary Magdalene. As if this were not heretical enough, the couple were alleged to have had children. This secret knowledge was whispered about in the halls of the most powerful and embedded even at the heart of the Merovingian dynasty, the early royal house of France. Further theories describe how Saunière found valuables stashed beneath the church at Rennes-le-Château by the local nobility and clergy as they fled the guillotines during the French Revolution.

Corjan spent years on the hunt for the truth, taking annual trips to the area around Rennes-le-Château with his father and traveling in person to every point of interest involved in the tangled web of the enigma. It turned out that the mysteries of Rennes-le-Château and Oak Island had much in common. In both cases the evidence was scarce, almost non-existent at some points, and the original stories were hazy and inconsistent to say the least. The final thing that these complex riddles also appeared to have in common was Nicolas Poussin, a French painter.

Christopher Morford started out as a musician and recording engineer during the heyday of industrial rock in Chicago after attending Berklee College of Music in Boston. He later settled in New Orleans, until the devastating Hurricane Katrina struck the crescent city. Chris then traveled to China and married the love of his life, Yan. The couple now live in South Carolina with their daughter Mia, where they own and operate a restaurant on Hilton Head Island. An active Freemason for more than 20 years, Chris is a member of several Masonic bodies, including the Scottish Rite, the York Rite, the Cryptic Masons, the Knights Templar, and the Royal Arch Masons. A member of the Order of the Élus Coëns, Mensa, and Intertel, Chris' in-depth esoteric interests led him to join the Gnostic Church, in which he has been ordained as a bishop. Soft-spoken and erudite, Chris is driven by a burning desire to discover the truth, especially truths hidden deep in history.

ACKNOWLEDGMENTS

A special thank you to Rick Lagina, who invited us to Oak Island, put us in a room together, and listened to our stories for hours on end; to everybody in the Oak Island team, who have helped, motivated, supported, and inspired us along the way; to everybody at Prometheus Entertainment and the Oak Island production crew, for their guidance and support; to those at A+E Networks and the History Channel, for granting us clearance, and for their guidance and support; to Erin King, who didn't get tired of us and gave us pixel-perfect GIS graphics; to Chris Donah, who introduced us to the heavens and now watches over them for us; to Mark Foster, who helped us with his super-smooth text-editing skills; to Martin Faulks, who introduced us to the world of publishing; and to Fiona Robertson, and all the people at Watkins, who believed in our manuscript. Thank you all for helping to make our dream come true.

Thank you, Monique, for putting up with me and all my hobbies gone way out of hand. Thank you Puck and Luna, for being the best kids in the world. Thanks, Mum and Dad, for dragging me into every church, castle, and museum in France when I was younger. I love you all so much. And thank you, Chris, for joining me on this ride—you are the fountain of knowledge, and I wouldn't have wanted to do this with anybody else.

Corjan

I'd like to dedicate this work to my daughter, Mia. May you never lose your sense of curiosity and adventure. Special thanks to my family for all your support—especially my wife, Stella, and my parents, Michael and Penny—for affording me the time for this research, and for all your help and encouragement. And my deepest gratitude to my esteemed colleague and friend, Corjan Mol, who made this book possible. Thank you for taking this journey with me.

Christopher

CHAPTER 1
THE LIGHT OF GOD

An end and a beginning

In a dimly lit chapel at the western edge of Paris, the answer to a great mystery unraveled.

We stood on French soil in a sacred space, in a chapel dedicated to the Virgin Mary. Our feet straddled an invisible line—an imaginary arch stretching out before and behind us, connecting distant points, both east and west, spanning half the globe.

We were at the end of a long road, yet had arrived at a new beginning. In this holy place we found ourselves surrounded by architecture adorned with fragments of now all too familiar symbolism, the significance of which we now fully understood.

After many months of searching, the meaning of these symbols fell into place, and we were finally able to decipher and reveal the story they told.

The building we were standing in was almost Romanesque in style and possessed an austere atmosphere. A spire ascended over our heads, unique and unusual in form. From the top of it rose a curious miniature tower that appeared to have been secretly whisked away from a medieval castle and erected right here. In turn, this tiny tower was topped by a five-pointed star: a pentagram, which is the ancient symbol of Jerusalem and of Mary, as she is the Star of the Sea. These two—the tower and the pentagram—were clues that we had been following for some time. They were tell-tale signs laid out before us that crossed a span of centuries, cropping up time and time again during the course of our investigation.

Whenever we caught sight of one of these clues, it would spur us on, indicating to us that the footprints we were following were not imaginary. We knew of no such spire that existed anywhere else in the world, and had not come across anything even remotely similar on any other church or chapel.

We strode purposefully to the center of the chapel, crossing a flat, oval paving stone that we knew was the capstone of a solitary pillar in the crypt below, standing guard in the middle of a circular chamber, sealed long ago. As above, so below. It seemed as though every statue whispered that phrase.

On our way, we passed a large rectangular slab that sealed the entrance to the subterranean vault. It was situated directly in front of the altar, and we had smiled at the inscription on it: *"Mementote Praepositorum Vestorum."* This was a quote from the Bible, Hebrews 13.7 (NIV): "Remember your leaders." It was a curious phrase, yet here, in this sanctified space, one of those very leaders was present.

The last rays of light from the setting sun illuminated the altar, shimmering down through the translucent body of a silent figure in the exquisite stained glass overhead. This was someone instantly recognizable to us: St Louis, King Louis IX of France, the legendary medieval sovereign who had impelled us to begin a journey that had us criss-crossing half the world, following the breadcrumbs which led, ultimately, to this precise location.

We stared at another pentagram, this time set into the marble floor directly in front of the altar—a most unusual sight in a church. This five-pointed star was flanked by the intertwined letters "A" and "M": *"auspice Maria"*—"under the protection of Mary." We had long dwelled on this phrase and discovered that, if we rearranged the letters, a new message emerged: *"Apius America."* "Apius" is the ancient name for the Greek God Asclepius, the fabled healer, so skilled at his craft that he could revive even the dead. We had spotted the staff of Asclepius, clearly shown with a serpent entwined around it, multiple times today. In France, it is depicted on the signs for pharmacies, and we also saw it emblazoned on the side of a speeding ambulance. The staff of Asclepius is often compared to Aaron's rod. Aaron was the brother of Moses and his staff transformed into a serpent. Aaron's rod is said to have been stored in that most sacred of artefacts, the Ark of the Covenant.

So much for Asclepius, but what of "America" and why tie the two together in the phrase *Apius America*? Every birth is accompanied by pain and suffering—and blood—and this is a nation that experienced all three as it came into being. America, home of the brave and land of the free. The newly forged America needed symbols to unite it, such as Benjamin Franklin's "Join, or Die" segmented serpent, and the five-pointed star. Where there are symbols, there are sacred artefacts—and sacred origins. We believed that we had traced some of those to this exact point. As in the East, so in the West.

What we had assembled was a curious mix—half treasure hunt, half case file— uncovering a tantalizing trail. From countless clues and observations we had woven a cohesive thread, visiting every location unearthed by our research, to see the evidence with our own eyes. We had also scoured every available original source and document, visiting countless libraries and archives—both in person and online.

What had become clear was that this was not some aimless quest. We were on the trail of a collection of some of the most sacred objects on the planet, artefacts that appear in some of the oldest religious writings in the world. Almost 2,000 years ago, the Romans stormed Jerusalem and rampaged through its holy places. The great treasures of King Solomon were stolen. Much later, these objects went missing, and their fate has been shrouded in mystery and intrigue ever since.

Our eyes drifted back to the Bible quote inscribed on the floor in front of the main altar. Hebrews 13.7. It is 13.7 m (45 ft) exactly when you convert the 30 cubits that is given as the length of the tabernacle—the tent housing the most sacred religious artefacts of the Jews while they traveled through the desert—in Exodus 26.16.

Wolfgang Pauli, one of the pioneers of quantum physics, was obsessed with the number 137. This number represents the fine-structure constant, a value that determines the distance between the lines of light inside an atom. Leading physicists consider the number to be at the very root of the universe.[1] In the 1950s, Pauli learned that, in Hebrew, the number 137 had another significance. A religious scholar had explained to him that, according to the ancient system of gematria, 137 is the numerical value of the Kaballah, an ancient esoteric store of Jewish mysticism that leads its practitioners to enlightenment. Pauli explored this extraordinary connection between mysticism and physics with his friend the psychoanalyst Carl Jung, leading to the publication of an article in *Nature* magazine in 1936, entitled "The mysterious number 137."[2] Pauli learned that the number 137 was found throughout the Bible—for example, it's the most common lifespan mentioned in the text. For us, the prime significance of this number is perhaps best described in the Hebrew verse 137 of the Jewish book *Tzava'at Harivash*:

Think that you look at the Shekinah which is at your side just as you look at physical objects.[3]

The Shekinah was the light of the world, the presence of God dwelling on earth, represented on earth by the seven-branched Jewish menorah, the giant golden candlestick fashioned by Moses following God's own exacting design, described in Exodus (25.31–32). The menorah illuminated the traveling tabernacle and, later, the holy of holies, deep inside King Solomon's Temple. The menorah had one central stem and stood on three legs (Talmud, Menachot 28b), supporting seven arms—137 again.

This meandering trail of clues had brought the two of us together and led us to this sacred space in France. Here in this chapel, as the mystery unfolded, we finally had the answer we had been searching for.

A meeting of minds
We first met on Oak Island—a tiny island, only half a mile by a mile (0.8 by 1.6 km) in size—that sits in Mahone Bay, Nova Scotia, which today is a territory of Canada

and one of the Maritime Provinces off its east coast. Oak Island is one of some 365 islands that are dotted throughout Mahone Bay. It has been uninhabited for most of its history, despite the area surrounding the island being home for many centuries to the Mi'kmaq people, one of the First Nations. Now a worldwide phenomenon, the small island has gripped the imagination of tens of millions of television viewers worldwide for several years.

This unassuming dot on the map would have remained insignificant and virtually unknown if a teenage boy named Daniel McGinnis hadn't climbed into his canoe to go hunting on the island in 1795. He noticed a strange indentation in the ground beneath a large oak tree that, curiously, was strung with an old ship's block and tackle. McGinnis decided to start digging with some friends—or so the story goes. Then again, perhaps it may be more accurate to say, "or so *one* of the stories goes" because there are multiple stories, as well as differing versions of each of them, and the only unifying feature of all these tales seems to be the fact that it is almost impossible to distinguish the truth from fiction.

It turned out that the early stories of Oak Island are based on hearsay, mostly relating to the eyewitness account of McGinnis' friend, Anthony Vaughn, recorded in 1849, but not published until 1862 in the *Liverpool Transcript*, a local newspaper. It was an old-school treasure story, though it didn't have a conclusive ending. More than two centuries later, it still doesn't. What eventually became "the mystery of Oak Island" has turned into an enigma that has spawned thousands of books and countless hours of television and video.

In April 2006, two brothers from Michigan, USA, bought half the island, inspired by a story from their own childhood that they had found in a *Reader's Digest* magazine in January 1965. Rick and Marty Lagina read in the now famous article how McGinnis and two of his friends had dug down into the indentation beneath that ancient tree only to find oak log platforms buried every 10 feet (3 m) down. When the hole grew too deep and dangerous to dig further, they abandoned it. It would remain that way for a further eight years, when both McGinnis and his friend John Smith settled on the island, keen to explore further.

The two friends were no doubt inspired by local legends concerning pirates who had roamed the area in the 16th and 17th centuries, such as Captain Kidd, along with tales of Spanish treasure fleets full of gold and booty, blown off course on their way from the Americas back to Spain. The *Reader's Digest* article also raised the prospect of more outlandish scenarios. One suggested that Oak Island could have been the hiding place for the jewels of Marie-Antoinette, Queen of France, beheaded along with her husband Louis XVI during the French Revolution. Another mentioned that, deep below the island, the missing original manuscripts of the works of William Shakespeare were secretly interred.[4] It's clear that Oak Island became branded as a real-life treasure island very early on and an absence of reliable facts, combined with the island's remote location, only fueled this reputation.

Six years after the first discovery, McGinnis, together with his accomplices, Vaughn and Smith, returned to the dig, thanks to the help of a local businessman, and the group of men began a more serious excavation of what had now been dubbed the Money Pit. At a depth of 91 feet (28 m), they drove a crowbar deep into the ground and hit something solid. They were convinced that this had to be a treasure chest or similar, but they could not complete their dig before the light failed. When they came back to finish the job the next morning, they found 59 feet (18 m) of water in the Money Pit, ruining their chances of claiming their treasure. This chain of events would become very familiar to treasure hunters over the next 200 years. Digs would flood, finds would disappear, and so it went on, the infamous tales of misfortune and disaster eventually becoming folklore. Treasure hunting on Oak Island also often ended badly for those involved, hence people have spoken of there being the *curse* of Oak Island.

The three original excavators eventually died, having failed to prise the Money Pit's secrets from the soil, but that wasn't the end of the story. A long parade of explorers and investors followed, each taking a turn to try their luck. The island frustrated them all and no real treasure has ever been found. Furthermore, no two explorers could ever agree on just what "treasure" meant on Oak Island.

However, there has never been a lack of theories. While individuals and teams dug deeper, in ever wider circles, others carried out local research, trawling through old archives and putting in the hours at home, online. These researchers developed an astounding range of scenarios concerning exactly *who* could have hidden *what* on Oak Island and *when*. This collection of theories forms a cross-section of world history, ranging from the times of the Roman Empire to the American Revolution, a timespan of some 1,200 years.

Some theories are clever and seemingly plausible; others look unlikely, to say the least, at first glance. For example, it is easy to imagine a pirate looking for a place to bury treasure close to where he commandeered a ship. However, it is harder to picture a 16th-century captain risking his life, crew, and ship for months on end, crossing the Atlantic Ocean, simply to bury someone's papers on the island. There is an exception of course, and that is when the cause is worthy of the effort and risk. This is where we both enter this tale.

It was in August 2019 when the two of us were first invited to Oak Island by Rick Lagina, who has run the search on the island since 2006, together with his brother Marty, and their business partner Craig Tester. While Marty and Craig focus more on the technical challenges presented by the island, including digging, drilling and scanning the ground—along with processing whatever comes out of the ground—

Rick adds his in-depth knowledge of the island's history to the equation. For Rick, the search is as much about revealing the history of the island as it is about securing the treasure.

Not long after the brothers had purchased the most promising section of the island and set up their search operation, the Laginas were approached by people from the American TV production company Prometheus, who proposed that this real-life treasure hunt could be filmed and presented as a reality TV series. Even though the brothers were convinced that no one was ever going to watch what they considered was their tedious day-to-day work on the island, they agreed to a pilot episode and the rest is history—on the History Channel.

As we finalize the manuscript of this book to send to our publisher, the TV series *The Curse of Oak Island* has just aired its 190th episode, closing its 10th season. Despite the excavation operation growing in scale and becoming more industrial every year, remarkably little has been found to date. But this has only increased the determination of the Laginas to unearth whatever is there. What was once a private dig with a shovel and a pickaxe more than 200 years ago is now an extremely complex operation that is filmed and recorded in real time. The result is a show that is watched by millions, and many of those viewers are addicted to it, poring over and picking apart every second of television footage aired.

Rick asked us both to travel to Canada to present an Oak Island theory and we arrived in the same week. Those presentations would be our take on the whodunit. At the time, we didn't know, or know anything about, each other. We were united only by our interest in mysteries and, even then, we had very unique perspectives and approached these mysteries from different angles. However, while we possessed very different CVs and qualifications, the research each of us had done separately touched on many of the same elements, such as the works of the 17th-century French painter Nicolas Poussin. Fortuitously, Rick Lagina believed that it would be useful if we compared our work and exchanged ideas.

Shepherds

It turned out that we have a lot in common other than the researching we had been doing. Furthermore, both of us were entirely new to the world of Oak Island. Chris had recently been introduced to the mystery by Chris Donah, an amateur astronomer who had been featured on the show in an earlier season. Donah had presented a theory that involved the projection of signs of the zodiac across Oak Island, pointing to possible locations where treasure might be hidden. Becoming intrigued by the mystery, Chris Morford developed a theory of his own, involving Sir Francis Bacon, Shakespeare, and the Freemasons, then sent it off to *The Curse of Oak Island* production team for consideration. The team was excited by his findings and, within a matter of days, he was invited to the island to give a presentation. His theory also involved the works of Nicolas Poussin and how clues left in his paintings could lead one to Oak Island. Poussin's name had surfaced in a few different theories involving the works of this 17th-century French classical painter, and there was a need for someone who could shed some light on Poussin and discover exactly how the painter could be linked to Oak Island.

This was when Corjan's name cropped up and he was highlighted as a possible expert on the subject. After a Friday night video conference, Corjan was invited to the island that same evening, and he was asked if he could be in Nova Scotia the following Monday. Corjan boarded a plane that weekend and arrived armed with a theory involving Poussin and Oak Island.

We both like a challenge and neither of us could resist one as intriguing as this. As Corjan was flying to Oak Island, Chris' theory involving Poussin had been selected to be presented on the show in what is known as a war room session. In between actual digging and assessing finds, *The Curse of Oak Island* team (which numbers some ten central characters, including the Lagina brothers) sits down in this so-called war room to discuss findings and theories with guests—guests like us. That week we both recorded our war room sessions. We also spent some time together privately, discussing our theories and points of view. What this led to was a breakthrough that became a defining moment in Season 7 of the TV series: the discovery of an object known as the Arcadia stone at the edge of the eye of the Oak Island swamp.

Approaching the subject from different angles, we had both focused on one of Poussin's paintings: *The Shepherds of Arcadia*. The artist painted two different versions of this scene, so we will refer to this one as *The Shepherds of Arcadia II*, because it was the second version he painted.

The Shepherds of Arcadia II is considered one of Poussin's defining masterpieces by art critics. Poussin produced the now famous work while in Rome, shortly after 1655.[5] It shows three shepherds and a woman gathered around a stone tomb featuring the inscription "*Et in Arcadia ego.*" The painting became very popular in the years that followed, especially in the 18th century when George Keete published a poem about it, "The Monument in Arcadia," while a prominent English aristocrat living at Shugborough Hall had one of his garden monuments adorned with a sculpted bas-relief of the work by acclaimed Flemish sculptor Peter Scheemakers the Younger.

In the 1960s, French investigative journalist Gérard de Sède's book *The Accursed Treasure of Rennes-le-Château* was first published.[6] In his book, de Sède claimed that the landscape depicted by Poussin in the background behind the tomb was intended to represent three hilltops in France, one of which was Rennes-le-Château itself. This idea triggered a flurry of books and documentaries. Nicolas Poussin, a man who hated pomp and ceremony, had posthumously claimed his place in the world of mystery theories and would never leave it again.

In 1991, British author and investigative journalist Henry Lincoln made some astounding claims in his book *The Holy Place*,[7] but all were substantiated. Lincoln discovered that the church in which Father Saunière had made his discoveries was one point of a giant five-pointed star that could be traced on a map of southern France. This pentagram was a little over 4 miles (7 km) wide and perfectly proportioned. Two of the other points of the pentagram were castles that had once belonged to the Knights Templar: Blanchefort and Bézu. Lincoln argued that this enormous pentagram, hidden in the landscape, was known about long before the structures that now occupied its extremities were built, meaning that the architects of the medieval buildings that followed had taken maximum advantage of the perceived protective nature of the pentagonal shape by constructing their fortresses at these exact locations. This sacred knowledge would have made Rennes-le-Château the logical place to hide valuable objects and relics, thereby adding a new layer to a much older mystery.

While researching his book, Lincoln employed the help of Professor Christopher Cornford. Although he came from a family of well-respected scientists and authors— he was a great-grandson of Charles Darwin—it was for his knowledge of art that Lincoln turned to him. He asked Cornford, who taught at the Royal College of Art in London at the time, to investigate Poussin's *The Shepherds of Arcadia II* from both an artistic and a technical point of view, and much of the investigation was based on X-ray images of the painting.

Cornford noted that Poussin had painted the staff each shepherd is holding before he began depicting the tomb itself, implying that there was an underlying geometric structure to the composition. Intrigued, the professor further analysed the painting and concluded that its composition was based on an underlying pentagram, sections of which, oddly, lay outside the frame of the painting. Lincoln therefore concluded that this hidden pentagram was the link between Poussin's painting and the Rennes-le-Château area.

When we arrived at Oak Island, we were both aware of this information and each of us had identified different connections between Poussin and the island. Chris had recognized a sickle-shaped inlet in Mahone Bay, where the island is to be found, which matches the shape of a curious shadow in *The Shepherds of Arcadia II*, and found that the poses of Poussin's shepherds were based on signs of the zodiac, constellations that could be used as a treasure map for the island.

Corjan had spotted an anagram for the inscription on the tomb, "*Et in Arcadia ego.*" He suggested that the phrase could be reshuffled to find the hidden sentence, "*gite neo Arcadia*," which is Italian for "take a trip to new Arcadia." When Poussin was painting the work in Rome, "Arcadia" was the name used at that time for what is now Nova Scotia.

Additionally, Corjan pointed out that while Poussin was completing *The Shepherds of Arcadia I*, he had also worked on a pendant, a sister painting that was intended to hang alongside *The Shepherds of Arcadia*, for the patron who commissioned both works. Poussin cleverly connected these two paintings by including a bearded River God on each of them. The sister painting was *Midas Washing at the Source of the Pactolus*, which depicts the mythological King Midas washing off the results of the curse that meant everything he touched turned into gold. At the end of the tale, when the King has finally washed off all the gold, the waterway becomes a gold river. It is worth noting that Oak Island lies at the mouth of the Gold River in Nova Scotia, resulting in a connection that is too obvious to miss. Combining the two paintings results in Arcadia (Nova Scotia) + Gold River, bringing anyone following these clues to within touching distance of the island.

Working together on the ground at the Oak Island research center, we discovered that Poussin had used the face of the female model in *The Shepherds of Arcadia II* before. In a self-portrait, painted five years earlier in 1650, he depicted the same woman. However, instead of the scarf that can be seen on her head in the painting of the shepherds, in the self-portrait she wears a diadem-like headdress, featuring an eye at its center. Traditionally, the third eye, or bindu point, is the eye that can see things beyond ordinary perception. We felt that this was compelling symbolism for a painter who took up as his personal motto "Keeper of secrets" ("*Tenet confidentiam*" in Latin). On closer inspection, we noticed that in *The Shepherds of Arcadia II*, the position where this third eye would be coincides exactly with the center of the pentagram discovered by Professor Cornford. It was the first of many secrets we discovered concealed in this enigmatic painting.

Crossroads

On Oak Island, there is a cross-shaped stone formation called Nolan's Cross, named after its discoverer, Fred Nolan, a surveyor by profession who spent much of his later life living on and exploring Oak Island until his death in 2016. Measuring 120 yards wide by 288 yards long (110 by 264 m), the cross consists of five huge, cone-shaped megalithic stones, with two forming the short arms of the cross, while the other three form the longer axis. In 1981, an excavation took place at the exact junction of the two short arms of the cross, unearthing what was dubbed the Head Stone because it appeared to have been sculpted to depict a face. This discovery caused quite a stir, inspiring thoughts of the head of Jesus resting in a similar spot at the center of the cross during his crucifixion. As with any find on the island, Nolan's Cross is disputed by some, who claim that the placement of the stones is arbitrary, purely a coincidence, a natural formation rather than deliberate.

However, having walked around the island many times and assessed the unique size and shape of each stone, coupled with their precise layout and alignment, we have no doubt that the cross is a deliberate feature. We also believe that Fred Nolan, who worked as a surveyor in Nova Scotia his whole life, would have been more than capable of distinguishing something made from a natural formation. Our conclusion has since been backed up by further analysis and a recent study of material taken from beneath the stones appears to confirm that their layout is indeed made, not naturally occurring.

Nolan's Cross became highly significant to us when we realized that you only need four stones to form the shape of a cross, but it has five. We found that the fifth stone could very well have been intended to illustrate how to superimpose a pentagram on top of the cross.

To help us with this thought, we called on Steven Guptill, one of the central *The Curse of Oak Island* team members who works full time on the island as a surveyor, documenting every find and recording the exact locations using extremely precise GPS equipment. Each find is subsequently recorded in a detailed 3D CAD model, which Guptill protects as though these virtual constructions were the crown jewels.

Once we had superimposed a pentagram star over Nolan's Cross on a surveyed map of Oak Island, with Guptill's help, we found that the center of this pentagram lay precisely on the edge of a pool of water, which is the only place on the island never to dry up, right at the center of a large, triangular-shaped swamp. On the TV show, this pool is called the Eye of the Swamp. Superimposing the pentagram over Nolan's Cross positions the head of Poussin's woman from *The Shepherds of Arcadia II* precisely on this pool.

Our discoveries, both in relation to the painting and projections on to the map, caused a commotion on the island and an emergency war room session was called, in which we were asked to present our findings. The entire cast attended, covered in mud and dirt as they had all been called in directly from their active digs without any time to clean up. There are no airs and graces on Oak Island.

We must have made a serious impression on the team members because, not long after, they excavated the site we had indicated at the Eye of the Swamp. They found a huge, buried stone—one of equivalent size to those used in Nolan's Cross, if a little rounder in shape. We were very pleased to learn that it was then christened—and is still known as—the *Arcadia Stone*.

Before we had to leave the island to fly home, Rick Lagina conveyed the thanks of the whole team and urged us to keep collaborating, having witnessed at first hand—and live on TV—what could happen if we combined forces and brought our different backgrounds to bear on such puzzles.

We have been an inseparable team ever since.

We returned to our homes in the Netherlands and South Carolina, determined to stay in touch, and convinced that we had only scratched the surface of something ultimately much grander in scale. There was every indication that what had happened on Oak Island was significant, and the Nolan's Cross find alone was reason enough for us to continue our investigations. On top of that, there was also the Money Pit, from which many artefacts have been recovered over the years. It made no sense for these objects—such as, to take only one example, fragments of human bone identified as originating from the Middle East—to have been found there, a very long way down beneath the surface.

The two of us had forged more than a bond on Oak Island; we had both experienced an epiphany. After many hours of discussion and comparing notes, we knew that we were searching for nothing less than the treasures of King Solomon—those ancient objects that had vanished long ago from Jerusalem and disappeared from the annals of history, entering into myth and legend. Chief among those treasures was the menorah, a sacred, solid gold object that had adorned the tabernacle of the Jewish people in the desert. The book of Exodus reveals how the design of this object was relayed to Moses directly by God, on top of a mountain. The menorah that resulted was a seven-branched lampstand, designed to illuminate the sacred sanctuary, the tabernacle (also known as the tent of the congregation or tent of meeting), which also held the Ark of the Covenant. Once the Jews had settled in Jerusalem, the menorah illuminated the entrance to the holy of holies—the most sacred room in Solomon's Temple. The menorah's iconic design would later become a symbol for the whole of Judaism, one that is recognized worldwide. It has also become synonymous with Israel, even to those who know nothing about its history.

The lost menorah

Thinking about our encounter on Oak Island, we suspected that Nicolas Poussin had himself been merely a conduit, an artist chosen to record clues that pointed to an ancient secret, one only ever whispered about. Something so significant and momentous that it had to remain hidden. At the time, we had no idea exactly what that secret was. We had experimented with "Arcadia," the old name for Nova Scotia and the theme of Poussin's painting. Were we meant to interpret it as two words: "*arca dia*," which is "*divine ark*" in Latin? Were we perhaps looking for the Ark of the Covenant described in the Bible and the rest of the treasures from the Temple, including the menorah?

What followed was a long journey that we will share in its entirety in this book. The keystone of our research was deciphering an inscription found on an inconspicuous and almost forgotten memorial to a hardly ever mentioned British prime minister. To our astonishment, the memorial features yet another 3D sculpted copy of Nicolas Poussin's *The Shepherds of Arcadia II*, and around this relief is inscribed a line from a poem by Latin poet Horace. The phrase reads, "*Desiderio nec pudor aut modus*," which means, "Grief has no shame nor limit," but, after a breakthrough, we established that the phrase is an anagram. It can be read as, *"Vos deduco id menora perditus,"* or "I lead you to the lost menorah."

This was the point when we knew that the long road we had taken—which culminated in us standing in front of this revealing inscription—had not been in vain.

But, to unravel this story for you and document the full significance of our journey—from our first meeting on Oak Island, our subsequent travails across the Middle East and Europe, right through to our final destination, the Chapel of the Virgin Mary in France—we first need to go back to this tale's ancient beginnings and reveal the secrets of the treasure of Jerusalem. Because that is where this story truly begins.

CHAPTER 2
THE ORIGINS OF THE MENORAH

The tent of the congregation

King Solomon ruled sometime between 970 and 931 BC and is one of the most well-known of the Jewish rulers—the great king of kings, famed for his exceptional wisdom and fabulous wealth. He was one of the kings, with David, of the United Monarchy, which comprised the nations of both Judah and Israel. "King Solomon's treasure" is a generic term for the collection of some of the most precious religious artefacts ever assembled in one place, which was in King Solomon's Temple, the first Temple, on Temple Mount in Jerusalem. It was the sacred, holy sanctuary of the Jews. However, the individual objects themselves were created many years before Solomon's reign, in the days of Moses, just after the emancipation of the Israelites from Egypt.

Many of the implements had a very specific nature and purpose, the design of which was outlined to Moses by God himself. Included among these, and possibly the most famous, thanks to a certain Hollywood feature film, was the Ark of the Covenant—said to have contained the tablets of the Law, the stone slabs engraved with the Ten Commandments that sealed God's covenant with the Israelites. It was atop the Ark, from the mercy seat, that God would speak directly through his oracle to the high priest.

Another item described in great detail by God, and constructed to his exacting standards, was the table of showbread. On it, a dozen loaves in two piles were set as offerings to God.

The final object God described to Moses was the menorah (Exodus 25.31–40, NRSV):

> You shall make a lampstand of pure gold. The base and the shaft of the
> lampstand shall be made of hammered work; its cups, its calyxes, and its
> petals shall be of one piece with it; and there shall be six branches going out
> of its sides, three branches of the lampstand out of one side of it and three
> branches of the lampstand out of the other side of it; three cups shaped

like almond blossoms, each with calyx and petals, on one branch, and three cups shaped like almond blossoms, each with calyx and petals, on the other branch—so for the six branches going out of the lampstand. On the lampstand itself there shall be four cups shaped like almond blossoms, each with its calyxes and petals. There shall be a calyx of one piece with it under the first pair of branches, a calyx of one piece with it under the next pair of branches, and a calyx of one piece with it under the last pair of branches—so for the six branches that go out of the lampstand. Their calyxes and their branches shall be of one piece with it, the whole of it one hammered piece of pure gold. You shall make the seven lamps for it; and the lamps shall be set up so as to give light on the space in front of it. Its snuffers and trays shall be of pure gold. It, and all these utensils, shall be made from a talent of pure gold. And see that you make them according to the pattern for them, which is being shown you on the mountain.

The 1st-century Romano-Jewish historian Flavius Josephus left us an account of the final form of the menorah, once it had been crafted. His description refers to a time when the lampstand had come to rest in the Temple in Jerusalem:

Affixed to a pedestal was a central shaft, from which there extended slender branches, arranged trident fashion, a wrought lamp being attached to the extremity of each branch; of these there were seven, indicating the honour paid to that number among the Jews.[1]

Facing the table, near the south wall, stood a candelabrum of cast gold, hollow. It was made up of globules (knobs) and lilies, along with pomegranates and little bowls, numbering seventy in all; of these it was composed from its single base right up to the top, having been made to consist of as many portions as are assigned to the planes with the sun. It terminated in seven branches regularly disposed in a row. Each branch bore one lamp, recalling the number of the planets; the seven lamps faced south-east, the candelabrum being cross-wise.[2]

When God gave instructions to Moses for the construction of the menorah and other items, there was no fixed temple to set them up in, and no plans to build one. Instead, God was to be worshiped in a portable structure known as the tabernacle: "And let them make me a sanctuary; that I may dwell among them" (Exodus 25.8–10, KJV). This sanctuary, also known as the tent of the congregation or tent of meeting, was to hold all the implements that God had so carefully outlined in intricate detail. Not only the Ark, the table of the showbread, and the menorah but also all their accompanying accoutrements—snuff dishes, tongs, pitchers, bowls—a whole array of objects, all designed to facilitate the worship of God in this sanctuary.

The tabernacle was the dwelling place of the Shekinah, a conduit to Yahweh during the travails of the Israelites, and they carried it throughout the Exodus and the years in the wilderness, until they had conquered and settled in Canaan. Although it was designed as a temporary structure, the tabernacle was still a substantial construction, comprising 48 wooden boards 16 feet (5 m) high, each overlaid with gold, along with four woven layers of curtains and coverings. The tabernacle would remain home to both the seat of God and the menorah for 440 years, long after the Israelites had settled in Canaan, and it moved from town to town as the power centers of the Israelites shifted.

The use of a lampstand or candelabrum as a cult implement goes back millennia and its role as a ritual object used in temples is as old as the concept of worshiping in a sacred space. There is almost always a conflation of light with sacred knowledge, and so the lampstand takes on a very special role in each cult or religion. Furthermore, the light in this case was generated by fire, which in itself was often seen as a metaphor for life in religious and spiritual circles. Therefore, finding such an object at the heart of Jewish religious practice is not surprising.

We must clarify here that while modern replicas of the menorah, such as those used in the home for the Jewish holiday of Hanukkah, feature candles, the original menorah first mentioned in Exodus was never designed to hold candles. This is a misconception that is often repeated throughout history by various commentators, so it is worth noting that the menorah was not a candelabrum but, rather, it held seven gold cups that would have been filled with oil and lit by means of a wick.

The instructions given in Exodus are very detailed and, for the menorah, it specified that it was to be made from "pure gold." There was a distinction between pure gold and ordinary gold, and the most sacred Temple implements were to be made from unadulterated, pure gold. The amount is also given—a talent of gold would be required. In today's terms, that is thought to be around 66 pounds (30 kg)—a substantial amount, especially as absolutely pure gold, not a diluted alloy, was to be used. However, as we will discover, the menorah was more precious than its weight in gold alone.

The final size of the completed menorah is not mentioned in the Bible, but it is detailed in the Talmud (Menachot 28b):

The height of the Candelabrum was eighteen handbreadths. The base and the flower that was upon the base were a height of three handbreadths; and two handbreadths above that were bare; and there was above that one handbreadth, which had a goblet, knob, and flower on it. And two handbreadths above that were bare, and there was above that one handbreadth that had a knob.

This means that the menorah was a considerable height, around 5 feet (1.6 m), making it around the same height as one of the Temple priests. It was also said to be more than 3 feet (1 m) across.

It is clear from these details that the menorah was a large, impressive object, designed to induce awe and wonder. Interestingly, it was only during the latter stages of our research that we realized exactly how big the treasures of the Temple were. If you take a stroll today around the old Jewish quarter in Jerusalem, you will bump into a modern life-size copy of the menorah, crafted by the Temple Institute for use on the day the new Temple of Jerusalem was built. Only when confronted by such a replica does it become clear that it would be no mean feat to transport or hide a treasure of this size. It also highlights how great a prize the menorah would have been for a foreign conqueror.

It is a similar story with the Ark of the Covenant, which the Bible says measured 2.5 cubits in length, 1.5 in breadth and 1.5 in height, which translates as 51½ x 31 x 31 inches (131 x 79 x 79 cm), almost the size of an office desk. While the menorah was hollow and weighed some 66 pounds (30 kg), the Ark weighed in at more than 661 pounds (300 kg). This, too, would have presented serious challenges to anyone wishing to carry it and the other treasures away or hide them from prying eyes.

Much has been made of the language used in the description of the menorah. The design of the lampstand clearly resembles a tree or shrub and words used to describe it in Exodus, such as "branches," "petals," and "calyx," only highlight this symbolism further.

There is another purpose of the lampstand in religious ritual. Shubert Spero, describes this purpose in the following terms:

> The most dramatic emphasis of the *Menorah*, however, lies in what it suggests is the fruit of the Jewish tree of life—light, the universal symbol of knowledge. "For the commandment is a lamp and the teaching is a light and the way of life, are instruction and reproof."[3]

The very nature of the menorah mirrors life and, as such, it is a metaphor for the light found in the pages of the Torah. This sacred knowledge will not illuminate by itself, it requires diligent work—dedicated study and teaching, as well as dissemination—if the light is not to be extinguished.

The construction and placement of the menorah

It is said in Exodus (31.1–6) that an individual known as Bezalel (whose very name means "in the shadow of God, son of light" and whose great-grandmother was Miriam, the prophetess and sister of Moses) was chosen by God specifically to construct the tabernacle, but the task of creating the menorah was first attempted by Moses himself.

We had come across a curious tale relayed in the Midrash Tanhuma in which Moses speaks to God and tells the Lord that he has forgotten the design of the menorah. God shows him again and reminds him that it is to be made of beaten gold. Moses still cannot grasp the design, so God says, "See it and make it." Moses is still struggling, whereupon God says, "Go to Bezalel and he will make it." This is what transpires and Bezalel is instantly inspired to throw the whole talent of gold into the fire and, miraculously, the menorah is suddenly in front of him, fully formed. This adds a curious layer to the mystery because all the other holy implements were shaped by the hand of Bezalel, even the Ark of the Covenant, but not the menorah, which, instead, appeared almost by magic.

When all the implements had been fashioned and were complete, Moses finally set the menorah in the tabernacle (Exodus 40.24–25, NABRE):

He placed the menorah in the tent of meeting, opposite the table, on the
south side of the tabernacle, and set up the lamps before the LORD.

This tent was to be the home of the menorah for centuries to come, even when the tabernacle itself was moved from place to place. Given the dimensions of all the individual elements, moving the hallowed collection must have been quite a spectacle.

Finally, after many years illuminating the tabernacle, the menorah was brought to Jerusalem by King Solomon, along with all the other holy implements, sometime around the year 950 BC. They were installed in the newly built Temple of Solomon, what we today call the first Temple, a structure that recreated the sanctuary of the tabernacle, only on a much grander scale. This was an elaborate, immovable, stone temple—a vast undertaking with, it is said, more than 19 tons (20 metric tons) of gold used for the holy of holies alone. The menorah was at the heart of this new exclusive place of pilgrimage for devout Jews. It was God's own light, and the only illumination allowed in the one place blessed by his presence.

CHAPTER 3
THE SYMBOLISM OF THE MENORAH

In the beginning God created the heaven and the earth. And the earth was without form, and void; and darkness was upon the face of the deep. And the Spirit of God moved upon the face of the waters. And God said, Let there be light: and there was light.

(Genesis 1.1–3, KJV)

The holy of holies in the tabernacle and later in the Temple of Solomon can be viewed symbolically as a microcosm of all creation, and the lamps of the menorah as representing the light brought forth to illuminate the deep. In Genesis we read that, in the beginning, there were two entities present. There was God and there was the Spirit of God, also called the Holy Spirit. The Holy Spirit is a divine mystery, yet in Proverbs (chapters 8 and 9), we get a glimpse into who she is. At the dawn of creation (Proverbs 8.27–30, KJV):

> When he prepared the heavens, I was there: when he set a compass upon the face of the deep:
> When he established the clouds above: when he strengthened the fountains of the deep:
> When he gave to the sea his decree, that the waters should not pass his commandment: when he appointed the foundations of the earth:
> Then I was by him, as one brought up with him: and I was daily his delight, rejoicing always before him

The Holy Spirit identifies herself as Wisdom personified, sometimes called Holy Wisdom or Hagia Sophia (Proverbs 8.1–5; 9.1, KJV):

Doth not wisdom cry? and understanding put forth her voice? She standeth
in the top of high places, by the way in the places of the paths. She crieth at
the gates, at the entry of the city, at the coming in at the doors. Unto you,
O men, I call; and my voice is to the sons of man. O ye simple, understand
wisdom: and, ye fools, be ye of an understanding heart.

Wisdom hath builded her house, she hath hewn out her seven pillars.

Take note of "She standeth in the top of high places" and "She hath hewn out her
seven pillars," as these lines will be of importance a bit later.

It should be clear at this point that the gender of the names given to the Holy Spirit
and to Wisdom, in both Hebrew and Aramaic (Ruah and Chokmah respectively),
are most certainly feminine.

We should also be getting a clearer picture of the relationship that this feminine
entity had with the Creator, she who was his "daily delight" and "rejoiced before him."

Jewish philosopher Philo of Alexandria (c.20 BC—c. AD 50) spelled it out quite
clearly in his work *On the Cherubim*. In a list of things he defines as "great mysteries"
(identifying himself as an initiate), he calls God the "husband of wisdom,"[1] thereby
unveiling the Holy Spirit as the wife of God.

Around the 2nd century AD, we are introduced to another feminine companion
of God: the Shekinah. This term first appears in the Targum Onkelos, an Aramaic
translation of the five books of Moses, which together are the Tanakh, the Torah.
Raphael Patai explains the usage of this concept in this way:

In actual usage, the term Shekinah, when it first appears, means that aspect
of the deity which can be apprehended by the senses. Whenever the original
Hebrew biblical text speaks of a manifestation of God through which He
was perceived by man, the Targum Onkelos interpolates the term Shekinah.
For instance, the verse "Let them make Me a Sanctuary that I may dwell
[w'shakhanti] among them," is rendered by the Targum Onkelos as follows:
"Let them make before Me a Sanctuary that I may let My shekinah dwell
among them."[2]

Throughout the Talmudic period, the terms "Holy Spirit" and "Shekinah" were
synonymous and used interchangeably.[3]

The term "Shekinah" means "to dwell" and the tabernacle of Moses was called the
"Mishkan," which is Hebrew for "dwelling."

The appearance of the Shekinah was a solution to a problem: how could God—an
immense, infinite being—dwell within the confines of the holy of holies, let alone

rest on the mercy seat of the Ark of the Covenant? He could not and, therefore, sent his consort, his Shekinah, in his stead.

We read in Proverbs at the beginning of this chapter how the Holy Spirit or Shekinah cries and "standeth in high places" and "hath hewn out her seven pillars." Let us recall how Moses was shown the form of the original seven-branched menorah on the mountaintop, and how its branches and buds took the form of a sacred tree of light. And here we have a connection to yet another goddess, who some scholars say was the wife of Yahweh: the ancient Canaanite goddess Asherah. Asherah was known by the titles "Queen of Heaven" and "She who treads upon the sea" or "Miriyam," which correspond to Miriam and Mary. Note that Mary is also called "Queen of Heaven" and "Star of the Sea."

Asherah's name translates as a tree or sacred grove, and her cultic object was the Asherah pole. This stylized tree would be found at her places of worship, in the high places around Jerusalem, and in Solomon's Temple itself, alongside the altar to God (2 Kings 21.7, NIV). In fact, we read in 1 Kings 3.3 (KJV) that "Solomon loved the LORD, walking in the statutes of David his father: only he sacrificed and burnt incense in high places."

The high places in and around Jerusalem were where the altars to Asherah and the sacred Asherah trees or poles could be found. We know this because there are numerous mentions of their destruction during the reigns and reforms of King Hezekiah and King Josiah in the Old Testament. There are more than 40 mentions of Asherah and the high places of her worship throughout the Torah. It does not seem outside the realms of possibility that the form Moses was shown on the mountain, a high place, as a template for the original menorah was perhaps a sacred Asherah tree.

This idea is further supported by the discovery of artwork and an inscription on what is known as the Lachish ewer—an earthenware urn with a dedicatory inscription to the goddess Asherah and what appears to be a seven-branched menorah flanked by two goats. This object was unearthed at the Bronze Age Fosse Temple archaeological site at Lachish, a Canaanite and Israelite settlement.

William G. Dever (former Professor of Near Eastern Archaeology and Anthropology at the University of Arizona) makes a solid case for Asherah being the spouse of God or Yahweh.[4] He praises the work of Ruth Hestrin, a curator at the Israel Museum, for discovering the connection between the Lachish ewer and a goblet discovered at the same site. The goblet features the same two goats, only they were now flanking the pubic triangle of the goddess Asherah. She then discovered that, on Bronze Age pendants depicting Asherah, one would find her sacred tree growing outward from her pubic triangle, reminiscent of the tripod that is often shown supporting the menorah. Connecting the dots, we seem to have a relationship here between the sacred tree of Asherah, consort of God or Yahweh, and the seven-branched menorah.

As strict monotheism took hold in Judea, the role of the goddess was diminished and eventually suppressed. The altars to Asherah on the high places were destroyed, as were her trees and cultic objects. Her devotees, priests and priestesses, were forced underground. However, teachings of the divine feminine had a resurgence in the 12th and 13th centuries, with the seeds of Kabbalah, the practice of Jewish mysticism, being planted in Spain and southern France. Cornerstones of Kabbalistic writings, such as the *Zohar*, would make an appearance and delve deeply into the nature of the Shekinah glory. This marked a period of tumultuous change and the emergence of several seemingly disparate events that, in fact, all had a connection to this mystery: the crusades, the founding of the Knights Templar, the construction of the first Gothic cathedrals, and the early compositions of the Arthurian and Grail romances.

Asherah, the menorah, and divination

As well as bearing the title "Queen of Heaven," Asherah was also known as "she who walks on the sea" and "Lady Wisdom," the latter being a nod to her association with the Shekinah and the Holy Spirit.[5] As mentioned, these titles are also connected with Mary. Furthermore, the name Miriam, Mar-Yam, Mary, means "she who treads on Yam," Yam being the God of the sea. It could very well be that Miriam was both a title and a given name. For example, to be a Miriam/Mary was to be a priestess/prophetess of "she who walks on the sea," and the curiously large number of Marys mentioned in the New Testament refer to these prophetesses. This is further substantiated by the sister of Moses and Aaron, the prophetess of the tabernacle, who is called Miriam.

Is it possible that the three Marys were priestesses of Asherah? Regarding oracles of the ancient world, such as the Oracle of Delphi, there were said to be three at any given time. It's not difficult to picture three priestesses with six arms between them, holding lamps in outstretched hands, divining the word of God. It should be mentioned that the holy of holies in the Jewish Temple was given the name "Devir," the literal meaning of which is "oracle."

There are clues scattered throughout these connections. As noted, Asherah was known as "she who walks on the sea." Stella Maris, or Star of the Sea, is another name that was used for the North Star, the Pole Star. The pole and tree of Asherah appear to represent both the celestial pole and the tree of life. The two are conjoined in a sacred metaphor, one made incarnate in the form of the menorah. Incidentally, the North Star is also known as the Star of Arcady, and both "Arcady" and "Arcadia" crop up time and again throughout our adventure.

Was the cult of Asherah kept alive and spread to the New World? And is Asherah the one who is "Also in Arcadia"? It is a tantalizing prospect and we will encounter clues later on in our journey that add weight to this claim.

The straight-armed menorah

Something that we became aware of during the course of our investigations was that the standard depictions of the menorah we are used to seeing are not entirely accurate, and a different form altogether was known of and present in early Judaic traditions.

The true form of the menorah was documented by Rabbi Maimonides, who was a Sephardic Jew, born in 1138 in Córdoba, Andalusia, in Spain. Maimonides was a prominent decisor, which was a legal scholar who interpreted the Torah and resolved or settled matters in Jewish religious law based on the sacred texts and traditions. He was also one of the most influential philosophers in Jewish history and that reputation lives on today. He traveled extensively during his lifetime, working predominantly in North Africa, where he trained in medicine and eventually went on to become the court physician of Saladin, a famous sultan of Egypt and Syria. There is also an inexplicable account included in *Ta'rikh al-Hukama* (*The History of Physicians*), penned by Egyptian writer Al-Qifti sometime between 1120 and 1235, that suggests Maimonides was invited to treat King Richard the Lionheart during the Third Crusade in the Holy Land, and the King of England asked Maimonides to accompany him back to London, so impressed was he by the physician's prowess.

Perhaps the greatest legacy of Rabbi Maimonides is the Mishneh Torah, a 14-volume treatise on Jewish law that he completed between 1170 and 1180, a time when the Third Crusade was being waged across the Holy Land. The book is colloquially known as the "Book of the Strong Hand," an allusion to the number of volumes it contains, as 14 is the value in gematria (the system of applying numerical values to Hebrew words) of the word "*yad*" meaning "hand."

In the pages of the Mishneh Torah, we discover that the menorah does not have the curved arms we often see in depictions of the holy lampstand. Instead, the menorah is clearly shown with seven *straight* arms.

We know that Maimonides made a long and dangerous pilgrimage to Jerusalem and he prayed at a place he described as "the Great and Holy House," which many have taken to mean a location on Temple Mount itself, even though at the time this spot was off-limits to all but Christians. There were long-abandoned and ruined synagogues on Temple Mount, as the crusaders had stormed the city, and it is possible that Maimonides received special dispensation to visit the area, because of his reputation. Whatever the true identity of the exact location, being able to pay his respects in Jerusalem was incredibly important for Maimonides, and he declared the moment as extremely significant. Is it possible that on his visit Maimonides became aware of some long-lost truth concerning the menorah?

If there was any doubt regarding the true form of the menorah depicted in the Mishneh Torah, Maimonides' own son, Abraham Maimonides, clarified the matter further, stating, "The six branches extended upward from the center shaft of the menorah in a straight line, as depicted by my father, and not in a semicircle as depicted by others."

Maimonides was not alone in his belief in a straight-armed menorah—an even earlier writer also alludes to this form. Rabbi Rabenu Solomon Yitzchaki, known as Rashi, was born in Troyes in France—a location that we will visit more than once in this book—in 1040. He became a well-respected Jewish scholar who wrote a famous commentary on the Torah and Tanakh. Rashi is explicit when talking of the menorah and he also states that the branches were straight:

From here and there in each direction diagonally, drawn upwards until they reached the height of the Menorah, which is the middle stem. They came out of the middle stem, one higher than the others: the bottom one was longest, the one above it was shorter than it, and the highest one shorter than that, because the height of their ends at their tops was equal to the height of the seventh, middle stem, out of which the six branches extended.[6]

In Rashi's commentaries it is made clear that the very word used to describe the branches of the menorah in the Torah itself, "ohbe," infers that they have to be straight lines, because this word refers to reeds found growing on riverbanks throughout the Holy Land.

It seems clear that this straight-armed menorah was much more than just one person's opinion on how the original menorah may have appeared. Rather, it seems that it was a long-held truth, finally revealed in medieval Judaic writings. Early carved inscriptions also show a straight-armed lampstand. Perhaps the oldest depiction to date is from Turkey. While exploring the ruins of a castle at Korykos, which today is the modern town of Kizkalesi in Turkey, Mark Fairchild, a professor of Bible and Religion at Huntington University in Indiana, discovered the remains of a building that had been built up against the exterior wall of the castle. A door lintel, discovered intact in the ruins, clearly displays a menorah with straight arms.

A second carving was found at Catioren, 4 miles (6.4 km) inland from Korykos, hidden among the rocks and trees. Fairchild documents why this site was never fully explored in the past:

The ruins of Catioren were surveyed more than 120 years ago by J. Theodore Bent, an Oxford-trained archaeologist who described the area as "given up to almost impenetrable brushwood, forest, and rocks." Not much has changed today; the brush is so thick that it is difficult to navigate the site. Perhaps this is why Bent failed to discover the synagogue menorah, which he never mentioned in his writings.[7]

The menorah found on this site has straight, diagonal arms, identical to that found in Maimonides' Mishneh Torah. Nearby inscriptions have been dated to the Hellenistic period, 300–50 BC, and it is thought that the synagogue itself was also built at this time. Up until then, the earliest example of a synagogue was found in Israel and dates to sometime in the 1st century BC. If, as the evidence suggests, Catioren dates from the Hellenistic era, then it would become the earliest synagogue found so far.

This would be a very important discovery, if verified, because the very age of these structures is what makes this such an intriguing prospect. If Professor Fairchild is correct and these are the earliest synagogues ever found, then the fact that the menorahs carved into their stone walls have straight arms tells us that this was the original way that Jews depicted the menorah and it proves to us that this is likely to have been understood as the true form of the lampstand. It seems from this evidence that the alternative form of the menorah, with curved, semicircular arms, was a much later invention, possibly arising after the original menorah had been lost for many years.

Some of the most well-known examples of a straight-branched menorah were created by the Knights Templar. Inside the guardhouse of the castle at Domme in southern France, in the 14th century a group of 70 Templars were held prior to being put on trial. During their incarceration, they scratched symbols into the stone walls, supposedly with nothing more than their nails and teeth. One clearly defined image is of the menorah, complete with straight arms.

Also during this time, the Templars depicted the crucifixion, set in what is known as a "house" or "roofed-square," a geometric shape with five points that was said to have been used by the Templars to represent the Temple of Solomon itself.

It looks likely to us, given all we now know about the Knights Templar (which you will also discover later in this book), that these knights were clearly aware of the true form of the menorah and its significance in the Temple of Solomon. That they chose to carve it shows it was a design they held close to their hearts.

However, this isn't the only example of a straight-armed menorah associated with the Knights Templar. In the 12th century, they built a commandery at Montsaunès, in Haute-Garonne, south-west France. The site was not chosen at random. It sits on a vital communication route between France and Spain, at a time when the Templars were on a new European crusade to wrest control of Spain from the Islamic Moors, who had gained a significant foothold on the Iberian Peninsula. A chapel was completed at the commandery of Montsaunès in 1180, during the tenure of Commander Ariol d'Aspet.[8] The d'Aspet family had been involved in the crusades since 1160 and had intermarried with the powerful Counts of Comminges. This Templar commandery was well connected to the early core of the Knights Templar, with one of its commanders fighting alongside its elusive first grand master Hugh de Payns himself in the Holy Land.

Today, the chapel, which is highly decorated, is almost all that remains of the Templars' settlement. It is now the church of Montsaunès, Saint-Christophe-des-Templiers, and much of the original decoration by the Templars is intact. It is a curious amalgam of symbolism and hidden meaning that provides an illuminating insight into the minds of the Templars. Rather than depicting biblical scenes, there is a proliferation of geometric, esoteric, and astronomical symbols, along with wheels, grids, checkerboard patterns, and a whole host of symbols that hint at Kabbalistic knowledge. When confronted with such a hodgepodge of symbolism, the overriding sense you are left with is that someone was trying to encode a great secret on the walls.

Among all this Templar paraphernalia is a depiction of the Jewish menorah on one of the walls, with clear, straight, diagonal arms pointing upwards.[9] The design is bold and deliberate and indicates that the Templars had intimate and precise knowledge of the design of the holy lampstand.

We believe that this truly was the original form of the menorah and the curved-branch version that we see today came much later. The straight-armed menorah was the tree of life, the Asherah pole, the light of the Shekinah, the secret fire of knowledge or gnosis, which leads later to the arrival of the wisdom goddess Ariadne, Mistress of the Labyrinth, the silk-weaving spider and Princess of Knossos (Gnosis), Crete, the place of bull worship.[10] This goddess was abandoned and rejected after leading her lover out of the darkness and into the light, which can be seen as a metaphor for being led out of the desert and into the promised land.

The conclusions are there for all to see, we believe. The Knights Templar had become guardians of this sacred knowledge, either through direct contact with the treasures of Solomon's Temple or via communication with those who knew of the true nature of these sacred objects. Wherever we see this ancient symbol—the straight-armed menorah—we must acknowledge that those involved in depicting it were inheritors of the same secret knowledge that Maimonides was passing on, and there is more than a nagging suspicion that they might even have seen the true menorah, the mother menorah, with their own eyes.

As a final note, the whole issue of the true form of the menorah becomes even more interesting when we consider that the symbol of the menorah itself is used worldwide to depict the Jewish nation as a whole, and it is present on the national emblem of the modern state of Israel. How curious it is that the curved-branch menorah is now used as this symbol rather than the original, straight-armed menorah described by Maimonides.

CHAPTER 4
THE JOURNEYS OF THE MENORAH

The Temple is breached

Despite the sanctity of the new stone edifice that was created as a permanent and inviolable home for both God and his treasures, the Temple of Solomon in the heart of Jerusalem, the menorah was not entirely safe there. The first assault on the Temple came not long after its construction. The Bible tells us that an Egyptian king known as Shishak stormed the kingdom of Judah and took Jerusalem around 925 BC, sacking the Temple and taking many of its precious objects back to Egypt (1 Kings, 14.25–26, ESV):

> Shishaq king of Egypt came up against Jerusalem. He took away the treasures of the house of the LORD and the treasures of the king's house. He took away everything. He also took away all the shields of gold that Solomon had made.

There are many problems with this story, not least of which is that we do not have corroborating accounts from Egyptian sources. Shishak is usually identified as Pharaoh Shoshenq I and, while we do have a series of reliefs at the Karnak temple complex, on the Bubastite Portal gate, that tell of Shoshenq I capturing towns in the kingdoms of Israel and Judah, including Megiddo and Adoraim, Jerusalem itself is not mentioned at all. This is odd, considering that such a city would have been a grand prize, worth celebrating.

It is possible that Shoshenq did capture Jerusalem and he did carry off Temple treasures, but if so, did he perhaps only take the raw gold and leave the religious artefacts, such as the menorah, behind? Were the most precious implements perhaps hidden away before the assault? We know that the Temple itself survived, so perhaps what happened was not a complete desecration of the Temple. We cannot be certain and instead have to rely on accounts from after the era of Shoshenq, which record that the menorah was still in Solomon's Temple. So, if this sack of the Temple really did occur, the menorah, along with the Ark of the Covenant and the other holy objects, somehow survived the incursion intact.

The next assault came some 450 years later and this time the Temple did not fare so well. The Babylonian king Nebuchadnezzar II launched a series of attacks on Jerusalem, and on the second attempt, in 586 BC, after a siege said to have lasted some 30 months, he finally stormed the city gates and the Temple was burned to the ground, its treasures ransacked. Disaster had befallen Jerusalem and much of the city's population either fled, were killed, or taken into captivity to Babylon, where they endured a long exile. Jerusalem itself was said to have remained deserted for the next 40 years.

However, after the destruction wreaked by the Babylonians, Darius the Great began construction of a second temple on Temple Mount and this was completed in 515 BC. Curiously, texts have been found that state the menorah was indeed present in this second incarnation of the temple, along with the table of showbread. The Ark of the Covenant, however, is clearly missing and it is never mentioned again, along with objects such as the urim and thummim, and Aaron's rod. Despite this loss, once again, the menorah, miraculously, seems to have survived another attempt to spirit it away.

Jerusalem and the temple at its heart were safe for another 500 years before the Roman general Pompey's great siege of Jerusalem in 63 BC, which led to the fall of the city. After his victory, Pompey apparently left the temple intact and he even visited the holy of holies. Josephus leaves us with the following account regarding what Pompey encountered:

> For Pompey went into it . . . and saw all that which it was unlawful for any other men to see, but only for the high priests. There were in that temple the golden table; the holy candlestick; and the pouring vessels; and a great quantity of spices: and besides these there were among the treasures, two thousand talents of sacred money. Yet did Pompey touch nothing of all this; on account of his regard to religion; and in this point also he acted in a manner that was worthy of his virtue. The next day he gave order to those that had the charge of the temple to cleanse it, and to bring what offerings the law required to God, and restored the high priesthood.[1]

What is not mentioned here is that simply by entering the temple, Pompey was desecrating it, as he was not one of the sacred priesthood tasked with tending to God's sanctuary. But perhaps history will overlook Pompey's transgressions in light of the fact that he at least left the temple intact.

A few years after Pompey's visit, Marcus Licinius Crassus, a Roman general who commanded enormous wealth and power, stole all the gold from the temple. Records do not state whether he touched the religious artefacts, such as the menorah, so we will assume that he left these in place and was satisfied with the amount of raw gold he had liberated.

Next, Jerusalem came under the control of Herod the Great, the Romans' puppet king in Judea. However, not only did Herod leave the temple intact but also, during his reign, the temple was completely refurbished and restored during a significant reconstruction that would see the temple regain the height of its former grandeur. Herod brought in architects from Greece, Rome, and Egypt to oversee the vast construction project. Some accounts say that this refurbishment took 46 years, so the temple was probably newly completed when the next disastrous phase in its history began.

By AD 70 Jerusalem was under Roman siege once more. The Jews had started a war of independence—the First Jewish—Roman War, known as the Great Revolt in Hebrew, a war that ended disastrously for the Jews. It is said that up to one-fifth of the entire Jewish population died as a result of this conflict, possibly as many as a million lives were lost. It was the Roman general Titus, later to become emperor in his own right, who oversaw the end of a lengthy and bitter siege of Jerusalem and, this time, the holy city was ravaged and the temple with it. The temple itself wasn't only sacked and pillaged, it was defiled, as the casualties piled up in the very sanctuary itself:

> Most of the victims were peaceful citizens, weak and unarmed, butchered wherever they were caught. Round the Altar the heaps of corpses grew higher and higher, while down the Sanctuary steps poured a river of blood and the bodies of those killed at the top slithered to the bottom.[2]

The second temple was utterly destroyed in revenge for the uprising, though many accounts state that Titus had not wished to see the temple destroyed and had instead wanted to convert it into a pagan temple, but his men were fueled with an insatiable desire for destruction and, after fire spread accidentally across the temple precincts, they threw firebrands into the temple and a great conflagration ensued.

The Jewish temple, God's own sanctuary, was no more and, ever after, Jews would have no central place to worship on Jerusalem's Temple Mount. The temple had stood as a symbol of God's covenant with the people of Israel and many now wondered why God had abandoned them. Some even questioned whether their covenant with God was finally over. Despite efforts to overthrow their Roman masters and regain Jerusalem during the next 60 years, a third temple would never be built and to this day there isn't a Jewish temple in the heart of Jerusalem. A few years after the destruction of Jerusalem, the Romans erected a new pagan temple on the site of the razed second temple. Today, Temple Mount is home to the Dome of the Rock, a Muslim holy site, and Jews have to be satisfied with offering prayers at the Western Wall, also known as the Wailing Wall, the last remaining vestige of Herod's great temple.

The menorah in Rome

The treasures from inside Jerusalem's temple were taken to Rome and paraded amid great fanfare. An account of this is given by Josephus, who writes of their entry into the Eternal city:

> The spoils in general were borne in promiscuous heaps; but conspicuous above all stood those captured in the Temple at Jerusalem. These consisted of a golden table, many talents in weight, and a menorah, likewise made of gold . . . After these, and last of all the spoils, was carried a copy of the Jewish Law. They followed a large party carrying images of victory, all made of ivory and gold. Behind them drove Vespasian, followed by Titus; while Domitian rode beside them, in magnificent apparel and mounted on a steed that was in itself a sight.[3]

The Arch of Titus, originally built on ancient Rome's main street, Via Sacra—a thoroughfare that passed from Capitoline Hill down to the Colosseum—and today can be found amid the spectacular ruins of the Roman Forum, is decorated with reliefs showing the procession of riches entering Rome. Prominently displayed in one of the scenes is the menorah.

This is a rare glimpse of an object that, up until then, had been secreted away inside the deepest recesses of the temple in Jerusalem. However, the menorah depicted on the Arch of Titus has semicircular, curved arms, not the straight-armed shape we would expect to see. This makes us wonder whether the sculptor was present on the day of the victory procession and saw the object with his own eyes or if a description of the menorah was relayed to him instead and it was incorrect. There is another solution to this mystery but it might be impossible to fully find out for certain, now that we are at such a great distance in time from the original events. However, we will return to this question at the end of this chapter.

In the panel on the Arch of Titus, the size and weight of the menorah can be seen clearly and it appears to take many Roman soldiers—triumphators—to bear it on their shoulders as the booty is paraded from Porta Triumphalis to the Forum Boarium. However, it is worth noting that, in more recent times, a widespread belief has grown among Jews, as well as other commentators, that the menorah is not being carried by Romans but by captives from Jerusalem. This alternative view on what is depicted in the relief was first posited by historiographer Gedaliah ibn Yahya in 1587, possibly for political reasons, but this viewpoint has been seized on by many who are moved by the idea that the panel shows not only the full brutality of Rome but also the indomitable nature of the Jewish captives carrying the menorah.[4]

The sacred artefacts from Jerusalem were deposited in the Roman Temple of Peace, built a few years before by Emperor Vespasian to house Rome's plentiful *praeda*—

looted artefacts captured from conquered cities and states. The Temple of Peace was said to have been one of the most impressive temples in Rome, and is described by Josephus as being shaped "in so glorious a manner, as was beyond all human expectation and opinion" (Me'ila 17b). It appears that this Temple of Peace acted almost as a museum, much like the British Museum in London today, and Vespasian had master works of sculpture displayed inside, along with innumerable artefacts the Romans had "liberated" from the peoples they had conquered. Vespasian's desire was to be viewed as the emperor who had unified the known world and brought peace to an extended empire. However, visitors to Rome, from all over the ancient world, went to view the collection inside the Temple of Peace and, along with such notions of peace and order, it would have been impossible for them not to have been reminded of Rome's darker side. These were, after all, the spoils of war.

The steady stream of visitors and travelers included Jews, who saw with their own eyes the treasures that once had resided in the temple in Jerusalem. One such visitor was Rabbi Shimon bar Yochai, a celebrated scholar credited by many with writing the *Zohar*, who traveled to Rome in the 2nd century AD from Judea. There is a surviving account in the Talmud of him seeing for himself the treasures taken from Jerusalem's Temple Mount, including the menorah. Together with Rabbi Elazar bar (son of) Rabbi Yosei, they saw (Me'la 17.b):

the curtain of the sanctuary in the city of Rome, and on the curtain were several drops of blood from the bull and the goat of Yom Kippur. When the emperor took them into his treasury Rabbi Elazar saw the temple vessels that the Romans had captured when they conquered Jerusalem, including the curtain.

The curtain in question was the *parokhet*, the veil that separated the holy of holies from the main hall of the temple in Jerusalem and so concealed the Ark of the Covenant and beyond. As mentioned, the Ark of the Covenant had already vanished by the time the second temple was constructed, which explains why the Ark was not appropriated by Titus and brought back to Rome. The curtain, however, must still have been kept in the holy of holies, even after the Ark had been removed, so the *parokhet* was brought back to Rome as part of the hoard from the temple.

Many other rabbis have stood in the presence of the sacred objects since, and Rabbi Simeon says of his visit, also made during the 2nd century AD, "When I went to Rome there I saw the menorah."[5]

The Temple of Peace was destroyed by fire in AD 192, but it seems that the menorah, and perhaps many of the other objects from Solomon's Treasure, were rescued and then secreted away. It is Byzantine historian Procopius who offers a suggestion as to where the menorah ended up in his *History of the Wars*. He first mentions briefly the sacking of Rome by the Visigoths and describes the removal of the treasures of Jerusalem, but he does not mention the menorah in this context. Instead, it is the later invasion by the Vandals and their destruction of Rome in AD 455 that Procopius focuses on.

It was from Carthage that the Vandals set out on their grand expedition to storm and capture Rome. Pope Leo I appealed to the Vandal king Gaiseric and begged him not to destroy Rome or murder her people. Gaiseric agreed to this and instead made do with plundering and pillaging.

Theophanes, a chronicler from the Byzantine (or Eastern Roman) Empire, leaves us with this image:

> Taking all the money and adornments of the city, he loaded them on his ships, among them the solid gold and bejewelled treasures of the Church and the Jewish vessels which Vespasian's son Titus had brought to Rome after the capture of Jerusalem.[6]

So, the menorah, and a great part of the treasure of Solomon suddenly had a new home in Carthage, but it was only a temporary respite in their adventures.

A return to Jerusalem

Almost 100 years after the Vandals' assault on Rome, in the year AD 533, the Byzantine emperor Justinian defeated Carthage on the North African coast and Procopius tells us that the treasures of King Solomon—the very same artefacts that Titus had brought home with him to Rome—were returned to Constantinople, the capital of the Eastern Roman Empire. The treasure is documented in detail:

> And there was also silver weighing many thousands of talents and all the royal treasure amounting to an exceedingly great sum ... and among these were the treasures of the Jews, which Titus, the son of Vespasian, together with certain others, had brought to Rome after the capture of Jerusalem.[7]

What Procopius says next is where the story turns from interesting to intriguing. He recounts a tale that, on the treasure's triumphant arrival in Constantinople, a Jew recognized the iconic treasures of Solomon and he approached the Emperor's cortège:

> These treasures I think it inexpedient to carry into the palace in Byzantium. Indeed, it is not possible for them to be elsewhere than in the place where

Solomon, the king of the Jews, formerly placed them. For it is because of these that Gaiseric captured the palace of the Romans, and that now the Roman army has captured the Vandals.

The message was clear: a curse would befall anyone who sought to possess the sacred treasures from Jerusalem, and the only place they could safely reside was in their rightful home on Temple Mount, in the sanctuary of God. When this dreadful news was brought to the ears of the emperor Justinian, he suddenly became afraid and ordered all the Jewish treasures to be sent forthwith from Constantinople and returned to Jerusalem, to avoid a calamity descending on the capital of the Byzantine Empire.

What Justinian did next is compelling. He began a construction project in Jerusalem, laying the foundations of what would become the Nea Church—the Nea Ekklesia of the Theotokos. Some writers have argued that the construction bears some resemblance to Solomon's own prodigious temple building and that Justinian was attempting to build a new temple in Jerusalem, possibly to reinstate the holy objects, including the menorah, in their rightful holy city. Did Justinian believe that he would break the curse if he did this?

Whether or not this was the case, Jerusalem at this time was a possession of the Byzantine Empire, so it makes sense that, even if Justinian only partially suspected the legend of the curse to be true, he still might have chosen to store this portion of the treasure in the city of Jerusalem where it had absolutely no chance of threatening his capital, Constantinople.

There is further, albeit scant, evidence which hints that the menorah and other temple treasures did, in fact, return to Jerusalem. This outcome certainly seems to have been believed by prominent Jews and scholars throughout the centuries since. During the Byzantine period, there was much Jewish messianic discourse throughout Constantinople and the Byzantine Empire and in it we find clues that demonstrate where the menorah had ended up after its many adventures.

In a text known as Otot ha-Mashiah (The Portents of the Messiah), written sometime during the 5th to 7th centuries AD, which deals with themes of Jewish eschatology, we find the following:

> The Messiah of the lineage of Joseph will come and fight a battle with the ruler of Edom. He will win a victory against Edom, kill great heaps of them, and also kill the king of Edom. He will devastate the province of Rome. He will recover some of the Temple vessels which had been deposited in the palace of Julianos Caesar and come to Jerusalem.[8]

Samuel Krauss, a Hungarian scholar, believed that the "Julianos" mentioned in this prophecy was the emperor Justinian himself, thereby linking this Jewish messianic text with the account we have from Procopius.

What is demonstrated clearly in this text is the power and inviolable nature of the temple treasures. They are given a key role in this eschatological narrative and the text suggests how potent they were—not only as symbols but also as physical objects. The menorah was conceived and designed by God, so it should be no surprise to find that this artefact assumed great significance in messianic texts such as this one.

However, there are other conflicting accounts in the various histories regarding the fate of the menorah. This is especially true of Procopius, as he not only tells us of its return (along with the other treasures from the temple) to Jerusalem but also, at one point, he tells us briefly that Alaric, King of the Visigoths, had taken the treasures from Rome to France. All the same, what does seem to be clear, reading between the lines, is that the temple treasures had become fragmented, finding their way into several hoards, in much the same way that there have been relics from the true cross, along with other items connected personally with Christ and the crucifixion, scattered throughout European cathedrals. A German historian famous for his works on medieval Rome, Ferdinand Gregorovius, concluded that Alaric only took some of the temple treasures, and the greater portion, including the menorah, "he must have left unheeded, since, together with the spoils acquired from the churches, some of the sacred vessels of the temple, brought by Titus from Jerusalem, were shipped by Gaiseric to Carthage."[9]

While we are not certain that Justinian's motives for returning the objects were exactly as Procopius states, one thing is evident to us: the chief treasures stolen from Jerusalem by the Romans all those years before—the menorah, the table of showbread, the trumpets, and probably several other important objects—were all returned to Jerusalem, and eventually housed at the Nea Church.

So, this most sacred object, the menorah, was now safe in Jerusalem once again, but there is one final twist in our tale. We are now no longer convinced that the menorah looted by Titus after the siege of Jerusalem and taken to Rome in AD 71 amid such splendor and procession was the *true* menorah of Moses' time, the original menorah that God ordered to be fashioned.

The clue that led us to this conclusion is found in that depiction of the menorah on the Arch of Titus. If what we have related in this chapter is correct, that Rabbi Maimonides revealed the exact form of the true menorah in the pages of his magnum opus, Mishneh Torah, then the original menorah of Moses' time had straight, diagonal arms. Yet, as we saw on the Arch of Titus, the menorah the Romans stole had curved, semicircular arms. We also know that this menorah was placed on display in Rome and many celebrated guests and visitors came to see it. If that menorah had possessed straight arms, then the design would have been remarked upon, but that is not the case.

There is another reason why we think the menorah on the Arch of Titus was shown with curved arms. In the first Temple in Jerusalem, there were several other menorahs in addition to the original from the time of Moses. When the Ark of the Covenant and the other holy vessels were moved from the tabernacle or tent of the congregation to the permanent Temple on Temple Mount, King Solomon created a further ten menorahs. These were designed to illuminate the *hekhal*, a sacred area just outside the holy of holies that contained the table of showbread, the altar of incense, and the original menorah. We are told of these additional lampstands in 1 Kings and 1 Chronicles. In 1 Kings 7.48–49 (ESV), we find:

> So Solomon made all the vessels that were in the house of the LORD: the golden altar, the golden table for the bread of the Presence, the lampstands of pure gold, five on the south side and five on the north, in front of the inner sanctuary.

It is also revealed that Solomon's father, King David, gave the precise weights of gold that should be used to make the new lampstands (1 Chronicles 28.11, 15).

> Then David gave to Solomon his son the pattern of the porch, and of the houses thereof, and of the treasuries thereof, and of the upper chambers thereof, and of the inner parlours thereof, and of the place of the mercy seat . . . the weight for the candlesticks of gold, and for the lamps of gold, by weight for every candlestick, and for the lamps thereof.

Today, it is still forbidden for Jews to create a replica of the original menorah and we wonder if this was also the case in Solomon's time. If so, it is not too much of a stretch to consider that when Solomon fashioned the ten additional menorahs to adorn his Temple, that he chose a slightly different design, to differentiate his menorahs from the original one described by God to Moses. The first menorah was thus unique and holy, gifted by God himself, and, as we have seen, it had straight, diagonal arms. We believe that the later menorahs created by Solomon would have had curved, semicircular arms. In this way, Solomon clearly delineated which was the original menorah, constructed for the portable tabernacle, and which were his later copies to illuminate his Temple.

Therefore, if the menorah held in Rome for all those years had curved arms, as is shown clearly on the Arch of Titus, we think it likely that the Romans stole one of these later menorahs. They were still precious artefacts, created as they were by King

Solomon himself and fashioned from gold, plus they were also kept at the heart of the Temple of Jerusalem, but they were not on a par with the original menorah and did not possess the provenance afforded to it by its origins in the time of Moses.

Looking back at Josephus' detailed histories, we found the following in Volume 6 of his *The Wars of the Jews*:

> A Jewish priest called Phineas handed over to the Romans some of the sacred treasures: two menorot similar to those deposited in the sanctuary, along with tables, bowls, and platters, all of solid gold and very massive.[10]

Perhaps here was the answer to the riddle: it sounds as though a Jewish priest misled the Romans by giving them not one, but two copies of the original menorah.

The Romans no doubt believed that they had captured the true holy artefact, but it now seems likely that the one, most sacred, menorah was hidden deep within Temple Mount long before the Romans ever desecrated the sanctuary and looted its treasures.

Experiencing multiple emotions—shock not the least of them—we realized that we had been pursuing a false trail. What we thought was the original menorah that we had glimpsed on the Arch of Titus, then followed across Europe to Africa, and finally back to Jerusalem, turned out not to be the true menorah. However, our pursuit of it had not been without reward and the journey had been an enlightening one that had taught us a great deal, even though we were not any closer to finding the true menorah that Moses had gazed upon. It was time to regroup and return to the hunt. There was one line of enquiry still open to us, one that could solve our dilemma.

Now that we had followed this tale of the stolen menorah closely associated with Rome to its conclusion, it was time to return to Jerusalem, because knowledge of the original, true menorah had not been entirely lost, and a group of religious idealists were about to stumble on this lost knowledge and begin a search for its ancient hiding place, deep within the sacred rock of Temple Mount itself.

CHAPTER 5

THE REDISCOVERY OF THE TEMPLE TREASURES

All our research up until this point hinted that the menorah—the original, the menorah of Moses—and many of the other remaining treasures from Solomon's first Temple had been buried deep below Temple Mount before the Romans had stormed the second temple and ransacked the holy sanctuary in AD 70, possibly even before the invasion of the Chaldeans in 597 BC. It was now looking likely that the treasures had remained hidden right up until the middle of the 12th century. We had picked up the scent of the true menorah and seen signs that it had surely been recovered, so it now seemed impossible for it to have remained buried beyond this time.

So, who had brought this ancient lost treasure to light?

The individuals responsible were members of the world's most recognizable and well-known religious order: the Knights Templar.

This fraternity of knights kept cropping up during our research, and you will encounter them again and again in this book. They run beneath events like an underground stream, sometimes burbling away deep below the surface, but at other times rising to the surface, to burst forth like a gushing spring.

Forged in the fierce heat of the crusades and founded in the year 1118, the Knights Templar—more prosaically named the Poor Fellow Soldiers of Christ and of the Temple of Solomon—rose to become a Christian order, the fame of which was based not so much on its devout religious figures as on the fierce warriors and defenders of the cross who made up many of their number. Their fighting prowess was due in no small part to the strict rules they adhered to, which included a vow never to retreat or surrender, and never to push forward without the proper command. Furthermore, their religious adherence to the concept of martyrdom was fundamental to the Templars and a linchpin of their ethos. This religious fervor resulted in them being quintessential fanatical crusaders.

St Bernard of Clairvaux, a man whom we will reveal as the 12th-century showrunner behind the Catholic Church, argued that the Templars were the epitome of all that was good and pious, and he wrote his *In Praise of the New Knighthood: A Treatise on the Knights Templar and the Holy Places of Jerusalem* in support of the fledgling order. In this book he elevated the Knights Templar above all other religious orders, citing their founding principles of obedience, poverty, and chastity, which are so directly bound to the teachings of Christ.[1]

Bernard's book addressed the doubts that Christians—and even some early Templars—had concerning whether Christians could be devout monks and warriors at the same time. A long line of popes had already sown the seeds here, and the crusades themselves, along with the Muslim threat to the Holy Land, had changed opinion and the political climate on this point. Suddenly the language itself also changed and we see phrases such as "Knights of Christ" and taking up the "gospel knighthood." The words of St Paul himself, with their suggestion of a spiritual warfare in the name of Christ, had always been prone to corruption and misuse, and it was then considered noble to take up the "sword of the Spirit" and wage war on those who threatened Christian holy sites. Finally, at the Council of Nablus in 1120, it was declared that "if a cleric takes up arms in the cause of self-defence, he shall not bear any guilt."[2]

Bernard also underlined the importance of martyrdom in his treatise:

How blessed is the death of the martyrs in battle! Rejoice, brave champion, if you live and conquer in the Lord; but exalt and glory all the more if you die and are joined in the Lord. Life brings its rewards and victory its glory, but a holy death is rightly considered preferable to both. "Blessed are they who die in the Lord," but how much more blessed are they who die for the Lord?[3]

After Bernard of Clairvaux's inspirational and reassuring words there were no longer any obstacles standing in the way of holy men wishing to take up arms and aid their brothers in the crusades. Malcolm Barber highlights the allure of this strange new alloy forged of religion and warfare:

Strong warriors on the one hand, and monks waging war with vice and demons on the other, were not unusual, but the combination of both was quite unique. Since they fought with a clear and pure conscience these men had no dread of death, confident in the knowledge that in the sight of the Lord they would be his martyrs.[4]

It was this very notion that fueled the legendary bravery of the Knights Templar on the battlefield. They would charge audaciously into combat knowing that, should they be killed, their place in heaven was assured.

The original official purpose of the Knights Templar was to provide protection to pilgrims traveling from Europe to the Holy Land. Jerusalem had become the great siren of Europe in the Middle Ages, and the taking of the city called out to every pious nobleman, yet the journey itself was perilous. The first true miracle to reveal itself to every pilgrim who reached Jerusalem, or the Holy Land, was his arriving there in one piece.

The journey from Europe was long and hazardous, far beyond anything we would come across today. Danger was quite literally around every corner, whether people went on foot, on horseback, or even by ship. Hardship was considered an integral part of the spiritual journey, yet, if you tried to put yourself in the worn shoes of a medieval monk making his journey to salvation, the challenges you would have to overcome in relation to travel, food, and health would seem almost unbearable. Furthermore, even if you managed to arrive in the Holy Land itself, your troubles had really only begun. It wasn't only robbers and bandits that presented a constant threat—even though they did, of course, make everyday life miserable—because, to confound matters further, many Muslim leaders actively called for the death of any Christian who dared to set foot in the newly conquered Crusader States. Aside from this grave Muslim threat, accounts from the time also describe attacks by pagans, and even lions. There were hundreds of ways to die once you started your pilgrimage.

It is certainly true that some travelers in search of the sanctity of Jerusalem believed that such dangers were part and parcel of a true pilgrimage and suffering and the threat of death were necessary evils—a price worth paying for redemption. However, after several large-scale raids by Muslims, with an attack close to the east of Jerusalem itself resulted in more than 300 deaths,[5] it soon became apparent that protection would need to be provided to these, often naive, pilgrims. This task was handed over to the Knights Templar.

According to the chronicles left to us by William of Tyre, who was Archbishop of Tyre, in the kingdom of Jerusalem, the Templars were created by Warmund of Jerusalem, the Latin Patriarch of the Catholic Church in the year 1118:

> In this same year [1118], certain noble men of knightly rank, religious men, devoted to God and fearing him, bound themselves to Christ's service in the hands of the Lord Patriarch. They promised to live in perpetuity as regular canons, without possessions, under vows of chastity and obedience. Their foremost leaders were the venerable Hugh de Payns and Geoffrey of St. Omer.[6]

It is Hugh de Payns who is usually attributed with the creation of the Knights Templar. However, William of Tyre was a native of Jerusalem and a well-respected chronicler, and his book is the only surviving first-hand account of the events of

12th-century Jerusalem, so we have to assume that his citing of Warmund as the instigator of this order is an accurate statement.

Warmund of Jerusalem was an intriguing character. Originally Warmund of Picquigny in northern France before his appointment as Patriarch of Jerusalem, he assumed great powers in his new role and reported directly to the Holy See. To us, Warmund came across as a curious mix of holy man on the one hand and military commander on the other; something that we saw later in the Knights Templar themselves.

In 1124, Warmund was appointed supreme commander of the crusader forces besieging Tyre because he was seen to possess greater authority than any other potential leader. He even replaced King Baldwin II while the King was held in captivity between 1123 and 1124. For us, this clearly underlined the notion that Warmund was one of the most powerful men in Jerusalem at the time.[7]

There is a further mention of the role of the Patriarch of Jerusalem in the prologue of the Rule of the Temple, the detailed code of conduct that dictated how the Templars should live:

we left it to the discretion of both our honourable father lord Honorius and of the noble patriarch of Jerusalem, Stephen [the successor of Warmund], who knew the affairs of the East and of the Poor Knights of Christ.[8]

Another statement by William of Tyre highlights the original guiding hand of the Patriach of Jerusalem, while also documenting a clear schism that developed later. These words were written by William in 1170, some 50 years after the establishment of the order:

they withdrew from the Patriarch of Jerusalem, by whom their Order was founded and from whom they received their first benefices. They have also taken away tithes and first fruits from God's churches, have disturbed their possessions, and have made themselves exceedingly troublesome.[9]

It therefore seems that Hugh de Payns was propelled towards his mission by the Church and, in particular, the Patriarch of Jerusalem. It was then left to Hugh de Payns to fulfil this task and bring the germ of the idea to fruition. Incidentally, we realized that, if William of Tyre's words were true, then during the 50 years since the formation of the Knights Templar, a rift had opened up between the Templars and the Catholic Church. Given the not insignificant privileges later afforded to the Knights Templar, we were curious to discover what might have caused this schism. But, before we turned to that question it was time to examine Hugh de Payns' origins.

Who was Hugh de Payns?

Originally from the Champagne region of France, Hugh de Payns swiftly rose from relative obscurity to become Grand Master of one of the most notorious religious orders in history. Hailing from a small village near Troyes, de Payns first visited Jerusalem in 1104 while accompanying another Hugh—the Count of Champagne—who was possibly a cousin. The two men returned to France after several years, but there was to be a second pilgrimage in 1114, and this time Hugh de Payns stayed on in Jerusalem. It was on this second visit that Hugh de Payns was called on by Warmund to begin what would become his life's work.

Hugh de Payns began by gathering the disparate bands of Christian fighters who had gathered around the Holy Sepulchre in Jerusalem into a more cohesive force. Some were already part of an order known as the Hospitallers, but Hugh de Payns used his strength of character to persuade a number of these men to follow his lead and form a new order. So it was that, in 1120, Hugh de Payns, along with eight knights, approached King Baldwin II of Jerusalem and the request to create the Knights Templar was officially granted; they were to be dedicated to the defence of Jerusalem and the protection of the many pilgrims who visited the city.

But there is something not quite right about this origin story. It must be remembered that the conquest of Jerusalem had triggered a flood of pilgrims, who were arriving in the city in large numbers, so a good question to ask might be: how much of a difference could nine knights have made in a city the size of Jerusalem? Accounts from the time show that the Knights Templar didn't increase in number until almost ten years later, so, realistically, how many pilgrims could these nine men protect and, if this was truly their aim, why did they not recruit further members? Despite these questions and lingering doubts, this is the accepted story of why the Knights Templar were founded.

The title "Templars" was shorthand for "the Poor Knights of Christ and of the Temple."[10] The titular temple in question was to be found on Temple Mount on Mount Moriah in Jerusalem, the lost Temple of Solomon—that most holy of sanctuaries which once contained the menorah and other treasures from the time of Moses.

This longer name for the order derived from the decision to move its headquarters away from the area surrounding the Holy Sepulchre, the knights setting up home instead in what had once been the al-Aqsa Mosque,[11] a striking building that sits at the southern end of Temple Mount. The mosque had originally been built by the Umayyads, a Sunni caliphate that ruled Palestine in the 7th and into the 8th century, establishing al-Aqsa in AD 705. Not to be confused with the Dome of the Rock, which also sits up on Temple Mount, the al-Aqsa Mosque is considered the third most holy site in Islam and its construction was elaborate and impressive, to the point where it was said to have been the most beautiful mosque aside from those in Arabia itself. Since the capture of Jerusalem by the crusader armies, al-Aqsa had been converted into a palace for the King of Jerusalem and was no longer an Islamic place of worship. It was here, in a decrepit wing of the palace, that Hugh de Payns and company took up residence and they would forever after be known as the Knights of the Temple.

A 12th-century account by Walter Map, an English medieval clerk and courtier, describes how Hugh de Payns worked tirelessly to secure a foothold on Temple Mount. In our opinion, this extract also seems to suggest that de Payns was on a very important mission and remained dedicated to his new cause:

> de Payns, who was neither sluggish nor easy to subdue, obtained, by his prayers, aid for God and himself, and contrived by every possible device to acquire as his own a great dwelling within the enclosure of the Lord's temple from the regular canons of the temple. Contenting himself with mean garb and scanty food he, under a vow, assumed for his fellows the full cost of horses and armour. By preaching, by prayers, and by all possible ways, he prevailed upon all pilgrims whom he knew to be mighty men of arms to abide in perpetual dedication to God's service.[12]

Accounts have been given of how the original nine knights remained alone in their new base on Temple Mount for nine years.[13] They also renamed al-Aqsa, calling it "*Templum Salomonis*," which means "Solomon's Temple." Again, we wondered how staying in their headquarters up on Temple Mount throughout those years was supposed to secure the safety of the numerous pilgrims they had sworn to defend.

Once the nine years had passed, in 1129, Hugh de Payns was sent to Europe by King Baldwin on a new mission: to gain support for the fragile Eastern kingdom. This trip ended up lasting several years and Hugh de Payns met with the Count of Flanders, the Count of Anjou, and even the kings of England and Scotland, in an effort to secure funding and men of arms for a campaign against Damascus itself.

Hugh de Payns' mission for Baldwin was a success, and his efforts achieved greater security for Jerusalem and the Levant. However, perhaps even more significantly, he also secured substantial support for his own organization, the Knights Templar. He received several sizeable donations in the form of land and property. Even more significantly, some of his new supporters pledged their allegiance to the Templars and joined the cause, promising to sail to Jerusalem.

Their reputation grew fast and, in 1134, when Afonso I, "the Battler," then King of Aragon, died after sustaining wounds at Fraga as a result of a disastrous rout fighting the Moors, his will revealed that he had bequeathed one-third of his entire kingdom to the Knights Templar. Hugh de Payns was building a solid foundation that would ensure the Templars a place in history. We are not privy to Hugh de Payns' exact negotiating technique, but it is clear that he must have had some very convincing arguments.

The final victory, however, came when Hugh de Payns secured an official papal blessing and recognition for the order at the Council of Troyes in 1129. There, its 68-point code of conduct, known as the Latin Rule, was established. The Rule was compiled by Bernard of Clairvaux, who played no small part in this story, especially in the founding of the Knights Templar. The Templars pledged to adhere to this Rule, which covered every aspect of their lives, from how they should pray and conduct their religious lives to what they should wear and eat and drink. One critical point in the Rule agreed at the Council addressed the issue that was still foremost for many: any knight who killed enemies of Christianity would not be committing a sin.[14]

The Council of Troyes is curious for several reasons, and the first question must be: why was the Council needed at all? Similar organizations, like the Hospitallers and, later, the Teutonic Knights, had been confirmed by a papal bull without the need to gather such a large number of dignitaries together. Furthermore, Troyes was more than 1,864 miles (3,000 km), as the crow flies, from the main theatre of action—Jerusalem. If we are to be persuaded that it was very important, then why was the Pope himself not present? He was represented by his legate, the Cardinal of Albano. Also, why were the archbishops of Reims and Sens there and what did those towns have to do with the whole affair? It would be many months before we found a connection that united all these places, but at this stage of our research we were puzzled by the scale of the Council of Troyes.

Perhaps the most remarkable point about the Council is that it took place in Hugh de Payns' home town of Troyes. This fact is mentioned in several accounts, most notably that of William of Tyre, where he is named as "Hues de Paiens delez Troies," which is "Hugh of Payens from near Troyes."[15]

No less than six of the original nine Knights Templar were present at Troyes, leaving just three of the senior Templars in Jerusalem to protect pilgrims—supposedly their *raison d'être*. This alone demonstrates how crucial the Council was for the order and the outcome was indeed a significant turning point for the Templars. With the papal blessing in place, and a religiously compelling—almost monastic—set of rules laid out, the Knights Templar would grow fast, their numbers increasing exponentially.

Barely 30 years after the first group of Templars had received recognition in Jerusalem and taken up residence in the al-Aqsa Mosque, Templars were everywhere throughout Europe and the Levant, and their holdings and possessions were impressive. By the time the Second Crusade was conceived—promulgated by none other than Bernard of Clairvaux—and had begun in 1147, the Knights Templar were not only in a position to take part in this new holy war but they would also lead it.

An ascent to wealth and power

Each individual member entering the Knights Templar had to give up all their worldly possessions, in line with the Rule (or the Rules of the Temple to give them their full title), but the order itself did not face the same constraints.

Fueled by a rapid rise in popularity after de Payns' tour of Europe and the Council of Troyes, it didn't take very long for the Templars to become extremely wealthy. It does make you wonder whether the "Poor Knights of Christ" part of their name was appropriate.

The order received numerous gifts and donations, including property and land, from all over Continental Europe and even beyond. It enabled the Templars to become bankers in all but name. They looked after the gold and possessions of pilgrims and travelers leaving for the Holy Land and Outremer, offering promissory notes in return. These could then be drawn against any of the Templar commanderies, whether London, Paris, or Jerusalem, or anywhere in between. The Templars were careful to place their fortresses and strongholds on every trade route between France, Jerusalem, and neighboring areas, forming a chain of safe passage for both pilgrims *and* commerce.

The Templars soon realized that they could loan out this capital and they used this newly found financial vehicle—along with their generous profits—to develop trade and commercial enterprises of their own, which further increased their wealth. They also rented out mills, leased ships, financed wars, helped run cities and collect taxes, and even raised the funds to ransom kings.

Hugh de Payns died in 1136, the circumstances of which are undocumented. However, just three years afterwards, in 1139, and a mere ten years after their official recognition at the Council of Troyes, Pope Innocent II issued a papal bull, *Omne Datum Optimum*, which means "Every perfect gift," that granted the Templars incredible privileges. The Pope conferred on them the right to wear their now iconic red cross on their white tunics. The Templars, and the powers that had created them, knew well the value of brand identity long before such things became commonplace. More significantly, the papal bull gave the Templars "the protection and tutelage of the Holy See for all time to come."[16] A further proclamation exempted the Knights Templar from all taxes, while allowing them to collect tithes from those who lived on Templar land.

At this point we began to realize that the Templars were involved in very different activities in the East compared to those in the West. While becoming a fighting force of redoubtable knights in the Levant, in their home territories of Europe they came to more closely resemble a civil administrative organization. In and around the Holy Land, one could find illustrious Templar fortresses, such as Pelerin, Montreal, Toron, and Le Destroit, often captured from their Muslim adversaries. In the homeland, the vast majority of Templar commanderies looked more like fortified farms, organized around a courtyard, with a monastery where members of the order were housed, usually with their own chapel on site. These commanderies served as administrative centers. For example, in Troyes, next to the commandery known as the "*maison du temple*" (or "house of the temple"), the Templars owned some 50 houses, which were rented out to inhabitants of the city. Several commanderies were organized around so-called "baileys," each of which were part of a larger province governed by a provincial commander based at a provincial house. There were nine such provinces: Portugal, Aragon, Mallorca, Castille and Leon, France and Auvergne, England and Ireland, Germany and Hungary, Northern Italy and Southern Italy, Apulia and Sicily.[17] The first three of these provinces all bordered Muslim territories.

What became clear was that the Knights Templar owned thousands of properties in total, all of which had to be managed, and administered—individually as well as collectively. The true success of the order wasn't due to the Templars' fighting prowess and fortress building, however impressive that aspect of the order was. Rather, it was down to their ability to organize people and assets successfully on a staggering scale, and, as a result, the order expanded at a break-neck speed. We knew there was really only one other organization in existence at the time that worked on the same international scale: the Catholic Church. It was likely that the Templars had, at the very least, received some coaching from their founding fathers in the Church.

One sign of the Templars' increasing authority, after the sweeping powers granted by the papal bull of 1139, is demonstrated by King Baldwin II's actions directly after the Council finished. The King of Jerusalem had been living in the palace in the old al-Aqsa Mosque complex, while a wing was occupied by the Templars. However, after the proceedings at Troyes, the King decided to move out of the newly named *Templum Salomonis* to a new location, which today is known as the Citadel of the Tower of David.[18] This became the new royal residence in Jerusalem for the Frankish kings, and the *Templum Salomonis* on Temple Mount was given over solely to the Knights Templar.

It took a little while for the enormity of this to sink in. The King voluntarily vacated one of the most legendary locations in biblical history, leaving it to a group of religious soldiers whose order hadn't existed only nine years before. This was surely a reflection of the power-shift taking place in Europe and the Holy Land, but was there more at play here? Clearly something of great significant had convinced Baldwin II that the Templars had a far greater claim to live and work on Temple Mount than did even the monarch.

Whatever the true reason for this move, the Knights Templar were clearly on the cusp of becoming a formidable power, one that straddled nations, due in no small part to the remarkable privileges granted them by the Pope. The question we were now asking ourselves more and more was: what could have spawned such sweeping concessions?

But before tackling that subject, we needed to examine even more closely the origins of the Knights Templar, and what exactly was behind their formation.

CHAPTER 6
THE KNIGHTS TEMPLAR: A CATHOLIC CREATION

We have seen how the Catholic Church had steered Hugh de Payns toward the formation of the Knights Templar, via Warmund, the Patriarch of Jerusalem. However, our investigations indicated that there was more to this than gentle nudging and encouragement. It now seems likely to us that de Payns was directed by a higher authority and had secret orders from the Church.

Bernard of Clairvaux

The role of Bernard of Clairvaux in particular cannot be overstated. He would later become one of the order's greatest champions, providing the Templars with access to the upper echelons of the Catholic Church, but Bernard also seems to have been instrumental in the formation of the Knights Templar, in those mysterious early years before de Payns sought official sanction for the order at the Council of Troyes in 1129.

Before Bernard became Abbot of Clairvaux, he was a monk at nearby Cîteaux Abbey and there is evidence of a connection between the brethren of this abbey and the foundation of the Knights Templar. A letter from a Master of the Temple, Philip of Plessis, to the Abbot of Cîteaux in 1202 sheds light on the role of Cîteaux Abbey:

> We need your prayers, in which we have faith in the Lord, to lift us out of the aforesaid calamitous tribulations we are suffering. And since our house had its origins in your house and your predecessors, it seems to us that we are bound by a special affection to you and you to us. Hence, when Brother Artaud and Brother Bernard of Borth came to us with their men, we welcomed their arrival and provided for all their needs as though they were our own.[1]

That line, "since our house had its origins in your house" is intriguing yet crystal clear at the same time. It hints at a deep connection.

There is also evidence from the later Templar trials that suggests Bernard was pulling the strings behind the scenes, even before he wrote his book, *In Praise of the New Knighthood: A Treatise on the Knights Templar and the Holy Places of Jerusalem.* In one such trial, held in 1310 at the Abbey of Sainte Genevieve, an extract recorded by the clerks of the Papal Inquisition Authorities reveals the following:

> your order of the Temple, founded at the Council for the honor of Your Mother, the Glorious St. Mary the Virgin and the Blessed Bernard, your Saint Confessor, elected to this office by the Holy Roman Church. It is he [Bernard] and other wise men, who have instructed them [the Templars] and entrusted them their mission.

> Holy Mary, Mother of God, defend your order, which is founded by your Saint and confessor, the Blessed Bernard.[2]

Was Bernard truly the original founder of the Knights Templar or was he merely the mouthpiece of some greater authority? In other words, was Bernard working directly on instructions from higher powers in the Catholic Church?

By the time Bernard wrote *In Praise of the New Knighthood* in the 1130s, the assignment he had passed on to de Payns and the other Templars was becoming clearer:

> What therefore is the end or result of this secular malitia, I do not say militia, if the killer sins mortally and the killed dies eternally? Indeed, to cite the words of the apostle: "He who ploughs ought to plough in hope and he who threshes does so in the hope of receiving the fruits."[3]

When he returned to France with his lord, the Count of Champagne, could de Payns have informed prominent members of the Catholic Church of his finds, his words perhaps reaching the ears of a young Bernard, who was still a monk at Cîteaux Abbey at this time but was about to rise swiftly through the ranks of the Church. Remember, the two men, de Payns and Bernard, were both natives of Champagne. Furthermore, one of the original nine knights who went on to form the first incarnation of the Knights Templar was an uncle to Bernard. This knight was André de Montbard, a man who would become the fifth Grand Master of the Knights Templar, and his sister, Aleth, was Bernard's mother.[4]

There was also a strong connection between Bernard and de Payns via another Hugh, the Count of Champagne. It was this Count who would donate the land for the foundation of the Abbey of Clairvaux, as an extension of Cîteaux Abbey. So, we see a clear conduit between Bernard and de Payns while the two men moved in the same circles in Champagne.[5]

Perhaps these revelations about de Payns hinted at something buried deep below Jerusalem. Bernard's mention of "he who threshes does so in the hope of receiving the fruits" is tantalizing as it could be a reference to a harvest that the Catholic Church hoped it might reap if only they put their backs to the plough.

Author and researcher Graham Hancock[6] suggests that, while in Jerusalem, de Payns became aware of Jewish Talmudic literature that described how the treasures of the Holy Temple were hidden below the holy of holies in secret rooms carved deep into the bedrock of Temple Mount prior to the invasion of the Chaldeans. One such example is found in the book of the Apocalypse of Baruch, thought to have been written in the 1st or 2nd century BC (2 Baruch 6.1–10):

> another messenger began to descend from heaven, and said unto them: "...
> I am first sent to speak a word to the earth, and to place in it what the Lord
> the Most High has commanded me." And I saw him descend into the Holy of
> Holies, and take from thence the veil, and the set-apart ark, and the mercy-
> seat, and the two tables, and the set-apart raiment of the priests, and the altar
> of incense, and the forty-eight precious stones ... And he spake to the earth
> with a loud voice: "Earth, earth, earth, hear the word of the mighty Elohim,
> and receive what I commit to thee, and guard them until the last times, so
> that, when thou art ordered, thou mayst restore them, so that strangers may
> not get possession of them."

In a further section of the text it seems that *all* the treasures from the Holy Temple were spirited away, not only the Ark of the Covenant, so possibly the menorah and its copies were as well (2 Baruch 80.1–3):

> the enemy had surrounded the city, the messengers of the Most High were
> sent, and they overthrew the fortifications of the strong wall, and they
> destroyed the firm iron corners, which could not be rooted out. Nevertheless,
> they hid all the vessels of the sanctuary, lest the enemy should get possession
> of them.

In later Jewish texts we read how a secret chamber had been prepared long before, even as far back as Solomon's time, should the treasures from the holy sanctuary ever need to be hidden:

> When Solomon built the Temple, he was aware that it would ultimately be
> destroyed. [Therefore] he constructed a chamber, in which the ark could be
> entombed below in deep, maze-like vaults.[7]

Divrei Hayamim II (Chronicles II; 35.3) of the Tanakh (Hebrew Bible) in the Ketuvim tells us that it is King Josiah who returns the Ark of the Covenant to the Temple following its removal and safeguarding by himself or a predecessor:

> And he said to the Levites who taught all Israel, who were holy to the Lord, "Place the Holy Ark in the House that Solomon the son of David, the king of Israel, built; you have no burden on the shoulders; now serve the Lord your God and His people Israel."

There are many other similar references and they all tell us roughly the same thing, that either some or all the treasures from the sanctuary were hidden and not lost. Hancock maintains that de Payns became aware of this crucial information *prior* to the formation of the Knights Templar in 1118, while on his first pilgrimage to Jerusalem in 1104 when he accompanied his cousin, the Count of Champagne.

Bernard displayed a deep affinity for the mystical Song of Solomon, also known as the Song of Songs, and created 86 sermons providing a detailed commentary on its content and meaning. Bernard was also said to have taken a great interest in the Kabbalistic schools that flourished in Troyes. So, stories—or even simply an indication—of the treasures of Solomon being so tantalizingly close to hand could well have inspired Bernard to take action. If Bernard shared these revelations with his superiors in the Catholic Church, this could explain what happened next.

In those early days prior to the formation of the Knights Templar, was a plan devised to recover the treasures? This could indeed have been the impetus behind de Payns' return to Jerusalem, and whether the guiding hand of Bernard or someone higher up the chain of authority pushed him into action, the result was the same. A few years after returning to Jerusalem, de Payns suddenly had the support and ear of Warmund, the Patriarch of Jerusalem, and joined forces with eight other knights to form the Knights Templar. Something as grandiose as the recovery of sacred Old Testament artefacts would have required decisive action, and the formation of the Knights Templar seems to have been the direct result of agreeing to do exactly that.

Bernard himself seemed to benefit from his position as founder—or catalyst—of the Knights Templar and he went on to wield significant power in the Church. During the Council of Étampes in 1130, called by King Louis VI of France to resolve the claims of two rival popes, Bernard was asked to intervene and judge between the two men. He eventually favoured Innocent II. Later still, in 1145, a disciple of Bernard's, Bernardo da Pisa, a fellow Cistercian monk, was elected pope, becoming Eugenius III. It would seem that Bernard was the power behind the throne and he quietly assumed the role of pope-maker.

A papal legal statement

We had followed the scant breadcrumbs of information scattered in the remaining documents that had survived down the ages and we now gathered all the pieces of evidence concerning the origins of the Knights Templar together and laid it out before us. There were only four contemporaneous chroniclers who wrote about the order's foundation, only one of which was a direct eyewitness. While this might not seem much to go by, we felt that the written statements we had in front of us spoke for themselves. Furthermore, there was one additional statement that revealed the hand of a pope and the Catholic Church. Innocent II, the pope selected on the basis of Bernard's judgment, inserted a sweeping legal statement in his papal bull *Omne Datum Optimum,* publicly claiming possession of whatever the Templars might find beneath their headquarters in Jerusalem:

> We establish that the house or Temple, in which you have assembled for
> the praise and glory of God and the protection of his faithful, as well as the
> liberation of the Church of God, with all its possessions and goods, which it
> is known to hold legitimately at present and which may be obtained in the
> future . . . will be under the protection and tutelage of the Holy See for all
> time to come.[8]

Omne Datum Optimum is translated as "Every perfect gift," but perhaps it is better translated as "Every gift perfect." Bernard's choice of pope makes it clear that the Catholic Church claimed ownership of everything and anything that the Knights Templar uncovered—all past and future finds included. From our point of view, this was the capstone confirming our theory: it was the Church itself that had set the wheels in motion, in effect ordering the creation of the Knights Templar, and initiating an expedition to search for something, or maybe some *things.*

The protection and privileges they later received from the then Pope clearly indicates that they succeeded in their mission, so what exactly did the Knights Templar end up finding and possessing? To answer that question we needed to return to Jerusalem once more, to discover what de Payns was up to on Temple Mount during the first few years of the establishment of the new order.

The Templars in Jerusalem

The newly formed Knights Templar base in the al-Aqsa Mosque was more than a convenient headquarters and, as you can probably guess from their name, it held symbolic significance to the Templars as crusaders. The nearby Dome of the Rock was known as the "Temple of the Lord" to the Christians, but the al-Aqsa Mosque was thought to be linked to the Palace of Solomon itself.[9] This whole area up on Temple Mount had been the holy precinct for the Jews and the site of the first Temple, a name that de Payns embedded in the very title of his religious order.

What is intriguing is that de Payns himself had convinced King Baldwin to allow the newly fledged order to take up residence in a wing of the royal palace, a building that was the al-Aqsa Mosque in all but name during the Christian occupation. As we have outlined, we suspected that de Payns was already looking for the treasures of King Solomon, the long-lost Ark of the Covenant, the menorah, and the many other Temple artefacts, so it would make perfect sense for him to ask specifically to be quartered in the old al-Aqsa Mosque.

What happened next is, perhaps not surprisingly, unknown. People will no doubt ask us where the records of what the Knights Templar found at Temple Mount are today. We cannot answer that question, although in this book we make the case that what they eventually discovered was recorded, but not in readily accessible documents or books. If written accounts of the Templar's finds had once existed, it is very unlikely that such documents would have survived to the present day or we would even be able to decode them if they did turn up (the Templars' use of codes and ciphers in their documents is well documented). We have assumed that the Templars destroyed any such records when the order was dissolved in 1312, if not long before. That is, of course, unless the Catholic Church seized any documents when they rounded up the Templars, to protect the secret that the Church had a hand in uncovering the treasures of Solomon's Temple.

What we *do* have today is proof that the Templars were excavating and searching at Temple Mount. To catch a glimpse of what they might have found during those first few years of confinement in the *Templum Salomonis*, otherwise known as the al-Aqsa Mosque, we need to jump ahead to the modern era.

CHAPTER 7
EXCAVATIONS IN JERUSALEM

Very little modern-day excavation has taken place on Temple Mount, due simply to the political situation in Jerusalem. Temple Mount is controlled by the Jerusalem Islamic Waqf, a religious trust that acts as guardian for the Islamic buildings on the site. As a result, excavations by the Israelis are very rare and when they do occur, they almost always trigger protests.

In the 1860s, Jerusalem suffered from a polluted water supply that was affecting over half the population, caused mainly by the fact that the city had no fresh water and relied on rainwater stored in underground cisterns. A team of six British surveyors, headed up by Charles Wilson, a 28 year-old British Army officer posted to the city with the Royal Engineers, began an investigation that would last eight months. Wilson's experience as a surveyor was key to his appointment, but he was also an amateur archaeologist and his knowledge of the history of the area would prove critical during his thorough survey of Temple Mount.

Wilson kept extensive records of the expedition and it turned out that many of the underground cisterns were remnants of subterranean features of the second temple. Some of the other cisterns were revealed to be flooded underground mosques.

These and other findings were published in Wilson's *Ordinance Survey of Jerusalem*, in three volumes, and they make for fascinating reading. His report reveals just how hollow the bedrock beneath Temple Mount really is, with the whole area having been pierced and delved into almost continually for thousands of years. The result of this is that the hill today is more like a honeycomb than a solid promontory.

Wilson studied the enigmatic section of bedrock enclosed by the Dome of the Rock at length. Here there is a sacred rock that to the Jews is known as "*Eben Shetiyah*," the "Foundation Stone," while to the Muslims it is "*al-Sakhrah*," the "Noble Rock." This sacred stretch of bedrock is thought by some to be the site of the holy of holies where the Ark of the Covenant stood, while others believe it to be the altar of Solomon's Temple.

Below this sacred rock there is a cave, which Wilson describes as follows:

The entrance to the cave is by flight of steps on the south-east, passing under a doorway with a pointed arch, which looks like an addition of the crusaders. The floor of the cave is paved with marble and produces a hollow sound when stamped upon, not merely over the mouth of the supposed well, but over nearly the whole surface.[1]

It turned out that there was a further cave below this first one but, despite finding a narrow entrance in the floor, Wilson was unable to descend any further. Local Muslim inhabitants maintained that the lower cave was the *"Bir al-Aruah,"* the "Well of Souls," and old crusader legends said that this was the spot where the Ark of the Covenant had once been hidden. Wilson had water stained with red dye flushed down this hole in the floor of the cave and he found that it drained out all the way to the base of Temple Mount and into the Kidron Valley. This revelation has led some Jews to believe that it proves the bedrock in the Dome of the Rock is the site of the original altar in Solomon's Temple, and not the site of the holy of holies, because such drainage channels would have allowed the blood from the many sacrifices carried out on the altar to flow away.

If that is the case and this was the site of the altar, then, mapping where the holy of holies might have been placed on Temple Mount in relation to the altar, there is another stretch of exposed bedrock on Mount Moriah and below that we have further evidence from Wilson's survey has multiple underground chambers. Almost all these forgotten subterranean rooms and tunnels remain unexplored and many have not been entered since Wilson's day.

It should be noted that, while the impetus for the survey was a petition raised by Arthur Penrhyn Stanley, the Dean of Westminster, in London, and despite the British War Office paying for Wilson and his team to go to Jerusalem, no solution to the water crisis was ever found.[2] It seems that once the survey began, all consideration for the original purpose of the expedition simply evaporated. We are left wondering whether the survey had other aims and the whole things was a subtle ruse. Were the British simply looking for lost objects, or even treasure, in the labyrinth of spaces below Temple Mount, much as the Knights Templar were all those years before?

Something significant that we must draw attention to in Wilson's comprehensive study is a find he made deep below the surface, some 40–49 feet (12–15 m) down, in an area that he said marks the original sanctuary wall. Multiple passages and chambers were found, all of which had been altered and adapted over the centuries. Wilson found evidence that seemed to point directly to the presence of the Templars:

the workmen have left their mark on the wall in the shape of a Christian cross, of the type used by the early Christians, or during the Byzantine period.[3]

Wilson then discovered a curious feature in this subterranean network of tunnels:

> At the farther end of the passage, to the west, the same large massive stones
> are seen until the eye rests upon a large perforated stone closing it up. This is
> the first approach we have yet found to any architectural remains about these
> old walls . . . It consists simply of a stone closing up the end of the passage,
> with a recess or alcove cut in it 4 inches deep. Within this recess are three
> cylindrical holes 5¼ inches in diameter, the lines joining their centres forming
> the sides of an equilateral triangle.[4]

An illustration accompanies Wilson's description and to us it was immediately
clear that we were looking at a representation of the *segol*, an ancient Hebrew
symbol imbued with meaning (see Figure 1). The *segol* is an upside-down
equilateral triangle of three dots. It has been used to signify the Jewish people
as a whole because the people of Israel are composed of Kohanim, Levites, and
Israelites. The three points are also said to represent the patriarchs Abraham,
Isaac, and Jacob. Additionally, the *segol* symbolizes the Sephirot of Chesed on
the Kabbalistic Tree of Life.

Figure 1   Illustration of the *segol* from Wilson and Warren's book recording
what Wilson found in a tunnel below the sacred rock of Temple Mount
(Wilson and Warren, *The Recovery of Jerusalem*, 1871)

There is another word in Hebrew, *segula*, that has as its root the word *segol*. *Segula*, often means "treasure" and is found in the Tanakh (Hebrew Bible) in the Torah, Shemot (Exodus; 19.5) and Devarim (Deuteronomy; 7.6). In Shemot (Exodus; 19.5) it says:

> Now therefore, if ye will obey my voice indeed, and keep my covenant, then ye shall be a peculiar treasure unto me above all people: for all the earth [is] mine

This association of treasure with the *segol* was promising in our hunt for the menorah. The mention of both "treasure" and "covenant" in the text of Exodus led us to consider that the word *segol* may have had much closer ties to the menorah in the past, an association that today has been forgotten.

The *segol* also has a value of 30 in gematria, the ancient Hebrew practice of assigning words a numerical value to create alphanumeric ciphers. We were already aware that 30 was a significant number, because it references one angle of a 30-60-90 triangle, which is a geometric shape that points directly toward Solomon himself. The reason for this association is again down to gematria.

There are no vowels in Hebrew, so Solomon's name was spelled SLMN, using the Hebrew letters *samekh*, *lahmed*, *mem*, and *nun*. The gematrical values of these letters are 60, 30, 40, and 50, respectively. These numbers total 180, the same as the sum of the interior angles of a triangle. Furthermore, if you add the values of *mem* (40) and *nun* (50) together, resulting in 90, you are left with three angles of 30, 60 and 90 degrees. We had named this geometric shape the Solomon triangle.

There was another place where we had also seen this symbol of three dots arranged in a triangle, as found by Wilson. It was on a map from 1612, created by Samuel de Champlain, founder of what is now Nova Scotia, one of the provinces on the Atlantic coast of Canada, where Oak Island is located. We will revisit this curious synchronicity a little later in this book.

Back to Temple Mount: is it possible that the large stone Wilson discovered marked with this symbol was the entrance to the hiding place used to store the treasures from Solomon's Temple prior to the Chaldean invasion? Using the *segol* to mark the final sealing stone could have been a code to alert anyone looking to recover the treasures afterwards as to their location.

Wilson and Warren seem to have believed that the room directly below this strange blocking stone was used solely for storing water, casually writing that "whatever has been there, it has been violently removed."[5] However, we have to ask whether something significantly more important than water was once stored in this room, as indicated by the presence of the *segol*. Evidence of Christian marks directly in front of this stone could be confirmation that the Templars not only dug extensive tunnels of their own below Temple Mount but also discovered older networks of tunnels that the Jews had created, forming a subterranean labyrinth below Solomon's Temple and the sanctuary. Does this stone mark where the Templars made their breakthrough and rediscovered the menorah, and possibly the Ark of the Covenant? Wilson and Warren's comment that something seemed to have been "violently removed" sounded very suspicious to us, especially because of the accompanying *segol*.

There is evidence from other Templar finds that they seemed to have a particular fascination with underground excavations. In 2019, while making a documentary series for National Geographic, archaeologist Dr Albert Lin discovered extensive Templar tunnels beneath a crusader fortress in Acre, which is about 80 miles (130 km) from Jerusalem. An underground feature on that site is thought to have been a "treasure tower" and Dr Lin speculated that the Templars moved copious amounts of gold and other treasure to Acre to be stored there. Apparently, the tunnels were dug specifically as a means of secretly moving the gold in and out.[6]

These discoveries at other sites leave tantalizing clues as to the modus operandi of the Templars and provide us with evidence that they routinely moved—and stored—valuables and treasure at points across their territories.

Sacred knowledge

While the physical evidence of what precisely the Knights Templar uncovered on Temple Mount has been lost to us, there is plenty of circumstantial evidence that they found something of great significance while digging into the underground labyrinth that is Temple Mount. They also clearly came into possession of sacred knowledge that they brought back to Europe and infused into the architecture of the Gothic cathedrals of this time, resulting in a sudden, unprecedented magnificence to all they had a hand in building.

The wisdom of Solomon is sometimes taken to be a character trait, but legend states that the King had a vast library of esoteric knowledge. This has mostly been lost to history, but works have come to light over the centuries that, it has been claimed, originated from this ancient library. One such is *The Lesser Key of Solomon*, which is a magical text focusing on demonology, among other esoteric topics. This work comprises five books, the most well-known of which is probably *Ars Goetia*. The books include details of magical geometry, astrology, and how to communicate with angels—and demons. The oldest part of the text appears to be *Ars Notoria*, a book that was mentioned by medieval Scottish mathematician Michael Scot in the 1200s. Curiously, *Ars Notoria* deals at length with how to develop eidetic memory, which is the ability to recall every detail of an image or object after observing it for only a short time.

The earliest ancestor to the Solomonic books on goetia is one called the *Hygromanteia, a Solomonike*. The earliest copy is from the 15th century, but it is highly likely that this work is based on earlier sources. As with most secret traditions, we may well never establish the true sources or precisely how long they was passed along "mouth to ear" before being written down.

Other works supposedly authored by Solomon had already been discovered and are present in the Apocrypha, including the book of Wisdom, a text seemingly composed in Egypt around the 1st century AD. Ecclesiastes and the Song of Solomon, also known as the Song of Songs, and can be found in both the Christian Old Testament and the Hebrew Bible.

A hidden library from Solomon's Temple would have been a precious hoard in its own right, as this lost storehouse would have contained the fabled wisdom of Solomon.

The Templars seem to have possessed an uncanny appreciation and understanding of architecture, and they were very skilled in this art. Moreover, the papal bull of Pope Innocent II bequeathed the Knights Templar the unique right to build their own churches, which is a curious privilege.[7] Examples such as the exquisite circular Temple Church in London, built in the 12th century, demonstrate their skill in design and construction. But where exactly did they acquire this knowledge?

It seems a strange coincidence that the Templars displayed this profundity of knowledge right after they had taken up residence at the al-Aqsa Mosque and begun their legendary delving.

The great Gothic cathedrals of France rose not long after the Templars were officially recognized in 1139. In Normandy alone, between 1194 and 1220, 15 great churches were erected, eight of which had great abbeys attached. Another 13 followed during the remainder of the 13th century, with five abbeys also built. In France alone it is estimated that between 1150 and 1250, 500 large buildings were constructed, of which well over 100 matched the size of the Gothic cathedrals in Reims, Amiens, and of Notre-Dame in Paris. Given the level of technology at the time, the sheer scale of the construction work executed over a span of 100 years or so is almost unimaginable. If you have ever stood before one of these great edifices, as we have on more than a few occasions during our research, you realize just what colossal effort would have been required to erect even one of them.

Sacred proportions and geometry feature prominently in the design of the Gothic edifices and seemingly Bernard of Clairvaux himself was privy to this newly rediscovered font of knowledge, and his own designs were incorporated into the north tower of Chartres Cathedral.[8] Then there are Bernard's curious words in one of his texts, now famous and often cited, which seem, at the very least, to point to an understanding of the sanctity of proportion. He asks, "What is God?" and declares: "He is the length and breadth and height and depth."[9]

A little later in the same text, Bernard expounds on his point:

> Again, what is God? . . . In one he is above all, in the other, he is within all.
> It is clear that nowhere in the Godhead is equality limited. It stands square
> on all sides and is utterly consistent. Consider his power as the height and
> his wisdom as the depth. They correspond to one another symmetrically and
> while the height is beyond reach the depth is equally beyond seeing into.[10]

Another point to consider is whether the Templars found some of this store of lost knowledge not deep underground but in the ranks of their Muslim adversaries. There is evidence that, despite being Christian zealots, the Knights Templar respected their Muslim adversaries as equals. It is quite possible that the Templars saw in Saladin and the Saracens kindred spirits. The Muslim warriors the Templars encountered while protecting the Holy Land were just as devout and devoted to their religion as the Templars were to Christianity. Both groups of fighting men believed strongly in the concept of martyrdom and neither side feared death, so it is perhaps not unrealistic to suppose that they had an admiration for one another. They may not have prayed to the same god or carried the same holy book, but they would have had an understanding.

We know the Templars employed Muslim intellectuals, translators, interpreters, and scribes, and we believe that there was a significant transmission of information from the East to the West, with Jerusalem at the heart of that transaction. The Templars clearly learned a great deal concerning mathematics, architecture, and sacred geometry from their Muslim contacts.

In a letter written by a curious figure known as Prestor John—a legendary king and Christian patriarch said to rule a kingdom hidden among the pagan hoards of the Orient, and claiming to be a descendant of the Magi—the Templars are accused of being in league with the Saracens:

> There are Frenchmen among you, of your lineage and from your retinue,
> who hold with the Saracens. You confide in them and trust in them that they
> should and will help you, but they are false and treacherous . . . may you
> be brave and of great courage and, pray, do not forget to put to death those
> treacherous Templars.[11]

This is more than likely a misinterpretation of the Templar's interest in Muslim sacred knowledge, but it proves that the Templars were known for taking the Saracens into their confidence.

Additionally, during their stay on Temple Mount, the Templars did not destroy the Dome of the Rock or the al-Aqsa Mosque but, in fact, incorporated elements of Islamic architecture into their own churches, and these same features also appear in the later Gothic cathedrals. This demonstrates that the Templars were not only tolerant of Islamic ideology but also willing to adopt some of this Middle Eastern culture's motifs. Whatever the true impetus and provenance, the Knights Templar were instrumental in driving cathedral building to literally dizzying heights. We were later to discover that five of these buildings would play a huge role in our search for the menorah.

Evidence of treasure

After all these compelling tales of treasure, coupled with the secrecy of the Knights Templar, we wondered if there were any remaining clues left behind that might confirm our suspicions that the Templars did indeed find at least some of the treasures from Solomon's Temple.

There are hints that something miraculous *was* discovered by the Templars. One letter from Peter the Venerable, who was then Abbot of the Benedictine Cluny Abbey in France, to Everard of Les Barres, third Grand Master of the Templars in 1150, uses language that suggests the menorah itself might have been uncovered:

> I have marvelled and rejoiced that like the shining light of a new star you have illuminated the world.[12]

Everard was only Grand Master for five years, after which time he retired to become a monk at Clairvaux, the spiritual home of Bernard, the man who we were now convinced had ignited the spark that had led to the creation of the Knights Templar.

We also thought that we recognized the menorah in some prominent Templar iconography, albeit in a concealed form. Perhaps one needed to look no further than the seals the Templar Masters of France used to stamp into the wax that authenticated their most important documents (see Figure 2). The first seal we have is from 1171, used by Master of France Geoffrey Fulcher. Like, his successors, Fulcher used an image consisting of three upward-pointing chevrons over either two or four arches.[13] Around the images, a Latin phrase is displayed. To read the line of words ("*mil templi sal*," which means, "Militia of the Temple of Solomon"), you have to turn the seal around until it is upside down. In the process, the three chevrons then look exactly like a menorah with straight arms.

To add to the intrigue, on the reverse side of the seal, the text reads "*secretum temple*," or, "the secret of the Temple." That is a very explicit message in our opinion. However, the image on the reverse is an enigma. It looks like what is known as a "panthée" or "abraxas"—a mystical creature with two tails, which deserves a book of its own—but here it appears to represent the almighty bringer of light in seven letters. Oddly, we knew it from the Harry Potter series because Abraxas is the name of Lucius Malfoy's father, as well as the name of a species of winged horses in J. K. Rowling's fictional world.

Next we see seven five-pointed pentagram stars. Do these represent the menorah? Around the Templar shown on the seal, the Greek letters iota, alpha, and omega are visible, which symbolize the Greek version of the so-called Tetragrammaton, letters for God's holy name, Jehovah, the bringer of the light.[14] Is this a third reference to the menorah?

| Geoffroy Fulcher
1171 | Andre de Coloors
1214 | Olivier de la Roche
1225 | Amaury de la Roche
1269 |

To read the inscription on the edge of the seals, one would have to slowly turn around the seal revealing the straight arm Menorah with it's 7 branches.

 The reverse of the seals displays a Panthee, or Abraxas with 7 five-pointed pentagram stars as well as the Greek letters Iota, Alpha, Omega.

Figure 2 Seals of the Grand Masters of the Knights Templar used to authenticate important documents (Paul de Saint-Hilaire, *Les Sceaux templiers et leurs symbols* (Paris: Pardès, 1996))

We had seen this motif with the three chevrons before. It was used in the coat of arms of the French Cardinal Richelieu, the supreme schemer of King Louis XIII and King Louis XIV during the 16th and 17th centuries. These same three chevrons were also used by a powerful family associated with this mystery, also based in France: the de La Rochefoucauld family (we will meet members of this family in Chapter 16).[15] Were these armorials intended to be held upside down to represent a menorah with straight arms?

We attempted to assess the full implication of the menorah hidden in plain sight on the seals of the Masters of France. Could it imply that, at some point in history, the menorah was not only rediscovered but moved, taken from the Holy Land and transported to France? If so, when might this have happened and who was responsible?

Going back to the Knights Templar, there is one event right after the foundation of the order that hints at a seismic shift during those early years when the Templars were based solely in Jerusalem, up on Temple Mount. Something that points very clearly to the discovery of a significant cache of sacred artefacts. What remains are only faint, lingering echoes, mere whispers of what happened, but these fragments of the story are still compelling.

In 1125, Hugh, Count of Champagne, patron of Cîteaux, sponsor of Bernard of Clairvaux, the most powerful man in France after the King himself, abdicated, stepping aside from all his official functions and titles. He set off for Jerusalem to join the Knights Templar, leaving his old life, even his pregnant wife, behind.[16] At the time, the Templars were little more than a dozen or so in number, so, it is clear that something truly momentous must have happened for Hugh to leave all his earthly possessions and family behind to join the order. The recovery of an Old Testament treasure, or treasures, would certainly explain his actions.

This was not the only strange twist in the tale of Hugh, Count of Champagne. Rather than leave his titles and possessions to his eldest son Odo, as was the custom, Hugh instead disinherited both his sons and left everything in the hands of his nephew, Thibauld the Great, the Count of Chartres. This single act united the Champagne region and the lands around Chartres under one house. Were we looking at the birth of a grand plan here? The Templar knight Hugh of Champagne died in 1126, but not before the ground was broken at Chartres, marking the beginning of what would become the largest underground crypt in Europe and over which would eventually rise what is arguably the greatest Gothic cathedral ever seen.

The question we now asked ourselves was: what if this building was designed to assume an additional role, becoming possibly the greatest reliquary in the world?

It is our belief that the Knights Templar, with the powerful Hugh, Count of Champagne now among its ranks and at the heart of the order, eventually intended to bring the rediscovered treasures from Solomon's Temple back to France at some point in the future, when Chartres was finally completed and consecrated.

An ascent to power

Historians would have us believe that, first, the Council of Troyes and then the papal bull of Pope Innocent II that enabled the Templars to grow into the monolithic enterprise that followed, came about simply because of the influence of Bernard of Clairvaux and the saintly reputation of the knights themselves. However, we no longer had any doubts that there was much more to this story. If the Knights

Templar had found something significant beneath Temple Mount, perhaps a major part of Solomon's treasure, perhaps the menorah or even the Ark of the Covenant, then this would have instantly elevated their position. It now looked likely to us that Pope Innocent II was not only well aware of the finds—through Bernard, the talisman of the Knights Templar—but also attempted to legally claim such treasures for the Church. The Pope's endeavors would ultimately fail and the Templars somehow always managed to keep the Catholic Church at arm's length— for a time at least.

These hidden riches—treasures that went beyond wealth itself due to their symbolic importance—clearly made the Templars immensely powerful and almost untouchable. From the mid-12th century onwards, kings and popes alike would have Knights Templar alongside them as attendants or advisers. King John of England even had a Templar beside him when he signed the Magna Carta in 1215. However, the power of the Templars, though it lasted for many decades, was merely transitory.

We have reason to believe that they would retain the treasures of Solomon for a little over 100 years before finally being forced to share ownership some time in the 1250s, after a disastrous miscalculation. Even after the Templars had lost full control of the treasures, they still retained much of their influence, wealth, and power, but this catastrophic loss clearly marked the beginning of their end. The Templars no longer had sole possession of their great bargaining chip and the protection they had enjoyed would vanish.

As you are no doubt aware, in 1312 the end arrived swiftly when Pope Clement V issued a new papal bull, *Vox in Excelso*, that ended the Church's support of the Knights Templar and called for the dissolution of the order. A second papal bull, *Ad Providam*, handed over almost the entirety of the Templars' assets to the Hospitallers. What had been started with such great hope by Bernard in France and Hugh de Payns in Jerusalem ended swiftly in fire and torment.

So, how exactly did the Templars lose everything after discovering the most powerful objects in the world, the fabled treasures of Solomon? Furthermore, the bigger question is: what fate awaited those sanctified items?

To address these questions, we need to return to France, go forward in time 100 years, and meet one of the greatest kings of the Western world—a man who was seen as the supreme Christian leader, a king of kings in the same league as King Solomon himself.

It is time for Louis IX to enter the story, a king closely entwined with the Knights Templar and, subsequently, the menorah and other Temple treasures.

CHAPTER 8
O JERUSALEM, O JERUSALEM

In August 1270, the great French king, Louis IX, lay dying in his tent outside the city of Tunis, in North Africa, amid the ruins of the ancient port of Carthage. This is the famed city that, as we saw in Chapter 4, had briefly housed the menorah and other treasures from Solomon's Temple, after being seized from Rome by the Vandals.

So it was that, at midnight on August 23rd, St Louis received the last rites from his personal confessor, Geoffrey of Beaulieu. By the early hours of the 25th, his condition began to worsen. His bed was covered in ashes (the mark of a penitent) and a huge cross was set up in the tent. It is said that, as he slipped away, his speech become ever softer until he was heard to utter a few final words, which included:

> O Jerusalem, O Jerusalem . . . I will go into your house, I will worship towards your holy temple, and I will give glory to your name.[1]

Perhaps these do not seem strange words for such a devout Christian, for whom Jerusalem would always be a clarion call, especially as he had been a crusading king, but the phrase "your holy temple" does seem to have some curious significance. It is rather an odd choice for a Christian because it sounds more like a reference to the Temple of the Jews that had existed on Temple Mount in Jerusalem and formerly housed the menorah and all the other sacred implements. "I will give glory to your name" could also be said to be an allusion to the Tetragrammaton, which is the name of God that was given to Moses on Mount Sinai: YHWH. As we went on to explore the secret life and passions of Louis IX, it would become clear to us that these last words were loaded with symbolism and reflected his secret life's work.

After his death, the body of Louis IX was boiled in wine to clean the bones. A tomb was erected for him in the basilica Cathedral of Saint-Denis, which consisted of a box covered with a cloth, along with an effigy of him standing upright—a precedent that broke with the usual tradition of depicting the dead monarch as a recumbent figure.[2] This striking, erect effigy of Louis IX has more in common with a cult image standing on an altar, hinting perhaps at the idolization of St Louis that would follow his death.

The great king was gone, leaving a legacy that would live on long after his death. However, now it is time to study his life in detail and examine exactly why he had referenced Jerusalem and the holy Temple in his last words.

The young King Louis IX

Louis was only 12 years old when his father, Louis VIII, died in 1226, having reigned for a mere three years.

Louis was crowned in Reims Cathedral but, because of his age, his mother, Blanche of Castille, ruled in his stead as regent until he reached a more mature age. Just what age that was is open to debate and the matter is not satisfactorily answered by the chroniclers of the time. Some say it was when Louis married Margaret of Provence in 1234, aged 21, but it is not clear that he was, in fact, ruling in his own right at that time. Even his marriage had been dictated by his mother, and it was a political union. Margaret was the daughter of the Count of Provence and she and her three sisters all became queens, Eleanor becoming Queen of England.

Even though Blanche had arranged the marriage, she was jealous of Margaret and hated that Louis' new wife deprived her of her son's full attention. Blanche would frequently interfere in their marriage and there are accounts that she was responsible for numerous difficulties between the King and his queen, to the extent that Louis even began to distrust Margaret and limited her powers and influence.

There appears to have been a long period when Louis and Blanche were co-rulers, and Blanche seemed reluctant to hand over power, having ruled for so long as regent. Even when Louis did finally begin to exercise control over the throne, there were hardly any changes in policy at all and it seems that Blanche was still pulling the strings. Louis' mother would remain one of the King's closest advisers throughout his life and she would also reprise her role, ruling France as regent while Louis went off to pursue the Seventh Crusade.

Louis seems to have gained confidence as he took control of military affairs in France. This occurred throughout the 1230s to 1240s when he personally led his troops, crushing the last of the rebellions in his kingdom. Under Louis IX, the extent of the royal powers were greatly expanded and the King ruled over an area roughly the same size as modern-day France. A parliament was established in Paris and the city itself grew in both influence and size.

The first time Louis and his mother had a serious difference of opinion was when he took up the cross and announced that he was launching the Seventh Crusade. This is perhaps understandable because her husband—Louis' father—had died while on the Albigensian Crusade against the Cathars, aged just 39, so she must have feared that her son would mirror his father's fate. She pleaded with her son, in tears, but this time she did not get her own way. Many commentators over the years have remarked that Louis IX's determination to lead the Seventh Crusade was born out of a desire to finally step out of his mother's shadow and assume the mantle of kingship. Here, at last, was something he could achieve for himself, and for Christendom.

Accounts of the Seventh Crusade describe Louis leading his men from the front and dashing into the fray with no care for his own life, such that there were times when he had to be physically restrained at times, lest he charge straight into the lines of the Saracens. It seems that, on the battlefront, fighting the holy war, Louis was finally free.

It was not only the crusades that became an outlet for Louis' growing religious fervour; he also grew to be an obsessive collector of Christian relics. The most prominent of these was the crown of thorns that Jesus had been made to wear prior to his crucifixion, as he was tormented and mocked in Jerusalem for being the "King of the Jews." In John's Gospel, the crown of thorns is put on Christ's head by Roman soldiers while Pontius Pilate, the Roman governor of Judea, is deciding his fate.

In an account from the 5th century, this crown of thorns was said to have been preserved in a church in Jerusalem, now lost to us—the Basilica of Mount Zion—along with other sacred relics from the crucifixion, including the post that Christ was bound to when he was scourged.[3] However, by AD 950, the crown of thorns had been transported to Constantinople and was safely stored near the Palace of Boukoleon inside the Church of the Virgin of the Pharos, along with other relics from the Passion including the holy nails, Christ's clothes, and a fragment from his tombstone.

In 1204, Constantinople fell to the crusader armies of the Fourth Crusade and Baldwin, Count of Flanders, was elected Emperor of the Latin Empire of Constantinople. The crusaders plundered the city for three whole days but the crucifixion relics of the Church of the Virgin of the Pharos survived and passed into the possession of Baldwin.

A year later, the barons of the Latin Empire secured a large loan from Nicolo Querini, a Venetian, using the crown of thorns as collateral and moved it to the Church of the Pantocrator in Constantinople. It remained there for many years until a further loan was taken out against the treasures in 1235, but this time the barons were unable to repay it, so they asked Louis IX to help. A deal was struck whereby Louis would settle all the debts and, in return, the crown of thorns would be transferred to France.

In the *Historia Susceptionis Coronae Spinea Jesu Christi*,[4] a 13th-century contemporary text by the Archbishop of Sens, there is a description of Louis taking part in a series of ceremonies to honor the arrival of this sacred relic. On August 19, 1239, he is said to have removed his own crown and worn a simple tunic (which has survived to the present day), then, barefoot, carried the crown of thorns into Paris.

Louis ordered the construction of a new holy church to store the crown of thorns, along with other sacred Christian objects from Jesus' Passion. Sainte-Chapelle, in the grounds of the royal Palais de la Cité, on the Île de la Cité in Paris, was built in the Gothic style and completed in 1248. Its west facade resembles the south side of the crusader Church of the Holy Sepulchre in Jerusalem. The architect of Sainte-Chapelle is said by some to be Thomas de Cormont, who had previously worked on Amiens Cathedral, gaining great experience, though others think it was Pierre de Montreuil, and some other names have also been mentioned.

Sainte-Chapelle is distributed across two floors, and the décor of the ground floor, which served members of the court, was relatively restrained, while on the first floor there is an opulent chapel that was exclusively for members of the royal family. Effectively, this inner sanctum was an ornate stone frame, designed to hold some of the most beautiful stained-glass windows in the world.

King Louis spent astronomical amounts of money on his quest to possess objects touched by Jesus. Aside from the sums paid to settle the barons' debts and secure the relics from the Passion of Christ, which is said to be some 135,000 livres, Louis spent a further 100,000 livres on the Grand-Chasse, which is a large, elaborate silver chest to store them in. To appreciate how vast these sums were, a livre (predecessor of the franc) was roughly equivalent to one troy pound (12 troy ounces, which is 0.823 of a pound, or 0.373 kg, rather than 16 standard ounces, or 0.4 kg) of silver. In contrast, the building and glazing of the Sainte-Chapelle cost *only* 40,000 livres.

The crown of thorns was a potent symbol for Louis IX. It reinforced his belief in the notion that the Capetian dynasty, the ruling house of France, was blessed with divine kingship, and professed to the world that its rulers were the *Rex Christianissimus*, the "most Christian kings." They could trace their line back to the great Old Testament kings, such as Solomon and David, and now, under Louis, with his ownership of the crown of Jesus, there was a sense that the royal line was creating a new Jerusalem in France, a heavenly kingdom on earth. This was not a new idea, judging by Pope Gregory IX's characterization of the French in 1229, which was that "the kingdom of France is distinguished above all other peoples of the world by being singled out for honour and grace by the Lord."[5] Also, the papal charter for the foundation of Sainte-Chapelle stated that, with the possession of the crown of thorns, Louis IX had been crowned with Christ's own crown. Perhaps this identification with the great biblical kings is what tempted Louis to proceed with his next religious acquisition, one that was not Christian in origin, but Judaic, with a much older legacy.

The treasure of the Knights Templar

During the 1250s there was a significant shift in power, one that imperceptibly changed the surface of the political world in Europe, generating ripples for several centuries. This event marked the beginning of the decline of one of the great powers of the known world: the Knights Templar.

The precursor for this event was the collapse of the Seventh Crusade, which from start to finish was nothing short of a catastrophe for the Christians. After some early gains, Louis IX's entire army was cut off in the Nile Delta of Egypt, just south of Damietta, a town that the crusaders had captured a few months before. Conditions were appalling and Louis and his men, starving from a lack of supplies, fell victim to disease. Louis himself was so ill with diarrhoea that he had the seat of his breeches cut out. His gums rotted, his teeth fell out, he was prone to constant nosebleeds, and he grew pale and weak. If the King was in such a sorry state, we can only imagine how his men were faring.

The Knights Templar fought alongside Louis' forces for the duration of the Seventh Crusade, under the command of Grand Master Guillaume de Sonnac. Spurred on by their initial success after landing at Damietta, where they won a decisive victory against the Egyptians, the two leaders marched south to Cairo and walked straight into a trap at the town of Al-Mansurah. A massacre ensued, with the Knights Templar caught up in the worst of the fighting, and they were destroyed almost to a man. The Grand Master himself was gravely injured and lost an eye in the fighting, yet, despite this, he managed to fight his way through the Egyptian lines with only two men remaining to fight with him. He lost close to 300 of his men in the ambush.

The Grand Master staggered back to rejoin Louis once more, but the Egyptians countered again and again. At the end, Guillaume de Sonnac lost his remaining eye and then his life.

Louis managed to retreat, but the reprieve did not last long. After clinging on and enduring much hardship, the final assault came at the Battle of Fariskur, and this time not only was the King's army utterly defeated by the Mamluks but also Louis was captured and taken in chains to Cairo.

It was a miracle that Louis survived the crusade at all, and he would surely have lost his life at Fariskur if it had not been for the actions of Jean de Catalogne, protecting his sovereign in battle.[6]

In a curious twist to our story, we found out that one of de Catalogne's descendants was a 17th-century French engineer who designed the Fortress of Louisbourg in Nova Scotia, a place that will feature prominently later in this book (in Chapter 19), but back to our story.

The capture of Louis IX, Europe's most powerful monarch at the time, was a stroke of genius by the Mamluks and it would prove to be the decisive blow in the campaign. They said that it would take a ransom of 800,000 gold coins to secure the King's release and, worse still, significant concessions also had to be made, including the return of territory gained by the crusader army at the beginning of the campaign. Sporadic fighting would continue for several months, but effectively the Seventh Crusade was over.

It is here that the man who would become the next Grand Master of the Order of the Knights Templar enters the tale. Renaud (which means "wolf" in old French) de Vichiers, then Marshal of the Temple, had been known to Louis before the crusade and the King had tasked him with hiring a Genoese fleet for the French troops.

When Louis' ransom was agreed, the French forces gathered together all the coins they could, including all that was stored at Damietta, but they were short by a significant sum. Jean de Joinville, one of the King's closest advisers, suggested that they send for the Knights Templar and ask the commander, Étienne d'Orricourt, and the Marshal of the Temple, de Vichiers, to loan them the money that they were missing. As the self-styled bankers of the European powers and the newly formed Outremer, also known as the Crusader States, they were the obvious people to ask. However, the commander refused to lend the money, despite having more than enough on his flagship, using the excuse that the Knights Templar at Damietta had no money of their own and all they safeguarded belonged to depositors. Commander d'Orricourt maintained that money lodged with the Knights Templar could only be returned to the depositor in person and they could not hand the money over to someone else, not even the King.

It was de Vichiers who came up with the solution, suggesting that if the King were to steal the money, then there was not much the Templars could do and, furthermore, they could then simply deduct the amount from the King's reserves, which were held by the Knights Templar at Acre in Outremer. Then de Joinville promptly took up an axe and was about to smash open one of the chests when de Vichiers handed him the keys.

With the ransom paid, Louis was released in 1250 but, rather than return to France, he accepted an offer of hospitality from the Marshal of the Temple, de Vichiers, who was acting leader of the Templars until a new Grand Master was appointed. So, the King sailed to Acre, a chief city in Outremer, where he spent the next four years.

It is said that the King spent much of his time engaged in personally strengthening the defences of what remained of the kingdom of Jerusalem. Using his great wealth and influence, he rebuilt the crusader-controlled strongholds such as Caesarea, Jaffa, and Sidon, even hauling buckets of earth with his own hands to aid in the construction of the fortifications. However, could there have been another reason for Louis tarrying in the Holy Land for so long? Was he perhaps there to further pursue his obsession with religious relics?

We've seen how the French king was one of the world's most avid relic collectors, and he was particularly fascinated by anything that had come into physical contact with Jesus himself. He already possessed the crown of thorns, along with the holy lance, pieces of the true cross, nails from the Passion of Christ, and the Mandylion—also known as the Image of Edessa—a piece of cloth bearing the likeness of Jesus himself. However, as well as his obsession with artefacts, Louis also used his time in the Holy Land to visit the locations detailed in the Bible and even negotiated access to Nazareth, so central to the story of the Nativity.

While Louis remained stationed in Acre, he continued his friendship with de Vichiers, Marshal of the Temple. They had known each other in France, before they left for the Holy Land, and Louis asked de Vichiers to be godfather to his new son, Jean Tristran, born in 1251. However, de Vichiers declined, citing Templar law, but another honor was conferred instead, one that this time de Vichiers graciously accepted: being appointed Grand Master of the Knights Templar.

This growing friendship between the two men did not last long. Only a year later, in 1252, there was conflict between Cairo and Damascus—two old rivals—and both sides approached the French for assistance. Louis was of a mind to support Cairo, thinking of the many crusaders still held there at the mercy of the Sultan, while de Vichiers and the Templars were keen to support their old allies, the Damascenes. Taking matters into his own hands, de Vichiers presumed to negotiate a secret treaty with Damascus and he then went to Louis to inform him of the new agreement. Louis lost his usual calm demeanor and flew into the rage of his lifetime.

The King instantly demanded that all the Templar Knights assemble before him, along with the Damascene ambassador. Louis then admonished the Grand Master, in front of his men, demanding that de Vichiers inform the ambassador that he had made a grave error and, furthermore, because the King's agreement had not been sought, all terms and conditions cited in the treaty were subsequently null and void.

With this done, de Vichiers and the assembled brethren were utterly contrite. They knelt before the King and asked for forgiveness. It is at this point that the Grand Master, keen to make good this gravest of mistakes, held out the skirt of his cloak to the King and he offered up to Louis all the possessions of the Knights Templar, including their most sacred treasures.[7] As we discovered in previous chapters, the Knights Templar were in possession of some of the greatest religious relics and objects on earth, including the treasures of Solomon that the Templars had unearthed in Jerusalem, and likely moved to their stronghold in Acre, a repository you may recall is known as the treasure tower.

What precisely happened after this schism between Louis and de Vichiers is shrouded in secrecy, but his misstep seems the point at which the Templars' inventory of sacred findings from the Temple in Jerusalem was finally revealed to Louis and when the Templars lost possession entirely of several artefacts from the Passion of Christ. We shall see the details of these when we reach the point in the story in Chapter 9 when Louis finally set sail from the Holy Land.

According to some accounts, de Vichiers went into exile after this reproach, ending his days in a monastery. However, others state that he died during a raid on Jaffa in January 1256.[8]

Some commentators have questioned why de Vichiers and the order made such concessions to Louis, especially as the Knights Templar were not known for bowing to royalty. For years their growing power had made them immune to the rules and regulations that most people had to adhere to. Formally, they were only answerable to the papacy, making them almost above the law—even those edicts passed down by the royal families of Europe. However, it seems that, in this instance, the Templars believed Louis to possess unique privileges and, as the greatest living Christian king, they also believed that he had been invested with divine authority, so should be obeyed. Additionally, it needs to be understood that this was a most severe transgression so required serious reparations. By handing over the pick of their Passion relics, and revealing that they possessed the menorah and other Temple treasures to Louis, they were safeguarding the Order of the Knights Templar, bringing the King into their confidence and asking him to share in their glory. This very political move seems to have saved their skin—temporarily, at least.

Because of its inclusion in the Old Testament, the menorah has always been a powerful symbol to Christians and it no longer remained simply a totemic object in Judaism. Here was a religious object of great significance, all of which was not lost on Louis, and he would have coveted the menorah because of its long history. We think it was at this point that the Knights Templar revealed not only the objects themselves but also their long-held plan to bring the hoard back to France and install the items in Chartres. Louis seems to have taken the bait and, together, the King and the Knights Templar brought forward the planned transfer from the Holy Land to France. The notion of bringing the menorah and the other treasures of Solomon back to France and securing them in the new holy kingdom he was establishing greatly appealed to Louis.

So, not long after this schism and power shift, Louis went home to France. Just before he had left his native land for the crusade, his mother, Blanche, had said to him, "Alas, my fine son, I will never see you again in this mortal life," and so it proved to be, because she died in 1252, at almost exactly the same time that the Knights Templar fell foul of Louis' temper. The official line is that Louis went home to attend to domestic matters, given that his kingdom was now being ruled by his brothers, Charles of Anjou and Alphonse, Count of Poitiers, where they acted as co-regents. There were also growing threats from England and Germany. However, we believe that Louis was keen to take possession of his latest acquisitions from the Knights Templar and ensure they were housed adequately, along with the Jewish treasures he now ordered the Knights Templar to bring over to France.

It was time for a quite remarkable journey, one that we have found evidence for in a historical record which is now almost entirely overlooked.

CHAPTER 9
LOUIS IX RETURNS TO FRANCE

Louis IX finally began his voyage home from Acre on April 25, 1254, accompanied by a wealth of treasures, if the accounts from the time are to be believed.

The King made the journey on an impressive ship named *Montjoie*, a nef (trade ship with three masts) that was said to be able to accommodate 400 passengers plus crew, along with 120 horses. Its name was the battle-cry of the Capetian kings, known as the "House of France," and it refers to Charlemagne's legendary banner, the oriflamme—a long, red, toothed banner, flown from the top of a lance—which had long been preserved at the basilica Cathedral of Saint-Denis, the burial place of the kings of old. Perhaps more intriguingly, it was also the name given to the hill from which the crusaders first set eyes on the city of Jerusalem.

The captain of the ship was a Templar described as "brother Remon" or "Hamon," who, we have established, was none other than the Master of Hyères, Raymond des Angles. It is clear that the *Montjoie* was specially outfitted for the journey. The vessel was complete with an exquisite royal tabernacle, in a similar style to that constructed in the time of Moses as a mobile temple when the Jews were traveling through the wilderness. This curious onboard temple was overseen by high priests clothed in the finest of robes—clergy entrusted with the task of protecting something of great religious value while it was transported across dangerous waters.

We are told in chronicles from the time that the ship was laden with holy relics and objects, so that is no secret, yet there was one among their number that had an extremely beguiling name. It was a relic of such importance that its very mention takes your breath away.

On St Mark's Eve 1254 (April 24), this mysterious object was brought onboard the *Montjoie*, which lay in the Templar harbor of Acre. It was shortly after Easter and the next day, April 25—the scheduled day of departure—was Louis' 40th birthday. According to the King's confessor, Geoffrey of Beaulieu, Louis:

saw to it that, before boarding the ship, the Body of Our Lord Jesus Christ was placed on board. He arranged for this sacred treasure to be placed in a most worthy and appropriate place and there he put up a costly tabernacle covered with a cloth of gold and silk.[1]

The precise Latin words Beaulieu used are *"corpus Domini Iesu Christi,"*[2] while Jean de Joinville, in a different account, describes the relic as *"le cors noftre seigneur qui estoit en la nef,"*[3] which means "the body of our Lord which was on the ship".[4] The pair of writers also describe additional holy relics of unknown provenance on board the ship, all headed for French soil.

It sounds almost unbelievable that Louis left Acre with the body of Jesus Christ on board his ship, but that is exactly what the eyewitnesses, in the form of these two chroniclers, recorded. Why did this knowledge remain ignored for so long? An account of such a significant discovery should surely be more widely known about and accepted.

Is there a chance that the chroniclers were referring instead to a sacred chalice with blessed hosts rather than the physical body of Jesus? A host would indeed be the transubstantiated Body of Christ for believers, as we still see in a Catholic mass today. If that were true, however, it does not explain the other holy relics on board the ship. Furthermore, why erect a tabernacle on a ship, at great cost, for a single voyage of only six weeks, and why insist that the priests dress in special robes?

It is evident to us that Louis accompanied an object—or objects—of extreme religious value from the Holy Land back home to France. Perhaps even the preserved, physical body of Jesus himself. If that was so, then this would directly contradict the story of the Ascension of Christ into heaven and would call into doubt Jesus' divine nature. We only have the words of the King's chroniclers to rely on here, and each of us must decide whether we take them at face value or not.

As noted, the *Montjoie* left Acre on April 25, the day of Louis' 40th birthday. At the time, people would have been aware of 40 as an important number. It was the number of years both David and Solomon ruled, according to the Bible, and it was the number of years the Jewish people spent in the desert.

The King's flagship was accompanied by 12 other ships—an interesting number given the claim that it contained the body of Christ, because Jesus had 12 disciples. On the third day out, the ship was hit by a storm and ran aground on the rocks just off the coast of Cyprus. A great panic spread throughout the fleet, but by some miracle the ship freed itself from the rock and was afloat once again. According to Joinville, "Brother Remon went to the King who was stretched crosswise on the deck, barefooted, clad in a simple tunic, and his hair in disorder, before the Body of Our Lord, which was in the ship."[5] Beaulieu describes the same scene, adding that the King lay "devoutly prostrate before the Body of Christ and the Holy Relics, humbly praying."[6]

In contrast to this and other storms they faced, the ships also experienced days with no wind and they drifted aimless, their sails slack. Despite the many setbacks, after some six weeks at sea the small fleet finally reached the Mediterranean coast of southern France. The Queen and the high priests who had accompanied the King, and even the crew, at the end of their strength after such an arduous journey, begged the King to drop anchor, but Louis steadfastly refused. The King had his heart set on the port of Salines d'Hyères. His destination was a small monastery in the town where a Franciscan monk awaited his arrival.

Hugh of Digne was a spiritual Franciscan and a Joachimite, an avid devotee of Joachim of Fiore, a millenarian prophet who foretold the "Age of the Holy Spirit." This new era was supposed to signal the end of the papacy and the rule of the Church, brought about by a female embodiment of the Holy Spirit, a papess.[7] After Louis and his entourage finally disembarked from the *Montjoie*, the King's retinue sat in awe as they listened to Hugh of Digne recount the changes that were to come. Louis was so impressed and moved by this monk that he asked Hugh to follow him and join his court, but the monk refused. His excuse was that he answered to a higher power and there was still much work to be done.

Then de Joinville himself intervened and tried to persuade the monk to at least accompany the King for a short time on his journey home, but it was to no avail. Hugh grew angry and insisted that he was needed elsewhere. Refusing the demands of his King was not to be undertaken lightly, yet there were no repercussions in this instance.

In the end, Hugh agreed to spend one day with the King. In this final meeting, Hugh made a lasting impression on Louis. He spoke once again of the coming of the age of the Holy Spirit, and invoked the rule of justice, recounting how the King must act in accordance with God's will because Louis was the chosen monarch during these dire times.

This, he said, was the end of the age of the Son of God, and the dawning of the new aeon of the Mother Goddess, the Holy Spirit, the Shekinah. Hugh spoke of the end of the papacy and offered a prophecy, a vision of the death of the Pope, and of Saint Bonaventure. His final proclamation announced the demise of one of the most powerful institutions in the known world at that time, the Order of the Poor Knights of Christ and of the Temple of Solomon—the Knights Templar.

With the King finally at Salines d'Hyères, back on French soil, something very strange occurred. The body of Jesus and the holy relics mentioned by the two chroniclers disappear entirely from the record. They are never mentioned again and do not appear in any account, document, or depiction thereafter. What happened to them after that day is entirely open to conjecture and we can only speculate on where they were taken and stored.

One of the very first places Louis visited on his return to France, after meeting with the monk Hugh, was the hermitage of Mary Magdalene at Saint-Maximin-la-Sainte-Beaume—a location believed to be the very spot where the woman who was said to be the wife of Jesus[8] was buried, and so the basilica Saint-Maximin-la-Sainte-Beaume was built on the site. What was Louis IX's reason for coming to this precise spot? Did he perhaps know of the old tales that spoke of the union of Jesus and Mary Magdalene? Is this where he brought the body of Christ itself? Did Louis want to reunite the man with his wife or did he simply bring this relic here as a mark of respect before taking the body of Christ elsewhere? We will never know for certain, but it is an intriguing visit that should not be forgotten.

Along with the mysterious body of Christ and other relics from the Passion, we believe that it is extremely likely that the Jewish treasures discovered by the Knights Templar, which included the menorah, were also aboard Louis' ship, the *Montjoie*, and this is the moment that they were finally brought to French soil. There is no record today of their inclusion among the relics on board the ship, but it seems the perfect opportunity to bring them back to France from Acre, where they had been safely stored in the Knights Templar's treasure tower. At this point, the collection of precious artefacts seems to have been divided up, so it is worth exploring what happened to the treasures. First, we will examine where Louis stored his bounty.

The King's treasury

On his return from Acre in 1254, Louis installed a collection of documents and objects in what was called the "Trésor des Chartes," a specially constructed annex attached to Sainte-Chapelle in Paris. Curiously, the Trésor blocked the view of the north side of Sainte-Chapelle from the main palace entrance in the Cour du Mai and seemed to occupy a prime location in the palace grounds, taking precedence over aesthetics and the architectural integrity of the site.

The Trésor des Chartes comprised three levels, according to Jérôme Morand's *Histoire de la Sainte-Chapelle*, published in 1790. Morand described the Trésor de Chartes only after it had been demolished but he had seen the building while it was still intact.[9] The ground and first floors served as sacristies for the chapel, with the first-floor sacristy called the "Revestiaire," while the third, upper level housed Louis' personal library, which was installed in 1254, along with other archives. This was the actual Trésor des Chartes but it was by this name that the entire building was later known.

This top level had a separate entryway from the courtyard by means of a spiral staircase built on to the buttress of Sainte-Chapelle. It was on this floor that Louis had his Passion relics on display: the crown of thorns, the Mandylion, the holy lance, and pieces of the true cross. The interior of this upper level of the Trésor des Chartes was lined with armoires under every window, and an altar stood in the middle of the apse.

The Revestiaire, or vestry, on the second level, was divided into three rooms: the vestry sacristy room, the Trésor des Reliques (where the relics not displayed in the chapel were located), and a third room known as the Gîte, a space where the chaplains who guarded the relics in strict rotation, as stipulated at Sainte-Chapelle's foundation, spent the night (they are not to be confused with the wardens, who were always present). Why the Trésor was built on to the lateral portals of Sainte-Chapelle remains uncertain, but it is possible the designers placed it to the east so that it would be close to the main altar, where the relics were displayed.

Beaulieu described how this annex was built after the completion of Sainte-Chapelle in 1248, on the very eve of Louis' departure for the Holy Land and the Seventh Crusade. Beaulieu also noted that when the King returned from the Holy Land, in 1254, he decided to put his archives and a library in a building beside the chapel (the name "Trésor" was not used at the time, only employed later, in 1330).[10] The construction of this annex seems like an afterthought, yet it would appear that Louis had a special role in mind for this new building. We think it is very likely that whatever artefacts Louis was carrying back to France on the *Montjoie*, they eventually found their way into the sanctity of the Trésor des Chartes, where they were added to Louis' already impressive collection of sacred relics.

There is another event in the historical record that goes some way to proving the Knights Templar were in possession of numerous holy artefacts. It also demonstrates to us that they were in a position to hand some of them over to Louis.

As preparations were being made in 1247 for the Seventh Crusade, Louis sought to motivate King Henry III of England to join his cause and, in particular, to send troops to bolster Louis' own forces. The French king knew that the English knights would be crucial to the success of this new crusade. Louis was also conscious that transporting the bulk of his French forces to the Holy Land would leave France vulnerable to an attack by the English, so this was another reason for wanting as many English knights as possible taking part in the crusade.

The Knights Templar were already committed to Louis' crusade, so they stepped in to help win over the English. Grand Master William of Sonnac, the most senior Templar Knight in England, arranged for an extremely potent relic to be sent to Henry III all the way from Jerusalem, in an effort to sway him to lend his support to Louis. This artefact contained nothing less than several drops of the holy blood of Christ. John J. Robinson describes this most holy of objects, quoting directly from an account made at the time by English chronicler Matthew Paris:

> the masters of the Templars and Hospitallers with the testimony of a good
> many seals, namely those of the patriarch of Jerusalem and the archbishops
> and bishops, abbots and other prelates, and magnates of the Holy Land, had

sent some of the blood of our Lord, which he had shed on the cross for the salvation of the world, in a most beautiful crystal container.[11]

Henry III not only accepted this generous gift but he also arranged an elaborate public procession to honor its arrival in England. This parade took place on October 13, 1247:

> The procession went from St. Paul's to Westminster Abbey, then to the palace
> of the bishop of Durham and back to Westminster. It was so drawn out that
> men had to be assigned to walk alongside the King to support Henry's arms,
> lest his tired muscles allow the crystal decanter to fall into the road. The
> bishop of Norwich celebrated the mass that day and followed it with a stirring
> sermon to emphasize the importance of this invaluable gift. "Of all things held
> sacred among men," he said, "the most sacred is the blood of Christ, for . . . its
> effusion was the salvation of the human race."[12]

What this tale proves is that not only were the Templars in possession of relics from the Passion, including an unknown quantity of the blood of Christ, but also that Louis was well aware of this before he left France to go on the Seventh Crusade. The fact that he returned from that very same crusade—and after losing the war—with many of these objects suddenly in his possession should make us all sit up and pay attention. This tale of the blood of Jesus being sent from Jerusalem all the way to London should also serve as a reminder that Louis and the Templars had previous experience of transporting the most precious objects in the known world over vast distances, by ship.

This episode once again reveals the true reach of the Catholic Church and highlights its connection with the Templars, because there is a description of the blessing of the holy transport by the Patriarch of Jerusalem. This was a man who had held exactly this same office when he had been instrumental in founding the Knights Templar in 1120.

The treasures from Jerusalem

Now it is time for us to turn our attention to the Knights Templar themselves and study their portion of the spoils from the Holy Land. After landing at Salines d'Hyères, the Templars went about safeguarding the treasures that they had uncovered in Jerusalem. We only know for sure that they possessed the menorah, but they could also have brought the Ark of the Covenant back to France. Indeed, we will soon reveal evidence that hints at this.

We have to admit at this point that we are not entirely sure who had legal ownership of the menorah and the other treasures of Solomon, whether they were now owned by Louis or if the Knights Templar retained possession of the artefacts once they were shipped to France. We get the sense that the Knights Templar still owned these objects outright, otherwise Louis might have stored them in the Trésor des Chartes at Sainte-Chapelle, along with his other artefacts. However, there is the possibility that he *did* own the treasures and simply wanted them stored safely outside the capital. If that was the case, then he may not have deviated from the Templars' original plan to store them at Chartres.

Who physically held the title to the Jewish treasures at this stage becomes academic. The Knights Templar guarded the treasuries of ruling monarchs right across Europe, such as at Temple Church in London, which served as the royal treasury during the reign of King John. France was no exception, and whether the Templars themselves owned the Temple treasures or they were simply safeguarding them for Louis, it fell to the Knights Templar to safely store and hide the menorah and other Jewish treasures. So, whoever owned them, the treasures ended up on Templar property.

The only question remaining for us was: could we find evidence that the Knights Templar did, in fact, secrete such ancient objects on French soil?

CHAPTER 10
A SACRED PENTAGRAM IN FRANCE

It was during Louis IX's reign that the great Gothic masterpieces were completed across France. The interior of the basilica Cathedral of Saint-Denis was completed by 1231. Notre-Dame in Paris followed in 1234. Royaumont Abbey was completed in 1235 and went on to become the resting place for members of Louis' family. Significant parts of Reims Cathedral were completed between 1244 and 1250. Chartres Cathedral was consecrated by Louis himself in 1260, and Amiens followed in 1264. Also, we must not forget the masterful Sainte-Chapelle.

There appears to have been a pattern of churches going up in flames between the 11th and 13th centuries, to be replaced by the Gothic masterpieces we see today. What was then new would become the dominant architectural style for around the next 200 years. The Knights Templar are thought to have been instrumental in its emergence, based in no small part on the knowledge that they had amassed throughout their years in the Levant. It was often Templar money that had funded the construction of these vast edifices and it was their masons who had laid the stones. Without the Knights Templar and their knowledge and administration, it would have been impossible to achieve.

The Knights Templar were obviously deeply connected with this crucial period of Louis' life, so we thought it would be worth examining in more detail a building in France that was synonymous with the Templars. It is vast and rose from the ground just as the power of the Knights Templar was itself waxing: Chartres Cathedral. Then we thought, could we find something that linked this colossal masterpiece—that stood astride Europe's biggest underground crypt—to Jerusalem, perhaps something hidden in the fabric of the cathedral itself?

The cathedral road trip

The Cathedral of Chartres was completed in 1252, two years before Louis' return from Acre, but the King himself was present when the cathedral was finally consecrated in 1260.

The monolithic building seems to have been designed for a very specific purpose. After some organization and planning, we met at a Paris airport and drove to Chartres to see the famous cathedral.

It is hard to describe the cathedral fully without feeling the need to devote a whole book to the subject. Also, unless you have stood in its hallowed spaces yourself and witnessed first-hand how all-encompassing and beautiful it truly is, then it is difficult to convey its sheer majesty adequately. The dizzying height of its vaulted ceilings, the slenderness of its filigree stonework, the thousands of hues of light that burst through the unrivalled and seemingly endless expanse of stained glass—everything seems to have been designed to shock and awe the viewer. Outside, its pinnacles are so tall it seems as though they graze the sky. Inside, the sense of scale leaves the visitor reeling. It is a vast stone exclamation that convinces everyone who witnesses it that miracles must surely have played a part in its construction. Chartres Cathedral is a testament to people's determination and will, crafted by those with a shared belief in an almighty God who they sought to rival through their command of stone, marble, iron, lead, wood, and glass.

Just inside the entrance on the right of the cathedral, two knights stand behind a single shield, reminding us that the Templars had a hand in the creation of this spectacular building. These two knights are part of a group of statues representing the zodiac, and these symbolize Gemini.

Even before we entered the cathedral our necks were starting to feel strained from looking up. Once you pass through the entrance portal and have taken in the breathtaking vaulted space that rises above you, your gaze is suddenly drawn down into the church itself and, finally, to a striking circular feature set into the floor. It is the famous labyrinth of Chartres, a circular, geometric stone construction, with a single, yet complex, sinuous path. Measuring approximately 42 feet (13 m) in diameter, the labyrinth is laid out across the entire nave of the cathedral, filling the space completely, and 11 concentric circuits wind their way to the center of the maze.

We had made sure to visit the cathedral on a Friday. On every other day, chairs are laid out over the labyrinth, but on Fridays the chairs are removed, so visitors can see the labyrinth in all its glory and walk its path.

It has been said that the labyrinth at Chartres was seen as an alternative to the journey to Jerusalem, a version of the pilgrimage for those who could not afford the real trip or who were too frail for a journey to the Holy Land. For this reason, the labyrinth came to be known as the "Chemin de Jerusalem," which means "the Jerusalem Road."[1]

It was evident to us that the labyrinth is somewhat reminiscent of the circular representation of Jerusalem you see on certain medieval maps. On the Hereford world map, which dates from around 1300 BC—approximately 100 years after the construction of the labyrinth at Chartres—Jerusalem is not only shown at the center of the map but is also depicted as a circle with a halo of ornamentation, like that found in Chartres.

So, there we were, far from the Holy Land, looking at a representation of Jerusalem. The labyrinth at Chartres has been dated from somewhere between 1215 and 1221, just after the construction of the nave had been completed. Shrouding the labyrinth from the outside world was the colossal Gothic structure, a cathedral that dwarfs the small medieval town it sits in. When it was first built, this effect would have been even more marked, looking ridiculously out of place compared to the skyline of the modest settlement that would have been there then. We had asked ourselves many times, why this cathedral and the labyrinth at its heart had been built on this exact spot. Then there was the question of its true relationship with the Champagne area, and why Count Hugh of Champagne had put so much effort into uniting Chartres with the Champagne region before he left for Jerusalem to become a Templar himself.

While we attempted to walk the labyrinth, navigating our way through several groups of tourists, we tried to unravel our own puzzle. We imagined the thousands of pilgrims, whose footsteps we were following in, traversing this very maze, some of them on their knees to repent for their sins, expecting salvation at the center. A description from 1640 notes that the center of the labyrinth was originally covered by a brass plate, complete with a depiction of the combat between Theseus and the Minotaur. This link with Greek mythology felt strangely out of place, especially when we were standing in what was essentially a Catholic structure. We wondered if Ariadne had also once been represented on the brass plate, as, in Greek mythology, Theseus only manages to escape the labyrinth after following Ariadne's thread.

We couldn't help but behave like proper tourists, our mouths open in awe as we looked at the architecture, taking photos, trying to take everything in, yet at the same time, we were interpreting what we were looking at, working out how it might weave its way into our body of research. It wasn't until we were standing on the walkway high up in the church and looked down that we made one of our breakthrough discoveries.

Viewed from above, we could see that the design of the labyrinth had a very clearly defined geometry. The maze was divided into two halves, with each half again divided into two, creating four main sections, or four quarters, of the main circle. We noticed that each half had what appeared to be three upward-reaching arms on each side of the small circle set at the center.

We immediately realized that two mirrored menorahs were staring back up at us.

The small circle at the center of the labyrinth was the central candle of both the upper and the lower menorah, so both clearly had seven arms. We suddenly had goosebumps and a profound feeling of enlightenment and revelation. Here it was, hidden in plain sight, two intertwined representations of a seven-branched menorah worked into the floor of the cathedral. This depiction had been there for 800 years, the stones that formed its design sitting above the largest underground crypt in Europe, with seven underground chapels. What was the story of this cathedral? Were we looking at one of the largest reliquaries in the world? Had the Knights Templar created a larger version of Louis' Sainte-Chapelle for their grandest relics?

Not for the first time, we had more questions than answers.

One of the most pressing questions was: why were there two mirrored menorahs in the labyrinth, not just the one. We suspected that this image was an expression of duality. As above, so below. After all, the buried menorah had been recovered from the earth and brought into the light by the Knights Templar.

We also realized that the mirrored menorahs could represent the two locations linked to this sacred object: its original home in Jerusalem, and its new residence in northern France. Perhaps this succinct explanation also reflected the menorah's true origins. God showed the exact form that the menorah should take to Moses on the mountain, so the form of the menorah was the heavenly prototype, perhaps a celestial menorah, a constellation, a sacred tree of light. Moses and Bezalel then acted on those instructions and fashioned the earthly version of the lampstand. In the labyrinth, in the sacred space of the cathedral, the two menorahs were reunited.

More cathedrals, more labyrinths

Back at our hotel, we had a lot to discuss. We recounted what we knew and set about compiling a dossier on the Chartres labyrinth. We discovered that there were several other labyrinths like that at Chartres found throughout France, albeit with slightly different shapes. We also found out that Louis had an association with many of the churches that housed those labyrinths.

One example is Reims Cathedral, which had a famous labyrinth that was—also famously—removed by the local clergy in 1779 because they did not approve of the children having fun following the lines of the maze during mass. The existence of this labyrinth, and even its design, are well documented and, in fact, its image can be seen all over France as it is the symbol used on plaques put up on buildings and other places by the Ministry of Culture to indicate that they are either protected historic monuments or remarkable heritage sites. We therefore instantly knew that our next visit had to be to Reims.

No fewer than 33 French kings were anointed and crowned at Reims—including Louis IX, whose coronation took place there on November 29, 1226. This signifies just how important Reims was to the French monarchy.

When we arrived in Reims it was late and already dark. We were fortunate enough to still be allowed access to the cathedral, as we arrived during the last hour of its being open. As a service to the public, the shape of the former labyrinth of Reims is sometimes projected on to the floor from the ceiling and during our brief visit, we were blessed to witness this.

As we studied the design before us, we could hardly believe our eyes. Although the labyrinth was shaped more like an octagon this time, not a circle, the two sets of seven arms above and below its center were unmistakeable. Again, we were rewarded with the sight of two menorahs facing each other.

We were now on the hunt for further labyrinths.

Another cathedral that featured in Louis' life was one constructed in the town of Amiens. This, too, had a labyrinth—one that was installed during the life of the King, in 1260. This was four years prior to an event that is now known as the Mise of Amiens, when Louis received King Henry III of England in that very cathedral and settled a dispute between him and his barons.

We visited Amiens the very next day.

We had thought that Chartres was the pinnacle in terms of jaw-dropping, show-stopping architecture, but we were about to be surprised once again. Amiens Cathedral is the largest in France, and that is saying something because there is some stiff competition, including Chartres. At Amiens, everything is constructed on a grand scale, yet it also manages to possess a subtle and delicate nature, which is quite a balancing act, one that only the master craftsmen of the time managed to pull off. At 476 feet (145 m) in length, it is 49 feet (15 m) longer than Chartres; its ceilings are also 16 feet (5 m) higher and it is an astonishing 139 feet (42.3 m) from the floor to the apex of the vaulted ceiling. The effect is further enhanced by the cathedral being only 48 feet (14.6 m) wide. People smarter than us have worked out that it was built to a 3:1 ratio, which focuses the eye on the vertical lines rather then the horizontal, giving the cathedral greater elegance than any others built around the same time.[2]

Our feet back down on the ground, we walked the labyrinth of Amiens. It is slightly smaller than the one in Chartres Cathedral, but appeared to follow the exact same path, though this time with angular rather than rounded turns.

The labyrinth looked pristine, modern almost, executed in exquisite black and white marble. This is because the original was destroyed in the early 19th century, but, fortunately for us, it was later restored, following the original specifications exactly, allowing us to appreciate how the original would have looked in the 13th century when the cathedral was finished.

Like Chartres, Amiens was a very special place to the Templars and, with this in mind, another feature in the cathedral caught our attention. The huge stained-glass rose window of the north transept featured a large, upside-down pentagram, with two points of the star at the top rather than only one—a symbol frequently seen on the tombstones of the Knights Templar. This emblem was also an early symbol for Jerusalem, still visible on the Tower of David today. It is a symbol that stopped being used in the Christian Church, so we wondered why the architects of this cathedral had placed it here, in such a prominent position.

Another night of intense research followed, in yet another hotel.

We knew that only a select number of cathedrals in France contained labyrinths. We had now visited three of them and all three mazes resembled two mirrored menorahs (see Figure 3).

Playing around with the names of the cathedral towns after a glass of wine, we realized that the first letters of Amiens, Reims, and Chartres spell out the word "arc." While we had stumbled on this half in jest, this unexpected revelation would prove to have significant consequences later on in our search.

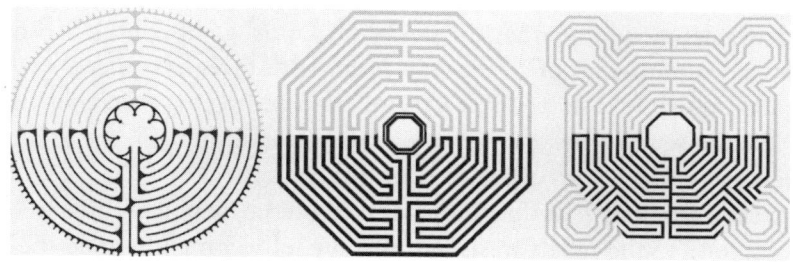

Figure 3 The labyrinths of Chartres, Amiens, and Reims (from left to right) each show two stylized, vertically mirrored menorahs with seven arms (Corjan Mol)

We continued our exploration of the central part of northern France with a trip to Sens, where Louis married Margaret of Provence in 1234. There we found another Gothic masterpiece from the same period as the previous three cathedrals we had visited.

Remarkably, Sens Cathedral also once had a large stone labyrinth that stretched across the nave. Studying the design on an information board, we found that, although less obvious than the labyrinths at Amiens, Reims and Chartres, here at Sens we could still distinguish the seven arms of a menorah hidden in the design. It looked rather like a photographic negative of the labyrinth at Chartres.

While at Sens, we learned more about the people who had worked behind the scenes to orchestrate the creation of these stone masterpieces. The work on what would become the cathedral at Sens was started in 1130 by Archbishop Henri Sanglier, an ally of King Louis VI.[3] Despite his strong connections to the King, the project only truly got underway after Bernard of Clairvaux became personally involved, writing a number of letters, some of which impressed on Sanglier the need to become humbler and more austere. The result of Bernard's intervention was that adequate funding was finally acquired to start construction.[4] The appearance of Bernard in this tale was intriguing, considering just how instrumental he had been in the creation of the Knights Templar.

After visiting the cathedral and admiring its stunning architecture, we settled with a coffee in the square outside. Sitting in the cool morning sunlight, we pored over a map of France on which we had marked the four labyrinth cathedrals that we had visited. Seeing their positions highlighted, we noticed that, if these four points were to be joined, they would create an almost perfect circle. Inside that circle was the whole of Paris, but the epicenter of the circle was slightly to the north of the city.

We turned to each other with more than a hint of excitement. This spot was a location we knew well—Royaumont Abbey, founded in 1228 by Louis IX and his mother (as Louis was only 14 years old at the time). This was the abbey that Louis visited more frequently than any other during his lifetime, the place that he helped build with his own hands, and the spot he designated to bury his wife and children.

It suddenly dawned on us that the design of Louis' great church at Royaumont was somewhat reminiscent of a menorah itself, with three entrances, each leading to a central nave that was shaped like a tripod, and ending in seven chapels north of the altar, like the seven arms and lamps of the menorah. In turn, the floor plan was almost identical to the layout of the cathedral at Amiens.

When we looked further at the points marked on the map, it seemed to us that we were missing one to the north-west, but we now fully comprehended the meaning of the ones we had found. Maybe we had sensed this when we looked up and saw the huge pentagram in the stained glass of the north transept of Amiens Cathedral.

We saw a giant pentagram plotted across the landscape of France, with four of its five points revealed in the form of cathedrals that each contained a tell-tale feature, unifying them: a labyrinth consisting of two mirrored menorahs. We now needed to find the missing fifth location to complete this vast pentagram.

After some provisional measuring and deliberation, we became convinced that the missing point could only be Rouen Cathedral. We then spent the rest of the day driving to Normandy, eagerly anticipating our visit to what is said to be one of the most beautiful churches in the world.

Approaching the city via a motorway, we noticed not one but two giant Gothic structures of similar size, standing very close together, but we ignored this for now, focused as we were on getting to the cathedral.

As we looked round Rouen Cathedral, we were very impressed by its sheer presence and demeanour, yet to our surprise and disappointment, we weren't able to find the tell-tale signs we were on the right trail that we had found in the other cathedrals. There were no pentagrams, menorahs, or even Templars. Worse still, there was no sign of a labyrinth in the cathedral and no mention of there ever having been one, so we left, unsure what this meant for our fledgling theory. Could we have become too wrapped up in the excitement of the chase and got ahead of ourselves?

We had planned to head straight to Royaumont after visiting the cathedral, but we suddenly remembered the second Gothic structure in Rouen—the one that we had seen from afar as we entered the city. We decided that it was worth a quick look.

Saint-Ouen Abbey church in Rouen is another undisputed masterpiece. It rivals the official cathedral and, in many ways, trumps it. Although it is no longer used as a church, and the former abbey it was once a part of is now the town hall, the building can still be visited and it possesses all the grandeur and glory it was blessed with in the Middle Ages.

As soon as we crossed the threshold of Saint-Ouen we knew that we had found our missing church. High up in the north transept was a massive rose window, mostly filled with a pentagram shape, supported by seven arches. We couldn't find a labyrinth, but we learned that the construction of this church had been interrupted many times and the designs were now lost, so the question of whether it had contained a labyrinth originally could not be answered. However, a helpful guide showed us the tombstone of one of the architects, which, to our surprise, featured not one but two figures. The guide recounted the legend of master mason and architect Alexander Berneval. According to the story, Berneval had just finished the pentagram rose window and, after taking a break, returned to find that his young apprentice had finished the rose window on the opposite side of the church. It depicted the tree of Jesse—a branching tree that displays the ancestral lineage of Jesus Christ, originating with Jesse of Bethlehem, the father of King David. This second stained-glass window apparently overshadowed the pentagram window by Berneval so, in a pique of jealousy, the master killed his apprentice.[5] Berneval was later tried and executed for this heinous crime and, in a strange twist of fate, both master and apprentice were buried together, as a lesson for posterity.[6]

Hearing this tale, we felt goosebumps rising again. We had heard it before in another form. It bore a remarkable resemblance to the story of Hiram Abiff, master mason and chief architect of King Solomon's Temple. There is also a version tied to the story of a carving called the "Apprentice Pillar," which is to be found in Rosslyn Chapel in Scotland.

At last we were able to fill in the blank space on our map. Our five locations were Sens, Amiens, Chartres, Reims, and now Saint-Ouen. The full pentagram was revealed in all its glory, stretching out across France.

We celebrated the next day by traveling to the very heart of the huge five-pointed star that we had drawn across the landscape of France. We sat in the gardens of Royaumont Abbey, sipping coffee and pondering our discovery.

This was surely the largest pentagram in the world, constructed on such a scale that we wondered how it had remained hidden for so long. Each of the labyrinths constructed at each of the points of the pentagram were completed during the 13th century, sometime between 1220 and 1280, a period in history that was crucial in our roadmap of the menorah's travels. Furthermore, four out of five of the pentagram's points we had identified from the mirrored menorah design used for the labyrinths, while the fifth point had a distinctive pentagram rose window. Although knowledge of it has been lost to history, it may also have had a labyrinth originally.

It had been chance that had led us to Saint-Ouen Abbey church, when the more likely candidate for our search, Rouen Cathedral, was right next door. However, the more we looked at Saint-Ouen, the more we realized that its secret had been hidden in plain sight. Saint-Ouen had also played an important role in the history of France, as it was there that the royal house of France was restored after the French Revolution, on July 4, 1814.

There are more than 100 Gothic churches in France, but only a handful have— or had—labyrinths. We went to see Saint-Omer, home of one of the original nine Knights Templar, Godfrey de Saint-Omer, but its labyrinth looked nothing like a menorah. The remaining few cathedrals that contained labyrinths merely possessed small engravings set in the wall or floor.

There was one other final candidate that initially we thought we simply had to see—the Basilica of Saint-Quentin. It has a labyrinth modeled on the one at Amiens, but once we discovered that it wasn't added until the late 1400s, it clearly wasn't part of the grand scheme we had uncovered, and so it was unrelated to the finds connected to our pentagram. With our comprehensive road trip almost complete, we were convinced that we now had the full story, so did not go to see it for ourselves. Yet, there was one major twist still to be played out.

It was nearly the end of our time in France and once again we were playing with the names of the cathedrals. We were thinking about our discovery of the word "arc" when something startling happened.

Did you know that you can draw a pentagram with one continuous line, your pen never leaving the paper? When we drew such a pentagram over our map, starting at Sens, we saw that we had spelled out the word "sacro." This was created using the first letters of Sens, Amiens, Chartres, and Reims, along with the "O" from Saint-Ouen (see Figure 4).

"Sacro" is Latin for "sacred."

There is no better word to describe the sanctity of the interior of a pentagram. This geometric device was not only an ancient symbol for Jerusalem, its use was much more widespread, not least as a symbol for protection. Pythagoras described the shape as ὑγίεια (hugieia), which means "perfect health."[7] A ring with a pentagram on it was found in Galpesos, Greece, that dated from the 6th century BC. This tradition continues to the present day, with a pentagram ring still thought to protect the person wearing it.

The symbol is also frequently seen on Knights Templar tombstones from the 12th century, particularly in Portugal.[8] As late as the 19th century, the pentagram was used by peasants as protection from the "evil eye." In the Middle Ages, when few could read or write, the protective properties of this symbol were universally understood. It is therefore not surprising that a giant pentagram—one uniting five prominent places of worship—had been chosen as the device to hide an equally large secret. Perhaps it was the greatest secret in the world, given the size of the sacred pentagram we had unveiled.

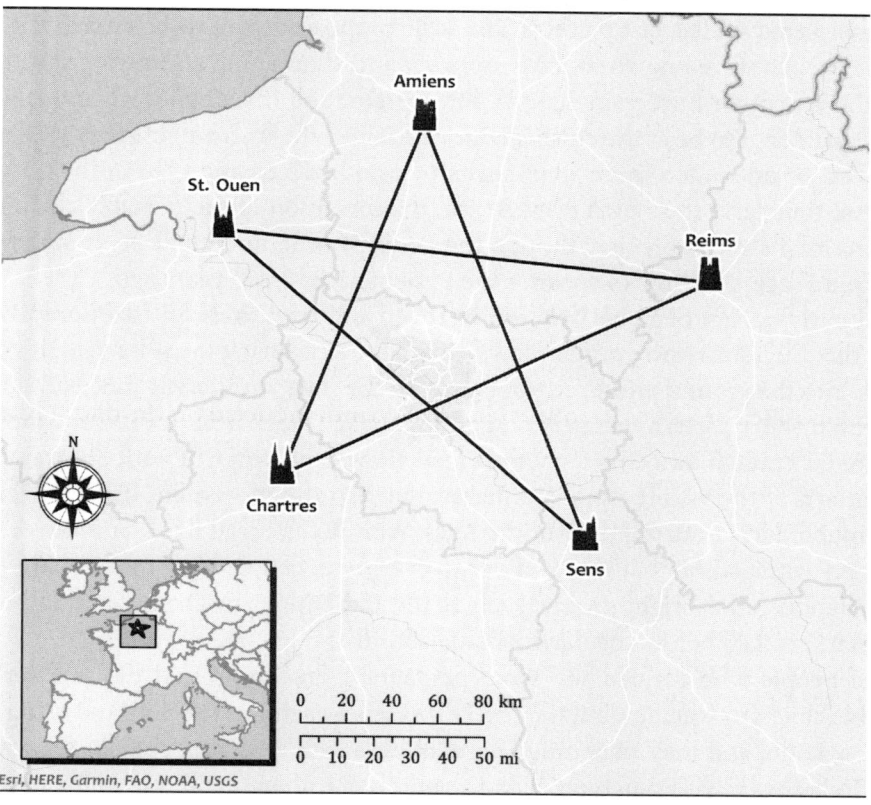

Figure 4 The sacro pentagram (Erin King)

With the reality of the sacro pentagram before us, we now started to wonder *how* the architects of this grand scheme had managed to achieve this.

Reims and Amiens lie almost 93 miles (150 km) apart, and there are almost 108 miles (175 km) separating Amiens and Chartres. To have visualized it alone is impressive, considering when it was conceived and constructed. It was before planes, so no one would have thought about or been able to look down on the vast area covered by the pentagram from the air. Where the sacro pentagram is, the highest vantage point would have been the summits of the cathedrals themselves, there are no great hills or mountains with far views. In 1254, when Louis IX returned to France, the high point would have been the spire of Chartres Cathedral, standing at 377 feet

(115 m) tall. Even if people had been able to stand on the very tip of the tallest of the two spires, it would still not have been anywhere near high enough to see any of the other sacro cathedrals. The shortest distance between any two cathedrals of the sacro pentagram is that between Saint-Ouen and Amiens, yet they are almost 62 miles (100 km) apart. So, the question remained: how had the organizers planned and completed such a vast project? The scale of the undertaking is hard to fathom.

The French were known to have more advanced mapping and cartography skills than those of other European nations. Yet, even in the 17th century, when the French were considered to be at the cutting edge of science, the instruments they were using consisted of not much more than sticks of wood, tables and charts, the ability to measure time, and their own eyes. At sea, the invention of the portable clock made measurements more precise, though the concept of latitude had been understood and used successfully on ships since the Phoenicians, 2,000 years ago.

The early science of global positioning relied almost entirely on astronomy. People knew that the stars slowly progressed through the sky during the solar year. If you set a stick into the ground and fixed your gaze on the stars at different times of the year, you could see a pattern emerge. If you observe the stars from a different location, and are far enough away from your original viewpoint, you will notice that not only the pattern of the visible stars is different but also the movement itself. The nights were much darker during the Middle Ages, with no artificial light, and the celestial night sky was a scene that was familiar to everyone. People were more aware of the constellations, and bright groups such as the Big Dipper or Orion were important way-markers well before the dawn of civilization.

The people who created the sacro pentagram on the ground did not yet have portable clocks or watches, but they had experience gazing at the stars and using them for navigation, and they were much more in tune with their inner clocks than we are now. Today, we rely so much on digital watches, our phones and other devices telling us what time it is every second of the day that we have lost some of our natural instincts about time and travel. However, we know that the Knights Templar gained detailed knowledge of such things in the Levant, and they brought many of the revelations back with them to Europe for the first time, including a comprehensive re-evaluation of astronomy. When the Templars arrived in Outremer, this Middle Eastern science of the heavens had been flourishing for over a thousand years. We even see evidence of this knowledge in the opening books of the New Testament, with the three Magi demonstrating their in-depth understanding of reading the sky after the appearance of the star of Bethlehem. The insights the Templars brought back to France were not only instrumental in shaping and guiding the construction of the Gothic cathedrals but they also made the laying out of the sacro pentagram possible.

We drew and redrew our sacro pentagram. We also realized that there are possible variations on the name, depending on which point is used to begin the pentagram. There were also some tantalizing anagrams. For example, "sacro" could become "arcos," bringing to mind the Ark of the Covenant—a nod, perhaps, toward the treasures from Solomon's Temple. We also considered whether the word was meant to be "arcas," the mythological king and namesake of Arcadia, which would be possible if the alternative spelling of the name Saint-Ouen had been used—Saint-Adouen.

Whichever turned out to be the right one, we knew that we had to look more closely at the five holy buildings that formed the huge star of our pentagram to establish whether there were further clues that might point to hidden medieval treasure and, specifically, holy artefacts from Jerusalem.

The saint that carried Christ across the water

During our exploration of the sacro cathedrals, we took hundreds of photos, documenting anything that we thought might be even remotely relevant to our search. Now came the task of sifting through all those images, to see if we could identify more pieces of the puzzle. We had also taken advantage of the gift shops at each site, so had also come away with an impressive library of books and pamphlets that described in great detail the history and architecture of each building.

Chartres Cathedral has been a magnet for professional and amateur researchers ever since its foundation, and many writers had exposed its connections with the Knights Templar long before we arrived on the scene. Two of Chartres' magnificent stained-glass windows feature the menorah in full colour, but perhaps that was not entirely unexpected, as many cathedrals contain such portrayals, drawing as they often do on the Old Testament, especially the book of Exodus. Often there is also a depiction of the Ark of the Covenant not too far away. However, at Chartres, we found something a little more explicit that piqued our interest.

We had taken many photos of the west portals of the cathedral, called the "Royal Portals," where there are several complex scenes carved on the arches and columns. Graham Hancock[9] describes how there is a clear portrayal of the Ark of the Covenant on a cart, being hauled off somewhere. In an older book about Chartres, historian Louis Charpentier remarks that, next to this depiction of the Ark, there is a sculpture of a knight hiding the base of the Ark under a cloth.[10] This scene marries up exactly with our understanding of events surrounding the appropriation of the treasures of Jerusalem, even if it was a surprise to see this carved in stone for all to see.

There were other unique details also revealed at Chartres. The base of the Ark was not shown here as the familiar golden vessel that supported two angels facing each other, instead, it appeared more like an ordinary wooden box with metal fittings and a lock.

What ties this depiction to the Ark of the Covenant is a Latin inscription carved below the image. Hancock records the wording as being, *"hic amicitur archa cederis,"*[11] which translates to something approaching "here is hidden, the Ark." However, Charpentier's reading of one of the words is different: *"hic amititur archa cederis,"* which means "here you will work through the Ark." Despite this difference, both meanings clearly imply that someone at Chartres had intimate knowledge of the Ark itself.

By this stage, we were convinced that the Knights Templar had rediscovered the menorah in the depths of Temple Mount in Jerusalem and that it had been brought to France, but was the inscription at Chartres proof that they had found the lost Ark of the Covenant as well? And had they brought it here to Chartres? If so, was this a sign that the menorah, and who knows what other treasures, had also been secreted in the cathedral?

When we studied our photos again, we noticed that on one of the three entrance portals at Amiens Cathedral, the same box was depicted—it was exactly the same proportions and shape, with identical fittings, and a similar lock. At Amiens there was no inscription to aid us, but historians have no doubt that the carving is a portrayal of the Ark of the Covenant. This is chiefly because it is flanked on the left-hand side by a statue of Moses holding the Ten Commandments, which, according to the Bible, were originally stored in the sacred casket (Exodus 25.16). On the right of the Ark sits Uzzah, recorded in the Bible as one of the men who drove the cart that carried the Ark (2 Samuel 6.3; 1 Chronicles 13.7).

What we found most striking about this scene at Amiens was that the Ark was not displayed on a cart but sheltering under a roof. Did the Ark of the Covenant find respite here at Amiens, and did it come to remain here for a time before being moved to its final destination at Chartres? We knew this was a tentative hypothesis but we were keen to see where it might lead us.

There are other connections that link Amiens Cathedral with the Knights Templar. On December 17, 1206, a crusader named Walon de Sarton arrived in Amiens, carrying a magnificent relic.[12] Looted from the imperial treasury of Constantinople during the Fourth Crusade, the knight was in possession of what was believed to be the skull of St John the Baptist, patron saint of the Knights Templar. This was therefore a potent symbol for any Templar and the importance of venerating this relic in the sanctity of the cathedral is almost beyond comprehension. The cathedral at that time would have been the earlier, Romanesque church, but a few years later, the grand, Gothic masterpiece we see today was begun.

As we now know, Amiens also takes prime position at the apex of the enormous five-pointed pentagram star we drew across this sacred region of France, the significance of which would not have been lost on a Templar such as Walon de Sarton, who would have been very familiar with the shape of the pentagram from his time in Jerusalem. He would have seen this exact image on the tombstones of his fallen brethren, because many of them had pentagrams etched on them.

A revelation at Amiens

While at Amiens, during our final visit, we realized that our sacro pentagram research had come full circle. We remember well that it was a Sunday morning and mass was in progress when we entered. We took our hats off and sat down with our backs to the entrance. A choir was singing majestically, making maximum use of the cathedral's acoustics. We began to realize that we had entered in the middle of a baptism, so took everything in while we waited, but could see the labyrinth.

When mass was over, we made our way to the north transept, complete with its upside-down pentagram rose window, the symbol forever pointing downwards. During our previous visit to Amiens, we bought what is probably the heaviest book in our collection—a compilation of descriptions of the cathedral made over the years by various historians, architects, and scientists. In the book, we had read that, in 1310, there had been a painting of St Christopher directly below the pentagram, set into the window.[13] We had hoped to find some remnant of this painting but, unfortunately, it had completely disappeared and not a single trace of paint was visible on the wall. We had, however, seen two statues of St Christopher in the cathedral. We were well aware how the French had concealed the giant pentagram out in the open, in plain sight, as it was so large no one would ever spot it. What if they had applied a similar methodology to their other secrets, hiding messages and ciphers in the everyday and the mundane, the truth visible only to a small group of initiates who possessed the required inside knowledge to crack the code.

The most well-known version of the legend of St Christopher was recorded in a work called *The Golden Legend*, written around 1260 by Jacobus de Voragine, who was the Archbishop of Genoa. His story relates how Offerus, a giant of a man by all accounts, went in search of Christ. One day, he encountered a child and helped him cross a river, wading through the water with the little boy on his shoulder. During the crossing, the waters rose and, as the current grew stronger, the child became heavier and heavier, until even the legendary strength of Offerus began to fail. When they finally reached the other side of the river, the child disclosed that he was, in fact, Jesus Christ. The crossing had not only been a test but also a lesson. After this miraculous meeting, Offerus was given the name Christopher, which means "Christ-bearer."

When we were standing in the cathedral, searching for traces of St Christopher, we suddenly realized that there was a parallel here with the records that were left by the chroniclers who had documented Louis' great voyage from Acre back to France. Just like Christopher, the King had been described as carrying Christ across the water, aboard the ship, the *Montjoie*. By carrying the body of Jesus Christ across the sea, Louis could himself be seen as a Christopher, a Christ-bearer. The relics disappeared after the King's return to France in July 1254, and all mention of them has since vanished, but we had always thought it likely that the Knights Templar had made a record of what was brought over on that crossing. Furthermore, we thought we knew where such an account could be concealed.

A few years after Louis' landing in France, the Templars began work on the interior decorations of the chapel at their commandery in Montsaunès, in the foothills of the French Pyrenees. You can still see their work today, the original paint still looking quite fresh on the walls. As we saw in Chapter 3, if you look up, high on one wall, you will spot a menorah with straight arms, just as it was described by Maimonides. That is remarkable enough, but the most intriguing feature to be found in the chapel is the large number of round rosette shapes, each with six petals, that have been dotted across the ceiling and walls. These are not simply random rosettes; they are identical to those used on 1st-century Jewish ossuaries. In the 1970s, respected French historian François Laborde thought the same, remarking that the odd "un-European" decorations in the chapel strongly reminded him of Jewish funerary decorations from the 1st to 3rd centuries.[14]

Ossuaries were part of Jewish custom in ancient Jerusalem and Judea for secondary burial of the dead. They are small stone boxes in which Jews would inter the bones of the deceased once their bodies had decayed naturally after their first burial in caves or stone tombs. If, contrary to the teaching of the Bible, Christ's body had remained on earth after his death, his bones would have ended up in an ossuary that featured rosettes just like the ones present at Montsaunès. Indeed, in a controversial documentary in 2007, *The Lost Tomb of Jesus*, directed by Canadian filmmaker Simcha Jacobovici, ossuaries are shown covered with these identical decorative shapes.

In Montsaunès, the rosettes assume an even greater significance because they surround a large image painted centrally on the ceiling. What we see here, in essence, is a copy of an image that pilgrims used to bring home from Jerusalem in the form of ancient ampoules, souvenirs that depicted the Church of the Holy Sepulchre, the tomb of Jesus. Typically what you find is a large cross standing beneath a vaulted roof, with chains hanging left and right. However, at Montsaunès, the painting extends further down, descending into what looks like a flight of stairs, beginning with a lighter version of the ossuary rosette and ending in a darker one. To our eyes, this could be interpreted as a map of the journey a sacred ossuary might take if it were carried down those stairs to be hidden beneath a church. Perhaps what was depicted here was even the ossuary of Christ?[15]

The inference was clear: the Knights Templar seemed to be recording the construction of secret underground crypts and using Jewish symbols to document the creation of those concealed spaces. Furthermore, there seemed a strong possibility that what we saw at Montsaunès was a depiction of a very special object, represented by an ossuary rosette, being moved west for nine weeks in a ship captained by the Knights Templar, eventually landing in a bay across the water (represented by the swirls in the design). This sacred relic was perhaps then placed under a cross or church, beneath what looked to us like a large rectangular slab. So, rather than leaving a written account of Louis' crossing with the body of Jesus Christ, the Knights Templar had instead codified the tale into this series of images at Montsaunès.

The story of St Christopher the Christ-bearer had thrown all our questions to the forefront of our minds and they all screamed for our attention. What on earth were we looking at here? A massive pentagram that comprised great Gothic cathedrals; stone labyrinths that featured stylized menorahs; rosettes depicting the transportation of the Ark; and then the stories of the body of Christ being carried across the water. We were clearly being shown that what we had searched long and hard for had passed from the Holy Land to France, but where to after that? Chartres? Amiens? Reims? Or all the above? The menorah here, the Ark there, and now the bones of Jesus. Would we ever find a way to prove any of this?

When we sat on a bench below the stained-glass pentagram at Amiens, where St Christopher was once painted on the wall, staring into the chapel holding the alleged head of John the Baptist, it suddenly felt too overwhelming, too much for two people to unravel.

We tried shutting the questions out for a moment, focusing on the here and now. How many Templars had sat here before us looking at this very scene? We turned our gaze to the other side of the cathedral for a moment. Though we had become accustomed to searching for mirrored images or features, at first we didn't spot anything of particular interest, but we decided to walk over to the south portal to give it a closer inspection.

Opposite the chapel of John the Baptist, on the far side of the nave, is the chapel of St Peter and St Paul. Looking down, we immediately spotted five large Maltese crosses set in the marble floor. This is the Cross of St John, symbol of the Hospitallers, now known as the Knights of Malta (part of the Order of Malta), an organization that inherited all the properties of the Knights Templar after their demise early in the 14th century.

Our attention was next drawn to a painting hanging above the altar in the chapel. According to the accompanying description, it was completed in 1751[16] and the subject is the adoration of the Magi—the three wise men from the East who had followed a new star in the heavens to find the infant Jesus. In this painting, the star of Bethlehem very clearly had five points. The symbolism was unmistakeable: we were looking at a pentagram shining a ray of light directly on Jesus. We had found yet another pentagram, albeit smaller this time, in a cathedral that stood right at the top of the much grander sacro pentagram, shining its light on Christ himself.

We had to follow the star. But where to?

The heart of the matter

The results of all the research we had completed up to this point were dizzying and we needed a way to steer a course through them all and out the other side. We realized that what we had to establish was whether there was any historical context which might point to the region covered by the pentagram having some special significance to France. If we were following a star, then we might as well start looking right at the heart of the huge five-pointed star that we had found.

As our pentagram was not entirely symmetrical, connecting all five points does not create a precise center where you would expect it. Instead, it delineates a central *area*. When we plotted the area on a map, we found that it corresponded almost exactly with the Forest of Carnelle, which was once part of the estate controlled by Royaumont.

Studying this in more detail on the map, we also found that the meridian (later known as the Paris meridian, which once challenged the Greenwich meridian as the prime meridian), a line once triangulated by Giovanni Domenico Cassini for King Louis XIV in the 17th century, bisected our pentagram, creating two perfect halves. That seemed to be more than a coincidence and hinted we were on the right track.

This meridian, which features in Dan Brown's *The Da Vinci Code*, but there is called the "Rose Line," runs from Dunkirk in the north to Mount Canigó in the south, and passes through some significant locations, including Saint-Sulpice in Paris, forming the central axis of France. We realized that the French had been working on such alignments since the Middle Ages, and it was still going on. On October 18, 1990, French President François Mitterand planted an olive tree to inaugurate the Garden of Human Rights, which is one section of the nearly 2-mile (3-km) long L'Axe Majeur (Major Axis) in Cergy-Pontoise. Designed by Israeli sculptor Dani Karavan and built during the 1980s, it is his grandest yet least-known work, perhaps eclipsed by his work elsewhere in Paris, such as the extension of the city's central axis towards the business district of La Défense, with its huge "Grand Arche." In all this, the French were merely continuing a tradition that they had started centuries before.

Nearby, on a cold Sunday morning, we clambered down a steep, muddy hill that meets the valley of the Oise river. It is an ancient, timeless landscape and we felt as though we had left the modern world far behind, despite the GPS device that was guiding us to our destination.

It took us the best part of an hour to finally achieve our objective: we were standing at the center of the sacro pentagram, deep inside the Forest of Carnelle in France, very close to Cassini's meridian (see Figure 5). We felt that we knew this place intimately after so many months of research and had an idea what to expect, but to see it first-hand was something else entirely.

In front of us rose a huge megalithic stone structure. We were looking at a dolmen, a covered corridor, which, together with smaller structures or chambers formed in this way are still one of the largest and best-preserved types of prehistoric monuments in France.

In French, this particular dolmen is called the Pierre Turquaise (the Turquoise Stone) and it is the largest in the region. Archaeologists have estimated that the structure was built during the Neolithic Age, around the beginning of the 3rd millennium BC. That means this monument was in existence some 2,000 years before King Solomon was born and, from our perspective, was built some 5,000 years ago.

On one of the pillars that supported the first massive flat stone of its roof, we could still discern a Stone Age carving. It appeared to be two circles, topped by a number of arches pointing upward.[17] Scientists have concluded that this is an image of the mother goddess, shown here with two breasts, and a collar around her neck. However, we instantly saw something else and, for us, it triggered memories of early images we had seen of the menorah. That raised some very interesting questions because this place was constructed two millennia before the first menorah of Moses had been shaped, so when was this image carved into the stone?

While touring the area the previous day, we had noticed that there had once been a Templar commandery only a short distance from this ancient site. This was a surprise discovery and, in our opinion, was no coincidence. The commandery was a fortified estate, known as Val Pendant, that stood strategically on a hill, overlooking the valley and much of the forest in which the Pierre Turquaise lies. It would have been an ideal location from which to monitor and protect this structure. Val Pendant is private property today but, hiking around it, we could see that the characteristic square tower remained, high up on the slope.

On the edge of the forest once stood the favourite haunt of Louis IX's father, Louis VIII, and his mother, Blanche of Castille. Now called the Château de la Reine Blanche (Castle of the White Queen), it was a formidable structure that today has all but disappeared. Louis IX often stayed there while Royaumont Abbey was being built because it was so close by. This forest seemed to have no shortage of ancient protectors.

Technically, the Forest of Carnelle was part of the domain attached to Château de Beaumont-sur-Oise, slightly to the north of it. That estate became royal property in 1223, when it was gifted to King Louis VIII. Lying on his deathbed three years later, the King made his son promise to build a magnificent abbey at the edge of the forest. The young Louis IX obeyed, aided by his ever-present and powerful mother, Blanche of Castille. Louis IX bought lands for it that he named Mont Regalis, or Royaumont, a French variation on Montreal.

Louis IX threw himself enthusiastically into the endeavor, spending the colossal sum of 100,000 livres. Even though he financed it himself, at the time this was two-thirds of France's annual income and more than half the Crown's annual revenues, which is still a staggering amount, even when you take into account that it was spent over a period of seven years. The first stone was laid in 1228, when Louis was 14 years old. As noted in Chapter 10, the boy king continued to be involved, visiting frequently and even performing the duties of an assistant mason during the building of the abbey.

In 1235, Royaumont Abbey was finally finished and its church consecrated. As also already noted, the floorplan of the church looked suspiciously familiar to us. Although, naturally, smaller than the cathedrals we had visited at Chartres, Amiens, and Reims, it was an impressive size, with three entrances, a long nave, and seven chapels behind the altar. In this way, it mimicked Amiens Cathedral. There is very little left of the church today, but it's not hard to imagine how spectacular it would have looked in its heyday.

The royal Royaumont Abbey was a direct subsidiary of the influential monastery of Cîteaux Abbey, and so it provided Royaumont with monks and servants. You may recall from Chapter 6 that it was Cîteaux which had been the first religious home of Bernard of Clairvaux.

Royaumont Abbey, then—this sacred place, at the center of our sacro pentagram— would have had a unique spot in Louis' heart too. He was able to bring to fruition his father's final wish, and he created the abbey in a location that was otherwise, to him, also the most treasured spot in the whole world. This was the place Louis assigned as the last resting place for his beloved wife and children, far away from the basilica Cathedral of Saint-Denis, which only later did he proclaim as France's royal necropolis. In 1249, while Louis was in the Holy Land with the crusader armies, fighting shoulder to shoulder with the Knights Templar, their commandery at Val Pendant was added to the Royaumont estate and with it, the dolmen of Pierre Turquaise.[18]

We spent around an hour at the megalithic monument, trying to gauge the energy of the place. Around the site we found traces of recent campfires and less-than-glamorous reminders that people exercise their dogs in the area. When we first arrived, muddy and sweaty from our long trek, we discovered that the site was not as secluded as we had thought. An access road and car park had been built on the other side of the dolmen that we were unaware of. It was now approaching lunchtime and, because we were visiting on a Sunday, cars began arriving in numbers, packed with families coming to picnic in the woods. This ancient, once sacred monument was suddenly quite busy.

We realized that we had miscalculated. This site wasn't the perfect spot for hiding treasure that we had first hoped it might be. Even before the road was built, the monument would always have drawn interest and so it would have been far too conspicuous. Over the centuries it would have attracted many nosy and inquisitive visitors, bringing unwanted attention. While it was an intriguing find, it was clear that this place could never have acted as a repository for sacred objects.

The day had not been a waste of time, however—far from it. The appearance of the Knights Templar once again, this time right at the heart of our sacro pentagram, was yet further vindication that we were getting closer. All the grand cathedrals at the points of our sacred pentagram were constructed with Templar insight and knowledge, and that work had been funded at least partially by them. Also, at the heart of the pentagram, King Louis, St Louis, had built a magnificent royal abbey, fulfilling a wish his father had uttered on his deathbed, and that resulted in a church with a floorplan in the shape of a menorah.

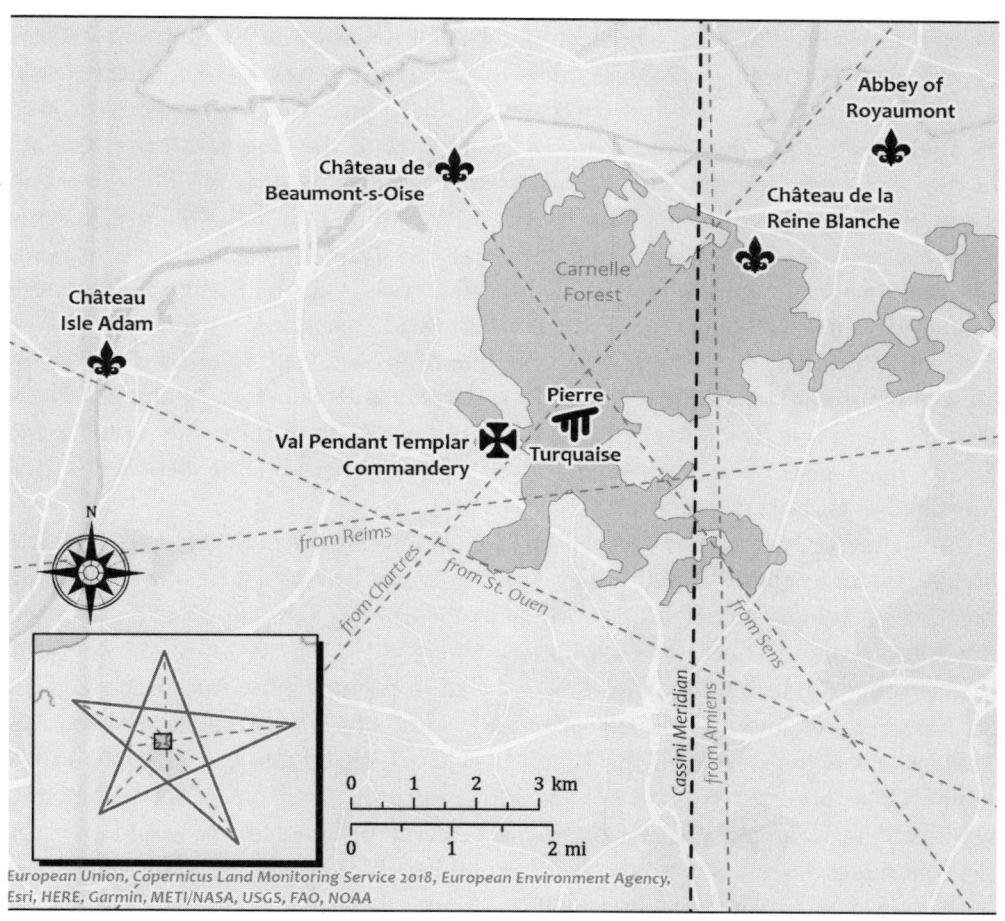

Figure 5 The center of the sacro pentagram (Erin King)

The Order of the Star

From our files, we knew that there was one French king who had more than a passing interest in the symbol of the pentagram star. Jean II, nicknamed Jean the Good, who reigned from 1350 to 1364, used it as his personal emblem and founded the chivalric Order of the Star at Saint-Ouen Abbey church—the "O"point in the sacro pentagram—in the second year after his coronation.

However, the order was short-lived. On September 19, 1356, Jean and his Knights of the Star strode on to the battlefield to confront the invading English armies with all the might and guile they could muster. The English were led by Edward, the Black Prince, who had been burning and pillaging his way deep into French territory. The two armies collided head-on, outside Poitiers in western-central France. Despite Jean's confidence, the resulting battle ended disastrously for the French. Jean was humiliated and captured after his army was devastated by the relentless arrows fired from the longbows of the English. Jean's Knights of the Star were almost entirely eradicated, bringing the order to a sudden and untimely end only four years after its inception. Among the fallen French knights was Guy de La Rochefoucauld, who had three chevrons emblazoned on his shield, representing the menorah. Jean was captured by two English knights, and we were staggered to discover that one of them was Edward Despenser.

During our early research into the menorah, we had found an image of Despenser in the *Tewkesbury Book of Founders and Benefactors*, which is a 16th-century illuminated manuscript from the famous abbey of the same name in the UK. In the pages of this beautiful manuscript, Despenser is clearly depicted with a life-size, seven-branch menorah.

It is a mystery as to why Despenser was depicted in such a way in a chronicle created for an English Catholic abbey. Did Despenser become aware of a compelling secret concerning the menorah unearthed by the Knights Templar when he captured the French king?

The other English knight who was involved in capturing the King was a certain Sir John Pelham, and he took Jean's belt and sword after his surrender. As a reward, Pelham was allowed to keep the King's buckle, which, to this day, features on his family's coat of arms. We had not encountered the name Pelham before but that would change dramatically later on, as our research progressed. We would discover that the direct descendants of the Pelham family still possessed intimate knowledge of the treasure of Jerusalem, almost 400 years after this event.

King Jean had to endure a series of humiliations and ordeals, and died in voluntary captivity in London in 1364, before he was able to raise the funds for his ransom. One of the first—and last—Knights of the Star was at Jean's side when the King drew his last breath. That knight was Pierre de Villiers.

Miraculously, Pierre de Villiers survived the battle at Poitiers and accompanied the King to England. With his master deceased, Villiers was free to return to France, where he took up a prestigious and powerful new role, becoming Grand Master of the Household for Jean II's son, the new French King, Charles V. The relationship between de Villiers and Charles V was so good that, in 1375, de Villiers became the official bearer of the oriflamme, Charlemagne's legendary banner and battle standard.

One of the first things Pierre de Villiers did when he was finally back on French soil was to purchase a château and lands at L'Îsle-Adam, in the Oise Valley. This is a mere stone's throw from the Pierre Turquaise discussed earlier in this chapter, which, you will recall is an ancient dolmen at the center of the sacro pentagram. In 1386, a few months before Pierre de Villiers' own death, King Charles V's successor, Charles VI, visited the estate at L'Îsle-Adam. When death finally claimed him, Pierre de Villiers had served three kings of France and had received the highest possible honors.

L'Îsle-Adam stayed in the hands of the de Villiers family and their role appears to have been to keep an eye on the heart of the sacro pentagram. The family also remained very closely connected to the kings of France. The descendants of Pierre de Villiers took up significant roles in the Order of the Hospital of Saint John of Jerusalem, also called the Hospitallers.

The family furnished the Hospitallers with its most illustrious Grand Master in 1521—Philippe de Villiers of L'Îsle-Adam. Under his command, 600 knights and 4,500 soldiers resisted a Turkish force some 100,000 strong for six months, echoing the legendary bravery of his predecessors in the Temple. It was Philippe de Villiers who finally settled the Knights Hospitaller on the island of Malta.

Regarding the Order of the Star, once Jean II had died, along with most of his knights, the order perished as well. We have been unable to find a single record that would suggest the order survived in any shape or form. However, the idea of creating an order to protect France's most treasured secrets would not be forgotten.

The menorah and the labyrinth

At this stage, we felt that it would be useful to explore briefly the links between the menorah of the tabernacle and Temple and the symbol of the labyrinth. This would help us to understand why the labyrinths found in the sacro cathedrals were used to conceal the lampstand of the holy of holies and, in doing so, illustrated the union of the two mirrored menorahs.

The similarity between the ancient labyrinths and the depictions of the menorah can be seen clearly in the unique 10th-century half-labyrinth depicted on the wall of the Basilica of San Michele Maggiore at Pavia—one of the oldest surviving labyrinths found in Italy.

However, labyrinths go back much further in time and one of the earliest found to date is that of Rujm el-Hiri in the Golan Heights, in the Holy Land, dating from sometime between 3000 and 2700 BC. These and other labyrinths have assumed mysterious significance throughout history, a case in point being depictions of the "Labyrinth of Solomon" as an alchemical device found in an 11th-century manuscript about alchemy deposited in the Biblioteca Marciana in Venice.

The labyrinths in the cathedrals in France that we have been looking at are based on the legendary labyrinth from the Minoan culture of ancient Crete, Greece. This is attested to by an account in 1640 of there having been images of the characters from the myth of the Minotaur adorning the center of the labyrinth at Chartres. These images were engraved on a brass plaque, long since removed, though the holes for the retaining bolts remain.

In Chapter 3 we looked at the tree of Asherah and how this stylized tree of life was a symbol of the goddess Asherah, the consort or wife of Yaweh or Jehovah. This sacred tree evolved into the menorah, complete with its blossoms and branches. A similar motif is found in the Minoan culture of Crete.

The Minoans are mentioned often in the Bible, Crete being called Caphtorim (Genesis 10.14). The Philistines were also said to be from Crete and, therefore, were, Minoan, and we must not forget that the Philistines were descendants of the son of Ham, who was the son of Noah. At the archaeological site of Tel Kabri in the western Galilee region of Israel, a palace has been unearthed that features Minoan frescoes. This places the Minoans in Israel some 3,500 years ago. Writer Simcha Jacobovici, mentioned earlier in this chapter regarding his documentary *The Lost Tomb of Jesus*, is also the author of *The Jesus Family Tomb*, and suggests that there was a Minoan presence at the time of the Exodus and that the people involved were part of the "mixed multitude" (Exodus 12.38, KJV) that followed Moses out of Egypt and into the desert.[19]

If so, did the Minoans mix with the Jewish people and, ultimately, influence the burgeoning religion of Judaism? Could the story of the golden calf be a reference to the bull cult of the Minoans? Is the Minoan serpent goddess and the Minoans' reverence for the serpent echoed in the brazen serpent of Moses? Most importantly, did this Minoan influence, especially the labrys (double axe) and labyrinth, reveal itself in the design of the menorah?

In the myth of Theseus, Ariadne, and the Minotaur, the Minotaur is given the name Asterion, "the starry one." This will come to have greater significance as we explore the alignments of the French royal family later in this book.

Thoughts about such links with Minoan culture and the very nature of the labyrinths in the French cathedrals left us better equipped to understand the sacro pentagram we had stumbled on, but we knew that we still had questions to answer. Who had been behind all of this? Were we looking at the execution of some grand scheme of the Catholic Church or was this a project for which the Knights Templar were solely responsible? Or was Louis IX the guiding hand behind all this? More importantly, perhaps, were we looking at a marker that pointed to the greatest treasure hoard in the world since ancient times, a vast sacred space designed to conceal and secure the world's most sacred treasures, those found by the Knights Templar on Temple Mount on the direct orders of the Pope?

It felt as though we were getting closer, but there was still much work to be done. Before we took on that challenge, we knew we had to take a final look at the last days of Louis IX to see if there were any further revelations.

CHAPTER 11

ST LOUIS

The most pious king

One lasting trait that Louis IX's defeat and capture in Egypt seemed to have instilled in him was penitence. When he finally returned to France, accompanied by his many treasures, he was almost a different man. Ever a fervent Christian, he became doubly focused on furthering God's cause, and he believed that the crusades had failed in the past because of the sins of the people taking part. So, he set about making a series of reforms to improve the purity and piousness of his own people. He outlawed prostitution, gambling, and blasphemy, and turned himself into a philanthropist and peacemaker, gifting huge tracts of land to secure peace rather than ride out and engage rebels in battle, as he had done prior to the Seventh Crusade.

During Louis' reign, France reached the zenith of its power and influence. It had the largest army in Europe, was the wealthiest kingdom, and was ruled by a leader who was seen throughout the Western world as the supreme Christian leader. Just as King Solomon was seen as a wise and beneficent ruler, so too was Louis, and he would often be called in to arbitrate in squabbles between other kings and lords in Europe.

Under Louis, the arts flourished, and not only architecture but many other fields as well, including painting and sculpture. He became a patron of many great artists and intellectuals, and Paris became a magnet for the gifted, while his court was the envy of the world.

If there was one thing that rivalled Louis' love of the arts, it was the passion he had for his religion. There were, of course, the grand gestures. The crusades spring to mind first, but he also funded many religious orders and charities, especially the Franciscans and Dominicans. He helped build a hospital for 300 blind patients in Paris and founded many others, including the Maison-Dieu at Compiègne, where Louis and his son-in-law, Theobald of Navarre, personally carried in the first patient. He was also the patron of Robert of Sorbonne, who founded the famous Collège de la Sorbonne in Paris, a center for theological excellence.

Possessing the religious relics and other objects that Louis did—the crown of thorns, the menorah, the nails of the true cross, the Mandylion, featuring Jesus' face, and perhaps even the body of Christ—seemed to instil a powerful sense of religious identity in him, and he saw himself as the bearer of significant holy powers. Modern scholars believe that Louis was the first French king to practice what is called thaumaturgic touch, which is healing through touch, known then as the "royal touch" or the "king's touch." Many people were reported to have come from as far as the regions we know today as Italy and Spain to receive this healing, as well as from all over France.

One of the commonest ailments that people turned up with was scrofula, a form of external tuberculosis that caused dramatic sores and growths on the face and neck. Also known as the "king's evil," it was a common belief that the touch of a king or queen was a cure, so Louis would lay his hands on these wounds in an effort to cure sufferers. The visitors expected to make a full recovery after their encounter with the King, which many did, but this was probably because scrofula can fade away on its own over time. However, that was not fully understood at the time, so it only lent credence to the legend of the King's miraculous powers of healing. It was even thought by some that Louis' miraculous powers could extend beyond the grave and so his preserved arm, held in the Poblet Monastery in Catalonia, was believed to still be able to heal the sick.

Louis' great Christian work was rewarded posthumously when, in 1297, he was canonized. Pope Boniface VIII presided over the proceedings and cited "*Rex pacificus magnificatus est*," which is, "the peaceful king is exalted," a line from the Old Testament (translated into Latin from the Hebrew Torah) that refers to King Solomon.[1] Given what we know about Louis' exploits, his perceived wisdom, his role as an arbiter, his healing powers, along with his secret knowledge of the menorah and the other Jewish treasures and implements, he would certainly have been proud to have been compared to Solomon, the very king who brought the menorah and artefacts of God to rest in the Temple in Jerusalem in the first place. Louis seemed to mirror this when he oversaw the construction of Sainte-Chapelle and its special places to house his collection of Passion relics, both those where pieces were on public display and those where they were hidden away, for his eyes only.

St Louis, as he was known thereafter, had become more than simply a king, a leader of the mortal realms. He had been elevated to the lofty heights of sainthood and, furthermore, he was a royal saint, the patron saint of the Capetian dynasty and, later, the royal house of Bourbon.

As a tribute to St Louis, a later French monarch from the house of Bourbon, Louis XIV, reserved his final phase of construction for a magnificent royal chapel at Versailles, completed in 1710, that is dedicated to St Louis. Up on the ceiling, St Louis can be seen praying piously while kneeling at a box covered with a shroud—a box the same proportions and shape as the Ark of the Covenant. In this chapel, all the scenes around St Louis that feature Jesus have links with the Temple in Jerusalem: an infant Jesus at the Temple, Jesus in the Temple with the doctors of the Law, and Jesus driving the merchants from the Temple. The ornate stonework around the altar includes depictions of the menorah, the table of showbread, and further images of the Ark of the Covenant. On the ceiling it states, "The Lord shall come to this Temple," and, above the altar, God's ineffable name in Hebrew is set in the center of a triangle at the altar.[2] Here, in stone, seemed to be a representation of a new Jerusalem, and the many secrets that it divulged were those that St Louis had gathered around himself.

It was later in this very refined space that Louis XVI was betrothed to Marie-Antoinette, and many other elaborate ceremonies were held below the kneeling St Louis. The most elaborate rituals, however, were those conducted by the secretive Order of the Holy Spirit, a Catholic chivalric order, the members of which came from the highest ranks of the French court and clergy, and whose Grand Master was the King himself.

We will explore much of this symbolism later but, for now, the inference should be clear: Louis may have passed away amid the wreckage of Carthage, but his secret plans regarding the menorah and the other treasures of Jerusalem did not die with him; in France, the secret of their existence was passed down the royal bloodline and kept safe among the inner circle of Louis' court. For several hundred years, this sacred knowledge would be treasured and preserved in the highest echelons of French society.

The significance of the fleur-de-lis

We cannot end this chapter on the life of Louis IX without remarking on the iconography of a symbol that came to represent France itself: the fleur-de-lis.

On the seal used by Louis throughout his reign, the King is depicted holding a fleur-de-lis. It is often shown with multiple petals and the design bears some resemblance to the seven branches of the menorah. Many medieval French texts specifically connect the fleur-de-lis—and the French lily in general—with the Temple in Jerusalem. Romano-Jewish historian Flavius Josephus had himself remarked years before that the calyxes and petals of the menorah resembled lilies. Brice Bauderon de Sénécé went further in his text of 1684, making the following observations:

> The lilies that are the principal ornaments of the mystic candlestick (the candlestick in the Temple) still render the most natural application of it to France; to which God has given this flower, as a sign of his alliance, and

a pledge of his love. This admirable flower thus serves as the principal ornaments of the magnificent Temple of Solomon.[3]

This is a fascinating development. If the symbol of the lily was said to have been gifted to France as a token of its allegiance to God, then this mirrors exactly the role that the menorah and other sacred objects created for the tabernacle were assigned to fulfil: the Ark and the attendant menorah were symbols of God's covenant with the Israelites. If the fleur-de-lis was indeed a symbol of God's devotion to the French people as Bauderon de Sénecé asserts, then this may suggest that the fleur-de-lis and the menorah were one and the same and that they became interchangeable in usage.

We know that the lily was used as a metaphor for purity in the days of Solomon, and it is found in his Song of Songs. The capitals on the columns in Solomon's Temple also took the form of the lily, so it would certainly be possible for the petals and stamen on the menorah to have resembled lilies. Given the meaning of virtuosity attributed to the lily in Jewish religious thought, there hardly seems a more appropriate flower that could have been used in the design.

We find the fleur-de-lis itself in use in Jewish art around the time of the second temple, so we have a clear precedence in this era. The symbol spread and was found throughout the Near East, as well as India, Rome, Byzantium, and beyond, before being brought to Europe. While there are legends stating that Clovis I of France used the fleur-de-lis in the 5th century, there is no hard evidence that the symbol had arrived in France until around 1060, when it was first adopted by King Philip I.

The fleur-de-lis was ever after closely linked with the French royal family and nobility. If it is true that the design was derived from the menorah and Solomon's Temple, then we suddenly see why the monarchy were so fond of this symbol. The fleur-de-lis is often associated with the divine right to rule, tied up as it is with the ancient kings of Judah and Israel.

One final revelation could prove that the fleur-de-lis predates even the kingdoms of Judah and Israel and this source is found in ancient Egypt. It turns out that the Egyptian hieroglyph for "plant," which is the symbol thought to represent the tree of life, comprised three water lilies in a very similar layout to that of the fleur-de-lis. It is worth remembering that the Israelites were captive in Egypt and lived there for many years, so they would have absorbed its iconography and symbols. Also, if you cast your mind back to Chapter 3, you will recall that the menorah is thought to represent the tree of life itself, so suddenly the link between the menorah and the fleur-de-lis is revealed: they really are symbols that share a common origin and meaning. When we are shown the fleur-de-lis we are being reminded not only of the menorah and its holy light but also the perennial themes of Asherah and the Shekinah once again.

When Louis IX is depicted holding a lily with seven petals on his personal seal[4] he may as well be holding a menorah. Such iconography could indicate that the menorah and the fleur-de-lis had become one in the mind of the King.

With the menorah at that time held safely somewhere on French soil, Louis would have known that everything the fleur-de-lis stood for and represented was then a part of his new holy kingdom, and this revelation only underlined Louis' position as the new king of kings among his peers.

However, this golden age, this new Jerusalem in France with St Louis at its helm, would not last forever. A shockwave was about to hit Europe, one that would have lasting consequences and reverberate for centuries to come. The Knights Templar were running short of friends and were swiftly being outnumbered by their enemies. When the tipping point finally came, the end was quick and brutal. With the Templars the official guardians of the treasures of the Temple, it is time to discover what happened to the menorah when the unthinkable happened and the Templars were felled.

CHAPTER 12
THE DOWNFALL OF THE KNIGHTS TEMPLAR

The relationship between the Knights Templar and the royal house of France deteriorated significantly after the death of Louis IX. The seeds of this decline had been sown during the disobedience of Renaud de Vichiers in the 1250s when, you will recall from Chapter 8, the Grand Master exceeded his authority and deeply offended Louis. It seems remarkable that de Vichiers all but disappears from the record after that event, as he had been close friends with Louis, who even asked him to be godfather to one of his children, though he had to decline the honor.

As we suggested in Chapter 11, it is possible that this sudden change of fortune had something to do with the Templars' loss of complete control of the relic and other treasures. Their whole *raison d'être* was to secure the Temple treasures from Jerusalem, so to lose absolute possession of them was clearly a disastrous turn of events. It seems impossible in our minds that the two occurrences are unrelated.

Much has been written about the demise of the Knights Templar by historians and academics, many of whom have spent their whole lives specializing in the subject. As we don't share that level of expertise, we decided our approach should be simpler and so agreed that we should form our conclusions based solely on written records and documents from the era when the Knights Templar existed, and that testimony is what we will draw on in this chapter.

The landslide that led to the destruction of the Knights Templar seems to have been triggered by nothing more than rumors to start with, spread initially by four Templars from the Aquitaine region of France who are sometimes referred to as the "four traitors." They were revealed in a deposition made to the Inquisition (set up by the Catholic Church to combat heresy) in November 1309 by a Templar called Ponsard de Gizy, the leader of the Templar commandery at Payns in the Champagne region. This was the same town that had been the home of the founder of the order himself, Hugh de Payns. During Ponsard's trial, a document that he had written was cited as evidence, and the following section was quoted:

These are the traitors who have uttered lies and slanders against the members of the Order of the Temple: the monk William Robert, who tortured them, Esquieu of Floyrac of Beziers, Comprior of Montfaucon, Bernard Pelet, Prior of Mas d'Agenais, and the knight Gérard of Boyzol, who came to Gisors.[1]

Ponsard's testimony not only disclosed the names of those who had first disseminated the rumors concerning the Knights Templar but also went into great detail regarding the content of the accusations themselves:

Afterwards, in the same place and on the same day, Brother Ponsard of Gizy, Preceptor of Payns, was brought before the same lords of the commission and asked by them if he wished to defend the said Order. He replied that the articles that were imputed to the said Order, namely that the Order denied Jesus Christ, spat on the Cross, permitted one brother to have sexual commerce with another, and certain other similar gross enormities arising from these, were all false. Whatever he and other brothers of the Order had confessed to concerning the aforesaid before the bishop of Paris or elsewhere were false.[2]

If there was any doubt, Esquieu de Floyrac, one of the four traitors named in the testimony, even boasted about having informed the King of France himself, in a letter to King James II of Aragon, a few years after the fact on January 21, 1308:

May it be manifest to your royal Majesty that I am he who exposed the actions of the Templars to my lord king of France, and may you acknowledge that you were the first prince in the whole world to whom I exposed their actions at Lerida. In the presence of your confessor, Brother Martin Detecha. In this you were unwilling, lord, to give full credence to my words at the time, which is why I had recourse to the lord king of France, who investigated the activities and brought them out into the daylight, particularly as concerns his kingdom; consequently he has fully informed the pope about their activities, as well as other princes, namely the king of Germany, the king of England and King Charles, and other princes.[3]

Further on, in the same letter, Esquieu de Floyrac provides the first hint of a sinister motive behind the spreading of the rumors:

My lord, remember what you promised me in your chamber at Lerida when I departed, that if the activities of the Templars were found to be proved you would give me 1,000 livres in rents and 3,000 livres in money from their goods. And now that has been shown to be the case, think fit to remember when the occasion arises.

It is nigh impossible today to establish conclusively whether there was a larger conspiracy at work here, and who might have concocted such an elaborate scheme. All we know for certain is that in November 1305, the French king, acting on information provided by Esquieu de Floyrac, raised the issue of an alleged heresy carried out by the Knights Templar during the coronation of the new pope Clement V in Lyon, France.

The King of France in this instance was Philip IV, nicknamed "the Fair," a direct grandson of Louis IX. The Pope himself does not appear to have taken much notice of Philip's claims at the time. Clement V had several Templars serving him personally, and he frequently met and conversed with Hugues de Pairaud, one of the leaders of the Knights Templar who held the title of Visitor of France, so it is obvious that the Pope was on good terms with the Templars. However, that's not the whole story, because Clement had a plan of his own in mind, and he wished to see the Knights Templar merge with the Hospitallers and the Teutonic Knights.

The reasons for this proposed union were manifold but the main consideration was wanting to create a single, crusading knightly order that might have a chance of withstanding the Muslim armies that now controlled the Holy Land unchecked. The Christian militia were fragmented into different orders at this time and faring badly on the battlefield: the Knights Templar had been forced out of the Levant entirely, even losing their headquarters at Acre, and were stationed now in Cyprus; the Hospitallers had fared no better and had been pushed back on to the island of Rhodes. So, a union between the three orders was thought to be a prudent move, but both the Templars and the Hospitallers eventually rejected such an idea—a move that in all likelihood accelerated what was about to happen next.

Over the next two years, Philip IV and his close adviser, the lawyer and keeper of the seals, Guillaume de Nogaret, mobilized the impressive administrative powers of France to bring the Templars to trial. At first glance, the King's motives appear to have been purely financial. The Templars had amassed unprecedented assets and the order functioned almost as an independent kingdom within France. The King had borrowed substantial sums of money from the Templars and he began to look to their strongholds and possessions with envy. Indeed, some of the King's valuables were stored in the Paris Temple, the headquarters of the Knights Templar, because it was considered more secure than the King's own facilities. Also, in 1306, riots broke out in Paris and Philip IV had to seek sanctuary in the large central tower of the Templar's stronghold.[4] This humiliating experience never left the King and it must have made him even more envious of the Templars' resources and the power they wielded.

However, the decision to turn against the Knights Templar was not solely driven by concerns about wealth and power, because the political landscape of France at this time was incredibly complex. Some historians have suggested that Philip the Fair was fighting an ideological battle with Pope Clement V for authority. Philip believed that he, more than anyone else, was entitled to be the Vicar of Christ on Earth.[5] In essence, the King had begun to believe that, as ultimate defender and figurehead of the Christian faith, he possessed a higher authority than the Pope.

The King and his advisers pressured the Pope to act against the Templars. Clement V was in poor health, so, not being in full possession of his faculties, he attempted to delay proceedings, but Philip was in no mood to wait for a reply. In an order dated September 14, 1307, the bailiffs and seneschals (stewards or administrators) of the kingdom of France, as well as appointed special agents, were commanded to initiate preparations to arrest the Templars.

The sole justification and legal foundation for Philip the Fair's decision was the Templar's alleged ill repute. In deepest secret, a simultaneous mass action was planned and, on the morning of Friday October 13, 1307, the King's forces swept into action, turning up at every Templar house in the country with arrest warrants, backed by the royal seal. They ordered the brothers within to surrender, after which they were taken into custody. Furthermore, the warrants gave the King's men the power to "seize their movable and immovable goods . . . until you receive further instructions from us on this matter."[6]

Jacques de Molay, Grand Master of the Knights Templar, was arrested, together with hundreds of other members of the order throughout France. The King had instructed the officials that they could resort to torture if needed, to extract a confession. Conveniently, this method of persuasion had been approved by the papacy in 1252 for those occasions when accused heretics refused to respond.[7]

Eventually, after immense pressure from the French king, the Pope caved in and joined the chorus. He issued a papal bull, *Pastoralis Praeeminentiae*, on November 22, 1307, that ordered the widespread arrest of all remaining members of the Knights Templar. At a stroke, the Knights Templar were no longer safe in any territory. What followed was a long period of interrogations and trials right across Europe, which led to the inevitable dismemberment of the Knights Templar as an organization, along with the execution of its leadership.

The Church's confirmation of this death knell came on March 22, 1312, when Pope Clement V issued a further papal bull, *Vox in Excelso*, in which he announced the dissolution of the Knights Templar and withdrew all papal support for the order. This was followed by another bull, *Ad Providam*, on May 2, in which the goods and lands of the Templars were given to the Order of St John (short for Order of the Hospital of St John of Jerusalem, better known as the Hospitallers, and operating today as the Sovereign Order of Malta).

There was one significant exception. The bull did not apply to the Templar possessions in Iberia, and Clement V left the matter of the Templar enclaves of Castille, Aragon, Mallorca, and Portugal unsettled, claiming them for himself, "until the Apostolic See makes another arrangement."[8]

After the publication of the papal bulls, the legal case against the Templars came to an end. The Grand Master of the Knights Templar, Jacques de Molay, was burned alive at the stake on the Île des Javiaux in Paris on March 18, 1314, closing a dark and sinister chapter in the history of Europe.

Now that we had gathered all this information, it was time for us to look at the aftermath of these events. We wondered what the implications of this sudden series of catastrophes were and what it might have meant for the treasures and sacred relics the Templars had brought to France from Jerusalem. Were the menorah and the other treasures and relics from the Temple in Jerusalem, which had, until this point, been safely stored in Templar strongholds, now in the hands of Philip the Fair?

The inner temple

Rumors of the Templar's alleged crimes had been spread by the King and his entourage for at least two years before the arrests. It seems to have been the perfect act of disinformation and when the carefully engineered trials of the Templars began, every detail was expertly recorded and documented; nothing was left to chance. Today, we still have more than 900 testimonies, dutifully recorded by the clerics of the papal Inquisition. We spent hours and hours sifting through every document we had access to, searching for any clue, however small, and tracing our way through the maze of testimonies.

One thing became apparent, which was that there appeared to have been a secret sect of initiates embedded deep within the Knights Templar, a secret chapter. In the testimony of Ralph de Prelles, a jurist of the King serving as witness to the prosecution, he states that, when he lived in the city of Laon, he was friends with a Templar called Gervais de Beauvais. Apparently, de Beauvais claimed more than 100 times in the presence of de Prelles and others that there was a division in the order so secret he would rather have his own head cut off than reveal the details to anyone.[9] Malcolm Barber elaborates on this strange revelation:

> There was also a point in the general chapter of the Order which was so secret that if Ralph de Presles or even the King of France should see it, those holding the chapter would seek to kill them, deferring to the authority of no one in this. Furthermore, Gervais had said that the Order had a small book of statutes which he would show to Presles willingly, but there existed another secret book which he would not show him for all the world.[10]

These statements by de Prelles attained more weight when we read the testimony concerning Hugh de Châlons, which is kept in the manuscripts section of the French national archives, held at the Bibliothèque nationale de France and quoted here in the original Latin with a translation below:

Frater Hugo de Cabilone nepos visitatoris et frater Girardus de Monteclaro, milites ordinis seu secte Templi, una cum quibusdam suis complicibus secte conceperant occidere regem.[11]

Father Hugh de Châlons, the nephew of the Visitor and brother of Gérard de Montclair, warriors of the Order or the Sect of the Temple, together with some more accomplices from the same sect, planned to kill the King.

Had we found a more sinister motive for the ruthless vendetta of Philip the Fair here? Was it possible that the King had become privy to the inner secrets of the Temple? A secret that his grandfather, Louis IX, had perhaps not even known about? And had Philip uncovered a subsequent plot to kill him or was this yet another smokescreen deployed by the King?

Whatever the real motive, and despite the secrecy of the final well-orchestrated pincer movement to arrest members of the order, the Knights Templar were clearly aware of the dangers that were amassing at their door. There was also a conscious move to attempt to conceal their most precious possessions before the wrath of the King finally descended on them. One example of such an event is recorded in another statement by Jean de Châlons, the Preceptor of Nemours and Hugh's father:

Item dixit, quod potentes ordinis prescientes istam confusionem fugiunt et ipse obviavit fratri Girardo de Villariis ducenti quinquaginta equos, et audivit dici, quod intravit mare cum XVIII galeis, et frater Hugo de Cabilone fugiit cum toto thesauro fratris Hugonis de Peraudo. Interrogatus, quomodo potuit tandiu istud fáctum teneri secretum respondit, quod nullus pro aliqua re erat ausus revelare, nisi papa et rex aperuissent viam, quia, si sciretur in ordine, quod aliquis loqueretur, statim fuisset mortuus.[12]

Then he said that, learning beforehand about this trouble, the leaders of the order fled, and he himself met Brother Gérard de Villiers leading 50 horses, and he heard it said that he set out to sea with 18 galleys and that brother Hugh de Châlons fled with the whole treasure of Brother Hugh de Pairaud. When asked how he was able to keep this fact secret for so long, he responded that no one would have dared reveal it for anything, if the Pope and the King had not opened the way, for if it were known in the order that anyone had spoken, he would at once be killed.

French historian Albert Ollivier has transcribed an oral legend in which it is said that the treasure of the Temple was loaded on to three carts and covered with hay on the direct order of Jacques de Molay on the very eve of the arrests.[13] This legend is impossible to verify, but we are inclined to believe the written accounts found in the legal documents that seem to point to the same revelation. The Knights Templar may have planned and made provision for such a betrayal, and when they sensed that the noose was tightening, acted accordingly.

The testimonies had slowly revealed their truth to us. There was definitely a secret and something clandestine had clearly been taking place, away from the public eye. Apparently, this secret was so potent that even a king would have to be killed if he were to discover it. Furthermore, if the testimonies were to be believed, certain Templars had indeed conspired to kill Philip IV.

This was not simply hearsay and the people interrogated in these accounts were not insignificant nobodies: Hugh de Châlons was a nephew of the Visitor of France, none other than Hugues de Pairaud himself. "Visitor" was one of the highest offices in the Templar hierarchy and de Pairaud was responsible for all Western Templar territories, except those on the Iberian Peninsula. He also held the title of Master of France at the same time.

Ultimately, Hugues de Pairaud was sentenced to life imprisonment in 1314 and died in captivity. According to the testimonies, Gérard de Villiers, de Pairaud's lieutenant, effectively the second-in-command in France, and Hugh de Châlons both escaped this fate.

Gérard de Villiers is last mentioned in an official document in February 1307, a few months before the Templars were rounded up. However, there is no mention of him being arrested or interrogated and Templar historians are unanimous in their conclusions that de Villiers escaped the trap set by Philip IV and Pope Clement V. The only question that lingers is: where did he escape to?

We believe that the hoard of treasure entrusted to the safekeeping of Hugues de Pairaud, Gérard de Villiers' superior, and held in Paris, must have contained the sacred treasures from Solomon's Temple. The Knights Templar had several impregnable strongholds at their formidable headquarters, the Paris Temple, at this time.

The Paris Temple was an independent city within Paris itself. The buildings of the Paris Temple comprised the impressive Grosse Tour, a great fortified keep with four turrets, along with a smaller tower called the Tour de César, which was designed to resemble the Church of the Holy Sepulchre in Jerusalem. Both these strongholds were built during the reign of Louis IX, when he came back from the Holy Land. The

Grosse Tour in particular is known for having stored many of the Knights Templar's prized possessions . We still believe that the menorah and the other Jewish treasures that the Knights Templar and Louis IX brought back to France in 1254 were stored initially beneath the great cathedrals that rose up during this era—the ones that are on the apexes of our sacro pentagram—but at some point, either when the Grosse Tour had been completed or maybe during the first years of Philip IV's reign, from 1285 onwards, the treasures were moved to Paris, where they would be much better protected than was possible in the cathedrals.

Something worth noting is that the Paris Temple sits within the inner pentagon of the sacro pentagram, so it would have been viewed as a sacred, protected space. Furthermore, the Paris Temple is positioned very close to the Paris meridian, which, originally, you will recall, was calculated by Cassini for King Louis XIV (see Chapter 8). In fact, if you follow this meridian south from Amiens at the top of the sacro pentagram, it cuts the pentagram in half.

When King Philip issued his arrest warrants and ordered his forces to claim all the possessions of the Knights Templar, he was counting on the great treasures that were stored at the Paris Temple still being there on the morning of the round-up. However, if we are to believe Jean de Châlons' testimony, de Villiers had fled with 50 horses when the first whispers of the growing plot against the Templars reached his ears.

Somehow, at the last moment, one day before the mass arrest was planned, two of the senior figures in the Knights Templar—Hugh de Châlons and Gérard de Villiers—seem to have been warned of the impending apocalypse that was about to rain down on the order. While they could do nothing to halt the arrests or stop the destruction, there was one last thing that they could do. They could steal the treasures of Solomon that were stored in the Paris Temple and attempt to move them out of France. We believe that this was done not only to secure the treasures for their order but also as a final stroke of revenge on King Philip, who had turned on them and was increasingly determined to put an end to the Knights Templar. It fell to de Villiers to retrieve the menorah and the other treasures, and the testimony from the trials goes on to claim that, after he escaped Paris on horseback with 50 of his men, he set out to sea with 18 galleys. So, where did de Villiers and his cohort ride to that night and how did he secure such a fleet?

Galleys were long, narrow, wooden vessels with a shallow beam (not that wide at their widest point) and a low freeboard (short distance between the railing and the water). They were propelled by rows of oars and usually sailed with one or two masts. Historians have theorized that if de Villiers did indeed escape France with a fleet of galleys, then he most probably did so from La Rochelle, the primary port on the Atlantic coast. There is a problem, though: La Rochelle is some 280 miles (450 km) from Paris, so this would have involved an almost impossible journey for men on horseback ordinarily, let alone at such a perilous time for the Templars. Further, the French authorities had been ordered to prepare for the arrests a month before the date they were to be actioned, so every official in France would have been on the lookout for Templars on the move, especially senior members of the order.

We know that there were galleys in the port of La Rochelle, as they were regularly used for shipping wine up and down the European trade routes, but the sheer distance from Paris still made us doubt that they were used by the Templars in the way put forward in the theory. We wondered if there was another answer to this riddle. Had de Villiers arranged another escape route in case such an emergency ever arose, one that was not so obvious?

We eventually identified another candidate for making the flight from France that was much closer to Paris but, at first glance, seemed unlikely as it is far from the coast. The city of Rouen is some 43 miles (70 km) from the sea, but the French had been building galleys there since 1226, at a shipyard called the Clos-des-Gallées, near the site of the oldest arsenal in France.

It was King Philip himself who had invested in the shipyard at Rouen, bringing in experienced Genoese shipwrights.[14] These shipbuilders turned what had once been a modest enclosure into an impressive galley yard, similar in scale to those you might have found in Genoa or Barcelona, laid out around a basin that branched off the river itself, with the entry and exit of vessels controlled by locks. This yard even included covered sheds to shelter the galleys during the winter. Crucially, the city was only 77 miles (125 km) from Paris—around a quarter of the distance from Paris to La Rochelle. This meant that de Villiers and his men would have been able to arrive safely in Rouen well before the order to round up all members of the Knights Templar came into effect. Once at Rouen, a fleet of galleys could have sailed along the River Seine to the Atlantic without attracting too much attention.

There was another significant difference, and that was between the galleys at the two ports. Those built at La Rochelle were trading ships, while the vessels constructed in the shipyard at Rouen were destined to be military ships.

The case for La Rochelle as the escape route contained many strong arguments in its favour, too, not least of which is the fact that the port had an old and powerful Templar commandery where de Villiers could have called in favours and been granted assistance. However, Rouen still felt like the smarter move, as it was a less obvious route, so had more chance of success: it is closer to Paris, and it had the more robust, warlike galleys available in the port.

Regardless of which of the two locations was the actual escape route, we were certain that de Villiers had fled France, and it was very likely that he had taken items of great interest—and value—with him. The question we next had to turn our attention to was: where had de Villiers sailed to with his precious cargo, especially when, with the arrest warrants then in force and Templars taken into custody in their thousands, the options for safe haven in Europe were then extremely limited?

Because galleys were notoriously shallow in their draught (the depth of water needed to float them) and sailed so low in the water, it made them too unstable to cross the open Atlantic Ocean. They were, however, well suited to skirting the European coast, offering de Villiers and those who had escaped with him a choice of destinations to seek refuge.

We must not assume that such a flight would have been easy, and success was not guaranteed. The Templars at this point were outlaws and it would have been a challenge for de Villiers to find a location that was safe enough to hide the treasure he carried and continue to be its guardian. If de Villiers had made the wrong choice, it would have resulted in imprisonment, or worse, and the loss of his precious cargo.

One obvious destination was Scotland—a country that then was still independent from England. France and Scotland had signed an agreement in 1295 called the Auld Alliance in an effort to keep an aggressive England at bay. This meant that if either Scotland or France was attacked by the English, the other would step in to help fight them off. This early NATO-like bond between France and Scotland was so strong that it lasted almost 300 years, until 1560. At the time of the mass arrest of the Knights Templar, Scotland was ruled by King Robert the Bruce, who was no friend of the Church. In fact, Robert had very recently been excommunicated by the Pope for stabbing to death a rival with a claim to the throne of Scotland. This bloody event had occurred directly in front of the high altar at Greyfriar's Monastery, greatly offending the Pope.

Robert was always in need of good fighting men and legend has it that a group of Knights Templar helped him win the battle of Bannockburn in 1314. Indeed, the Knights Templar had maintained a presence in Scotland since the early days of the order and, as we saw in Chapter 5, it was one of the locations visited by the first Grand Master of the Templars, Hugh de Payns, in 1128, when the Scottish Temple had been handed land and estates. However, there are no remaining records of French-speaking foreigners turning up in Scotland in the 14th century,[15] so, once again, we had to turn to the Inquisition records for answers.

We discovered that there were not many Templars in Scotland in 1307. Of the few brothers present, Walter Clifton and William of Middleton were rounded up and arrested, while others, such as Thomas Totti, were recorded as "escaped," although most would be caught later. Almost all the Templars in Scotland appear to have been of English origin.

Clifton and William testified that they were the only remaining members of the order in Scotland. Both had lived at Ballantrodach and Clifton had served as the Master of Scotland.[16] What was also revealed was that the Scottish Temple was answerable to the Master of England. The records relate how Hugues de Pairaud, Visitor of France, had visited Scotland twice and William met with him. One witness at the trial testified that de Pairaud would visit England, while the Visitor of England would travel to Scotland where he would call the brothers into the chapter general, "so that their secrets could be communicated."[17]

Once more, here was confirmation that the Templars not only retained and protected great secrets but they also had the capacity to disseminate this privileged information within their order over vast distances. Just as in France, the Templars in England and Scotland performed essential banking services to the Crown. In Scotland specifically, the king's almoner was almost always a member of the order. To facilitate the religious and financial interests of the Knights Templar, there was frequent travel between Scotland, England, France, Cyprus, and the Holy Land, underlining that here was an organization which operated as an independent and supranational entity.[18]

The Scottish arrests in 1307 were carried out by an English administration that was occupying southern Scotland at the time of the papal decree against the Templars. The Inquisition trials that followed took place at Holyrood Abbey in Edinburgh. On Sunday, November 17, 1309, Clifton and William gave their testimonies and they made the following statement regarding the Templars of Scotland:

> *qui, habitu rejecto statim fugerunt quum audiverunt captionem confratrum suorum, ultra mare, prout dici audivit et pluribus aliis, nunc rebus humanis exemptis.*[19]

who, having cast off their habits, had immediately fled, across the sea, when they heard their brothers had been caught, as he heard it said, and many other men, who were now dead.

This was exactly the kind of evidence we had been looking for. Here was a direct reference to several Knights Templar apparently fleeing, after disguising themselves by casting off their regalia and traveling incognito. Furthermore, they had escaped overseas. However, given that this testimony was given in Scotland, it naturally followed that Scotland could not have been the place where the Templars in question had fled to.

Aside from this, there is another reason why Scotland was not a safe refuge for the persecuted Knights Templar, despite what is often claimed. The new Scottish King, Robert the Bruce, had already made two powerful enemies: Pope Clement V, who had excommunicated the Scottish monarch, and the King of England, who Robert was waging war against. It would not have been in Robert's interest to incur the wrath of the King of France by harboring a handful of knights who were fugitives in the eyes of French law. The Auld Alliance between France and Scotland also made such a breach of trust unlikely, because Robert desperately needed to keep the French on his side and wouldn't have wanted to lose the protection afforded by such an alliance.

We therefore decided that, despite the rumors that had sprouted up over the centuries, it was unlikely that Gérard de Villiers and his company of outcast Templars had fled to Scotland. So, what were the alternatives?

A single Templar, even several, could have successfully escaped to Ireland, some remote parts of Germany, or even Denmark, where they might have attempted to live in rural backwaters, their presence perhaps going unnoticed, but it would not have been easy, especially given the language barrier. Such a life also seemed incompatible with the stature and character of someone like Gérard de Villiers.

Through the recorded statements of Ponsard de Gizy—the leader of the commandery at Payns quoted earlier in this chapter—we knew that de Villiers had been involved in a similarly treacherous situation that had occurred some years previously, only just escaping with his life. When Acre had finally fallen to the Muslims in 1291, the Templars lost all their possessions in the Holy Land, but they had managed to cling on to a fortress on the tiny island of Ruad (also called Arwad), off the coast of Syria. This fortress acted as a temporary staging post between the Holy Land and the Templars' new headquarters on Cyprus, and was only 2 miles (3 km) from the coastal town of Tortosa (also called Tartus), which the Templars had recently lost.

De Gizy recounted a story that he had heard from an old Templar Knight, who described how Gérard de Villiers and a small band of friends had fled the island barely one day before it was finally overrun by the Mamluks.[20] Many of de Villiers' comrades were either killed or taken prisoner in the final assault, so it was a miracle that he escaped.

Fleeing the last Templar foothold in the Holy Land and abandoning his brethren would not have been easy for de Villiers because it violated every Templar rule that he valued. However, it is very possible that he had greater concerns that day. We know that he would later be personally responsible for some of the greatest treasures the Templars owned so, perhaps on this earlier occasion, in a similar manner to his flight from Paris mere days before the Templars were outlawed, he had something precious to safeguard that overruled all usual protocol. If that was the case, then it is likely that his brothers in arms held the Mamluks at bay long enough for de Villiers to make his escape from the island. For us, this signaled a pattern, it indicated a clear precedent, and its conclusion was suddenly glaringly obvious: in 1307, de Villiers performed a repeat of the disappearing act that he had pulled off in Tartus.

Both Gérard de Villiers and Hugh de Châlons vanished entirely from the record after the testimony of Hugh's father, which seems very suspicious to our minds. It cannot be a coincidence that the second-in-command of the French Templars fled on the eve of the arrests and subsequently went missing, along with the nephew of the Visitor and Master of France. The documented testimony from the trials—given by someone who knew them both personally—does not state that de Villiers and de Châlons escaped together, but there is evidence that this is precisely what happened.

Like historian Ollivier, French investigative journalist Gérard de Sède claimed that the two Templars not only fled together but also they left Paris with three horse-drawn carts, each laden with hay, under which they had concealed the treasure from the Paris Temple.[21] He also cites a single-page document from August 1308, held at the Bibliothèque nationale de France, that had been inserted into a letter by Pope Clement V entitled, "these are the names of the brothers that have fled."[22] This document is also referenced in the works of renowned German Templar researcher Heinrich Finke. The insert mentions, "Gérard de Villiers and Hugh de Châlons who had armed 40 brothers."

According to de Sède, of minor nobility himself and well connected with the French institutions and archives by profession, the fugitives had headed towards Normandy and probably boarded ships in one of the ports on the Atlantic coast, headed for Scotland. We have already outlined why we disagree with his suggestion that Scotland was the final destination, but one of the claims of this theory vied for our attention: Rouen and its royal shipyard of military galleys is situated in Normandy.

So, if de Villiers did not set sail for Scotland, where did he chart a course to?

There was a country in Europe where, even during such tumultuous times, a group of 50 Knights Templar might find shelter, support, and a safe place to hide treasures, and that was far enough away for them to escape the clutches of the French king. Crucially, it was a country where they could remain Templars, true to the oaths they had sworn. Finally, this location could be reached safely by galley from France, making this destination a tantalizing prospect.

That country was Portugal.

CHAPTER 13
LIFELINE: THE KNIGHTS TEMPLAR IN PORTUGAL

Like de Villiers during his miraculous escape, our research had led us to a new country and a new chapter. Up to the point when we discovered this, we had not paid much attention to Portugal, but in that moment it was clear that we needed to begin a new branch of research, and what we found was extremely revealing.

Portugal had been home to one of the oldest—if not *the* oldest—Templar commanderies in Europe. By 1126, the Templars had already been given land in Fonte Arcada, in what is now northern Portugal. We had to look at that date twice because it was three years earlier than the Council of Troyes, so three years before the Knights Templar had been officially inaugurated.

We wondered if this revealed the hand of the Catholic Church. Had it been making preparations even at this early stage, already confident that its plans would come to fruition? Whatever the true implications, it is clear that the Knights Templar and the Portuguese rulers had close ties.

On June 2, 1128, the feast day of the Templar patron saint, John the Baptist, Prince Afonso Henriques defeated his mother's troops and officially became the Count of Portugal, at only 18 years old. Immediately following this, a few months after the Council of Troyes, Afonso donated a castle to the Knights Templar at Soure, but that is not all. The Prince joined the order himself at the same time.

I make this donation, not by command or persuasion of somebody, but for God's sake, and for remedy of my soul, and my parents, and the heartfelt love that I have you, and because your guild and all your works I am Brother, I, the Infant Dom Afonso rubric with my own hand this letter.[1]

With the help of the Knights Templar, Afonso began to transform Portugal into an independent kingdom. The decisive moment came in 1147 when, to our astonishment, we found that a central role was played, yet again, by Bernard of Clairvaux.

In 1146, Afonso had sent a Templar named Pedro northwards to request help from Bernard. Afonso was eager to gain the ear of Pope Eugenius III, in an effort to persuade the crusaders of Northern Europe to come to Portugal's aid and assist with driving out the Moors from Iberia. Afonso also asked Bernard to include this Portuguese cause of "Reconquista" in his own preachings in France and the Low Countries, adding new spiritual weight to Afonso's campaign.

Bernard worked his magic and used his charm once again, eventually securing the blessing of Pope Eugenius III. This is no great surprise, given that the Pope had once been a pupil of Bernard's, and it was Bernard's great influence that had seen Eugenius installed in the role the previous year. To seal the deal, in July of 1146, a monk was sent to Portugal from Clairvaux with the necessary documents, accompanied by a personal letter from Bernard to Afonso:[2]

> To Afonso, Illustrious king of the Portuguese, Bernard, in name Abbot of Clairvaux, the prayer of a sinner, if that is of any worth. We have received the letters and greetings of your Highness, rejoicing in him "who commands deliverances for Jacob." What we have done in this matter, the outcome will reveal for us, and you will also discover from the outcome; you will discern our readiness to act from the care we have taken or at least from our known friendship. Pedro, the brother of your Highness, and worthy of all glory, related the matters enjoined on him by you, and is now fighting in Lorraine, after roaming in arms through France; and he is soon to fight for the Lord of hosts. Brother Roland, our son, is bringing letters conveying the papal concessions. May you commit to your care him, our brothers residing with you, and myself.[3]

So it was that, in May 1147, 164 ships set sail to Portugal from Northern Europe, as recorded by French historian Odo of Deuil. Heading out from Dartmouth in England, this fleet of ships carried crusaders from Frisia, Flanders, Germany, France, and England. The contingent arrived in Porto on June 16, where the crusaders met with an ecstatic Afonso, who was thrilled to see the reinforcements.

Two weeks later, Afonso and the fleet set a course for Lisbon, where they laid siege to the city on July 1. Afonso had promised the newcomers as much plunder from the city as they could carry. The Moors surrendered the city four months later and most crusaders never left Lisbon, settling there instead. The capture of Lisbon was to be the crowning achievement of Afonso's "Reconquista," and this victory became the decisive turning point the King had needed.[4]

Miguel Real reveals that all this was because Afonso was on a mission:

It was supposed to be through Templars and through the vision of King Alfonso Henriques in the Battle of Ourique (1139) that a sacred territory would be established, a country, a nation whose destiny would be to establish the messiah mission in Europe, Portugal as a country chosen by God, a messiah state.[5]

Throughout the campaign, Afonso relied heavily on the support of one man in particular—Gualdim Pais, a soldier from the northern regions of Portugal, who fought valiantly alongside him. Afonso made him a knight in 1139, after the Battle of Ourique. Pais then departed for the Holy Land to fight with the Knights Templar, and he gave a good account of himself in battle for five years under the tutelage of Templar Grand Master Robert de Craon, who succeeded Hugh de Payns after his death in 1136. Pais' reputation propelled him up the Templar ranks and eventually he became Grand Master himself, of the Knights Templar of Portugal in 1157.

As Grand Master, Pais made good use of the lands donated to the order by Afonso, founding several Templar strongholds. The most impressive of these was at Tomar and the huge defensive structure, built in only one year, became the Templar's official Portuguese headquarters. Not far from Tomar, Pais built an equally formidable fortress at Almourol, on an island in the River Tagus, that guards the road leading to Tomar. After Pais' death in 1195, an inscription honoring his achievements was carved into a marble slab over the gate of Almourol castle:[6]

AD 1208. Master Gualdim from noble birth, born in Braga, lived in the time of Afonso, illustrious King of Portugal, left the secular military, when the light suddenly appeared, went to Jerusalem as a Knight of the Temple, lived a hard life for five years, fought many battles with his Master and his brothers, moving against the kings of Egypt and Syria, being captured at Ascalon, went to Antioch, fought many times for the surrender of Sidon, after five years of military experience, he came back to become Preceptor of the House of the Temple in Portugal, founded the castles of Pombal, Tomar, Zêzere and this that is called Almourol, and Idanha and Monsanto.

We were curious why Pais had left King Afonso and Portugal in 1139, especially when he had just been made a knight. We also wondered why Afonso had allowed one of his most reliable lieutenants to leave. The answer can perhaps be found in the short sentence inscribed on the marble plaque: "*ut lucifer emicuit.*" "Lucifer" means "light" or "light bringer," which in English is, "as the light (or light bringer) suddenly appeared." Taking into account all that we had learned up until this point, this statement seemed yet another explicit reference to the rediscovery of the menorah by the Knights Templar, as the menorah was the most famous lampstand, the bringer of light.

We found this revelation even more significant because, as we described in Chapter 7, Templar Grand Master Everard Les Barres had made similar allusions to a "new light" in his letter to Cluny in 1150. Pais and Everard were contemporaries and it seems clear to us that the discovery of this most sacred object was the impetus for one of Portugal's, if not Europe's, most formidable fighting men to travel to the Holy Land. The menorah needed to be defended and who better to ensure its safety than Pais.

Before we leave Pais, there are a couple of curious facts about the man that left us puzzled. The first is his name. It appears that "Pais" was a Portuguese version of the name "Payns." It is a strange coincidence that Gualdim Pais should share the same name as Hugh de Payns, the founder of the Knights Templar. It also turned out that Pais died on Friday, October 13, 1195—yet another Friday 13th, to go with the day the Knights Templar were arrested. Was this an accurate date or was it yet another clue left to us in the historical record?

Afonso Henriques officially became the sovereign King Afonso I of Portugal in 1179. His status was recognized by the Pope and sanctioned via a papal bull, *Manifestis Probatum*. Afonso had a curious symbol that he used to sign official documents during his reign, rather than use his own name. He used a stylized circular seal showing the capital letters "PORTUGAL," configured in the form of a cross, with the letter "R" inserted a bit below but between the "G" and "AL." Some authors have theorized that this implies a link between Portugal and the Holy Grail because this device morphs the word "Portugal" into "Portugral" or "Portu Gral," which is Portuguese for "Port of the Grail."[7] This appearance of the Holy Grail was a pleasant surprise for us and, yet again, here we had another coded reference to a sacred object from the Holy Land. We do not want to become distracted by the Holy Grail at this point, but we saw its emergence here as a clue that we were on the right path.

Afonso's part in our story was almost over, but he had played a key role. By the time Afonso came to the end of his life in 1185, he had established Portugal as a strong, independent kingdom and had pushed the Moors southward beyond Lisbon, defeating no less than five Moorish kings. He had also created a safe haven for the Knights Templar and aided their cause greatly, even going so far as to donate one-third of his estates to the order.[8]

The Order of Christ

Relations between the Portuguese monarchy and the Knights Templar remained strong long after Afonso was placed in his tomb. This loyalty was keenly demonstrated in 1307 when King Dinis I, a direct descendant of Afonso Henriques, politely refused to arrest any Templars after they had been outlawed. The King simply chose not to accept the accusations. Even after the Pope had officially dissolved the order, Dinis safeguarded their possessions "for the benefit of the nation" while he worked on a more permanent legal solution to the problem, petitioning both Pope Clement V and his successor, John XXII.

The eventual compromise was agreed in 1319, when King Dinis founded the Ordem de Cristo, which means the Order of Christ. This stroke of genius by Dinis was simply a rebranding of the Knights Templar as, although it had a new name and a new identity, it comprised the same individuals with the same holdings. The order even had a new, updated logo. The familiar red cross used by the Templars was altered subtly, with the curved lines squared off and a smaller, narrower white cross simply inserted in the center, to symbolize the Templars' atonement for their sins. In this way, Dinis had miraculously safeguarded the possessions of the Knights Templar. Across the rest of the Western world, the Order of the Knights Templar vanished entirely, but in Portugal, the organization found continuity. It had a new name, but the core of the order, along with its aims and possessions, remained unchanged—and it even had the Pope's blessing once again.

There were some changes, however. The Portuguese king now had the statutory right to nominate the Grand Master of the Order of Christ. This almost imperceptible detail in its statutes would have significant implications further down the line, and it became a crucial part of our overall theory.

If our calculations and conclusions were correct, the contingent of Gérard de Villiers and Hugh de Châlons arrived in Portugal sometime towards the end of October 1307, their precious cargo safely aboard their galleys. If they had sailed into Lisbon and followed the River Tagus, de Villiers and his men could have navigated all the way to Almourol. From there, it would have been a case of simply covering the last 7 miles (12 km) to Tomar on horseback—or they could have remained on the water if they had traversed the minor Zêzere and Nabão rivers.

By 1307, the Templar's headquarters at Tomar had grown into a formidable stronghold, a virtually impregnable fortress that sat on a hill overlooking the valley and river. Curiously, just as with Jerusalem and Rome, the location chosen for the foundation of Tomar has seven hills. In the streets below the fortress, Pais had a church built, Santa Maria do Olival, which means Saint Mary of the Olive. It became the Templar's pantheon, a hallowed place where their grand masters were buried. On the edge of the central square in Tomar, Pais had also founded a church dedicated to John the Baptist, the Templars' patron saint.

The heart of the Templar's headquarters in Tomar, their castle, was built around an impressive octagonal chapel. Its rotunda, or *charola* in Portuguese, is a marvel of medieval architecture, inspired by the Church of the Holy Sepulchre in Jerusalem, as was the Tour de César at the Templars' Paris Temple. Pais started construction in 1160, but the chapel only arrived at its current architectural form between 1230 and 1260, during which time a number of murals were added to the walls. When the French refugees arrived in Tomar and set foot in the *charola*, they would have been greeted with a magnificent scene painted on the north wall. Today, the mural is extremely faded, unfortunately, but enough remains of the design to discern what it once depicted. What you see is a large, bent figure with a dark-brown face, carrying a child on his shoulder. The child is holding aloft a sphere surmounted by a cross and, at the top left of the mural, a monk is lighting a lantern to illuminate the scene.

When we saw this image for the first time, we knew instantly that we were looking at St Christopher carrying Christ across the water. This was the same image that we had talked about during our visit to Amiens Cathedral, when we had been looking for a painting of St Christopher. The story and mural both reflect the legend of Christopher carrying Jesus Christ in the form of a child across a river in full flood. St Christopher was sometimes depicted with a dog's head, which explains the saint's dark face on the Tomar mural. One version of the parable even tells how Christopher only became fully human after Christ's revelation.

Here, then, at Tomar, was another version of this scene, packed full of meaning and intent. St Christopher was carrying Christ across the water. This was exactly what Louis IX's chroniclers had told us the saintly king had done, carrying the body of Our Lord Jesus Christ across the water from Acre to southern France, "on board" the ship *Montjoie*, captained by Knights Templar. Staring at this image at Tomar, after everything we had discovered, we wondered if there was further meaning embedded in the scene.

As happens today, mural decorations were usually the last part of any building project to be completed, painted directly on to the stone or plaster, so this dates the *charola* mural to around 1260, shortly after Louis IX had returned from the Holy Land with the sacred treasures. We had seen many images of St Christopher before, but this one was such a great size that it screamed out to us. Here was a message from the 13th century, hidden, again, in plain sight. While it clearly represents the body of Jesus, equally, it displays the Light of the World that Christ represents, which is also wedded to the menorah—both have the same meaning. The monk lighting the lantern appeared to us to be revealing or reinforcing this metaphor. Was this confirmation that de Villiers and de Châlons had been carrying the menorah with them on the final leg of a journey that had seen the Light of the World rescued first from Jerusalem and now France?

One thing was now certain, Tomar was the ideal location for de Villiers and de Châlons to come to. Also, this was not somewhere that they chose at random or in haste; this had been planned, possibly long before. In 1307, at a time of great persecution and fear for the Knights Templar, there was no safer place in the whole world for a Templar and his treasure than the order's headquarters at Tomar in the heart of Portugal. Whatever treasures de Villiers and de Châlons had brought with them to Tomar, they would be safe here—for a time, at least.

Barbara Jursic, a specialist in Portuguese literature at the University of Ljubljana, Slovenija, allows us a glimpse of the power that was gathering in Tomar:

> It was in Tomar that the Knights of the Order of Christ were planning new projects that reached ecumenical proportions. Templars dreamed of an empire, a land that would allow them to rise against the evil fate that struck them elsewhere. Portugal was a safe haven, a land they helped to build and where they, hand in hand with the King [Dinis], were conceiving very ambitious plans for those times.[9]

The menorah at Tomar

Such a monumental escape and the safe deposit of the Templars' most treasured artefacts would have left a lasting impression on those knights who lived at Tomar, so it occurred to us that there had to be references to this great event embedded somewhere in the fortress itself. We set about searching for any clues that might confirm our suspicions.

In 1357, the fortress of Tomar became the official headquarters of the newly established Order of Christ, the rebranded Knights Templar. In the years that followed, the stronghold was transformed into a crossover between a monastery and a royal palace. It eventually came to be known as the Convento de Cristo or the Convent of Christ.

Over the years, the royal house of Portugal forged ever stronger ties with the Order of Christ, culminating, in 1420, with the appointment of Prince Henry the Navigator, the son of the Portuguese king John I, as the new Grand Master. After Prince Henry's death, the position remained in the royal family for a long time, until Portugal's most illustrious king Manuel I assumed the role.

Manuel began to enlarge the Convent of Christ as soon as he became king. As part of this expansion, the *charola* was decorated with a number of large oil paintings. One of those, found today on the eastern wall of the octagonal chapel, depicts the resurrection of Christ. We see Christ hovering in the air, holding a cross on a pole that supports a white flag with a slightly darker but also white cross. The design looks similar to the crusader flag of St George, and Christ is often seen carrying this design in similar scenes from the late 15th and early 16th centuries. However, in the Tomar version, the red cross is replaced by a white one, in much the same way that the red

Templar cross was replaced by a white one during the transition from the Knights Templar to the Order of Christ. In the background of the scene, a city and a harbor are depicted, which have been identified as 16th-century Lisbon. The ships in the harbor, many shown with full sails, are pointed inland, heading towards the east, where the entrance to the River Tagus can be found.

The inference to us was clear. Here was Christ, resurrected over Lisbon, holding a crusader flag with a white cross, just like the one belonging to the Order of Christ. The pieces were all here. King Manuel I had clearly used the *charola*, the private inner sanctuary of the Order of Christ, to record a defining moment in its history, adding to the earlier imagery present in the chapel. First, the Templars had depicted the miraculous rescue of the sacred relic and treasuress in the 13th century, carried over the water from Acre to France, and now their successors, the Order of Christ, had recorded them being transported from France to Portugal, via the harbor of Lisbon.

Under Manuel's leadership, the fortress evolved into a more regal and monastic building and, significantly, the original entrance to the castle was closed off. The Almedina gate, known locally as the "blood gate" was positioned centrally in the huge walls of the medieval structure. Over the gate, on each side, a large, round Templar cross was sculpted into the stone, symbolizing that the site was a place of great importance for the order. This cross was identical to that used over the eastern gate of the church in Fonte Arcada. The inside of the arched gate featured a central capstone with an even more intriguing symbol: a cross surrounded by four dots. It is very badly worn today but, from a distance, and in a favourable light, the image is still visible.

This was one of those instances where fate plays her hand and deals you just the card you need. While visiting the magnificent medieval synagogue in Tomar, we had been told a story about this very symbol. It transpired that, in times of persecution, Jewish people were unable to safely display images of the menorah because it would immediately identify them as Jews. Instead, they used a covert symbol, of a square cross with four dots. We experimented with this symbol and found two ways to change this apparently innocent symbol into a seven-armed candelabra, by joining the dots together with the central cross (see Figure 6).

For any knight leaving the Tomar fortress to head into battle, or set off on a mission, this covert menorah symbol would be the last thing they would see before leaving the safety of the stronghold. The image on the capstone appeared to have been added to the arch above the gate after its construction, but it was impossible for us to establish exactly when. However, after uncovering all that we had so far, we were certain that it had been carried out after 1307, once de Villiers had arrived in Tomar with his precious cargo.

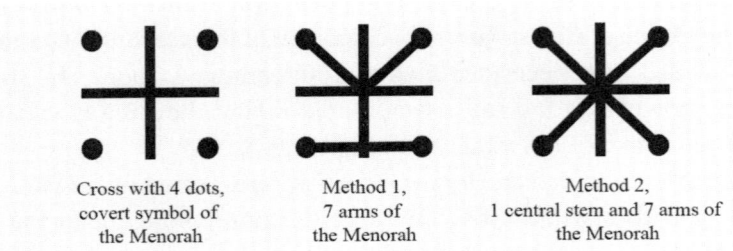

Cross with 4 dots,   Method 1,   Method 2,
covert symbol of   7 arms of   1 central stem and 7 arms of
the Menorah   the Menorah   the Menorah

Figure 6 The cross with four dots—the secret substitute sign for the menorah
(Corjan Mol and Christopher Morford)

Perhaps more intriguing, for us and our quest, this exact same symbol had been found on Oak Island. Sometime in the 1930s, a treasure hunter by the name of Gilbert Hadden discovered a large, inscribed stone on the north side of the island, on the shore of Joudrey's Cove. The inscription proved fatal for the stone, being too intriguing to resist. The explorers believed the markings indicated that something was below the stone and, because the stone was too large to move, they decided to use explosives to blast it out of the way, so the stone was now in pieces. On one of the few remaining fragments that were left on the island, an enigmatic inscription was visible. There was a letter "H," a cross with four dots, and the letter "O" with a dot at the center. This fragment thus became known as the "HO-stone." Sadly, the stone disappeared from the island in the 1980s, but, fortunately, it was photographed before it vanished.

There is a very simple interpretation of this HO-stone that dovetails neatly with our narrative and growing theory. If this were indeed a treasure marker, "H" could represent "*Hierusalem*," the old name for Jerusalem. The cross with four dots would indicate the menorah, and the "O," or circle with a dot, is an old symbol representing gold. Remarkably, this concise cipher translates into nothing short of, "the golden menorah from Jerusalem." Finding this message halfway across the world would have seemed impossible had we not been on this very trail for months. Now, in the larger context of our research, the discovery made perfect sense and the full implications of this message from the HO-stone on Oak Island were not lost on us.

The Age of Discovery

As we dug deeper into the history of the Order of Christ, we began to realize that its history was closely intertwined with the Portuguese Age of Discovery. Although it was Henry the Navigator who kicked off this new age of exploration and enlightenment, it was Manuel I who really pushed world exploration to new heights by sending out numerous exploratory fleets. What we did not expect to uncover was that most, if not all, the great Portuguese explorers were active members of the Order of Christ.

Barbara Jursic sums up this new era of exploration by men we would know today as Knights Templar, had their order not been dissolved:

> Simultaneously, a common thread could be linked between Jerusalem—Rome—Lisbon. Lisbon is a symbol of the new Paradisiacal Empire born from Portugal and the Portuguese. According to the Portuguese intellectuals and historians sharing this conviction, Order of Christ, direct heir of the Order of Templars, took on the mythic destiny and took Portuguese navigators around the world where they were able to spread the new values of the Empire of the Holy Spirit. The idea of this empire is strongly linked to king D. Dinis' wife, queen Elizabeth of Portugal, also known as the Saint Elizabeth of Portugal who allegedly brought the cult to Portugal from her native kingdom of Aragon and spread it around Portugal and its islands (Azores and Madeira), whereas during the age of discoveries, worshiping of the holy spirit also spread across Brazil through the Order of Christ, known as the spiritual leader of the overseas campaigns.[10]

Between 1419 and 1637, the Portuguese explorers Madeira, Cabral, Dias, Corte Real, Almeida, Da Cunha, Vasco da Gama, Magellan, and Texeira expanded the map of the known world beyond anything that had been seen before. Without a single exception, they were Knights of the Order of Christ. Their voyages were all financed by the order, the cross of the order was emblazoned across their sails, and they drew on the order's extensive expertise in the field of navigation, a body of knowledge that dated all the way back to the crusades.

> It should not be forgotten that Prince Henry the Navigator started discoveries under their [Order of Christ] flag which would probably not have been possible without the broad knowledge of maritime affairs, navigation techniques and astronomy, which the knights had acquired in the East and passed to their younger brothers.[11]

As well as its advanced navigation techniques, the Order of Christ was also responsible for initiating and financing numerous innovations and breakthroughs in shipbuilding, all of which gave the Portuguese a head start when it came to exploring the seas. At this early stage in our Portuguese education, we didn't appreciate quite how significant these revelations were or how crucial they would turn out to be in our search for the menorah.

A movement westwards

The question we now had to consider was: did the menorah and other treasures remain in Portugal after de Villiers had miraculously brought them there? Despite the relative safety of their new home, did the Knights Templar, in their new guise as the Order of Christ, decide that they needed to find a more permanent home for the sacred treasures? Was this the perfect moment, as Portugal was sending out vast fleets to the furthest reaches of the world, for the descendants of de Villiers, and the Order of Christ, to take advantage of this great age of exploration and send the treasures out on a journey of their own?

In August 2021, the BBC reported on archaeological research that proved Norse or Viking explorers had founded a settlement at L'Anse-aux-Meadows in Newfoundland as early as 1021. These seafarers had settled on both the Orkney and Shetland islands, off the north coast of Scotland, from the 8th century onwards, and from there they ventured further and further west, arriving in Iceland in 960 and then Greenland ten years later. While this Nordic age of exploration was taking place in the north, other Norse travelers had also ventured as far south as Paris and, in 885, their legendary leader Rollo even dared to besiege the city, though they failed in the end to storm and take the city.

Their impressive expansion proves that the Norse people were in possession of both incredible navigational skills and the shipbuilding prowess needed for such long-distance voyages. It is claimed that their push into North America extended as far as Delaware. Back on the European mainland, Rollo set about attacking France and managed to have an area of the country ceded to him by Charles III, as settlement in a treaty, and it became known as Normandy, named after Rollo's own people, the Normans. Later, 100 years after Rollo, the Byzantine emperor established his elite force, the Varangian Guard, which consisted predominantly of battle-hardened Norse warriors. So it was that they set foot in the Holy Land long before any crusader ever did.

The Knights Templar counted among their ranks many members from Normandy, such as the fabled Geoffrey de Charnay, the Preceptor of Normandy, who was executed by Philip the Fair alongside Jacques de Molay. Norman families would have had extensive knowledge of the sea route to North America, because their ancestors had been making that journey for hundreds of years.

We cite the story of these early Norse explorers at this point because it seemed obvious to us that when the Knights Templar began to feel the heat of the fires stoked by Philip the Fair and the Pope, the sea route from Europe to North America would have been known about and kept secret among many Templar families for almost 300 years. If you were looking for the ultimate hiding place for something of great value, then such an escape route might have been too tempting to resist. The old world of Europe and the Holy Land was full of intrigue and treachery, so the New World, which was still mostly unexplored at that time, must have held great appeal.

There is one place on the Atlantic coast of Canada that has dated and documented evidence of European activity from as early as the 1200s. There are structures and earthworks built by human hands that were found in a swamp and are so far unexplained, including a cobblestone road, which is a completely unique feature in the region, as nothing even remotely similar has been found elsewhere in Nova Scotia.

That place is Oak Island, 600 nautical miles (1,111 km) south of L'Anse-aux-Meadows. The features in question in the Oak Island swamp have been dated to between the 13th and 15th centuries.

On 18th-century maps, Mahone Bay, in which Oak Island lies, is indicated as a place that is, "remarkable for being seen at a great distance."[12] This refers to the white cliffs of Aspotogen Hill, the highest point on the Canadian Atlantic coast, which happens to mark the entrance to the bay. This small detail is important because it highlights Mahone Bay as a landmark that would have been relatively easy to spot from sea, especially at a time when mapmaking and cartography were still in their infancy. Many of the earliest maps were handmade and unique, passed down from generation to generation, so having notable landmarks was crucial to navigation. There is strong evidence on Oak Island of early medieval contact with Europeans and we believe this is because the cliffs at the entrance to Mahone Bay acted as a gateway marker to early navigators and could be accurately marked on maps.

We believe that the Knights Templar, or the Order of Christ, had the necessary knowledge and the means to have made such a crossing from Europe to the Atlantic coast of North America and Oak Island in the 13th century, probably setting out from their new headquarters in Tomar, Portugal. All that now remains is a strong enough motive for undertaking such a perilous journey.

As we have seen, Europe was no longer safe for members of the order. The dissolution of the Knights Templar, a result of the political schism at the heart of the old world that had nearly wiped out everything the Templars had worked for, authorized by the very office that had created the order in the first place, the papacy, would have shaken every survivor to the core. While de Villiers and his followers had found sanctuary in Portugal, they must have feared that there would be another shift and would have been watching for another fault line to open. What if next time they were not as fortunate, what if their treasures were uncovered and taken from them? While the Pope and others had such a long reach, a more permanent solution was needed.

Even though we cannot be clear as to the exact date, we believe that someone in the newly founded Order of Christ made a decision, one that was not that hard to make given the circumstances in which they found themselves. They had a duty to protect the sacred objects that they had recovered and retained with such hardship—objects so key to their religious beliefs and ideals.

If the dating of the scientific finds on Oak Island are correct, and there is no evidence to suggest that they are not, then the prime candidates responsible for leaving such remains are the Knights Templar, or at least their successors, the Order of Christ. The knights had not only the resources to make such a journey but also the navigational knowledge needed for such an undertaking—knowledge that was jealously guarded in those days, so only known by a very few.

We are convinced that a select group of the knights—Knights Templar or the Order of Christ—fled across the Atlantic with great treasure aboard their ships. When they landed at Oak Island and hauled this precious cargo on to the island, they unwittingly left behind tell-tale evidence while excavating their earthworks and building the structures that have since been found in the swamp.

We are hopeful that further evidence may come to light on Oak Island that enables us to say with more certainty exactly when these knights landed and secured their treasure on the island, if it was de Villiers, his descendants or voyagers from much later. For now, all we can say for sure is that our research indicates the menorah was brought to Oak Island between 1254 and 1450.

Ex-Templars, newly established as members of the Order of Christ, would have possessed explicit knowledge of this island via their Norman roots, or even through their Scottish ancestry. Either way, the route would have been preserved and kept secret throughout their order as a true back door, an escape route into the wilderness of the mostly unexplored west, if needed.

There is also evidence that the Catholic Church was still scheming in the background and protecting the menorah. In 1456, in the papal bull *Inter Caetera*, Pope Callixtus III declared Santa Maria do Olival in Tomar to be the mother church of every church established overseas, including North America. This meant that the Prior of Santa Maria do Olival, the Grand Master of the Order of Christ, would have ecclesiastical authority over all overseas territories and its inhabitants. This edict seemed another broad legal stroke designed to align the interests of the Church with those of the order it had helped found.

With the menorah now residing in Nova Scotia, it is time to turn our attention to this part of—what was then—the New World.

CHAPTER 14
THE MENORAH IN ARCADIA

With the power once invested in the Knights Templar handed over to the Portuguese military Order of Christ, and the menorah then in all likelihood in Nova Scotia, a great responsibility passed to this order, as its members were tasked with safeguarding the menorah and whatever other Temple treasures had traveled with it. This role was more important than ever because the New World—that great wilderness in the West—was opening up and explorers were charting its coasts as they did so.

In September 1522, 18 Portuguese sailors landed back in Spain after completing the world's first sea voyage around the globe—a journey that had been initiated by a Portuguese member of the Order of Christ, Ferdinand Magellan. Inspired by the event and at the request of rich merchants, King Francis I of France tasked an explorer from Florence, Giovanni da Verrazzano, to search the coast of North America and find a new passage to the Pacific Ocean.

In March 1524, da Verrazzano arrived in the area around Cape Fear—a prominent headland that juts out into the Atlantic Ocean on the coast of modern-day North Carolina—and he made his way north from there, following the coast. On July 8, da Verrazzano wrote a long letter to his patron, "the most serene King Francis." In his letter, known as the Cèllere Codex, he described his voyage and adventures:

We continued to follow the coast to the northeast which we baptized "Arcadia" on account of the beauty of the trees. In Arcadia we found a man who came to the shore to see who we were. He stood suspiciously and ready for flight. He watched us but would not come near. He was handsome, naked, with olive-coloured skin, his hair fastened back in a knot. There were about 20 of us ashore, and as we coaxed him, he approached to within about two fathoms of us, and showed us a burning stick, as if to offer us fire. And we made fire with powder and flint, and he trembled all over with fear as we fired a shot. He remained as if thunderstruck, and prayed, worshiping like a monk, pointing his finger to the sky, and indicating the sea and the ship, he appeared to bless us.[1]

It would take until 1566 before the name "Arcadia" appeared officially on a map, where it covered the area known today as Nova Scotia, Canada, but the area da Verrazzano had given that name to was bigger. Over time, Arcadia was shortened to "Acadia," a name that is still used today. It encompassed what is now Eastern Canada and included New Brunswick, Nova Scotia, and Prince Edward Island, along with the Gaspé Peninsular and parts of Maine that extended as far as the Kennebec River.

Columbus' discovery of the Americas had created a firestorm of curiosity back in the old world. In the years that followed, at least 16 expeditions were organized by England, France, and Portugal, headed in the direction of the northern regions of America, all of which ended in disaster or failure. The French came closest to occupying the new territory and establishing a colony after an expedition in 1541, led by Jean-François de La Rocque, Sieur de Roberval, the newly appointed Viceroy of New France, and his Captain General of the fleet. They had spent several years exploring the new continent, even going so far as to claim possession of the territory in 1534 and naming it La Nouvelle-France for King Francis I, along with raising a 10-metre (33-ft) cross bearing the words "Long Live the King of France." Fort Charlesbourg-Royal was established, which would later become Québec City, but the fort only survived for two years and the French were finally forced out without gaining a foothold. First Cartier then de Roberval returned to France but, a few years later, de Roberval's entire fleet vanished on the way to the New World and he was presumed dead.

Despite these setbacks, the shores of North America were frequently visited by European fishing ships, and one eyewitness from the time states that there were no fewer than 100 vessels fishing there. These maritime people, from Basque, Portuguese, Breton, and Norman ports, spread the word and kept the dream of a precious land of opportunities, tantalizingly out of reach, alive in the minds of the European kings.

It was in 1604 that the French finally succeeded where so many had failed before in the two centuries that had passed since Columbus first landed in America. It was during the reign of the French king Henry IV, of the House of Bourbon, otherwise known as Good King Henry, that a nobleman from the court known as Pierre Dugua, Sieur de Mons set out on a new expedition across the Atlantic, accompanied by a number of dignitaries. They headed for Nova Scotia, a region that was marked on maps from the time as La Cadie, and, on landing, they established the settlement of Port Royal, which comprised a few dwellings and a surrounding palisade.

It had long been known that the entire continent of North America was inhabited and explorers had found indigenous peoples in every habitat, even on remote islands. Despite this, the King of France claimed this newly colonized territory for himself and it continued to be referred to as New France. Much happened during those early years, most of it undocumented. As one writer put it, it was:

impossible to find on this continent any other spot so interesting, at that time, as Acadia was. The most thrilling dramas of America in the seventeenth century were played in the waters of the Bay of Fundy (Baie Française). . . . It is to America what Greece once was to Europe and the Bay of Fundy evokes almost as many memories as the Aegean Sea.[2]

There were attempts by the local inhabitants to drive out the newly arrived French, some of which were temporarily successful, but that wasn't the only danger. Disease and the harsh weather probably took more lives than the indigenous people did. Thus, Port Royal itself was soon destroyed but, despite these adversities, the newcomers adapted, intermarried with the locals, and clung on. Slowly, and after much sacrifice, New France began to grow into a prosperous colony.

The Jesuits were one of the first religious orders to exploit this nascent community, and between 1611 and 1764 some 320 Jesuit priests and brothers set sail from France to take up their mission in North America. As well as being devoted to bringing Catholicism to the New World, they also ended up being vital empire-builders, recruiting First Nation peoples and utilizing their skills at warfare to defend the burgeoning state of New France. They also negotiated trade alliances and set up a network of civilian experts who were willing to deliver medical advances and services to the colony. The Jesuits published a book annually entitled *Relations de la Nouvelle France*, in which they promulgated the ideas of a greatly expanded French empire.

It was during these early days that a fascinating figure entered this tale: Samuel de Champlain, a French explorer, navigator, cartographer, ethnologist, and chronicler—among a host of other interests. He came from a long line of mariners and had inherited a broad knowledge of the sea, so maybe it's not surprising that de Champlain ended up as one of the first men to venture to New France, securing a place aboard that early voyage by Pierre Dugua, Sieur de Mons. So, how did he come to be a part of that pioneering expedition?

As a young man, it was war that helped lead de Champlain into adulthood, and he used his time with the French fleet to further sharpen his skills and perfect his already detailed knowledge of navigation and seafaring. He took on the role of quartermaster sergeant and used what he learned about commerce and trade via the western sea routes to supply the King's army in Brittany. His abilities soon caught the attention of his superiors and he rose through the ranks.

While fighting in Brittany, de Champlain met several men who had sailed to the newly discovered lands in North America and their stories ignited a passion in the young soldier. Over the next few years, he became obsessed with the idea of this New World across the Atlantic. King Henry IV shared his interest, though for his own clandestine reasons, so he seized on de Champlain's enthusiasm and put him to work.

Henry had converted to Catholicism in 1593 and he issued the Edict of Nantes that year, making religious tolerance law and finally giving Protestants in France substantial rights. Henry's own father had created the French dynastic, monarchical Order of the Holy Spirit to unite the nobility around him after the fierce religious wars. The order was institutionalized with extreme pomp and ceremony. The King of France was to be its Sovereign and Grand Master and he personally selected every single member.

It soon became an exceptional honor to be a member of the Order of the Holy Spirit and no expense was spared for the regalia and elaborate dress. The order's emblem was a downward-facing dove, representing the Holy Spirit, and it had seven tail feathers and seven feathers on each of its outstretched wings. The dove was laid over an eight-pointed star, like the Maltese Cross of the Hospitallers, heirs of the Knights Templar. The emblem was hung from a cordon bleu, which is a blue riband, the color blue being reminiscent of the blue robes of the Virgin Mary. The downward-facing dove itself reminded us of the menorah, its seven tail feathers rather like the seven branches and lamps.

The King of France automatically assumed the position of Grand Master of the order shortly after his coronation in Reims Cathedral, which is one of the five points of the sacro pentagram. We suspected that, through the Order of the Holy Spirit, the royal house of France had long kept alive the secret that France had once recovered and possessed the menorah and other treasures from Jerusalem. If so, Henry IV must have been determined to finally track down and recover this lost holy object, one that he, as the French king, felt he had a divine right to own. Rumors that the menorah was in Nova Scotia had abounded for decades in the Vatican, as well as among members of the Order of Malta and the Hospitallers, even the Medici. These tales had reached the ears of King Henry.

One clue that the Vatican certainly had knowledge of the menorah can be seen in a fresco commissioned from Raphael as part of a grand scheme to decorate the reception suites of the Apostolic Palace at the Vatican. Known as *The Expulsion of Heliodorus from the Temple*, painted between 1511 and 1512, and found in the Room of Heliodorus, it shows the then Pope staring at the menorah, which is positioned in the distance in the center of the painting. On the right, a large, Ark-like box is being hauled away.

Ten years later, between 1520 and 1524, the final freso of the series was painted in the Hall of Constantine, completing the commission. Known as *The Donation of Constantine*, Raphael's assistants (Raphael died in 1520) gave prominence to the striking figure of Philippe de Villiers, Lord of L'Îsle-Adam, the estate in the Oise Valley in France that neighbors the Pierre Turquaise, the ancient dolmen that sits at the heart of the sacro pentagram. Philippe de Villiers, a direct descendant of Gérard de Villiers, who had fled France with the Templar treasure in 1307, was the Grand Master of the Knights Hospitaller at the time. He can be seen clearly behind the figure of Constantine, who is kneeling before the Pope, de Villiers in his full regalia with the white Maltese Cross emblazoned on his chest. He is standing upright, the only person dressed in black, positioned as though supporting one of the twisted columns that flank the altar of the early St Peter's Basilica at the back. The columns had been donated by the Roman Emperor Constantine, who claimed that they had been a part of Solomon's original Temple. Intriguingly, it appears that three prominent circles have also been incorporated in the painting, in a three-dimensional triangle formation, perhaps recalling the Hebrew *segol*—the ancient symbol consisting of three circles arranged in a triangle that was used to conceal the hiding place of the menorah and the treasures of the Temple.

Having become aware that the menorah had moved and was likely to be in Nova Scotia, Henry believed that it was his destiny to be the king who restored the treasures to France, and he endeavored to return them to the protection of the Order of the Holy Spirit.

To this end, Samuel de Champlain was immediately pressed into service and he began undertaking secret missions for the King. Author David Hackett Fischer has found evidence of such missions:

> In 1595, he received extra pay for a "certain secret voyage in which he had made an important service to the King." Whatever that "secret voyage" and "important service" may have been, the army's paymasters were now referring to him as the sieur de Champlain. He was soon an officer himself . . . then an aide to the highest-ranking marshals in the royal army, and finally got his own command. It was exactly the same sequence that would later occur in his American career. Some of his opportunities might have come from the King himself.[3]

Several years later, the King moved de Champlain to his court, appointing him as his geographer—a position that enabled him to carry out the King's orders without raising anyone's suspicions. One of the tasks de Champlain undertook was to travel broadly and learn all he could from the Bretons, Normans, and French Basques, many of whom took part in whaling voyages to Labrador and the islands. Slowly, de Champlain gained a detailed knowledge not only of the territory across the sea but also of the many voyages that were rumored to have been made in the past to the region. He was especially keen to hear tales of the journeys made by the Portuguese and the Order of Christ.

The first journey de Champlain made to the new territory of Acadia in 1603 was aboard a ship owned by his uncle, François Gravé du Pont, a soldier turned fur trader, and an excellent sea captain. His uncle had been trading furs from the 1580s onwards and routinely sailed between his hometown of Saint-Malo in France and the new lands on the other side of the Atlantic.

It was on March 7, 1604, that de Champlain returned to Acadia, this time as a member of Pierre Dugua, Sieur de Mons' now legendary expedition, aboard the ship *Don-de-Dieu*, meaning "Gift of God." Henry had given de Mons exclusive rights to colonize lands in North America between the latitudes of 40 and 60 degrees. As de Mons had also been given exclusive rights to the fur trade in the region, the team sought the help and experience of du Pont, who planned to follow them a month later on the ship *Bonne Renommée*, bringing provisions for de Mons' expedition. As de Mons and de Champlain would be arriving much earlier, they had agreed that a cross with a letter attached would be placed at Campseau (Canso) on the easternmost point of the Acadian peninsula. That way, du Pont would be informed of the *Don-de-Dieu*'s progress and whereabouts.

In early May, de Mons and de Champlain reached the shores of Acadia but they missed Campseau. They decided to wait for the *Bonne Renommée* to show up, which took much longer than they had expected. On May 27, a Frenchman, and a number of "savages"—local First Nation people—were sent off in a sloop to scout the coastline for the missing ship. They finally found du Pont and his ship three days later, in what de Champlain describes as the Bay of Isles (La Baye des Îlles) in his journal. The *Bonne Renommée* handed over the promised provisions and the two ships parted company, each going their own separate ways.[4]

This whole episode occurred very near to Mahone Bay, where Oak Island is situated. We had come to believe that Henry had asked de Champlain to confirm the stories that the menorah had been hidden in Nova Scotia by the Portuguese all those years before. So, as you can imagine, we were keen to discover if de Champlain had actually been in Mahone Bay on this occasion and whether or not he surveyed the area and the island itself.

We knew that, according to certain sources, Mahone Bay was once called La Baye de Toutes Îlles, but we quickly found out that it did not bear that name when Samuel de Champlain was in the area.

We also knew that de Champlain was renowned as an excellent cartographer. We therefore decided to download high-resolution copies of his maps from the French National Archives and then studied every possible detail. The first comprehensive map of Acadia drawn by de Champlain was published in 1612, together with his exploration journals. We quickly noticed that he indicated one La Baye de Toutes Îlles on the coastline of Acadia, but it was positioned much further to the north-east than Mahone Bay. His maps are so accurate, even today, that they can be closely compared to modern maps and it's easy to distinguish the many bays and coves along the shore, along with other features. The real Mahone Bay was identifiable on the map, indicated by the letter "V." He dotted letters and numbers over the map, the meaning of which he explained in the legend at the foot of the map. However, we gasped and held our breath when he read de Champlain's explanation for "V":

Martires ille

This means "island of martyrs."

We now sensed that we were closing in on the truth. Clearly, de Champlain had landed on "Martires ille," and he described the bay in his journal on May 8, 1604:

Departing from Cap de la Hève, we went as far as Sesambre, an island so called by some people from St. Malo, and distant fifteen leagues from La Hève. Along the route are a large number of islands, which we named Les Martyres, since some Frenchmen were once killed there by the savages. These islands lie in several inlets and bays.[5]

We wondered if this could be a reference to the Knights Templar. After their order was destroyed by Philip the Fair and the Pope, "*Les Martyrs*" sounded a very apt description, and also matched the oath that the Templars took when entering the order, swearing to lay down their lives to defend Christendom. We knew that many Knights Templar had fled overseas after the purge, so could some of them have made their way here, to this island, only to meet their fate at the hands of the First Nations peoples?

There is another tantalizing clue in a Portuguese map of North America by 16th-century mapmaker Bartolomeu Velho. In 1508, a Portuguese family living on the Azores islands claimed parts of the coast of Nova Scotia.[6] The result of this can be seen on Velho's 1560 Portolan map of the Americas. On the line demarcating latitude 44.5 degrees, he indicated a bay, flanked by "I. Barcelonas" (Island of the Barcelos), called "Gulfo de San Bernardo" or Gulf of Saint Bernard—a clear reference to St Bernard of Clairvaux, who was responsible for the foundation of the Knights Templar. This is the exact same bay indicated by Samuel de Champlain on his map as "Martires ille" or "island of the martyrs," drawn 52 years later at latitude 44.5, the precise location of Mahone Bay. So, here we had two mapmakers from different countries, working in different centuries, both describing Mahone Bay with names that are closely associated with the Knights Templar.

We had earlier concluded that Gérard de Villiers and Hugh de Châlons had probably fled to Portugal rather than taking to the Atlantic Ocean, as a 14th-century French galley would not have been able to make the trip across open water, so we were puzzled by these findings. Was someone referencing the Templar origins of the Order of Christ, who we knew sailed over to Nova Scotia?

While staring at de Champlain's map from 1612 (see Figure 7), we noticed a few oddities. Across the top of the map, the following text was written:

Carte geographiqve de la Novvelle Franse faictte par le Sievr de Champlain saint tongois cappitaine ordinaire povr le roy en la marine.

This is written in the Roman Latin style, in which "u" and "v" are interchangeable, but even so, it has a few odd spelling mistakes. "Faictte par" (made by), for example, is normally written as "faicte par," with one "t." Similarly, "cappitaine" (captain) is usually written with one "p." Last, "Franse" should be written as "France," with a "c" instead of an "s." We compared the text to other writings by de Champlain and concluded that he knew full well how to spell these words after finding multiple instances of them written correctly. These mistakes had to be intentional, but what was their purpose?

We know that "tt" is sometimes used to indicate the "triple tau," a symbol used by Freemasons to represent the Temple of Jerusalem, but which is also said to be a "clavis ad thesaurum," meaning "a key to a treasure." We were almost about to dismiss this link entirely when we spotted two small square Templar crosses on the map. In two locations to the north-west of Martires ille, de Champlain has written "s'te," followed by a square Templar cross. This was probably intended as an abbreviation of "Sainte Croix," which means "Holy Cross," a term frequently used in placenames in the New World, but "Sainte" is usually written with only one "t." Here, therefore, we have two more instances of seemingly wrong spellings, making three "t"s in total. Our initial thought—that perhaps the triple tau had been intended—suddenly became more likely.

We then noticed that there was a wolf drawn over the heart of the Acadian peninsula, and it seemed to line up diagonally with the two Templar crosses. We decided to draw a line through the two crosses to see if our assumption was correct. The line passed through the heart of the wolf and, what's more, it also hit two letters on the map—"L" and "I."

This was the point at which we started to realize that we might be dealing with intentional clues hidden in the map. "LI" can be read as Roman numerals for "51," which definitely caught our attention, as it is a number that is very familiar in esoteric circles. It represents several concepts, and almost everybody knows of the mysterious area in North America that is labeled "Area 51." More importantly, when the "5" is read as an "S," you get "S1," which evokes the symbolism of the serpent and the pole, the snake and the rod. It is like the staff of the Greek God Asclepius, entwined by a snake, or the imagery of St George or, in France, St Michel, piercing the dragon.

We zoomed out and looked at the map in its entirety. Dominantly placed in the middle is a pair of compasses, open, sitting on a ruler, which is in between a navigational compass on the right and a sun of the same size on the left. The pair of compasses has been drawn as a perfect equilateral triangle, with corners of 60 degrees. This shrieked of Masonic influences.

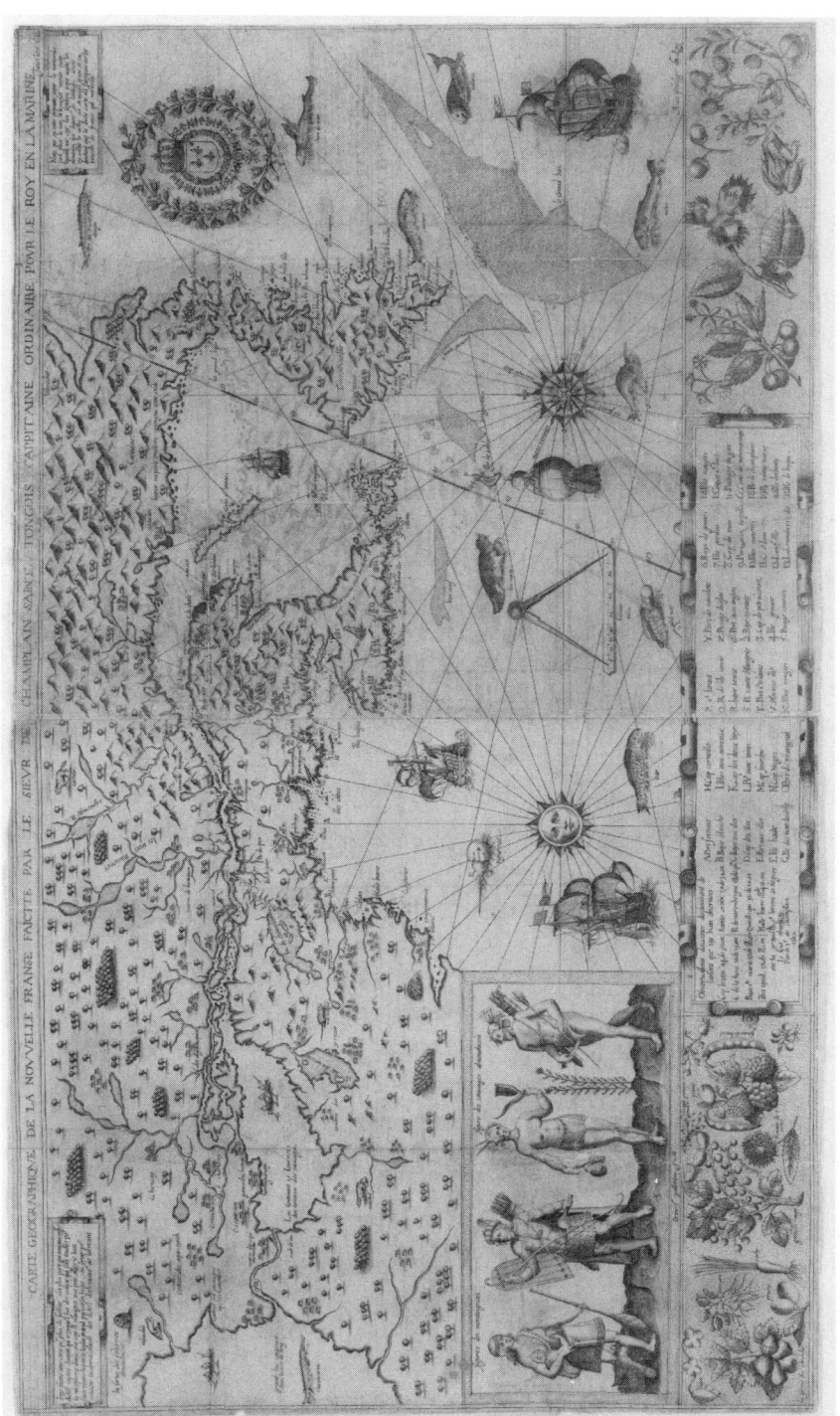

Figure 7 Map of New France by Samuel de Champlain, 1612 taken from

https://upload.wikimedia.org/wikipedia/commons/c/c3/Samuel_de_Champlain_Carte_geographique_de_la_Nouvelle_France.jpg

We decided to use the pair of compasses as the diameter for a circle, with the top as its center. The circle we drew hit the "V" signifying the Martires ille in Mahone Bay, and we knew immediately that we were on to something. Enclosed inside our circle was an animal. Although de Champlain called it "lou marin," it was clearly a seal. Was that a clue? Were we supposed to think of another type of seal? The Latin for seal is "*sigillum*" or "*sigil*." Now we were sitting up and taking notice.

We looked at the Martires ille shown on de Champlain's map. As we mentioned, de Champlain added a legend to his map, placing letters over prominent features: bays, inlets, islands, and so on. Above and to the left and right of the Martires ille there is an "O" and an "R." "Or" is "gold" in French. We turned again to the "lou marin" wording by the seal and looked these words up. There are various French names for the animal but "lou marin" is not one of them. Instead, we found "loup de mer." We could understand the use of "marin" instead of "mer," but "lou" without a "p" was certainly strange. Then we spotted the anagram: "lou marin" can be rearranged as "or lumina," meaning "golden light." That seemed a very concise way to refer to the menorah—the solid gold lampstand known as "the light of the world."

This hidden word gave us an idea, and we now began searching for very specific letters that were marked out across the map and referenced in the legend. When we found what we were looking for, we joined them together with a line. Some 15 minutes later, we were staring at the outline of Ursa Major, the constellation of the Big Dipper, the shape formed by the positions of the seven letters on the map (see Figure 8).

Ursa Major is also known as the Great Bear, "*ursa*" being Latin for "bear," and this constellation is strongly linked to the name Arcadia. In Greek mythology, Callisto, the daughter of the King of Arcadia, was seduced by the supreme god Zeus and she bore his son, naming him Arkas. There are several different versions of the myth, but the central theme is that Callisto is turned into a bear by Zeus, Artemis or Hera. When Arkas grows up, he becomes King of Arcadia and, just as he is about to kill a bear (not realizing it is his mother), Zeus intervenes and rescues Callisto, taking her to the sanctuary of the sky, where she resides ever after as Ursa Major.[7]

"Arcadia," the early name for Nova Scotia and New France, shares a similar etymology to the word "*ursa*." "Arcadia" is derived from the Greek "*arktos*," which can mean both "bear" and "north," giving Arcadia the full title of "land of the bear" and "northern land," both of which fit the location of Arcadia perfectly.

The discovery of Ursa Major on de Champlain's map was not the whole story. There are also the letters "V," "R," and "S" marked around Mahone Bay, which can be read as "urs," the old French word for, once again, "bear." Clearly de Champlain was labouring this point and making us focus on his embedded constellation of Ursa Major. Seven letters marked along the coast form the shape of the Big Dipper, which are: A, E, H, M, N, O, and R. Rearrange those letters and you end up with the word "menorah."

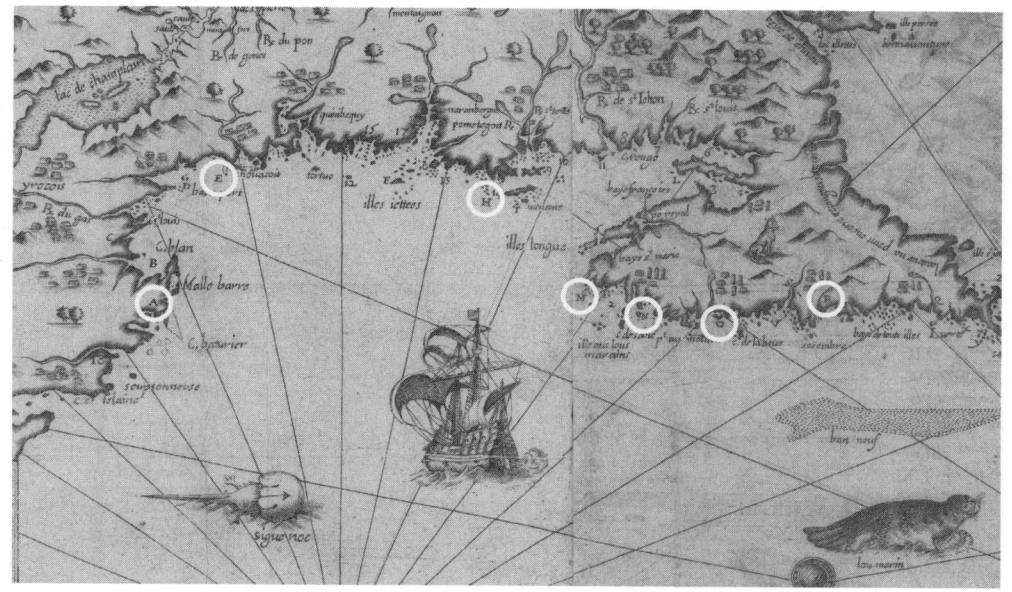

Figure 8 The letters to spell "menorah," hidden in the shape of Ursa Major, on Samuel de Champlain's map of New France, 1612 (Corjan Mol and Christopher Morford)

As if this were not astounding enough, the final star marked on the map, labelled with an "R," represents Alkaid in Ursa Major, the name of this star meaning "the leader." Was that a clue?[8]

During the Middle Ages, Alkaid was one of a group of so-called "Behenian" stars thought to aid occult practices and each was assigned a unique symbol. Alkaid was given the symbol of the menorah.[9] We were not sure what to make of all these details at this stage, but the "R" that marked this star seemed significant here and needed further attention.

We stared again at the map and looked deeper. As we noted earlier in this chapter, the Martires ille, marked by a "V," is between the letters "O" and "R," which together make the French word for gold, "or." This word was also highlighted when we found the anagram of the words by the seal as a result of using the compasses and noticed the Latin for seal, *sigillum*. The anagram of "lou marin" was "or lumina," meaning "golden light."

There was another letter near the "V"—an "S." What is odd about this "S" is that it is the only one of the letters on the map relating to the legend that is tilted. We found that it is at an angle of 60 degrees. We decided to draw a line through the "S," as if piercing an "S"-shaped serpent on the map. This also created a line at 90 degrees to the "L—I" line we drew earlier in the chapter connecting the Templar crosses. The new line cut right through a small island, just off the coast of Mahone Bay, sitting bang in the middle of the two uprights of the letter "V." That small island is Oak Island. This also meant that we had now used both a square and compass, very Masonic tools, and by doing so had pierced a serpent and pinpointed Oak Island.

We were very excited, but also cautious, regarding exactly what we had found here. We were worried that our imaginations were influencing us too much, yet this information seemed to have been marked accurately on the map originally. The Templar crosses were clearly real, and so was the wolf. That much could not be denied. Furthermore, we knew of one famous Templar "wolf." That was Renaud de Vichiers, as "Renaud" is old French for wolf. He was the Grand Master whose disobedience forced him to offer all the sacred treasure of the Knights Templar in 1251 to Louis IX, the king who would eventually become St Louis and sail back to France in 1254 carrying a hoard of holy items. Was de Vichier the wolf de Champlain was pointing to?

We decided that we needed to carry out further research to bolster our theory. While studying the map for additional clues, we stumbled on a new anomaly. In the legend, de Champlain used letters and numbers. However, while almost every character was included and depicted correctly, there was something strange about the number 1 used. In fact, it was not a number "1" at all. Instead, de Champlain had drawn a symbol we had never seen before. It looks like a bit like a triangle but with a little tail dangling from it. The symbol had been used to highlight "Port aux anglois" on the map, which turned out to be the bay that would later become the harbor of Fortress Louisbourg in the 1740s.

Louisbourg was the largest and most important French fortress in Acadia, but when de Champlain drew his map there was no Louisbourg and it would be least 100 years before construction began on the fortress. Why, then, was this spot so important to de Champlain?

To help us solve this mystery, we searched every book on ancient symbols that we could find. It took us several days before we finally identified the strange "tailed" triangle. It turned out that de Champlain had deliberately made our job harder by taking one of the medieval alchemical symbols for gold and then mirroring it.

Our heads were spinning. Had de Champlain left us a treasure map? Had there once been gold in what was later the bay of Louisbourg?

If there had been, then there did not seem to be any references to it. Gold had been found on the Acadian peninsula, but that was far away from Port aux anglois. Oak Island itself lies at the mouth of the Gold River, one of the places where gold was discovered, but the bay that would become Louisbourg was not known to have any gold, so de Champlain marking this spot with an ancient symbol for gold was curious.

We turned our focus back to the legend. At first glance, the name "Port aux anglois" appeared to contain another possible spelling mistake, but the word "English" was written as both "anglais" and "anglois" in the 17th century, so we gave de Champlain the benefit of the doubt and looked deeper. Because the strange symbol was used in place of the number 1, it was the only deviation among the numbers in the legend. We decided to check for anagrams and were soon rewarded.

It turned out that "Port aux Anglois" can be rewritten as "Axonis Portugal" or "Axis of Portugal." "Axonis" could mean "parallel", in the sense of a latitude. We looked at the map again and noticed that "Port aux anglois" had been written in the column directly below the pair of compasses, which are between the navigational compass and the sun. We realized with a jolt that the sun is one of the oldest symbols used to represent gold. This was the second reference to gold that we'd found on the map. We felt like we were closing in on the prize.

There was only one horizontal line on the map, drawn halfway down and joining the compass, compasses and the sun. If an axis had been concealed on the map, this had to be it. The line crossed a diagonal scale that de Champlain had included on the map to indicate latitude. Our horizontal line, the Axonis Portugal, crossed this scale between 41 and 42 degrees. We instantly checked Google Earth to see where those latitudes would lead to in Europe. To our great surprise and delight, we were taken to northern Portugal and the earliest known Templar commandery at Fonte Arcada.

The final hidden clue on the map is positioned between the line "Port aux anglois," our "Axonis Portugal," and the pair of compasses, directly below the Acadian peninsula. The feature in question on the map is a depiction of a curious sea animal. W. F. Ganong, who translated the works of de Champlain at the end of the 19th century, had no idea what this creature was. To our eyes it appears to be a cross between a hotdog and an oyster, but de Champlain himself simply described it as "uit de mer," which, loosely translated, is "sea creature."[10]

It took a couple of days to unravel this mystery and the final revelation was a shock to say the least. This strange sea creature actually exists, it is a species of jellyfish that was named after a very specific warship: the Portuguese man o' war. In fact, the Dutch name for this creature is "Portugees Oorlogsschip" or "Portuguese Warship." This clue could not have been more obvious. By including this rare jellyfish at this precise point on his map, de Champlain was demonstrably declaring that the Portuguese had been here.

The full implication of this discovery began to sink in. The Portuguese had dominated the world seas during the 15th and 16th centuries, and their explorers and navigators had been members of the Order of Christ, the rebranded Knights Templar. Gérard de Villiers had not been able to cross an ocean in a French galley but, 100 years later, the Portuguese were more than capable of making such a journey in their ships. Their small, highly manoeuvrable caravels, developed to perfection under Henry the Navigator, opened up the world, leading to the Portuguese Age of Discovery and bringing the worlds of Europe and North America closer together. There is a monument in the harbor of Nova Scotia's capital Halifax honoring the Portuguese explorer Joao Fagundes, dated 1520. Halifax lies only 49 miles (80 km) from the Martires ille, which is today known as Oak Island.

The map de Champlain drew seemed full of references and imagery that all pointed to the Portugeuse. To the right of the Martires ille is a place called "sesembre." There is another place that goes by that name: Sesimbra in Portugal. The town is situated very close to Lisbon and has a natural harbor on the Atlantic coast, making it a prime location for sending out ships to Nova Scotia.

We were now convinced that Samuel de Champlain, the founder of New France, had recorded a number of hidden messages when he published his journals and maps in 1612. The tale they told was unmistakeable. He had even used the same symbols we had latched on to at the beginning of our journey: the cross of the Knights Templar, a wolf, gold, coupled with the added symbolism of the serpent and the pole, by drawing our attention to the number 51 (LI in Latin).

We knew what this meant; it was a tale that we had been following for months. The menorah had been moved at some point in the past, taken from the sanctuary of Tomar and the shores of Portugal, then transported to a new home, one that was deemed a far safer resting place. Amid the relative obscurity of Oak Island, the menorah could be concealed and kept out of reach.

It was now apparent to us that King Henry IV of France had finally received confirmation from de Champlain that the rumors were true: the menorah was in Nova Scotia, and its location had been identified as Oak Island in Mahone Bay.

This great unspoken secret would remain at the heart of the French monarchy for many years, until it finally emerged in the most unexpected of places. The menorah would remain in its new hiding place for some time, yet the next piece of evidence that proved this concealment had indeed taken place would not come from Oak Island itself, nor even Nova Scotia. Instead, it was found back in France, at the heart of the old world.

We now turned our attention to one of the most remarkable clues we had stumbled on so far—a grand location in France that pointed directly to the menorah, hidden on Oak Island.

CHAPTER 15
THE VERSAILLES ALIGNMENTS

It was the end of the afternoon and we were walking across an endless expanse of cobblestones. Stretching out before us was the largest royal estate on the planet, spanning some 3 square miles (8 sq. km). Despite maintaining a steady pace, we hardly seemed to be drawing closer to the entrance gates. We were heading towards what was the center of the world in the 17th century. The French have many large buildings, yet the structure before us, with gold leaf highlighting details of the roof, windows, statues and railings, defied description, in much the same way that it is impossible to convey to someone just how large the Grand Canyon is if you have never stood looking over the edge. This place was equally breathtaking—a vast, beautiful, harmonious mountain of stone, but built by talented human hands.

We were at the Palace of Versailles—the mysterious and regal complex that was to lead to a staggering breakthrough in our research. The palace today is a grand spectacle, brimming with opulence and showstopping exuberance, but it had very humble beginnings. What was once an insignificant, rural hunting lodge became one of the world's greatest palaces almost overnight. However, that is not the whole story. We discovered that Versailles had been created with a very specific purpose in mind, from the outset.

Today, we associate the Palace of Versailles most closely with Louis XIV, the Sun King, a ruler who focused all of his almost unlimited power and wealth on this one spot. Louis was the longest-reigning monarch of any sovereign nation in history: he ruled for a total of 72 years and 110 days. He was also the absolute monarch of France, ruling at a time when the King had complete control over the country. He is said to have declared "*L'état, c'est moi!*," which means "I am the state!" and whether or not he did utter those exact words, the sentiment itself cannot be denied. Like his predecessors, Louis subscribed to the view that he ruled by divine right, which elevated the King above other mere mortals. In a famous speech given in front of the Sun King by Jacques-Bénigne Bossuet, the court preacher and confessor, this point was driven home:

Kings reign by Me, says Eternal Wisdom: *"Per me reges regnant;"* and from that we must conclude not only that the rights of royalty are established by its laws, but also that the choice of persons [to occupy the throne] is an effect of its providence.[1]

The passage Bossuet quotes here is from Proverbs 8 (v. 15, ESV), about the blessings bestowed by Wisdom, and seems to have been chosen very deliberately. The proverb clearly establishes Wisdom as an entity separate from God. She (Wisdom) says later, "The LORD possessed me at the beginning of his work, the first of his acts of old" (v. 22, ESV). God's first act was to command, "Let there be light." This clearly shows that Wisdom is the light, the very same light that is represented by the Shekinah and the menorah. These terms are interchangeable. The Shekinah = Holy Wisdom (Hagia Sophia) = the light = the menorah. When we hear of the wisdom of Solomon, it is this light they are referring to. In his speech, Bossuet was confirming that Louis derived his kingship from Wisdom and was chosen by Providence, the goddess with the third eye. This belief was underlined in the painting by Charles Le Brun of a three-eyed Providence[2] crowning Louis. It is worth noting that this same eye of Providence was later adopted as an important symbol of Freemasonry.

So, how did a king of such stature as Louis come to inherit and inhabit his beloved home of Versailles? Charles Perrault, author of *Cinderella* and *Little Red Riding Hood*, famously wrote of Versailles:

The king had hardly said that there should be a palace than a wondrous palace emerged from the earth.[3]

It's a striking quote, but it obscures the true beginnings of this story and glosses over much of the intrigue. While we stood in line to enter the golden gates to the palace, we recalled what those beginnings were.

The dawning of Versailles

In 1561 a parcel of insignificant, swampy, uncultivated land was purchased by a man named Martial de Loménie. At the time, Martial was the Secretary of State for Finance to King Charles IX. The plot consisted of 202 acres (82 ha) of land, within which lay a ruined castle and a hamlet known as Versailles.[4] Martial de Loménie built himself a manor house on the land and used his influence to convince the King to allow the hamlet to hold weekly fairs, elevating its status somewhat. The site was inhabited as early as the 8th century but the name "Versailles" only appears from the 11th century onwards. In Old French, *"versail"* means "ploughed field," and the site had once contained cultivated fields, ancient vineyards, and orchards, despite the prevalence of marshland in the region.

This parcel of land sits about 12 miles (20 km) south-west of Paris, occupying a position along one side of the Val de Galie, an ancient valley the main river of which vanished long ago, to be replaced by a maze of small streams and waterways, resulting in a boggy and very damp stretch of land. The air at that time was said to be unpleasant and unhealthy due to the numerous pools of stagnant water and people mostly avoided the area like the plague.

The purchase of this unassuming plot of land triggered a sinister chain of events. An Italian from Tuscany by the name of Albert de Gondi made a name for himself in the court of King Henry II and became Councillor of State, then French Ambassador to the Imperial Court in Vienna. He eventually managed to embed himself in the household of Catherine de Medici, Henry II's tough-as-nails Italian wife, who became queen regent after his untimely death during a jousting tournament. Albert de Gondi became one of her closest advisers. It was a time of almost constant civil and religious conflict in France, and a war raged between the ruling Catholics and Huguenot Protestants. During one of the Catholic raids to arrest prominent Protestants, Martial de Loménie, the owner of Versailles, was arrested. He was held in a small cell in the Paris prison of Châtelet for four months. While he was suffering the discomfort of the 16th-century French penal system, de Loménie was visited by de Gondi. What exactly was discussed isn't recorded, but the end result was that de Loménie signed over his office to de Gondi and, furthermore, he agreed to sell his entire Versailles estate to him for a nominal sum—a sum of de Gondi's own choosing.

It is clear that de Loménie believed his act of contrition had saved his life, but it was not to be. On August 22, Catherine de Medici met with de Gondi and her other advisers. It is generally assumed that the decision to eliminate the Protestant leadership of France was made that night. The city gates were closed and, as the bells rang out at midnight, a massacre unfolded in the streets of Paris[5] that raged until August 24, the feast day of St Bartholomew the Apostle—a date that the occult-driven Catherine may have chosen specifically because this violent episode was nothing short of a blood sacrifice.[6]

Protestant nobles and thousands of ordinary folk were hunted down and killed. Scores were settled. The Royal Notary at that time, Pierre de l'Estoile, described in his memoirs how, during the events that followed, de Loménie was strangled in his prison cell on the orders of de Gondi himself, with approval from Catherine, her words being, "so he could have his lands."[7]

With Versailles secured, de Gondi continued to buy more land surrounding the estate and his family became the dominant power in the area. This unremarkable, still mostly uncultivated, region soon attracted the interest of King Henry IV, who enjoyed hunting in the woods of the valley. In 1607, Henry took his young son, the Dauphin, along with him. It was this six-year-old boy who would later become Louis XIII.[8] King Henry's doctor, Jean Heroard, described how the King and his son hunted together near the old stone windmill of Versailles, ending their day at the Château de Noisy, owned by de Gondi. It was the young Dauphin's first hunting trip and, despite the boy's tender age, it would mark the beginning of a long line of kings called Louis who would all become fascinated—if not obsessed—with Versailles.

We realized early on during our hunt for the truth that the de Gondi family deserved closer inspection, and we found some curious details relating to Albert de Gondi in particular.

It was clear that the family, with its origins in Italy, had extremely close links with the house of Medici—the powerful political dynasty that originated in Florence. Albert's parents, Antoine de Gondi (also known as Antonio Guidobaldi) and Marie-Catherine de Gondi (born Marie-Catherine de Pierrevive), found great favor with the household of Catherine de Medici, wife of the future Henry II of France. Marie-Catherine de Gondi in particular was held in high regard by the Queen Consort and she occupied several important roles in the royal household, including, most notably, governesss to the "Children of France," as the royal offspring were known.

It seems that Antoine de Gondi's own rise to fame began with his marriage to Marie-Catherine de Pierrevive. There is strong evidence that the female members of the de Gondi family were incredibly influential in the royal court.[9] Catherine de Medici was only 14 years old when she took Marie-Catherine de Gondi into her employ, looking on her governess as a mother figure. Marie-Catherine's own son, Albert de Gondi, was only three years younger than the Queen Consort and so Albert grew up being seen almost as a brother to Catherine de Medici. This relationship seems to have been the reason for his role as the most important confidant and aide to the Queen Consort. His royal apprenticeship at Catherine de Medici's side during those years would have served him well, and he went on to continue to take up positions of power in the courts of Catherine's husband, Henry II, and Henry's successors, Henry III and Henry IV.

Both Albert de Gondi and his brother, the Cardinal Pierre de Gondi, were two of the first individuals to be inaugurated into the newly formed French dynastic, monarchical Order of the Holy Spirit (L'Ordre du Saint-Esprit in French), founded by Henry III in 1578. The institution would become the pinnacle of all the royal orders. As noted in Chapter 14, its emblem was a downward-facing dove that reminded us of the menorah, as the dove's seven tail feathers are reminiscent of the seven branches and lamps. No less than six members of the de Gondi family were installed in positions in the order in the years that followed, the final de Gondi to join the order being Pierre de Gondi, who was admitted in December 1661.

We shall put the de Gondis aside for a moment to return to the object of their affections, Versailles. We had now entered the palace grounds and crossed its pristine marble courtyard to enter the main, central building. Countless stone faces stared at us, their features frozen in time. Charlemagne, Joan of Arc, and an endless line of kings, cardinals, and once-famous dignitaries and artists lined the vast central hallways of the ground floor. All this grandeur was designed to impress and overwhelm visitors and we, too, experienced its full assault on our senses. Having studied the early incarnations and architecture of the building, we realized that we were then standing in what had been the old hunting lodge at Versailles.

King Henry IV of France was assassinated in 1610, leaving his title to the young boy who then became King Louis XIII. The newly crowned King found himself inexorably drawn back to Versailles—a place of innocence and escape in his youth— and, from 1617 onwards, Louis spent more and more time in the area, hunting throughout Noisy, Rocquenfort, Vaucresson, and Marly.

Louis decided to build his own hunting lodge at Versailles in 1623, on the site of that old familiar windmill, which had been situated on a promontory above the swamp.[10] This modest hunting residence, built by Huau, the King's Master Mason, rose above the mists of the marshland, where it witnessed a curious power shift in Europe.

The Queen Mother, Marie de Medici, wife of the late King Henry IV, tried to persuade Louis to remove Cardinal Richelieu, the King's extremely influential chief minister. Louis retreated to his property in Versailles, where he was met by Cardinal Richelieu himself. In an apparent volte-face, Louis placed his complete trust in Richelieu. This event, ultimately, led to the end of the Medici influence in France, and that Versailles was the place where that transition began feels significant. Versailles came to be in Louis' possession through the machinations of Catherine de Medici and Albert de Gondi, yet it was at Versailles that the transition of power from the Italian Medici family to the French house of Bourbon truly began, leading in the end to the overarching dominion of Louis only a few years later.

Many in Louis' court questioned his love of Versailles. The Marquis of Bassompierre described it as a "puny château" and pointed out that it "would not inspire vanity in even the simplest gentleman," while others criticized the squalor and the stench of the stagnant waters in the summer. These critics endlessly compared the lack of amenities and absence of sophistication at Versailles with the sheer opulence of the Louvre and Tuileries palaces in Paris. However, Louis grew increasingly disillusioned with the French capital and preferred the simplicity of life at Versailles.

Louis continued to build at Versailles and it slowly shook off the squalid image of its early years, turning from a hunting lodge into a small château, much more suitable as the home of a king. One curious feature was introduced: seven arches were added to the east face of the château, a feature that was illuminated by the sun each morning, like seven candles. The grounds received a glowing recommendation in 1639's *La Voyage de France*, in which Claude de Varennes implored visitors to Paris to travel to Versailles, citing it as a must-see.

Louis was ever proud of Versailles and continued to selectively invite dignitaries and notable foreign emissaries to stay there. However, it is said that while Louis brought his queen, Anne of Austria, to Versailles, he never allowed her to stay overnight, reinforcing the view that Versailles was the exclusive playground of the King, a male-dominated fortress that kept the realities of the world outside at bay. We began to wonder what secrets Louis was keeping close to his heart in his new sanctuary.

With his château complete, Louis cemented his relationship with Versailles further in 1632 by purchasing the surrounding Seigneury de Versailles from Albert de Gondi's son, Jean-François de Gondi, Archbishop of Paris, for the princely sum of 66,000 livres. With the entire estate now in royal hands, plans for elaborate gardens were drawn up and work on them began.

The reshaping of Versailles continued throughout Louis' life, but the work did not stop when he died. It was not only continued by his son but also expanded on a dramatic scale. It was under the patronage of Louis XIV that Versailles truly began to take shape and it was during his reign that Versailles was opened up to the wider world. Louis XIV created the vast palace we were standing in, the starting point of which had still been a modest country seat up until he took it over from his father.

Louis XIV and the great secret at Versailles

Inside the palace, Louis was omnipresent. Countless paintings and statues of him surrounded us, showing a handsome, confident man with piercing dark eyes. The King radiated a unique presence, described by his contemporaries as his "terrible majesty." They adored his persona almost as much as they feared it. A few of Louis' portraits show him as a young boy with much softer features and inquisitive eyes, his form buried beneath the robes and regalia of his office. We wondered what it was like to become one of the most powerful men in the world at only five years of age. Louis had only brief moments with his father at Versailles before his unexpected death plunged the young Louis headlong into the intrigue of the French monarchy.

The young Louis was denied Versailles during his formative years. His mother, Anne of Austria, ruled as regent while Louis gained sufficient maturity, and she much preferred the Palais Royal in Paris, so they lived there primarily. It was not until he was 21 that Louis turned his attention to the old hunting grounds he had known as a very young boy, echoing the experience of his own father. Legend has it that Louis began hunting again in the area around Versailles, but we believe something else stirred within him, compelling him to turn Versailles into something grander, and so it was that he began his own series of dramatic renovations from 1660 onwards, turning in particular to the gardens and the landscape surrounding the château.

Our research revealed that, in all probability, the early landscaping works were initially carried out by two men—first, Jacques Boyceau and, later, Claude Mollet, a man who had been First Gardener to Henry IV and Marie de Medici before being appointed by Louis XIII. Both Boyceau and Mollet wrote extensive treatises on the art of landscape gardening, highlighting the use of sacred geometry and precise alignments on a huge scale. Their written works also document the scientific instruments they used to create such features.[11] However, we know it was Boyceau, the first gardener at the site, who was responsible for creating Versailles' central axis. It was first documented on what is known as the "Plan du Bus."[12]

We continued our tour of the interior of the château. We saw Louis pointing at a burning tower on a big sculpted relief at the entrance to the royal chapel. We climbed the stairs and walked through the hall of mirrors, as unique in size and form when it was first conceived as it is still to this day. We stood in Louis' bedroom, noticing the little sofa at the foot of his bed where his valet and personal aide Alexandre Bontemps would sleep.

It dawned on us that, in the 17th century, this would have been a crowded place, more akin to a city than a palace. Louis was never alone in his day-to-day life. Depending on the day in question, there would be 3,000 to 10,000 people on the estate, all following very strict protocol, with everything centered on the Sun King. We imagined how, every morning, the whole world would be waiting for him to rise from his bed, which faced east, on the central axis of his awe-inspiring palace.

By now we had completed our tour of the King's private quarters and had stepped out into the gardens. We were excited and a little nervous. We had spent weeks studying maps and plans of them. What we had discovered was breathtaking, and it still made us reel. We had found that something extraordinary had been concealed in the layout of Versailles when the gardens were constructed, something that had remained hidden for centuries. We only discovered it because we were eagerly following the trail of the lost treasures of Jerusalem and they had led us here.

Louis had the elaborate gardens designed in such a way that they depict a giant menorah, delineated on a truly massive scale (see Figure 9). If you look at a plan of the gardens, you will slowly see the menorah take shape, with its seven straight-armed branches pointing upward. In the middle, its central candle sends rays of light in all directions. The palace building itself is right at the heart, sitting at the center of the 3-mile (5-km) axis that begins with the avenue leading up to the central gate, where two other diagonal avenues converge to meet it, forming a huge, and perfect, 60-degree tripod.

The menorah depicted here, on such a staggering scale, bore a striking resemblance to the very earliest depictions of the menorah, shown with straight arms. You will recall that we discussed in Chapter 3 how Rabbi Maimonides had popularized the idea that the menorah had originally been made with straight arms. His book containing that idea, the Mishneh Torah, was in Louis' possession. It was even translated into French in 1678 on the orders of the King's First Minister of State, Jean-Baptiste Colbert.[13] It appeared that Louis and his inner circle shared our theory that the straight-armed menorah was the original version, the form we had come to know as the *true* menorah, and it was this form that was introduced into the layout of Versailles.

We walked toward the central portion of the upper gardens, where you can see the central axis of the royal estate stretch down the hill, seemingly without end. It is a grand perspective and, fortuitously, that day it was bathed in the glorious fading light of a perfect French evening. It was April 25, the birthday of Louis IX, the very same day he left Acre, carrying what was described as "the body of our Lord Jesus Christ" and "Holy relics." We sat down at the top of the giant stairway that cascades down to the lower section of the gardens, watching the sun go down along the middle of the central lamp of the Sun King's giant menorah. It felt as though someone had lit this giant lampstand for St Louis' birthday. We watched in devout silence, getting goosebumps, while the sun dropped towards the horizon, sending out dazzling reflections across the water of the Grand Canal just before it sank out of view. The handful of people around us sighed in pure delight, which was followed by a spontaneous burst of applause that concluded this sacred moment.

We sat there in silence. We suddenly had to remind ourselves that this hidden menorah we were sitting in was not the only secret written into the landscape of Versailles. There was another, perhaps even more significant, revelation.

We had discovered that the central axis of the gardens formed part of a very exact alignment, one laid out with almost unbelievable precision and accuracy. In the distance, at the start of the Grand Canal, we saw a statue of the God Apollo standing in his chariot, being pulled out of the water by seven figures. We imagined Apollo taking off over our heads and flying far into the distance, along the menorah's axis in a south-easterly direction. If we had been able to ride with him in his chariot as he headed across the sky, following a dead straight line, we would eventually have landed on Temple Mount in Jerusalem, where the menorah had once stood, along with all the other treasures of Solomon.

If you were to do the same, in the opposite direction, to the north-west, Apollo would take you across the Atlantic to Nova Scotia, some 3,106 miles (5,000 km) away. We had ascertained that the central axis of the Versailles menorah aligned with the spine of a cross-shaped megalithic formation on Oak Island known as Nolan's Cross.

Figure 9 The giant menorah with straight arms, as seen on a map of the domain of Versailles from 1715 by Naudin in the year Louis XIV died, image by Corjan Mol, based on https://gallica.bnf.fr/ark:/12148/btv1b8446022m

The sun had now completely disappeared below the horizon. As the light faded, the stars became visible. The sun had set within the constellation of Aries, bowing reverently at the feet of the Holy Lamb, the Hi-Ram, the Golden Fleece of Jason, and, just to the right of the pentagon formed by the head of Cetus, the sea serpent at the center of the celestial sea.

We realized that we were sitting atop a grand reveal, kept secret throughout the centuries. Versailles is positioned grandly in the middle, a massive, figurative menorah, while on either side are the two locations where it had remained hidden throughout its long history. The line drawn through these three sites rose like a royal arch around the world—an arch in the sky, an *arc en ciel*, French for rainbow, or arch in the heavens, an arch that later royal arch masons would depict, formed of seven of the signs of the zodiac. We suspected that there was another clue here, one pointing to the esoteric symbolism of the menorah itself. Furthermore, the layout on the ground was mirrored in the sky by means of celestial alignments of stars and constellations that carried enormous symbolic significance and added an extra layer of depth to the narrative, one that we would soon fully unravel.

The question for now was, how was it that this alignment linking Jerusalem with Oak Island, along with a 3-mile (5-km) menorah, had remained hidden for so long at Versailles? You may also be asking: how had we come to discover this astonishing feature? You are about to find out.

CHAPTER 16
THE ALIGNMENT DISCOVERY

It was our friend and colleague, the late Oak Island researcher Chris Donah, an avid and skilled amateur astronomer, who initially inspired us to look for alignments at Versailles. Chris had suggested that the mysterious feature found on Oak Island known as Nolan's Cross pointed towards Temple Mount in Jerusalem. He had raised this possibility during one of his war room discussion sessions with the team of *The Curse of Oak Island* television show. The segment never aired, but we continued to mull over his research long after our meeting and the three of us shared many insights over the following weeks.

It didn't take long for us to realize that the giant menorah we mapped for the gardens at Versailles (see Chapter 15) was pointing in exactly the same direction, so we sought to verify our findings and dig deeper. What we could never have expected was how accurately this alignment had been crafted. The central axis in the gardens at Versailles pointed with astounding precision directly to Temple Mount in Jerusalem. Needless to say, such a discovery astounded us but, at the same time, we realized that we needed to be both extremely careful and absolutely sure of our findings before going public with any of the details. So, we set out a number of rigorous criteria that we applied to the Versailles alignments, to qualify and validate our research signs—and to ensure that we didn't include any spurious results that might skew our investigation.

The first of these criteria we labeled the "what" and it applied to any *directional* alignments that we identified. We agreed between us that at least one place had to physically point to the other one, as delineated by one of its features (a path, an axis, or a roofline, for example). We also declared that any such alignment had to be very precise, so we approached Erin King to check that our conclusions were valid. As she is a seasoned geolocation and geographic information system (GIS) expert and a consultant on *The Curse of Oak Island* show, we asked her to validate our alignments using her industry-grade software and maps.

Our second criteria was the "why," concerning the *motive*, that any two places linked by our directional alignments had to be contextually connected. For example, a menorah design laid out on the ground that was linked via a directional alignment with Temple Mount in Jerusalem would meet our criteria because the menorah sat in Solomon's Temple at that location.

Moving on to the "how" criteria, we vowed to only consider technology that would have been available at the time Versailles was constructed and developed, so sometime during the 17th century. Based on the written works of the royal gardeners Jacques Boyceau and Solomon de Caus, followed by the latter's chief mathematician, Allain Mallet, we had no problem concluding that the French had both the scientific knowledge and the tools to align designs and buildings across very large distances, even as early as 1610. However, judging by the sacro pentagram of Gothic cathedrals we had uncovered, there was more than a suggestion that the French had been in possession of such skills much earlier than we currently accept.

Finally, our "when" criteria related to *historical context*. Where we identified a historical link with an alignment, we set a requirement for there to be at least some circumstantial evidence from the time the alignment was created. For example, the memoirs of Madame de Montespan highlighted Louis XIV's obsession with alignments pointing to specific places. They describe the King handpicking a pentagonal plot of land for the citing of the Royal Observatory in Paris, for example, a location that was itself aligned with the Palace of Luxembourg in Paris.

Using these guidelines to keep us on the straight and narrow, we proceeded with caution. We needed to visualize the alignments clearly, in 3D, so we made use of Google Earth Pro and Erin King continued to assist us to make sure we got things right. As we discovered, Google Earth is very reliable at modeling the Earth and so we found that we could use it to draw a straight line across the topography that would then follow the curvature of the Earth with great precision. This suite of software tools opened up a whole new world for us and we were able to gain insights into the French landscape and architecture that would have been impossible even a few years ago.

Why Versailles?

We had always wondered why Versailles had been chosen as the location for Louis XIV's grand palace. As we have seen, it was an inaccessible, unremarkable marshland that many of the first inhabitants of Versailles found deeply unpleasant. This unfavourable location, coupled with our examination of the precise global positioning of the locations in question led us to suspect that Versailles' location was chosen deliberately.

We noticed that the palace sat perfectly on the numerically meaningful coordinates 48.48 degrees. We know that the French were aware of this synchronicity when the idea of a grand palace at Versailles was first conceived because these coordinates are documented on various maps from the time. Furthermore, the alignment that points to Temple Mount in Jerusalem lies at an angle of 291 degrees. When we saw that number we suddenly realized precisely what the French architects responsible for laying out Versailles had achieved.

291 degrees at latitude 48.48 can be declared as:

$$2 + 9 + 1 + 4 + 8 + 4 + 8 = 36$$

In the 16th century, 36 was the numerical value of the name "Arcadia" when a number is given for each letter of the alphabet (A = 1, B = 2, C = 3 and so on). Though this may look contrived to some observers, this method of substituting numbers for letters was a common way to encrypt correspondence at the time, and the protagonists in our story were not only aware of this method for concealing information but also most of them were using it in one form or another. Versailles was, for those with eyes to see, identical to a numerical Arcadia, as it were.

There was another aspect to the number 36 that was impossible for us to unsee once we had spotted it. It tied in perfectly with the rest of our research. The interior angles of a pentagram comprise three different angles: 36, 72, and 108 degrees. The 36-degree angle is the foundation here, while the 72- and 108-degree angles are both multiples of it. In other words, numerically, Arcadia was one of the corners of a pentagram while the other two were made up of its multiples.[1]

Numeric and linguistic theory aside, we found another reason why this very spot was chosen to build on. Versailles turned out to be the ideal place to point to a number of prominent sites from the crusades era, tying them together into a unified design.

The menorah at Versailles was not as regular as we expected, and neither was the giant Latin cross that appears, made up from the gardens' many lakes. Looking at the original plans, the measurements behind all the construction works had been executed with military precision, so any deviations like this had to be deliberate. This made us suspect that the entire layout of Versailles had, from the very beginning, been conceived to conceal a whole host of alignments, so it was time to see where the lines led us.

One of the first alignments we found at Versailles (after initially establishing the Jerusalem connection) was the one to Oak Island. We presented our findings on television during Season 8 of *The Curse of Oak Island* TV series, revealing this discovery to an audience for the very first time. We did, however, include the caveat that the alignment to the island had a deviation of some 0.7 degrees. This might not sound like much, but if you extend that line halfway across the world, from France to Oak Island, you find that such an error is soon magnified and it creates a variation of around 25 miles (40 km) on the ground, which makes it impossible to claim with any certainty that this alignment was ever intended.

During our research for Season 9 of the show, we realized that there *was* a perfect alignment from Versailles to Oak Island, but it clearly wasn't between the central axis of Versailles and the spine of Nolan's Cross.

One of the defining features of Versailles is its symmetry, and Louis always insisted that this design aesthetic should be adhered to religiously. Even the village of Versailles that neighbored the palace had to follow this rule, expanding outwards from the estate in a symmetrical fashion, to retain and maximize the beauty of the surrounding area. Louis had a term for this: "the royal symmetry."

Therefore, when the King announced the location for a new royal chapel, it came as a great surprise to the courtiers and nobles of Versailles because it appeared that no one had given its positioning any serious thought. Its location would violently break up the otherwise perfect symmetry of the palace and gardens. From 1685 onwards, Louis rejected several proposals for the placement of his supreme place of worship but, in 1687, he finally settled on the location of what proved to be his last great work at Versailles. Even though it was always called a château, a castle, by its maker, Versailles didn't have a single tower. So, to put it politely, the new royal chapel stuck out from the north wing of the palace like a sore thumb. It was a public relations disaster and many individuals in Louis' court deeply resented the fact that the King had broken the symmetry of his—and their—home so recklessly. The situation was not helped by the fact that this new chapel was also now the tallest structure in the whole estate.

Just why the Sun King broke his own golden rule of the royal symmetry has never been explained satisfactorily, until now. We felt that we could finally offer an answer: the royal chapel at Versailles aligns very precisely with the spine of Nolan's Cross on Oak Island.

If you were to walk along the spine of Nolan's Cross, heading east, and you then continued across the floor of the Atlantic Ocean, you would eventually come face to face with the altar that sits in Louis' chapel at Versailles. We had little doubt that this was the reason for the strange and sudden break from the symmetry of the rest of the palace. Was it necessary for the King to correct an alignment that had been laid out imperfectly by his father? To us it felt very much as though Louis had realigned his menorah to Oak Island, creating a dramatic landmark at Versailles in the process.

Louis was very explicit when it came to the significance of this new place of worship and its alignment. If you stand in front of its altar, you will see the menorah sculpted on the wall to your left, the image closely resembling the one depicted next to Edward Despenser in the *Tewkesbury Book of Founders and Benefactors* after the capture of Jean II.

The Latin cross

Next, we returned to looking at the Latin cross, formed by the Grand Canal at Versailles, that sits at the heart of the representation of the menorah (shown in Figure 9). The horizontal arms of this cross are not of equal length but, based on the drawings from 1679 made by the original designer, architect Jules Hardouin-Mansart, that was exactly how it had always been conceived. This was no error. Hardouin-Mansart's plans were, as always, executed to perfection. Therefore, something else was going on behind the scenes and this encouraged us to look deeper.

We discovered that the horizontal arm of the cross was aligned with Château de La Rochefoucauld, some 223 miles (360 km) to the south-west of Versailles, in the Charente département of France. This had long been the ancestral home of the de La Rochefoucauld family, previous generations of which had their origins deep in medieval history, long claiming descent from the Lusignan kings of Jerusalem.[2] The family's coat of arms features the very same three chevrons we had found on the seals of the Templar Masters of France that we looked at in Chapter 10. When viewed upside down, these chevrons bear an uncanny resemblance to the menorah. Moreover, Cardinal de La Rochefoucauld had been Louis XIII's chief minister until Cardinal Richelieu took over. What is perhaps most striking about this transfer of power is that when Richelieu was made a duke by the King in 1629, he chose these very same three chevrons for his coat of arms, a motif that had been on the shields of the de La Rochefoucaulds since the Middle Ages (see Chapter 7), even though Richelieu had no links with that family whatsoever.

Obviously Temple Mount in Jerusalem had been the location of Solomon's Temple long before Versailles ever came into being and the same is true of Château de La Rochefoucauld. The earliest incarnation of the château dates from the 11th century at the very latest. All the same, someone deliberately wanted Versailles to point to the Château de La Rochefoucauld.

Another alignment we discovered excited us greatly: Versailles points directly to Chartres Cathedral. This revelation held great significance for us because Chartres was central to the main thread of our overall hypothesis, so to find Versailles also shouting the name Chartres thrilled us.

Working backwards, if you draw a line from the center of Chartres Cathedral to Versailles, it bisects the left-hand side of the tripod of the menorah that we traced in the landscape into two perfect halves, in effect splitting the 60-degree triangle that forms the base of the menorah into two triangles, each with angles of 30, 60, and 90 degrees (see Figure 10). You might remember that these are the exact same triangles we classify as Solomon triangles (see Chapter 7). Finding two Solomon triangles shaped by a direct line between Versailles and Chartres felt significant to us, and a good omen for what was to come.

We allowed ourselves a moment to reflect on our discovery. That Chartres, with its labyrinth design of two menorahs, should be aligned with the tripod of the Versailles menorah, creating two Solomon triangles, was more than we could have hoped to find. Here we found vindication, proof that we were not chasing our tails.

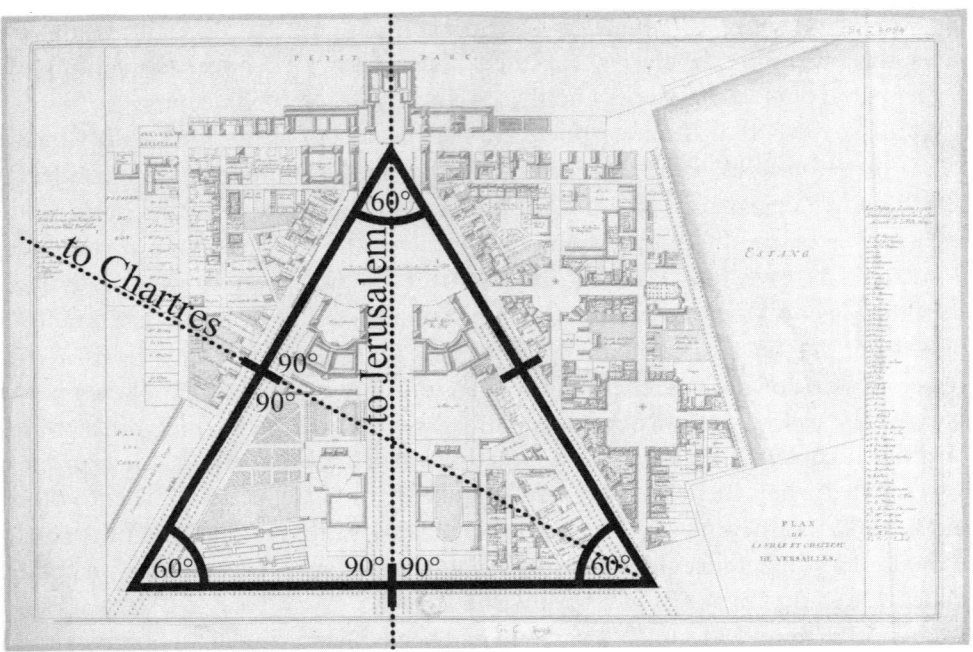

Figure 10 The tripod of the Versailles menorah in 1685 with its alignment to the cathedral of Chartres, image by Corjan Mol, based on https://gallica.bnf.fr/ark:/12148/btv1b530636814. r=Plan%20de%20la%20ville%20et%20chasteau%20de%20Versailles?rk=21459;2

There was now little doubt in our minds that the Versailles menorah was configured to point at very specific locations, each of which was already relevant to our body of research.

That was not the end of this branch of our research, however. We realized that the French had not ceased embellishing their alignments after the completion of the palace at Versailles. In 1720, five years after the death of Louis XIV, the city of New Orleans was founded on the Gulf Coast of North America. It carried the name of Philippe II of Orléans, the king regent of France who ruled the country during the minority of Louis XV (as he became king at the age of five). French engineers had hand-picked the site for the town and they did the same for the location of its church, which today is known as the Cathedral-Basilica of St Louis King of France— the same St Louis who initiated the Seventh Crusade and who, we believe, was privy to knowledge of the treasures of Solomon being brought from the Holy Land by the Knights Templar to be secreted deep within the holiest sanctuaries in France.

When you enter the Cathedral-Basilica of St Louis King of France in New Orleans (interestingly, situated just off Chartres Street), it is impossible to miss a huge mural, high above the altar. It depicts Louis IX, St Louis, calling for the Seventh Crusade.

If you were to start at the altar of this cathedral and head out in a straight line towards France, you would discover that it is aligned precisely with the central axis of the Versailles menorah. This line, starting at New Orleans, passes, in turn, through Oak Island, then Versailles, and, onwards, finally ends at Temple Mount in Jerusalem.

By now, we were beginning to be less surprised by our discoveries, but this alignment seemed beyond anything we could have expected. We realized that what had begun almost as a game to us was becoming serious. In short, we had to consider that we had uncovered something remarkable. Everything appeared to fit. There was a grand scheme—Louis XIV's great work, if you like—of alignments, lines of sight, symmetry (even deliberate asymmetry), sacred geometry. All of it cleverly concealed over centuries, yet out in the open for all to see, if you know where to look.

However, we felt that one puzzle remained. We had expected to find an alignment pointing toward the sacro pentagram that we had discovered earlier, but we could not find one—not at first, at least. Then we realized that Amiens Cathedral, at the very top of the sacro star, is counter-aligned with the only pentagram shape found in Louis XIV's gardens. This garden within the gardens is called the Star Grove—a pentagon-shaped element that stands out prominently from the greenery surrounding it and the rest of the Versailles gardens. It originally featured a fountain at its center, shaped like a mountain with five star-shaped channels. Here, finally, was an indication that Louis XIV had been well aware of the symbolic and sacred pentagram etched into his homeland when viewed from above.

Nicolas Fouquet

At the same time that these alignments were being created and refined at Versailles by the guiding hand of Louis XIV, a sinister turn of events took place—one that had its roots in the affairs of the King's father, Louis XIII.

The royal court was notorious for the intrigues, plots, and counter-plots that arose among the various courtiers and political figures that surrounded the house of Bourbon. Louis XIII had not wanted his wife, Anne of Austria, to rule as sole regent on his death and he left instructions for a regency council to be set up instead. However, just four days after he died, Anne had the last will and testament of her dead husband annulled, overturning his wish. This act left the way clear for Anne to become queen regent of France and to rule in her own right with no interventions from anyone else. To aid her plans, she quickly installed Cardinal Jules Mazarin—a skilled diplomat originally from Italy who had served both Cardinal Richelieu and Louis XIII—as head of her new government, giving him the role of First Minister.

Cardinal Mazarin was a man of great cunning and skill, and it was through looking into his machinations that our research led us to another curious character—one Nicolas Fouquet. Fouquet had been appointed Superintendent of Finances in 1653 by Cardinal Mazarin himself, effectively becoming the Finance Minister of France. It was a marriage of convenience and came about mostly because Fouquet had inherited a small fortune. Cardinal Mazarin urgently needed funds to prop up the grand plans of the French state. Fouquet's own money, and that of his extended family, were suddenly a very tempting proposition. That's not the whole story, of course, because as well as deep pockets, Fouquet was no stranger to the world of finance. He had learned a great deal from members of his wife's family, the Jeannin de Castilles, who were embedded in the financial institutions of France.

Fouquet had a deeply layered background. At times he appears to be no more than a shadow, but his hand was evident in some key events that were closely linked to our research. Fouquet's father, François IV Fouquet, was a confidant of Cardinal Richelieu's and he had helped establish three companies between 1627 and 1628, all of them created to exploit and expand the French influence in New France across the sea. However, two of these companies operated out in the open while the third was a much more clandestine affair.

The first of these entities was the Company of New France, otherwise known as the Hundred Associates, which counted among its number Samuel de Champlain, the explorer and cartographer who had hidden a number of secret messages in his map of 1612 (Chapter 14). The foundation of this company was first suggested by Isaac de Razilly, a prominent member of the Knights of Malta who had been raised in their service since he was a child. He was a brilliant naval captain who worked for Cardinal Richelieu and defeated the English fleet at La Rochelle in 1625—though he lost an eye in the ensuing combat.

A year after the victory, de Razilly sent an inspired memo to Cardinal Richelieu, urging him to focus his attention across the Atlantic on Acadia, which was now, to all intents and purposes, New France. Richelieu answered the call and pledged to sail new settlers to the burgeoning territory as well as maintaining the Catholic faith in the region.

Nicolas Fouquet's father, François, was put in charge of a second entity, the Company of the American Isles, tasked with trading and religious affairs in the new overseas territory.

The third organization was the highly secretive Company of the Blessed Sacrament. It had been founded by Henry de Lévis, Duc de Ventadour, who was Viceroy of New France—a title that declared he was the King's representative on the American side of the Atlantic. His coat of arms showed the now familiar three chevrons, but also three pentagrams. This company appeared to be nothing less than a vehicle for the Order of the Holy Spirit, set up to do its work. The Company of the Blessed Sacrament maintained a rule of absolute secrecy and it obliged members "not to speak of the company to those who do not belong to it and never to make known the names of the individuals composing it."[3] The company kept no printed materials of its dealings and written minutes were kept only when absolutely necessary.

We started to suspect that this organization was tasked with identifying the exact spot where the menorah that had been taken to North America (then New France) by the Portuguese Order of Christ was buried, and, if possible, take possession of it.

It is worth noting that the Company of the Blessed Sacrament was founded in France at a convent on rue du Saint-Honoré, a stone's throw away from the exact spot where the Church of Saint-Roch would later be constructed. Among those involved with the company were some legendary French figures: Vincent de Paul, once the house preacher of the de Gondi family, who would become one of France's most revered saints; Jean-Jacques Olier, who founded the Society of Saint-Sulpice (a member of which—Paul de Chomeday, Sieur de Maisonneuve—founded Montreal in Canada) and would control much of New France; Jacques-Bénigne Bossuet, Louis XIV's court preacher and personal confessor; Louis Fouquet, brother of Nicolas Fouquet. The company's emblem was a Eucharist inside the sun, shown as a small circle inside a larger circle.[4] Bossuet would go on to state (in 1652) that the mission of the Company of the Blessed Sacrament was to "Build Jerusalem at the centre of Babylon."[5]

As an intriguing aside, it is worth mentioning that, in 1631, Louis XIII himself wrote a personal letter to the Archbishop of Paris, Jean-François de Gondi, asking him to acknowledge and confirm the Company of the Blessed Sacrament, but de Gondi refused without giving a clear reason. The insult was not forgotten and, as we have seen, Louis XIII gradually excluded the de Gondi family from all affairs of state after his purchase of Versailles from them in 1632. We felt that this was another sign that the de Gondis had served their purpose and were needed no more by the royal house of France.

Louis XIII's wife, Anne of Austria, appears to have had a special attachment to the Company of the Blessed Sacrament. It was only abolished by her son, Louis XIV, after her death. As an indication of his different approach to state affairs, immediately afterwards, he founded the Royal Academy of Sciences—an organization that seems have been created to finish what the Company of the Blessed Sacrament had started: to pinpoint exactly where the menorah was hidden and claim it once again for France. This was a decision that was to bear fruit, as we will see.

Having established what these three companies did, we turned our attention back to Nicolas' father, François IV Fouquet. A magistrate and businessman, he built up an impressive library at his house in rue de Jouy in Paris, where, along with a large collection of rare and specialist books totaling more than 15,000 volumes by the time he died, he displayed old maps, ancient coins, and medals.[6] It was in his library that captains returning from New France and Acadia would convene to recount their adventures and detail their finds. Curiously, in the entrance to the library stood a long dugout canoe that once belonged to the Huron tribe of Canada. Flanking the entrance were two large globes, one of the earth and one representing the heavens.[7]

Fouquet's mighty library eventually passed to his son Nicolas. After his father died, Nicolas had it moved to the estate he had bought at Saint-Mandé, on the outskirts of Paris. Once installed in the new house, Nicolas Fouquet hired Pierre Deschampneufs to catalogue and curate the collection, no doubt due to the size of the library, which had now grown to some 27,000 titles. This library is today known as the second most important library in the whole of 17th-century France,[8] inferior only to that of Cardinal Mazarin himself. However, Fouquet's collection would not remain intact for long.

Acclaimed French historian Michel Vergé-Franceschi argues that Nicolas Fouquet was himself a secret member of the Company of the Blessed Sacrament, possibly even its chairman.[9] Nicolas' brother, François Fouquet, Archbishop of Narbonne, was definitely a confirmed member and is known to have financed the company. Given the circumstances, it would have been unusual for Nicolas not to have also been a part of this secretive organization.

It will probably never be known exactly how much influence the Fouquets wielded in the esoteric arena of French affairs, but some clues can be gleaned from Nicolas' dealings. As his power and hold over the French court increased, he started to collect art on an impressive scale. In 1655, he sent his brother, Louis Fouquet, to Rome to buy works of art on his behalf, to embellish his new château. Louis Fouquet spent almost a year in Rome and he enlisted the help of a renowned Frenchman, Nicolas Poussin, one of France's most famous classical painters. Poussin lived in Rome and was at the height of his fame when Fouquet approached him for assistance. The two men appear to have become very well acquainted and Poussin advised Louis Fouquet on a number of acquisitions.

On April 17, 1656, Louis Fouquet wrote a now notorious letter to his brother Nicolas in France.[10] The letter seems to suggest discussions between Nicolas Poussin and Louis Fouquet involving a great secret, and possibly a hidden treasure or hoard.

We had the letter translated by Charlotte Wheatley, a bilingual linguist who speaks French and English, and now have a greater understanding of its contents. Here is the relevant passage from Charlotte's translation:

I have given to M. Poussin the letter in which you have honoured him by writing to him; he expressed all the joy imaginable. You would not believe Monsieur, neither the hardships that he has taken in your service, nor the affection with which he takes them, nor the merit and the probity that he brings to everything. He and I, we have projected certain things that I may discuss with you entirely in a short time, they will give you, through M. Poussin, advantages (if you do not want to despise them) that kings would have great trouble taking from him, and after him maybe nobody in the world will ever recover in the centuries to come, and furthermore, this would be without much expense and might even turn to profit and these are things so great to search for, that whatever there is on earth right now can not have better fortune or even be equal.

We felt this clearly indicated that Fouquet and Poussin were discussing alignments and sacred geometry with a view to their pointing to and identifying specific locations, both in France and beyond. We believe this intention marries up with the coded knowledge that Poussin was secreting in his paintings at the same time. It appears to have been during this exact timeframe that Poussin completed the painting discussed in Chapter 1, a second rendering of *The Shepherds of Arcadia*, so we added "*II*" to its title (it is also known as *Et in Arcadia ego*). As you may recall, this work depicts the lost utopia of idyllic bliss known as "Arcadia," an area in Ancient Greece that became a popular subject to write about throughout medieval European literature. Poussin's work features a group of shepherds and a lone woman looking at a stone tomb in the center that has various inscriptions on it.

The mention of Arcadia in this instance is intriguing. As you may recall, "Arcadia" was also the name given to the large peninsula on the Atlantic coast (now known as Nova Scotia, Canada) after it was discovered by explorer Giovanni da Verrazzano while he was in the service of King Francis I of France in 1525 (see Chapter 14). In the 17th century, the name "Arcadia" was shortened, becoming "Acadia," a name still used today.

As demonstrated earlier, if Versailles was a metaphor for the legendary mythical idyll that was ancient Arcadia, a *numerical* Arcadia, then its counterpart was a very *real* location, also called Arcadia at one time, which lay on the other side of the Atlantic Ocean, an area that also included Oak Island—the tiny speck of land so accurately aligned with the royal chapel of Versailles.

CHAPTER 17
VERSAILLES: THE INFLUENCE OF NICOLAS POUSSIN

Nicolas Poussin is an intriguing figure. From humble beginnings, he would go on to become a leading painter, founding the French classical baroque style. He was born in Villiers-en-Désœuvre, which translates as "Villiers with nothing to do." This described the village perfectly and explains why Poussin was keen to leave as soon as he could. In France, the names of villages are usually tied to old family surnames, so we tried to find connections between this village and the family of Templar Master Gérard de Villiers, without much success.

Wherever the name came from, Poussin ran away from his parents' home when he was 18 years old. He found refuge in Paris, in the ateliers of Flemish masters Ferdinand Elle and Georges Lallemand. However, despite serving his apprenticeship in Paris, it was Rome that Poussin had set his sights on and, in 1624, aged 30, he finally made the city his home. By now his artistic skills were well advanced and the powerful Cardinal Francesco Barberini became one of his patrons. For him, Poussin painted *The Destruction and the Sack of the Temple of Jerusalem*, a painting destined to be a gift for none other than Cardinal Richelieu. Against a background of chaotic looting amid the columns of the Temple, a golden menorah can clearly be seen being carried out of it on the left-hand side. After vanishing from history for many years, this painting was rediscovered in 1995 by art historian Sir Denis Mahon, restored, and then donated to the Israel Museum in 1998.

This painting was followed by the first of *The Shepherds of Arcadia* paintings, completed between 1627 and 1628, the same period when Richelieu and Fouquet's father were busy founding the three illustrious companies. *The Shepherds of Arcadia I* as we had come to call it, to distinguish it from its more famous later version, was painted alongside *Midas Washing at the Source of the Pactolus*. They were pendants, twin paintings, intended to hang side by side. The commissioner was Giulio Rospigliosi, who later became Pope Clement IX and had the paintings installed in his private apartments at the Vatican. At this point we had to remind ourselves that paintings like these were never created as public works. The thought that they might end up in the Louvre to be viewed by millions of people each year would have been impossible for the painter and his patron to imagine at the time. Rather, these were private works for exclusive rooms in the Vatican, where only a very small inner circle around Rospigliosi would have had access to them.

The theme and composition of *The Shepherds of Arcadia I* were borrowed from Guercino's *Et in Arcadia ego*, commissioned by Cosimo II de Medici in 1618. It is thought that it was de Medici himself who had come up with the phrase in the inscription, "*Et in Arcadia ego.*" Both Poussin's versions of *The Shepherds of Arcadia* have been extensively studied by experts and amateurs alike. The paintings also feature in another mystery that we had been involved with in the past: the mystery of Rennes-le-Château.

Countless books have been written about the enigma of Poussin's paintings in connection with this location in France, but what was relevant to our research here was that it had been suggested "*Et in Arcadia ego*" was an anagram. The sentence, which means "And in Arcadia I" is simply bad Latin, as it is missing a verb. This inspired people to rearrange the letters of the sentence to form a new Latin sentence, such as "*I tego arcana Dei*," which means "Begone I conceal the secrets of God." As you can imagine, this new sentence did nothing to calm the frenzy surrounding Rennes-le-Château.

Like a simple cipher (A = 1, B = 2, and so on), anagrams were a popular way to code information in the 17th century, especially in France, where King Louis XIII went so far as to employ Thomas Billon as his royal anagrammatist in 1624. With this in mind, we considered that further information may have been hidden in the sentence, "*Et in Arcadia ego.*"

During Season 7 of *The Curse of Oak Island*, in the "Tryptich" episode, Corjan suggested that "*Et in Arcadia ego*" was an anagram for "*Gite Neo Arcadia*," which is Italian for "Go on an excursion to New Arcadia." Now, searching for more layers of information in the sentence, Chris suggested that there was another, tantalizing way to rearrange the letters, as "*Ariadne goetica.*"

Ariadne is a mythical Greek princess, whose thread led Theseus out of the labyrinth. It is to her crown, the constellation Corona Borealis, that the shepherds in the center of the painting are pointing. The shapes formed by the legs and arms of the two shepherds—one kneeling, the other glancing back at the woman—are those of the constellations of Hercules and Boötes respectively. Ariadne's crown lies directly between them in the night sky. The term *goetica* refers to the collection of magical grimoires attributed to King Solomon that instruct the reader on the evocation of demons and spirits. One of these demons was Astaroth, which, astoundingly, is one of the names of the brightest star in Ariadne's crown. Of all the *sigils* (seals) presented in Solomon's books, only two feature pentagrams: the *sigils* of Venus and Astaroth.

Through his "pent-aleph" ring, King Solomon was said to have subjugated 72 of these entities to his will and forced them to build his Temple. In light of this, we thought that this intriguing anagram warranted more research.

In 1638, 13 years after Poussin first depicted the menorah in *The Destruction and the Sack of the Temple of Jerusalem*, he produced a second copy of the painting, called *The Conquest of Jerusalem by Titus*. It was again commissioned by Cardinal Francesco Barberini, but this time presented to Prince Eggenberg, Imperial Ambassador to Pope Urban VIII. In this new image, the slaughter and carnage of the sack of the Temple of Jerusalem is more evident and, again, the menorah is clearly visible in the composition.

The year 1640 would see Poussin return briefly to France, though it was not to be a happy episode. Cardinal Richelieu had bullied and cajoled Poussin until he finally moved to Paris to take up the position of First Painter to the King, Louis XIII. Poussin was asked to decorate and embellish the Long Gallery of the Louvre, among other artistic endeavors. Rather than being an honor, Poussin reluctantly endured the next 18 months, declaring them to be among the worst of his life, due mainly to the workload and Louis being very demanding. Poussin took the first opportunity to escape back to Rome in 1642, claiming that he was going to fetch his wife. Fortunately for Poussin, Cardinal Richelieu died later that year and the King shortly after, freeing the artist from his obligation to return to Paris. Curiously, on his arrival back home in Rome, Poussin had a ring engraved with a lady holding a ship aloft, a design that bears a remarkable resemblance to a medieval nef, much like Louis IX's *Montjoie*, as depicted in a 13th-century illuminated manuscript.[1]

During our combined stay on Oak Island in the summer of 2019 we had spent some time together studying an iconic self-portrait of Poussin, painted in 1650. This research gave us the opportunity to peer a little closer into the mind of the maturing artist. The painting was replete with Masonic influences. We spotted a hidden pentagram present in the composition that joined the black, pyramid-shaped onyx ring on his finger, the artist's eyes, and the headdress of Venus, who is in a curious position on the left edge of the composition. This was clearly the same woman Poussin would later use in *The Shepherds of Arcadia II*, but she is depicted in the self-portait being embraced by two open arms, her headdress featuring a third eye. We were aware that the third-eye (also known as the bindu point) is said to see things beyond ordinary perception. The door in the background of the portrait is blocked by three large, framed canvases, which brings to mind various old Masonic rituals in which three veils must be passed. In the foreground, Poussin looks out at us from his canvas. Clearly, here is a man telling us that there is more to his painting than meets the eye. Unlike most of his contemporaries, Poussin was known for working alone, and his work was in such demand that he was given free rein to choose his own themes and compositions. Looking into his eyes, we wondered what his secret was.

In this same year of 1650, Charles Le Brun, another famous French artist, who had been tutored by Poussin, featured Nicolas Fouquet in one of his works (see Figure 11). Fouquet is portrayed in an austere black robe with a white collar and sleeves, almost clerical in appearance. He holds a folded piece of paper and sits next to a locked book. Behind him is a curtain that has been partially pulled to one side, tantalizingly revealing a portion of a painting. Painted in dark, muted tones, the curtain reveals two figures standing on a boat. One figure is fully visible, holding a wooden oar.

To our absolute amazement, we recognized him instantly as the same man painted as a kneeling shepherd dressed in a blue shift in *The Shepherds of Arcadia II*. As for the second figure, only his lower legs are visible, but it is notable that he is wearing one sandal, not two. As mentioned earlier in this chapter, it is our belief that the kneeling shepherd in *The Shepherds of Arcadia II* represents the constellation Hercules and, if that is the case, then we have to assume we are looking at the same character in this scene by Charles Le Brun.

The well-known one-sandaled associate of Hercules is Jason, captain of the legendary ship the *Argo*. Hercules joined the Argonauts on their quest for the golden

Figure 11 Nicolas Fouquet by Charles Le Brun, 1650, image taken from https://upload.wikimedia. org/wikipedia/commons/b/b7/Nicolas_Fouquet_par_Charles_Le_Brun.jpg

fleece—Aries once again, as at sunset in the gardens in Versailles (in Chapter 15). It is worth mentioning that, in the *Argonautica* (the Greek epic poem by Apollonius Rhodius), Hercules is attacked by six-armed giants while guarding the *Argo*. Hercules defeats them all and leaves them strewn on the beach of an island, like anthropomorphic menorahs. Strangely, Rhodius thought it necessary to mention that some lie with their heads on the sand, while others are inverted, their heads in the water. Mirrored menorahs, perhaps?

Charles Le Brun and Nicolas Poussin had been close friends and they had both worked for Fouquet, as well as for Louis XIV. Both also once held the prestigious title of First Painter to the King. We therefore couldn't simply dismiss as coincidence the two using each other's figures in a painting in such a symbolic way. Incidentally, Le Brun also appears to have used exactly the same model Poussin did for Providence or Venus. In Le Brun's drawing,[2] the woman with the third eye is seen placing a crown on the head of Louis XIV.

In 1674, eight years after the death of Nicolas Poussin, Charles Le Brun, who had succeeded his friend as the most famous painter in France and First Painter to the King, was commissioned to paint a grand fresco inside the cupola of the chapel at Château de Sceaux. This estate was the home of the man who would become Fouquet's nemesis, Jean-Baptiste Colbert. Louis XIV would later make it the designated home of the Dauphin, the crown prince of France.

Le Brun took to his commission with zeal and produced what is arguably the most imposing of all the scenes he painted. The original has not survived, but we were lucky enough to find engravings (see Figure 12) and sketches[3] of it, as well as a very good full-size copy of the work inside the dome of the church at Mondaye Abbey, near Bayeux in Normandy.[4]

The scene is almost surreal. At the center there is a bearded figure representing God, looking down towards the edge of the dome. When we followed his gaze we couldn't believe what we were looking at. On the railing that encircles the composition, there is a shovel, casually lying there next to an an urn on the rail near an angel who is holding a large, seven-armed menorah, half covered by a length of cloth. Slightly to its right, we recognized the only human figure in this enormous scene, one who is painted all in white. It is Nicolas Poussin, staring at the menorah, tucked into the background of the composition. The angel holding the menorah looks like he is about to jump down to Earth with it.

On the other side of the dome, we spotted a group of angels carrying what appears to be the Ark of the Covenant. But is it? We thought when we first saw it that there was something very odd about it—the Ark looked smaller than usual. Then it dawned on us; this was only the lid of the Ark of the Covenant. We searched every tiny bit of the painting but the main *box* of the Ark was nowhere to be seen.

So what exactly is being shown here? This scene had been intended to adorn a private chapel, in a private house, destined for the successor to the throne of France. Had we just seen the menorah, freshly dug up with a shovel, transported back to France? And what about the lid of the Ark of the Covenant? The *arca dia*. Our heads were spinning. The outline of an old secret was forcing itself on us in ever more explicit images.

The completion of the Château de Sceaux was celebrated in July 1677 in the presence of Louis XIV, who prayed in the chapel before attending a performance of the opera *Cadmus and Hermione* by his court composer Lully. The prologue showed Louis XIV as Apollo slaying a serpent.[5]

Figure 12 Engraving by Girard Audran of Le Brun's fresco, originally in the cupola of the chapel at Château de Sceaux (Museum of Art and History, City of Geneva)

We had the feeling that a plot was slowly becoming clearer before our eyes and we tried to connect some more of the dots. We knew that the Knights Templar had been key players in the recovery and restoration of the menorah. Was there anything to suggest that Poussin had been privy to a great secret about the Templars?

173

A year after he had painted his curious self-portrait, in 1651, Poussin painted *Landscape with Buildings*, an image that represents the artist's idealized landscape. We found it intriguing that this painting featured two men riding one horse, a motif that seemed to strongly recall a well-known Knights Templar seal of two knights riding one horse. On closer inspection, we spotted something wrong with the reflection of the two men that appeared in the river. One of the men was not reflected in the water. We were convinced that this was deliberate and had been contrived in such a way for the purpose of drawing attention to this part of the image. There are also shepherds in the foreground of the painting, cryptically pointing the way.

We turned our attention to a final clue, an artefact Poussin had carried on his person throughout his life, right up until his death. Today this object is in the Louvre, though sadly it is not on display. The artefact in question is a small wax figure, made by his own hand, as his own copy of the carved figure of *Sleeping Ariadne*, a 2nd-century BC Roman statue depicting the lovelorn mistress of the labyrinth that today resides in the Vatican Museum.[6] Why had this figure captivated Poussin and why, above all the other models he made throughout his career, was this the one he carried everywhere he went?

The original *Sleeping Ariadne* was acquired by Pope Julius II in 1512. Pope Julius II is also relevant to our story because his coat of arms includes a large oak tree and acorns. He created the famous Vatican Swiss Guard for his personal protection and their helmets feature an oak tree and acorns to this day.

The *Sleeping Ariadne* sculpture was only the second acquisition by Julius II for the Vatican collection. The first was the statue *Laocoön and His Sons*. We would discover that this was no accident and the two were intertwined. The *Laocoön and His Sons* statue once resided in the palace of Emperor Titus—the very emperor responsible for raiding the Temple of Jerusalem.[7]

We therefore took a closer look at the first sculpture. We saw a Trojan priest and his two sons being attacked by serpents, sent by the gods as Laocoön and his sons had offended them. In the heavens, Laocoön was known as the Ophiuchus constellation, the serpent-bearer. Mythology is often multifaceted, multilayered, and in this instance, Ophiuchus/Laocoön was also regarded as Asclepius, the father of all physicians, whose healing powers were so great, he could raise the dead, which is remiscent of the story of Lazarus.

Asclepius was a son of Apollo, the same God whose chariot departed from the Grand Canal of Versailles in the direction of Jerusalem. However, there is a twist: the artist and mystic William Blake made the claim that *Laocoön and His Sons* is a copy of a statue that resided in the Temple of Solomon, and depicts not a Trojan priest but, rather, Yahweh and his two sons, Adam and Satan, and their mother, the Serpent Goddess.[8]

We were quite perplexed by Blake's claims, but they did give us the idea to investigate what serpentine links we could find associated with the *Sleeping Ariadne* statue. We soon found that it was the labyrinth itself that provided the key. The labyrinth, which can only be conquered with Ariadne's guidance, has long been associated with a coiled serpent and, indeed, in the Vatican statue there is a snake on her upper arm, in the form of a bracelet.

We knew that Minoan snake goddess figurines had been found during excavations at the Palace of Knossos on Crete, where Ariadne, according to Greek myth, was said to have been a princess, as the daughter of King Minos of Crete. Images of a figurine that dates from around 1600 BC, discovered at the palace and restored by Sir Arthur Evans, show a goddess or priestess holding two serpents, one in each raised hand. The similarity of this to depictions of the Ophiuchus constellation is quite obvious and it was clear to us that here we had a feminine interpretation of this ancient constellation. The goddess or priestess figurine wears a crown, her breasts are bare, and she wears a "sacral" knot. This last is an important symbol because it represents holiness. The knot occurs throughout Minoan art, often in conjunction with the "labrys," the double-headed axe from which the labyrinth evolved. We thought it was worth pausing for a moment to ponder that, through these ancient tales of the holy knot of the serpent goddess, there was a link to the origin of the Order of the Knot, one of the names of the Order of the Holy Spirit.

Back to the starry skies: if Laocoön was depicted as Ophiuchus, where, then, would we find Ariadne? We believed that she would be sleeping beneath her crown, which is the constellation of Corona Borealis, known since antiquity as Ariadne's crown, fashioned, in another myth, by Vulcan and presented by Venus to the newly betrothed Ariadne.

So, what lay beneath her crown? It was none other than the Serpens constellation, which means "serpent." We had found serpents in many places: coiling around Laocoön; climbing the staff of Asclepius; and lurking in the tree of knowledge in the Garden of Eden. The serpent is an age-old symbol of wisdom. It was almost impossible not to recall the wisdom attributed to the Holy Spirit, and its accompanying symbol, the dove. In Matthew 10.16 (KJV) we are told, "be ye therefore wise as serpents, and harmless as doves." It seemed clear to us that both symbols—the bird and the serpent—come together in the form of the Holy Spirit.

The main star in the Corona Borealis, the jewel in Ariadne's crown, is named Alphecca, but it went by other names. One is Gnosia, a nod to both "gnosis," which means "knowledge," and Knossos, the ancient city and palace on the island of Crete, home of Ariadne. The star's other names were Gemma, for "gem," and Astaroth, the demon of the pentagram, mentioned in Chapter 15. Astaroth gives mortals power over serpents—the same Astaroth who was the adversary of St Bartholomew. This is the very same pentagram that we had found adorning Amiens Cathedral, one of the five labyrinth cathedrals that form the sacro pentagram and which were so very important to the mystery we were attempting to unravel. Regarding Amiens, alchemist Fulcanelli wrote, "Ariadne, the mystic spider, has escaped from Amiens, leaving only the trace of her web on the paving stones of the choir."[9]

All these things formed a daunting web of clues, buried far back in time, but we started to see their implications on the ground ever more clearly. We suddenly realized we had been following strands of Ariadne's web that stretched right across the world, from Jerusalem to Versailles and on to Nova Scotia. This point was really driven home when we realized that the latitude of the Alphecca star was recorded by Johannes Kepler in 1627 as 44.33 degrees, only a little over 2 miles (3 km) from Oak Island in Acadia.

What were we to read into this? Was there a group of individuals who used these connections interchangeably? Was there a secret tradition whereby labyrinths = Ariadne = Serpens = Asclepius = Astaroth = pentagrams = gnosis = Alphecca and 44.33 degrees latitude?

What we do know is that, in 1684, Louis XIV commissioned a full-size copy of the original Ariadne from the Vatican, which he installed in the gardens at Versailles.

Returning to Nicolas Poussin and his own beloved miniature statue of Ariadne, on arriving in Rome, he was befriended by Cassiano dal Pozzo, an avid art collector, alchemist, historian, and scientist whose grandfather had been First Minister to the Grand Duke of Tuscany. Poussin's friendship with dal Pozzo would last 34 years, until dal Pozzo's death in 1657.

Secretary to Cardinal Francesco Barberini and a nephew of Pope Urban VIII, dal Pozzo surrounded himself with the finest artists, scientists, and thinkers of the day. He was a member of the prestigious scientific institution Accademia dei Lincei, along with its founder Federico Cesi, and it should be noted that the shepherdess in Poussin's *The Shepherds of Arcadia II* is modeled on the Cesi Juno, an ancient statue of the goddess in Cesi's sculpture garden.

So it was that dal Pozzo would become—and remain—Poussin's most loyal patron and supporter. Poussin once declared himself "a disciple of the house and museum of cavaliere dal Pozzo."[10] As such, Poussin would have been well versed in all aspects of mythology, astronomy, and the latest scientific discoveries of the day. It is certain that dal Pozzo would have been among the first to secure a copy of the Rudolphine Tables, the most accurate star chart at that time, created by famed astronomers Tycho Brahe and Johannes Kepler, published in 1627. Undoubtedly, therefore, Poussin would have been privy to this work, which records the aforementioned latitude of the star Astaroth, in Ariadne's crown.

Earlier in this chapter we theorized how the phrase "*Et in Arcadia ego*" could have been intended as an anagram for "*Ariadne goetica*," a clear reference to both the labyrinth/serpent mistress and the main star in her crown named for the Goetic demon Astaroth. When we studied the image of the Goetic seal of Astaroth we immediately recognized the pattern of three dots clearly marked at each of the five points of the pentagram. Here again, we had the Jewish *segol* represented, the symbol found deep below Jerusalem that marked the spot where possibly something of great importance had been concealed.

For final confirmation, we visited the Louvre and sat down on a bench facing *The Shepherds of Arcadia II*. It was a lot smaller than we had imagined, measuring only 33 inches tall by 47 inches wide (85 by 121 cm) wide. Notwithstanding its size, the scene grew to great stature in our minds, until it encompassed everything. We saw how it mirrored the patterns in the sky:

- the four figures are enclosed in a pentacle, the pentacle of Astaroth;
- the kneeling shepherd represents the constellation of Hercules, also known as Engonali, the Kneeler;
- the backward-glancing shepherd forms the constellation of Boötes;
- between these two constellations lies Corona Borealis, the crown of Ariadne, which is what the shepherds are secretly pointing at, as Hercules is pointing to both the word "Arcadia" and the main star, so he was telling us where to look on Earth.

The Rudolphine Tables of 1627 clearly showed the main star of Ariadne's crown at 44.33 degrees latitude. In that same year, Poussin created *The Shepherds of Arcadia I* or *Et in Arcadia ego*. We propose that the bare-breasted shepherdess the artist depicted was our now familiar Mistress of the Labyrinth, wearing her laurel crown.

The mouth of the Gold River in Mahone Bay, just above Oak Island on the map, lies at latitude 44.33.

In Poussin's second version of the painting, Hercules is telling us to look to Arcadia, at the latitude of Ariadne's jewel, just above a sickle-shaped landmark. That landmark looks exactly like the sickle-shaped bay of Chester, part of Mahone Bay, Nova Scotia. Just above the tip of that sickle, we found ourselves again at latitude 44.33.

Was this the great secret that the Fouquets were discussing with Poussin in the letter from 1656 (see Chapter 16)? It is an intriguing prospect.

We sat there in the Louvre for over an hour and didn't leave until we made one final observation. Perhaps this was another instance of secret knowledge hidden in the simplest way—in plain sight.

Just like the menorah, we could see seven of the arms of the figures in the painting (see Figure 13).

Figure 13 Nicolas Poussin's second version of *The Shepherds of Arcadia* (Peter Horree / Alamy)

The journey of *The Shepherds of Arcadia*

We dug through our books and our collection of research documents on our laptops to draw up a conclusive timeline of this painting, *The Shepherds of Arcadia II*. We discovered that the picture had quite a history.

It was originally commissioned by Giulio Rospigliosi in September 1655, who became Pope Clement IX. The painting passed from his estate after his death in 1669, and found its way into the collection of Chevalier Henri Avice, who was not only a collector of Poussin's work but also a skilled engraver. A few years later, in 1685, the painting turned up at an auction in Paris, where it was described as "Shepherds who find the tomb of Igiezy, famous Arcadian shepherd on the shore of the Ladon river."[11] In 1685, the painting came into the possession of art dealer Charles Antoine Hérault at precisely the time that the Marquis of Louvois had asked Henri de La Chapelle-Blessé to find a Poussin painting on the direct order of Louis XIV.[12]

The Marquis of Louvois acquired the painting (listed at that time as *Pasteurs d'Arcadie*) for some 6,600 francs and the picture finally headed to Versailles. It was hung in the Sun King's Petit Apartment, at the heart of the palace, on the central axis of the giant menorah.

After Louis XIV's death in 1715, the French court moved to the Louvre and Philippe II of Orléans became the king regent during Louis XV's minority (he was five years old when he came to the throne). *The Shepherds of Arcadia II* moved to the Louvre during this transition and it was recorded there by art collector Jonathan Richardson Jr during one of his visits to the palace. He described the work as "Clorinda coming to the Shepherds, from Tasco, his Fade Coloring."

The court and the painting returned to Versailles in 1722, where Louis XV kept it in his Oval Cabinet. This was a curious location because it was, in effect, his science room, which contained a collection of astronomical instruments that he frequently used himself. *The Shepherds of Arcadia II* was hung among all this scientific equipment, hinting that it was not simply a decorative picture. The Oval Cabinet was next to the King's unofficial bedroom, and both rooms were used for informal and discrete conversations and negotiations. A magnificent automatic clock was installed in the Oval Cabinet in 1754, which led to its final name of Cabinet de la Pendule. Outside the room, Louis also had a sundial placed that contained a golden image of the sun with a small hole in the center. Inside the room, there was a north—south-aligned copper strip in the floor, called the Versailles meridian. Louis used the clock and this meridian to set the official time across his entire kingdom, calculated from the time the sun would hit the Versailles meridian on the solstices.

The Shepherds of Arcadia II was viewed in this very spot by Thomas Anson, a young MP sent on a mission to France by Henry Pelham, then British Prime Minister, to negotiate the signing of the famous Treaty of Aix-la-Chapelle in 1748. The painting was still hanging there when Benjamin Franklin passed this room on his way to meet Louis XVI in 1778.

After the French Revolution, Poussin's masterpiece ended up on the Liste Civile and was estimated to be worth 10,000 livres, according to the Durameau inventory. The painting survived the upheaval and was left hanging alongside the equally famous clock.

In 1809, following a restoration in the workshop at the Louvre, *The Shepherds of Arcadia II* became part of the collection of Napoleon I. The Count of Forbin subsequently selected it for the collection of the new National Museum and the shepherds made their final journey to the Louvre, where the painting still hangs today. The bench we had been sitting on stands more or less exactly on the Paris meridian, the north—south line that was triangulated to be France's axis for Louis XIV by Giovanni Cassini, an alignment that is also known as the Rose Line in Dan Brown's *The Da Vinci Code* (see Chapter 10).

A final note on the painting. Many sources and art antiquarians list the painting as being from 1638, or thereabouts, but Anthony Blunt, a notorious British art historian who was not only a Soviet spy but also the undisputed expert on the works of Nicolas Poussin, concluded that *The Shepherds of Arcadia II* was completed in 1655 or shortly after. This would mean that it was painted *after* the famous self-portrait that contains the Masonic symbolism. This date makes much more sense in our opinion than the earlier one, so we are inclined to agree with Blunt's assessment.[13]

Nicolas Poussin died ten years later, in 1665, in Rome, where he was buried in the Basilica di San Lorenzo in Lucina. The French ambassador in Rome, Châteaubriand, raised a monument to Poussin above the artist's mausoleum in 1820 that includes a bas-relief from *The Shepherds of Arcadia II*. Below this image there is the following inscription, taken from an obituary by Giovan Pietro Bellori:

Parce piis lacrimis vivit Pussinus in urna. Vivere qui dederat nescius ipse mori. Hic tamen ipse silet si vis audire loquentem. Mirum est tabulis vivit et eloquitur.

Spare your pious tears, Poussin lives in this urn. He who gave him life knows no death. He is silent here now, but you would be surprised if you would hear him speak. He lives and speaks through his paintings.

This perhaps sums up Poussin's work throughout his lifetime and, as the inscription tells us, he may now be silent, but if you understand what he was trying to say in his lifetime, you can perceive him proclaiming loudly through his many artworks. Poussin clearly had a tale to tell us long after he was lying in his grave.

The fall of Nicolas Fouquet

Events began to move fast after the notorious letter about Poussin between the Fouquet brothers was sent (see Chapter 16). Immediately after it was written, Basile Fouquet, another of Nicolas' brothers, became the Chancellor of the Order of the Holy Spirit and he took up a position as head of the secret police, working directly for Cardinal Mazarin, protector of his brother. Then, in 1656, only six months after the letter, Nicolas Fouquet signed a contract to buy the Château de Vaux-le-Vicomte, a grand estate some 37 miles (60 km) south-east of Paris, for the astronomical sum of 600,000 livres.

Nicolas Fouquet carried out extensive work at Vaux-le-Vicomte, at great expense. The man responsible for the impressive remodeling of the gardens was André Le Nôtre, an architect and gardener who had begun his professional career with Louis XIV's brother Gaston, duc d'Orléans. Nicolas Fouquet hired Le Nôtre when he acquired the estate, and the stunning gardens that followed were the result of this man's genius. Many commentators over the years have suggested that Louis XIV became jealous of the lavish gardens and architecture at Vaux-le-Vicomte and that was the reason for what Louis would do next. However, there seems to be much more at play at Vaux-le-Vicomte than simple jealously and we believe that the King was aware that Fouquet was himself closing in on the lost treasures from Jerusalam.

In the Château de Vaux-le-Vicomte there are many oddities. Indicated visibly in its marble floors, there are strange alignments that to date remain unstudied and unexplained. Inside the house, Fouquet displayed a painting of the menorah, standing at the heart of Solomon's temple,[14] which is perhaps another hint that he was searching for this object.

Amid all the grand works and building plans, time was running short for Fouquet, whether he knew it or not. Louis XIV had achieved maturity in 1651, so could have taken over then, but he allowed Cardinal Mazarin to continue to run the country in all but name. This changed on Mazarin's death in 1661, when Louis decided not to appoint anyone else as First Minister and declared that he would rule himself, alone. It was an unprecedented move. At that time, the financial affairs of the kingdom were in a parlous state and the King desired to install a trusted adviser with the required administrative and financial skills. He found all this and more in Jean-Baptiste Colbert. The son of a merchant from Reims, with Scottish roots, Colbert had served Cardinal Mazarin diligently, even if he hadn't always agreed with him, and it appears that this was exactly what Louis needed. Colbert was installed as Controller-General of Finances and, even though he was almost 20 years older than the King, they would become very close, creating an indomitable team. The first man to witness their combined power was Nicolas Fouquet.

There had always been a good deal of suspicion that Fouquet was embezzling funds that should have gone to the Crown, and claims and counter-claims were rife at court. Colbert was therefore tasked with fabricating a case against Fouquet. Eventually, in August 1661, Louis contrived to have Fouquet arrested at Nantes, fearing that the minister would use his great influence to flee or manage to secure his release should he be taken into custody in Paris. Making the arrest fell to Charles de Batz de Castelmore d'Artagnan, the musketeer who has been popularized since in the famous book by Alexandre Dumas, *The Three Musketeers*, and the movies that followed subsequently. The King was so wary of Fouquet escaping and seeking revenge that he had d'Artagnan guard Fouquet for the three years it took to resolve the criminal proceedings against him and he was then finally incarcerated.

During our research into Fouquet and his family, we had always been aware of their connections to the Company of the Blessed Sacrament, Nicolas Poussin, and France's dealings in North America. Nicolas Fouquet wasn't officially a member of the Order of the Holy Spirit, so we wondered why its emblem featured prominently at the entrance of his Château de Vaux-le-Vicomte. He was not a registered member of the Company of the Blessed Sacrament either, yet his fingerprints were all over it. He financed its founder, the Duke of Ventadour, by buying his title of Viceroy of New France, providing Fouquet with detailed insight into all of Acadia's affairs.[15]

Fouquet's estate at Château de Vaux-le-Vicomte and his huge library at Saint-Mandé were both seized by Colbert on behalf of the French state and, with this sweeping move, all evidence of the North American treasure in Fouquet's library then became the property of King Louis. Colbert arrived in person at Fouquet's great library and carried out a thorough search and it was he who found Fouquet's escape plan to flee to Belle-Isle—a document was hidden behind a mirror in Fouquet's office.

At the command of the Chancellor of France, Pierre Séguier, a prominent member of the Order of the Holy Spirit, an inventory was created of Fouquet's library. The Chancellor's written reports expressed simple wonder at the extraordinary contents of the house. Some finds in particular seem to have garnered the attention of the new owners of the library. Not long after the seizure, two Spanish monks turned up at Saint-Mandé with a letter of authority from the Marquis of Louvois, the French Secretary of State for War, to study Fouquet's books.[16] They allegedly took notes regarding a rare Spanish book stored in a room filled with hundreds of religious texts, including Korans, Talmuds, Mishnahs, and old interpretations of the Bible. We now know, it was in this very room that an original copy of a book by Jewish philosopher Moses ben Maimon, commonly known as Maimonides, was kept. This book was the *Yad Hazaka* (mentioned in Chapter 3), and it was in its pages that the menorah was depicted with straight arms. We believe this is what inspired Colbert to order Louis de Compiègne to complete and publish his translation, thereby securing a French version for the library of King Louis.

At this point, we remembered that Colbert's family originally came from Troyes, in Champagne, where they had been bankers. Their coat of arms displayed a single coiled serpent. We couldn't shake the feeling that perhaps there was secret knowledge held in Colbert's family even before their most famous member took up his position in the Sun King's court.

We also discovered that the Company of the Blessed Sacrament went into serious decline exactly when Fouquet was imprisoned. Had the whole *raison d'être* of the organization suddenly disappeared? Had King Louis personally taken over control of the search for the Jewish treasures in North America and was Colbert then his instrument?

Nicolas Fouquet's brother, Louis, the famous letter writer, made a curious comment at the time of the arrests. He suggested that Saint-Mandé, the location of Nicolas Fouquet's library, should be burned to the ground.[17] We wondered if he was trying to ensure that something remained hidden in the shadows with this wish.

In the end, it wasn't only Nicolas who fell foul of King Louis. One of his brothers, François, was exiled to Alençon, in Normandy, while another brother, Louis, was exiled to Villefranche-de-Rouergue, in southern France. A third brother, Basile, did not escape the retribution of King Louis either—he was also exiled and stripped of the title of Chancellor of the Order of the Holy Spirit. The Fouquet dynasty had been stopped dead in its tracks, its knowledge handed over to King Louis.

Nicolas Fouquet would spend the rest of his life imprisoned in the fortress of Pignerol. However, he was not idle. He manufactured his own ink from soot and vinegar, choosing to both further his own cause and denounce King Louis.

Something that adds further intrigue to the story, which has been suggested by some—including French author Alexandre Dumas in *The Vicomte of Bragelonne: Ten Years Later*—is that the mysterious prisoner known as the Man in the Iron Mask became the valet of Nicolas Fouquet at Pignerol. There was apparently no danger of Fouquet revealing the identity of this masked prisoner as neither man was destined to see the outside world ever again. Furthermore, both François-Michel Le Tellier, Marquis of Louvois, and Jean-Baptiste Colbert employed Bénigne Dauvergne de Saint-Mars, the Officer-in-Charge of the donjon at Pignerol, in an attempt to get Fouquet to reveal his secrets. In 1673, Fouquet wrote directly to the Marquis of Louvois, seeking to receive a royal pardon in exchange for information. In this letter Fouquet stated:

> I have been occupied for a long time in examining the best possible service that I could do to His Majesty, and God has enlightened me regarding certain things in such a significant way and about such important, easy and glorious designs that it would do him a real displeasure if they would be lost without him knowing about it.[18]

The French phrase Fouquet uses in the letter is "*des lumières d'affaires si grandes et des desseins si importants.*" "*Lumières*" feels extremely significant, as it means "multiple lights." He also specifically introduces the word "designs." We feel this choice of words was very deliberate and clearly Fouquet was hinting—and not too subtly either—at what he knew. We believe that he was dropping a direct reference to the hiding place of the menorah, concealed in North America.

It appears that King Louis had already secured all of Fouquet's secrets, whether from the officer of the donjon at Pignerol or maybe from one of Fouquet's brothers. All we know is that he had secured the information somehow and, by the time Fouquet had written his letter in 1673, the King had even acted on it.

We believe that, by 1670, King Louis knew the precise location of the menorah, so no response was given to this final attempt by Fouquet and no pardon. Fouquet would take any remaining secrets to the grave, spending his last 15 years incarcerated inside

Pignerol. While he was allowed only one visit from his wife during his imprisonment, curiously, King Louis allowed Louis Fouquet, the letter writer, to spend an astonishing four months with his brother in 1679, a year before his death. Even more curious, during those four months, the two Fouquet brothers received the royal gardener André Le Nôtre, who was on his way back from a visit to the Pope and the Vatican. Do these visits signify a last attempt by the King to acquire Fouquet's secrets?

Nicolas Fouquet finally died in 1680. To this day, it is not known what he discussed with his brother and Le Nôtre during his incarceration. All we do know is that, four years later, in 1684, Louis Fouquet was fully reinstated and was even granted a royal pension of 35,000 livres. An intriguing footnote to this story is that the tower of Pignerol is almost a doppelganger of the tower found at the top of the spire of Versailles Cathedral.

Versailles refined

With the arrest of Fouquet, King Louis swept in and took the disgraced Superintendent of Finance's entire complement of artists, architects, and gardeners into his own household. Notable among these were master gardener André Le Nôtre, distinguished architect Charles Le Vau and painter Charles Le Brun. So it was that, in 1661, a new figure emerged as the chief designer and architect of the royal estate of Versailles: André Le Nôtre, the man who had been responsible for the splendor of Château de Vaux-le-Vicomte.

This changing of the guard would see Versailles altered dramatically as Le Nôtre turned his attention to what would become his magnum opus. However, as we now know, the designs were not entirely of his own hand and many features were clearly dictated by the King and his inner circle, who had a message that they wanted secreted in the many avenues at Versailles.

Today, Le Nôtre's fame is well documented, but he also received great respect in his lifetime from his peers, including Italian architect Gian Lorenzo Bernini. Thierry Mariage highlights a revealing anecdote that demonstrates the significance of Le Nôtre's work at Versailles:

> Pope Innocent, who was still living, having learned from Monsieur the Duc d'Estrées, ambassador of France, that Le Nôtre was in Rome, wished to see him and granted him a fairly long audience . . . the pope had him rise and asked to see the plans of Versailles that he had heard so much about.[19]

Mariage goes further, claiming that Le Nôtre's work will have significant ramifications throughout the wider world:

As curious as it might seem, the Versailles project and its extension into the south-western region of Paris . . . was the testing ground for cartographic and surveying techniques that led to a global conception of national territory.[20]

Throughout his reign, King Louis urged the Royal Academy of Sciences to focus on and develop cartography, refining and advancing the art. Curiously, many map-making projects, as well as the hiring of mathematicians and astronomers, were financed directly from the treasury of the royal building accounts. This highlights how important this work was to the development of Versailles, and the gardens and landscape around the palace became a blueprint for the technology that would follow.

As if the central motif of Versailles—the grandly illustrated menorah—and an alignment linking the palace with both Temple Mount in Jerusalem and Nova Scotia on the other side of the world, were not a strong enough message, in 1661 Le Nôtre began to reshape the central axis of Versailles.

Something we discovered that happened during Le Nôtre's tenure is that scientific advances at the time meant King Louis' inner circle must have suddenly become painfully aware that the chief alignment forged in the landscape at Versailles—the main avenue—did not point accurately to Oak Island in Nova Scotia. The margin of error was less than one degree, but this axis was deemed so important that a correction appears to have been made to the layout of the gardens. To mark the adjustment, Le Nôtre designed the Grotto of Thetis in 1665—a large marble structure, complete with statues that depicted the descent of Apollo, the Sun God, as he plunged into the sea at the end of his daily travails across the sky. Here, Apollo echoed the grand Apollo Fountain on the opposite side of the gardens and the Sun God's procession across the heavens depicted in the architecture of the grotto mirrors the arc of the alignment present at Versailles as it sweeps from Jerusalem to France, then over to Nova Scotia, east to west—the same path and direction the sun follows.

The statues comprising the scene in the grotto were themselves laid out in a configuration that resembles the menorah—yet another coded reference. Grottoes had long been viewed as sacred places where homage would be paid to local divinities found alongside water sources and holy wells. From the Roman Empire onwards they were also referred to as "*nymphaea*," meaning "fountains consecrated to the nymphs."

The Grotto of Thetis was demolished only a few years after it was built, as the north wing of the Palace of Versailles was expanded and the new royal chapel ordered by Louis XIV—the one that caused such a commotion because it broke the palace's symmetry—was created exactly on this spot. Today, only the sculptures remain, which have been scattered throughout the gardens, but the desired effect was achieved. The correction to the chief alignment had been not only noted but also etched into the landscape of Versailles forever.

When we looked at the Grotto of Thetis in detail, a few features jumped out at us. The exquisite underwater decoration of the interior of the grotto featured shells, semiprecious stones, mirrors, mosaics, and, to our surprise, the same mythical River God that is featured in Poussin's *The Shepherds of Arcadia I* and *Midas Washing at the Source of the Pactolus*. We now realized that this same River God was depicted on a panel that can be found at the entrance to King Louis' new royal chapel—a scene that shows Louis XIV crossing the River Rhine. In the grotto, the River God can be seen above the central arch, and he was added to several other locations in the gardens as well. We were convinced that here was another coded reference, representing the underground stream, pointing to the secrets concealed in Poussin's artworks.

We spotted something else very interesting too. Looking at Le Nôtre's original designs for the grotto, he labeled the feature "Crypta Versailles." Remember this as you will encounter the phrase towards the end of this book. Another feature also grabbed our attention. Woven into the design of the three gates to the grotto were maps of regions of the world. The middle gate featured North America, with particular emphasis given to the northern part of the Atlantic coast, precisely where Acadia lies on the map.

During the reign of Louis XIV, and under the guiding hand of Le Nôtre, 15 groves were created at Versailles. One such feature created by Le Nôtre in 1665 was the Labyrinth Grove. Of course, the "labyrinth" in the name immediately grabbed our attention and it is a curious feature when considered together with the menorah that Le Nôtre also delineated in the landscape. Sadly, the Labyrinth Grove deteriorated and was also destroyed, though not until the late 1770s, when it was replaced and replanted to become the Queen's Grove.

One final, curious feature that Le Nôtre installed at Versailles in 1670 is the Bosquet du Marais, otherwise known as the Bosquet du Chêne Vert. "*Marais*" is French for "swamp" and here Le Nôtre created an artificial pool complete with sculpted, metal reeds and an iron oak tree that had painted tin leaves and water that spouted from its branches. The end result was a manicured swamp with the emphasis on the central oak tree.[21] The Bosquet du Marais was destroyed in 1704, replaced by the Apollo's Baths Grove, but for the few years that it stood in the gardens it might have represented a message to those who were in on the plot: Versailles pointed to a faraway oak tree in a swamp.

When one enters a church, all the statues are usually placed so that they face you. Not so the funerary bust of Le Nôtre in the Church of Saint-Roch in Paris. Instead, his marble effigy is staring towards the back of the church, his head clearly turned in that direction. France's most famous gardener, the master of the line-of-sight device in landscape design, has been immortalized with his gaze fixed on a life-size copy of the Ark of the Covenant that is flanked by two menorahs. These gilded replicas of the sacred treasures are situated in a small round chapel at the back of the church, the domed ceiling of which features a giant Templar cross. This little-known church, larger in size than Notre-Dame Cathedral, is tucked away on rue Saint-Honoré, which is the beginning of the famous street lined with the haute-couture fashion boutiques of Paris, rue du Faubourg Saint-Honoré.

When we visited Saint-Roch, the caretaker of the church told us of a secret tunnel, connecting it to the adjacent Palais Royal. It was by means of this tunnel that kings and their spouses gained access to a stone staircase hidden inside the wall that leads to two concealed alcoves high above the altar, so they could attend mass without being seen. The caretaker was kind enough to take us to these vantage points and we witnessed Marie Antoinette's personal solid silver crucifix, still hanging on one of the walls.

We also noticed that it isn't only Le Nôtre who is curiously aligned in the church. A statue of Louis XIV's First Painter, Pierre Mignard, also has his eyes fixed keenly on the treasures of Jerusalem.

We now felt that we had compiled enough evidence to fully understand the motive behind the creation of Versailles itself and why the house of Bourbon, through the actions of Albert de Gondi, had secured this site. By constructing a grand royal palace on this spot, they were able to straddle the alignment that linked Jerusalem with Oak Island in Nova Scotia—creating an invisible thread that stretched right across the world, one that only those who kept this great secret alive would recognize. Moreover, the arms of Versailles' giant menorah and the rays of light emitting from its central lamp connected a number of sites that were associated with St Louis and the Knights Templar, highlighting key points of the menorah's journey. We had already plotted alignments pointing to Jerusalem, La Rochefoucauld, Chartres, New Orleans, and Amiens, among others, but, as we collated all our research and began writing this book, we found one more that tied the whole story together.

With now-familiar, uncanny precision, we discovered that one of the rays of the Versailles central lamp points straight to the center of the circular Templar church in the Convent of Christ in Tomar, Portugal, which was the headquarters of both the Knights Templar and their rebranded successors, the Order of Christ. This was the final proof we needed that all the locations where the menorah had been concealed throughout its long history were encoded in the landscape of Versailles: Jerusalem, Chartres, Tomar, and Oak Island.

With this new revelation came a final question: if the precise location of the menorah in North America was now known to Louis XIV, how could it remain on Oak Island for much longer?

The time had come to turn to the activities of the French in Acadia and Nova Scotia, and reveal what they had planned for the treasures of Solomon. To begin that search, we first needed to take one final look at de Champlain's map of Arcadia.

CHAPTER 18
THE SERPENT AND THE POLE

Ever since that point in time when we were studying de Champlain's map from 1612 and discovered the "51" or "SI" hidden in it, we had been pondering what it might mean and why he had used this symbolism. You will recall from Chapter 14 that de Champlain had highlighted the letters "L" and "I" by linking them via a hidden axis, one that connected two Templar crosses and passed through the heart of the wolf shown on the map.

We found that "SI" signifies many things, both religious and esoteric. It stands for a serpent and a pole or a snake and a rod, as evident in the staff of the Greek god Asclepius, as well as the caduceus, a staff associated with Hermes that has two snakes entwined around it. Then there is the Nehushtan, which was a bronze serpent on a tau cross (shaped like a "T"), erected by Moses in the desert. A serpent and a pole have also been used to symbolize the Archangel Michael, as he defeated a serpent or dragon, and St George, who pierced the heart of a dragon with a lance.

From this it is clear that de Champlain was making a statement when he concealed this symbolism in his map. We then wondered what the full significance of this was for our quest to find the menorah.

We had already concluded that the Templars used the knowledge they discovered in the Holy Land to create the giant sacro pentagram, with its vast Gothic cathedrals constructed at each point of the star. The question now was whether this was also the case for the serpent and the pole. The fact that de Champlain had hidden this symbol on his map by using Templar crosses suggests that these two things were linked. Perhaps by highlighting "51" or "SI" this way, he was simply saying that the Templars had been involved with and active in Acadia. We had discovered that the second incarnation of the Knights Templar, the Order of Christ, brought the menorah to New France, and de Champlain also seems to have been aware of this information.

While we pondered this, we decided that it was time to look at the serpent and the pole in a literal way. A staff has been used as a walking aid and a sign of authority since ancient times, while a serpent has been used to symbolize wisdom for even longer. Huge numbers of books have been written about the symbolism of each, but it occurred to us that, in this instance, perhaps a far simpler message was being conveyed.

What we were being shown was a walking stick combined with knowledge. Perhaps the serpent and the pole in de Champlain's map merely represented a body of knowledge that had traveled. In that case, they could represent a piece of information that had been carried across the Atlantic. Once we allowed this idea time to percolate, things began to fall into place.

In Chapter 15 we discussed the Company of the Blessed Sacrament—a secret club of influential men who offered unflinching support to Louis XIII and his wife, Anne of Austria. One of its members, Jean-Jacques Olier, founded a new religious body in 1641, which was a seminary, and the Society of the Priests of Saint-Sulpice, named after the church in Paris that was their headquarters. These Christian mystics, or Sulpicians, as they are also known, played an active role in the development of New France, and when Louis XIII died, they continued this work under the banner of Louis XIV. In 1657, the first four Sulpicians were sent across the Atlantic to act as missionaries to both the indigenous population and the French settlers. One of their number ended up founding Montreal on land given to them by Richelieu's Company of New France, otherwise known as the Hundred Associates. According to the company's minutes, in 1668, while the Royal Academy of Sciences in Paris discussed the ways in which mathematics might aid navigation, more Sulpicians traveled to Acadia to begin converting the local Mi'kmaq population, a First Nations people, to Christianity.[1] The question we asked ourselves was whether this was their sole ambition or something else was behind their mission. The year 1668 was some seven years after the arrest of Nicolas Fouquet. By this time, Louis had acquired his secrets and his members of staff, and was homing in on the location of the menorah.

Five years after the foundation of the Sulpicians, ground was broken for a new church at Saint-Sulpice in Paris. It was an enormous project, one that was not fully completed until 1870, but the one constant from the very beginning was the society's motto and iconography: the serpent and the pole. It seems to have have had two mirrored meanings for them. First, there is the image of the Virgin Mary crushing a serpent under her feet, found in both the Sulpicians' large churches, in Paris and Montreal, which represents Mary conquering evil. Then, there is the image of the serpent as wisdom, wrapped around a staff. The most explicit example of this is seen in the design for the altar of the Church of Saint-Sulpice, completed in 1704 (the rendering of the design is kept in the Hermitage Museum, St Petersburg; the altar itself was destroyed during the French Revolution). In what almost looks like an origin story, on top of a large altar, the Ark of the Covenant is supported by two cherubim, as you would expect, but in this instance, on top of the Ark, there is a large cross encircled by a snake.

The logo of the Sulpicians also features the letters "A" and "M" intertwined, meaning "*auspice Maria*," "under the protection of Mary." The organization has survived to the present day and you can still see the AM logo over the gate of their seminary in Montreal. It has proven impossible to establish for certain whether or not this phrase existed before 1641, when the seminary and Society of Saint-Sulpice was founded, but what we do know is that from 1624 to 1647 Thomas Billon was the official "anagrammatist" to Louis XIII and his wife Anne of Austria. It was Louis himself who laid the first stone for the new church and he was closely acquainted with the Sulpician's founder, Jean-Jacques Olier, and his mentor, St Vincent de Paul.

At this point it would be helpful to elaborate a little on Billon's role and the function of anagrams at that time. It was Billon's job to find amusing, and mystical, anagrams of people's names or the names of saints and so on. He worked predominantly in Latin, which was the language of choice for anagrammatists because it was the pre-eminent language for scientific writings. On rare occasions, anagrams were created in other languages, so "Charles James Stuart" could become "claims Arthur's seat" or "François de Valois" (who sent da Verrazzano to North America) could become "*de facon suis royal*." Sometimes, a mix of Latin *and* another language was used.

Anagrams were a source of entertainment, used to create pseudonyms (so French writer François Rabelais became Alcofribas Nasier), but they were also often employed to conceal information. Scientists such as Galileo and Robert Hooke recorded their most important results in the form of anagrams, to stake their claim on a discovery while at the same time prevent anyone else from claiming the credit. For example, when Christiaan Huygens discovered Titan, Saturn's largest moon, in 1665, he communicated the news to John Wallis in an anagram:

admovere oculis distantia sidera nostris vvvvvvvcccrrhnbqx

meaning, they carried distant stars to our eyes + code

When unraveled, this anagram becomes:

Saturno luna sua circunducitur diebus sexdecim horis quator

meaning, with Saturn, his moon circles itself around in 16 days, 4 hours

Educated and literate people were trained to use and spot anagrams and, at the time that de Champlain's map was published and the Sulpicians embedded "*auspice Maria*" into their logo, this linguistic device was very fashionable. Anagrams, therefore, were extremely prevalent and would remain so for at least another century.

Perhaps it was Billon himself who had created the *auspice Maria* phrase, because it turns out it is an anagram that conceals the words *"Apius America."* "Apius" is the old Greek name for the god Asclepius, wielder of the serpent and the pole, and "America," of course, is the name that was given to the entire newly discovered continent in 1507. Forming close by, in part of that huge continent, was the then new French territory that the Sulpicians would be so influential in building into part of what became Canada.

It was said that Asclepius learned the secrets of medicine from a serpent. This called to mind again the phrase from Matthew 10.16 (KJV): "be ye therefore wise as serpents, and harmless as doves." The dove is also a key symbol, used for the Holy Spirit, and another link with Mary.

However, what connection might Asclepius have with Mary? Could this be a reference to the temple dedicated to Asclepius unearthed in Jerusalem? It was that very same temple of healing which featured one of the pools of Bethesda, where Jesus healed a crippled man. Throughout the temple slithered non-venomous snakes. In John's Gospel (5.2–9), this Asclepeion is described as having five porticoes, referencing the shape of the pentagram once again. The temple was located adjacent to (less than 98 feet or 30 m), and shared a grotto with, the purported home of St Anne and Joachim, making this the birthplace and childhood home of Mary. The crusader Church of Saint Anne (built in 1138) still stands on the site, and France has a fascinating claim on this part of Jerusalem, as it is French territory. Thus, even though this spot lies in the Holy Land, when you stand on the foundations of the home of the mother and grandmother of Jesus, you are, in fact, standing on French soil.

As the serpent represents knowledge and wisdom, this hints at something we had wondered for a while. Another word for "knowledge" is "illumination" or "light." As noted in Chapter 15, the menorah has long been seen as a metaphor for wisdom and illumination in Judaism. Is it possible that the serpent and the pole represented not only the transmission of an idea, of knowledge, but also symbolized the journey that the original "light of the world," the menorah, made as it was taken from Europe to New France?

If we were right, then by the time the Sulpicians' missions to Acadia occurred, the menorah was already in New France, hidden by the Portuguese long ago. The French were closing in on their prize and, to pinpoint the exact location, they turned to the best and the brightest minds in the world.

In April 1670, two years after the Sulpicians began to push deeper into the Acadian peninsula, a ship called the *Saint Sébastien* left the port of La Rochelle on its way to New France. On board was an astronomer called Jean Richer, who had been assigned the task of taking detailed measurements to establish the precise latitudes and longitudes in the new territory. His mentor, Italian astronomer Giovanni

Cassini, was creating a map of the world on the floor of the new Royal Observatory in Paris, a building erected on a pentagonal plot of land, hand-picked by Louis XIV, and perfectly aligned with the Palais de Luxembourg in Paris. Cassini called the map his planisphere—a very large, circular, flat representation of the Earth, much like the modern 2D map projections that we use today. Cassini had already established the Paris meridian, a line that split France into two halves, running from Bray-Dunes, near Dunkirk, in the north to the mountain peak Canigó in the Pyrenees in the very south. We had already discovered, to our utter astonishment, that this line bisects the sacro pentagram perfectly. Cassini's meticulous measurements also led to adjustments being made to the map of France, reducing it in size, leading Louis XIV to exclaim, "You have cost me more territory than all my enemies."[2]

The Paris meridian had been created by taking measurements between peaks in the landscape, a process called triangulation. As members of the French Royal Academy of Sciences were more than aware that Richer would not be able to make use of tall buildings or the summits of mountains or hills while surveying at sea, of necessity, they provided him with a simple instrument made out of pieces of wood that he used along with his eyes, tables, charts, and the measurement of time. The highly accurate, portable marine clocks produced by Dutch mathematician Christiaan Huygens were essential in this endeavor and resulted in a breakthrough.[3] The more accurately you could keep track of time, the more reliable were the measurements produced by the survey.

Richer became a celebrated scientist, who is still recognized today for his incredibly accurate latitude and longitude measurements, yet there are more than a few question marks hanging over his expedition to Acadia. First, it was organized at very short notice on the direct order of Louis and his First Minister, Jean-Baptiste Colbert. The *Saint Sébastien*, originally meant to sail to the Indian Ocean, was instructed at the very last hour to reroute to Acadia. Second, no records of the scientific experiments performed in New France have ever been revealed.

Although Richer is well known for comprehensively documenting his later voyage to French Guyana, which was the norm for such explorations, the Acadia expedition was conducted in secrecy. While we have no doubt that extensive details were recorded and maps *were* made, they were not made public and have since vanished.[4] Richer's later writings provide some clues as to where his ship sailed and where he took his measurements, but they give us only scant details. For example, Richer recorded the coordinates of Fort Pentagouet on August 6, 1670, and, even though he then sailed the Acadian Atlantic coast until August 18, we have no full account and not a single map remains.[5] This is disappointing for many reasons, not least of which is that Richer would certainly have sailed past Mahone Bay and Oak Island, yet there are no details of what he did there or what he discovered.

Despite the lack of documentation, we are convinced that this was the moment the French pinpointed Mahone Bay on the world map, with the precision necessary for the accurate alignment of the soon-to-be-built royal chapel at Versailles. We knew that we would never be able to prove this point categorically, not unless Jean Richer's notes from Acadia suddenly came to light, but in our eyes the curious lack of expedition notes only strengthened the plausibility of this discovery having occurred. If you want to keep something secret, you simply keep it to yourself and destroy the evidence. All we could do was keep dissecting the timeline and focus on the strong circumstantial evidence that substantiated our theory.

With everything we had discovered so far, the picture was becoming much clearer and, although it was impossible to pin down some of the dates precisely, we felt that we had enough information to reach a firm conclusion. We knew that, in 1670, the exact latitude and longitude of the menorah in America was recorded by Jean Richer. The knowledge of the light had therefore traveled from Europe to the new continent of America and would then travel back to France. *Apius America*.

CHAPTER 19
SECRETS OF LOUISBOURG

Yet again, de Champlain points the way

As we saw in Chapter 14, on his revolutionary map of New France or Acadia of 1612, de Champlain curiously had highlighted what would become the bay of Louisbourg. He had marked it with three dots, supposedly representing islands in the bay, yet we found that, when we compared these dots to modern maps, there were no islands anywhere in the vicinity. If the three dots did not signify islands, then why had de Champlain drawn them there?

Intriguingly, the three dots resemble the *segol*, the ancient Hebrew symbol of an equilateral triangle of three dots. This is the exact same symbol that was found deep below Temple Mount in Jerusalem (see Chapter 7) and was likely to have been used to mark the hiding place of the hidden Temple treasures. The symbol is also likely to have been closely associated with the menorah itself in ancient times. That this was marked on de Champlain's map was as close to "X marks the spot" as we could possibly have hoped for. Further, there was de Champlain's mirror image of the alchemical symbol for gold directly below, so we felt that de Champlain was begging us to delve deeper.

The first thing we discovered when we started investigating the history of Louisbourg was that it had been at the heart of a war fought between the French and English, a war that, ultimately, would decide who was to control Acadia and the wider region of what would become Canada.

On November 30, 1706, Louis XIV received an anonymous note urging him to build a stronghold at Havre à l'Anglais, which means the English Harbor, a bay lying on the easternmost edge of Cape Breton.[1] Seven years later, in 1713, a group of 250 settlers landed there and named it Louisbourg, after their King.

Approval for the construction of a great fortress on this site was granted by Louis in 1715, which proved to be one of the last decisions he made before his death. The fortress at Louisbourg would quickly become one of the largest on the continent and documents from the time show that it was the most expensive military construction ever undertaken outside Europe. The reason for such seeming extravagance was simple: this was heavily contested territory and the English were harrying French towns and settlements right across the region.

The French designed the fortress at Louisbourg to last for an eternity but, unfortunately, it had a number of weaknesses that, ultimately, led to its demise. In 1758 it was captured for the final time by the British and systematically levelled— even its foundations were completely destroyed. However, in the 1960s and 1970s a grand project was initiated by the government in Nova Scotia to restore the fortress to its former glory. A major section of the fortress and the surrounding town were reinstated, based on thousands of original designs and drawings showing what it looked like in the 18th century. Every year, large groups of tourists enjoy the many historical re-enactments that are put on by a dedicated group of employees and volunteers, often in period costumes, and the result is an authentic recreation of what the atmosphere of the fortress must have been like in its heyday.

We, too, will now travel back in time, but not to the golden era of Louisbourg. Instead, we shall consider the years immediately before its destruction.

An expedition to save Louisbourg

The decline of Louisbourg began in January 1745, when the fortress first fell, unexpectedly, to the British. From that moment on, a curious chain of events began to nudge the fortress towards the center of our research and storyline.

As a response to the British threat and the capture of the fortress, the French assembled the largest military force ever to sail to the New World, under the command of Jean-Baptiste-Louis-Frédéric de La Rochefoucauld de Roy, Duc d'Anville. The expedition was tasked with retaking Louisbourg and driving the English from Acadia. All told, 11,000 men were assembled on 64 ships.[2]

Despite the lengthy preparations, and careful planning, the expedition quickly descended into chaos and the fleet was plunged headlong into disaster. It took the armada three months to reach New France and when they finally did arrive, hundreds of sailors had already died, falling victim to vicious bouts of scurvy, typhus, and typhoid, with hundreds more seriously ill. In the end, only 44 vessels reached the harbor of Halifax. As if to underline the depth of the tragedy, the fleet's own commander, the Duc d'Anville, died within a week of their arrival and he was solemnly buried on George's Island, in what is now Halifax Bay. After a number of further miscalculations, and disastrous military decisions, with many more men dead, what remained of the fleet eventually left Acadia to return to France, leaving it largely under English control, including the fortress at Louisbourg.

After the French had failed in their attempt to win back their most prestigious stronghold in North America, they were forced to enter into negotiations with the British, who were also joined by the Netherlands and Austria–Hungary. Events in

Acadia were part of a wider conflict that is known as King George's War, a contest between France and Great Britain, along with each side's native allies in New England and Nova Scotia. In France it is known as the Third Intercolonial War. Not all that occurred during that war is relevant to our story, but there are some startling details that we need to draw your attention to.

In the summer of 1748, the British government, headed by Prime Minister Henry Pelham, agreed to send a member of Parliament (MP) on an important mission to France. The MP in question was Thomas Anson, who represented the constituency of Lichfield and was the older brother of the famous Admiral George Anson. Anson traveled from the family estate of Shugborough Hall in Staffordshire to the European mainland, where the negotiations between the two powers were in full swing.[3]

This extraordinary expedition, at a time when Britain was still—officially at least—at war with France, appears to have been Anson's own idea. He took it on himself to establish what stance the French had taken, what their motives were, and what it might take to persuade them to accept a peace agreement. As with Anson's life as a whole, this French mission is puzzling, and also quite out of character. It has been suggested that Anson only became an MP to please his sister-in-law, Lady Anson, as he had a close relationship with her. A letter that Anson wrote to George reveals that he had very little interest in the "Cabal, Intrigue and . . . Huddle of politics,"[4] so it is curious that he should not only take part in but also initiate this mission to France.

Anson arrived at The Hague on May 19, 1748. He then met with the British negotiators in Breda and Brussels before traveling on to Paris, arriving at the end of June. From there, Anson traveled to Versailles in early July, spending four days and nights negotiating with France's Foreign Minister, the Duc de Choiseul, alongside the hosts at the palace, King Louis XV of France and his chief mistress Madame de Pompadour. A surviving letter from Lady Anson to Thomas Anson remarks, "[but] how trifling that must sound, to one who spent four days at the magnifique Palais de Versailles."[5]

Anson shared many interests with Louis XV, most notably a fondness for architecture and construction. It is also known that Anson went horse riding with the King. Crucially for our story, the two men spent time together in the Cabinet de la Pendule, the room where, you will recall (see Chapter 17), the King kept a very highly advanced clock and had the Versailles meridian strip installed in the floor. This was also the room where Louis hung Poussin's painting *The Shepherds of Arcadia II*, which was directly aligned with the central axis of the Versailles menorah.

While it is impossible to verify, we have to consider whether Louis XV revealed the existence of the giant menorah in the landscape of Versailles, and relayed the significance of both the imagery and the direction in which it pointed. If so, Anson would suddenly have understood just what was hidden at the end of this grand alignment, far across the sea, in Acadia.

A few months after Anson's departure from Versailles, in October 1748, the Treaty of Aix-la-Chapelle was finally signed. France lost a great many of its foreign and colonial possessions, but there was one property over in Acadia that they regained control of. Against all the odds, the fortress at Louisbourg was handed back to the French.

Why the British agreed to this one concession has never been answered satisfactorily. The British held a position of power throughout the negotiations and, from the point of view of political control in North America, it made no sense to return this fortress to the French. Handing back Louisbourg meant that the British had to start from scratch in Halifax, where they founded a new capital, leaving what was essentially the front door to Canada in French hands. We have to wonder whether there were greater powers at work. Ultimate responsibility for the decision fell to Britain's King George II and his prime minister, Henry Pelham. Both men agreed to the return of Louisbourg to the French, much to the chagrin of the British generals at the time. It is almost as though there was a greater—and clandestine—international agreement at play here.

On October 24, 1748, Anson wrote to his brother, George, and made this intriguing statement regarding the signing of the Treaty of Aix-la-Chapelle:

> If I had no other Reason to like the Peace than the Astonishment and Dejection it has thrown the Party into, that would be alone sufficient Recommendation, but I have many more.[6]

Whatever the real reasons for the complex political machinations, both at home and abroad, the end result was that the French were once again in control of Louisbourg. Now we needed to establish exactly why the French wanted this stronghold back so desperately and what secrets it might once have concealed.

Louisbourg's mysterious tunnels

When the Canadian government finally began to rebuild Fortress Louisbourg in the 1960s and started the groundworks, two tunnels were discovered, in the shape of a Latin cross.[7] It transpired that the entrance to these tunnels had been blocked up and disguised. According to the current curators of the restored fortress, the tunnels were constructed by the French and never discovered by the British. The tunnels head away from the fortress, running outwards from the edge of the main structure, the King's Bastion.

The archaeologists who discovered this subterranean feature referred to it as a "countermine tunnel," and it was said to have been constructed to enable the defenders at Louisbourg to place explosives directly beneath the feet of any forces besieging the fortress. However, the placement of the tunnels, coupled with their size, seems to make very little sense. A single tunnel appears to run out under the field, completely dwarfed in size by the width of the fortress.

To add to the mystery further, on an old French map from 1744, held in the Louisbourg archives, the tunnels are indicated by what appears to be a Templar cross marked on the wall of the King's Bastion, where the entrance to the tunnels was found. This underground feature is quite simply a conundrum, and it is still unknown to this day what these tunnels were originally designed for, and what exactly was once stored here, deep beneath the fortress.

The addition of the giant menorah to the landscape of Versailles, along with the alignment of its central axis, which points straight to Oak Island in one direction and Jerusalem in the other, proves to us that Louis XIV, and his successor, Louis XV, had been well aware of the existence of the menorah and it having been hidden somewhere on the Atlantic coast of New France. The French were searching for the treasures of Jerusalem again after the Portuguese had moved them to Acadia, and multiple clues crop up over the centuries on the maps from this era, as we have seen.

We knew that, during the course of his expeditions, de Champlain had gained final confirmation that Mahone Bay in Acadia, New France, was where the Portuguese had relocated the Temple treasure, and Isaac de Razilly, Lieutenant-General for New France and a prominent member of the Order of St John (short for Order of the Hospital of St John of Jerusalem, better known as the Hospitallers, and operating today as the Sovereign Order of Malta), had backed this up after de Champlain's death. Then, in 1670, Jean Richer and Giovanni Cassini at the Royal Observatory pinpointed the exact location of the hidden menorah on Oak Island, extremely precisely.

At the beginning of the 18th century, French Acadia began to come under intense pressure from the British, to the extent that the settlers must have realized the menorah was no longer safe on Oak Island—a location that was almost impossible to defend. We estimate that the menorah was retrieved and transported to Louisbourg sometime in the early 1720s, where it was secretly deposited in the cross-shaped tunnels under the main fort. Incidentally, in the 1720s the the central axis of the giant menorah was extended towards New Orleans, indicating that something significant happened around that time.

When the fortress fell suddenly to the British, they did not discover the tunnels that ran below the structure, and they had no idea that the menorah was right below their feet. Against all the odds, the menorah remained hidden.

When, after Anson and Pelham's intervention, the British handed Louisbourg back to the French, they ensured that the menorah stayed in Acadia. The handful of individuals who secretly knew of the menorah's location—an international collection of the world's most powerful men and women—and were working behind the scenes to keep its existence classified, had gained more time and the menorah was once again safe, for then at least.

We realized that this curious episode in history deserved closer examination, so we turned first to Anson, whose meeting with Louis XV had apparently led to the signing of the Treaty of Aix-la-Chapelle, and the return of Louisbourg by the British to the French.

The Ansons and Shugborough Hall

On returning home to Shugborough Hall in August 1748 after the negotiations in France, Anson immediately employed the services of architect Thomas Wright and Flemish sculptor Peter Scheemakers the Younger. Anson was keen to create his own paradise in the grounds of his estate, which he envisaged as a small, idealized version of Elysium or Arcadia set in the pretty vale of the River Trent, and he commissioned multiple follies and monuments to be constructed, many of which emulated the architecture of ancient Greece.

The most memorable result of Scheemakers' commission was the construction of a stone folly in the grounds of Anson's mansion known as the *Shepherd's Monument*. This feature resembles a stone portico with Doric columns. Between these is set a finely sculptured marble relief that, in fact, is a mirrored copy in stone of Poussin's second version of his painting, *The Shepherds of Arcadia II*—the same painting that had brought the two of us together on Oak Island at the beginning of our adventure. The exact same imagery is present on the stone panel, so we find the shepherdess, the three men, and the tomb with the inscription "*Et in Arcadia ego.*" The relief is set in an arch, which provides the illusion of a grotto or the entrance to a cave.

This folly has attracted notoriety in more recent years after being featured in a book by Michael Baigent, Richard Leigh, and Henry Lincoln entitled *The Holy Blood and the Holy Grail* (Delacorte Press, 1982), in which the authors suggest that Poussin was a member of the Priory of Sion and included secret codes in his paintings. Since the book brought the *Shepherd's Monument* to the public's attention, numerous theories have been proposed, most of which center on a stone plaque that sits below the main carved relief of the shepherds and so on. The plaque features a ten-letter inscription in two lines: "O.U.O.S.V.A.V.V" and "D." and "M." on the line below with a large space between them. Various attempts have been made to decode this inscription over the years, some more plausible than others, but a conclusive solution has not yet been found.

The Shepherds of Arcadia became a significant and perennial theme in the life of Thomas Anson and his family. In September 1750, his sister-in-law Lady Elizabeth Anson, married to his brother, Admiral George Anson, wrote to Thomas about "a very material discovery," leading her to prolong her stay with him (her husband stayed too). In further correspondence with Thomas, Elizabeth addressed him as "my shepherd." A year later, she bought an original sketch of Poussin's first version of the painting, *The Shepherds of Arcadia I*, from Jonathan Richardson, a collector (see Chapter 17). She had a picture of herself painted with this image in the very same year. It was a portrait by Thomas Hudson in which she is holding the sketch in her hand, like a scroll. The original Poussin painting was acquired by William Cavendish, 4th Duke of Devonshire, a close friend of the Anson family, and it remains in the family's possession to this day. All these events seem to have been triggered by Thomas Anson's visit to Versailles, when he was negotiating the Treaty of Aix-la-Chapelle in the very room where Poussin's *The Shepherds of Arcadia II* hung.

The first known reference to the Scheemakers' *Shepherd's Monument* panel was made in a letter from Lady Anson in September 1756, but historical researcher Andrew Baker puts forward a convincing case that it was probably completed as early as 1750.[8] If that date is correct, then it looks as though the signing of the Treaty of Aix-la-Chapelle was the impetus for the commissioning of the panel, and the recreation of Poussin's *The Shepherds of Arcadia II* was a celebration of ensuring the continued safety of the menorah.

Lady Elizabeth Anson died in 1760 and some have suggested that the *Shepherd's Monument* was then dedicated to her, perhaps with the stone plaque and mysterious inscription added after her death. In this instance, the monument becomes not the shepherd's monument, but the shepherdess'. According to James Stevens Curl:

A friend of Anson, William Bagot (1728–98) of Blithfield Hall, not far away from Shugborough, mentioned (1772) how nature pours:

Profuse her verdure & her flowers,
Her earliest, freshest bloom,
Embroidering all the hallow'd ground
With blue-bells, daisies, violets, round
Your shepherdesses tomb![9]

Lady Anson and her brother-in-law Thomas were known to have had a very deep friendship, and she would regularly stay at Shugborough while her husband was away on naval duties for extended periods. Thomas and Elizabeth shared many interests, and traveled together.[10] Some have suggested that there was a romantic connection between the two. Thomas himself never married and, instead, seems to have been devoted to Lady Anson, whether this was platonic or otherwise. As we have already seen, he apparently became an MP solely to impress her.

There is another painting of Lady Anson at Shugborough Hall, this time completed by John Vanderbank, that depicts her dressed as a shepherdess. This image seems to highlight the pair's fascination with the Poussin image, and it points to an undercurrent that ran through both their lives. In an undated letter from Lady Anson to Thomas, there is also a curious allusion to the two of them role-playing beside the River Sow, which ran through the estate at Shugborough, with Thomas dressed as a shepherd and her as a shepherdess. The text of the letter is in French, but translates as:

> Kind Shepherd . . . Delightful rivers . . . happy moments . . . days filled with gold and silk . . . flowered valleys . . . shadowy hills . . . clear and undulating waters . . . and above all Shepherds and Shepherdesses.[11]

Their fascination with both versions of Poussin's *The Shepherds of Arcadia* seems to allude to a shared, hidden secret. To add to this air of mystery, unfortunately, Thomas Anson destroyed most of his own correspondence shortly before his death, so we will perhaps never know conclusively what secrets he took to his grave and precisely what role he played in securing the menorah.

Baker leaves us with this tantalizing glimpse of the man who made the Treaty of Aix-la-Chapelle possible:

> Thomas Anson seems to have been a man of modesty and secrecy. No-one could have been more self-effacing. Very few documents in his own writing are known to exist. The only substantial collection of his letters that survive are to his brother George, now held in the British Library. Those letters are mostly about politics and business, although they do contain evidence of some very dramatic incidents. There are few allusions to anything artistic, or about the development of the house and gardens. There are no extant estate management records from Thomas's lifetime.[12]

Anson seems to have been a master of remaining invisible and unremarkable, while at the same time steering momentous events from behind the scenes.

The menorah and *Le Grand Esprit*

On the evening of October 17, 1750, two years after Louisbourg had been returned into French hands, the ship *Le Grand Esprit*, which means the great universal spiritual force, docked in its harbor. The vessel was owned by Michel Rodrigue of La Rochelle, a man who worked directly for King Louis XV. Rodrigue was the only ship owner to directly recruit and train his own men for his vessels and ventures, leading to him having a reputation for being a very reliable partner and contractor. *Le Grand Esprit* was captained by one Etienne Coindet, also from La Rochelle.

We believe that the *Le Grand Esprit* was in Louisbourg for one reason alone: to retrieve the menorah and other Temple treasures that had been stored in the underground tunnels below the fortress and move them somewhere safer. Louisbourg was in a precarious position and the French must have known that they might not be given a second chance. It was a miracle that the British had not discovered the secret tunnels and hiding place when they had occupied the fortress then razed it to the ground. The time had presented itself to secure the treasures and carry them safely out of harm's way. As it turned out, this move was fortuitous, because, only a few years later, in July 1758, Louisbourg fell once again to the British and the French did not regain control that time. However, Louisbourg had served its purpose, it had kept the menorah and the treasures safe. The question we now had to consider was where *Le Grand Esprit* headed next with its precious cargo.

The Oak Island Money Pit

Based on carbon dating of the wood found deep in the Money Pit on Oak Island, it is now generally assumed that this curious feature was constructed sometime in the 1750s. This raised some intriguing questions for us. Did the French attempt to create a remote hiding place for the menorah, somewhere the treasure could reside safely, away from prying eyes, after Louisbourg became too precarious a repository?

It is our understanding that the menorah had already been on Oak Island in the past, probably hidden in the structures that have since been found in the swamp, after it was brought there from Tomar by the Portuguese remnants of the Knights Templar, the Order of Christ. It seems to have rested on Oak Island for many years before the menorah was later moved to Louisbourg. Did the French turn once again to this island once the *Le Grand Esprit*'s crew had rescued it from Louisbourg and is that when and why the Money Pit was first constructed?

The Money Pit has baffled treasure hunters for more than 200 years and a full understanding of this mysterious feature still eludes us to this day, which shows how well it was built. So, it seems a perfect hiding place for something as precious as the menorah and the treasures of Jerusalem.

The French had believed Louisbourg to be the strongest fortification in the whole of the New World, and they obviously believed that the menorah and other treasures would be safe there. As we have seen, that trust was seriously misplaced, but fortunately for the French, the miscalculation did not come back to haunt them and they retained possession of the menorah, against all the odds.

It seemed obvious to us that the menorah was then headed back to Oak Island and the newly constructed Money Pit, but a chance discovery we made next would highlight just how wrong that assumption was. The menorah was destined for somewhere much grander.

CHAPTER 20
HENRY PELHAM AND THE LOST MENORAH

On March 6, 1754, the British prime minister, Henry Pelham, died unexpectedly. Today, he is probably the least well known of all the British prime ministers, but is there more to his story than appears to be the case at first glance? We believe that he took a great secret to his grave and he should, in fact, be celebrated for his part in a great historical drama.

While impossible to prove, because of a lack of documents from the time, there is more than a hint that Pelham was an honorary, silent member of the Order of the Holy Spirit (along with Thomas Anson, see Chapter 19)—the secret supranational organization tasked with protecting the menorah and other treasures from Solomon's Temple. Pelham had been a high-ranking Freemason, assuming the mantle of Grand Master of the Grand Lodge of England, and he moved in rarefied social and political circles. We were also acutely aware that Pelham was a descendant of Sir John Pelham, the knight who had captured Jean II of France at Poitiers in 1356 alongside Edward Despenser, who we mentioned in Chapter 16 is depicted next to a life-size menorah in the *Tewkesbury Book of Founders and Benefactors*.

After Pelham's death, a memorial was erected in the gardens of his house—Esher Place, in Surrey, near London—featuring three sculpted panels and a dedication by his private secretary, John Roberts (see Figure 14). Pelham's memorial is—like the man himself—mostly forgotten, one of hundreds of similar monuments dotted throughout the UK. However, there is one feature of Pelham's memorial that made us sit up and pay attention.

Unbelievably, one of the sculpted panels features a copy of Poussin's painting *The Shepherds of Arcadia II*. Our curiosity was piqued even further when we discovered that the monument had been sculpted by the very same artist who had created the *Shepherds Monument* for Thomas Anson at Shugborough Hall—Peter Scheemakers the Younger from Flanders (see Chapter 19).

Figure 14 Prime Minister Henry Pelham and his private secretary, John Roberts by
John Shackleton, after Richard Houston, *c.*1752 (©National Portrait Gallery)

By now we were very familiar with this artist's work, having studied the themes
he wove into the *Shepherd's Monument*. As discussed, Anson was not only a
contemporary of Pelham's, but Pelham had also personally approved Anson's
mission to France to secure the Treaty of Aix-la-Chapelle. So, for both men to
have a sculpted copy of Poussin's famous scene in the gardens of their estates felt
extremely significant.

The *Shepherd's Monument* at Shugborough Hall is not the only work by
Scheemakers that has courted controversy and spawned conspiracy theories. The
artist was also responsible for the *Shakespeare Monument*, installed in Poet's Corner
in Westminster Abbey in 1741. Shakespeare can be seen very clearly pointing to
a line from his play *The Tempest*, highlighting in particular the words, "solemn
temples." Researchers have since made much of this, suggesting that the line refers
to Solomon's Temple in Jerusalem.

If Scheemakers had a history of concealing such hidden meaning in his
sculptures, was there anything to be found in the monument he carved for Pelham?

Pelham acquired Esher Place in Surrey in 1729, and he hired William Kent to make significant renovations to the property, with the aim of turning the estate into his country retreat, somewhere to escape the bustle of London in the summer. There had been a house on that spot as early as the 13th century, but since then Esher Place had had quite a history. At one point, it was owned by the famous Cardinal Wolsey, who was the Archbishop of York and chief minister of Henry VIII in the 16th century, but later was held there under house arrest after he fell out of favor with the King because he was unable to achieve an annulment of Henry's marriage to Catherine of Aragon. Esher Place is only 3 miles (5 km) from the more famous Hampton Court, a palace that Wolsey was responsible for renovating, and he moved into Esher Place specifically so he could oversee the works being carried out at Hampton Court. In the end, Wolsey had to content himself with Esher Place, as he reluctantly handed over Hampton Court to Henry in an attempt to deflect the King's wrath. As an interesting aside, Wolsey originally acquired what would become Hampton Court from the Order of St John of Jerusalem, otherwise known as the Hospitallers.

Pelham's original house has since been demolished and all that remains is Waynflete's Tower, a grand, much earlier gatehouse that Pelham altered significantly. Some of the foundations of Pelham's house, along with other remnants from the grounds, can still be seen and are accessible to the public. The house during Pelham's tenure had elaborate gardens that featured a fashionable Chinese bridge, a temple, and a grotto. The latter is the only structure from his time that has survived to the present day, aside from one other key monument—the aforementioned memorial to Henry Pelham, which is tucked away in a stand of trees, up against a hedge along the boundary with the neighboring property.

What we discovered when we inspected the details of the memorial closely might make this seemingly neglected tribute to an almost forgotten former prime minister one of the most significant monuments in the whole of the UK.

Standing some 10 feet (3 m) tall, the memorial consists of a square pedestal supporting a large urn. There are three sculpted panels with Latin inscriptions and the front panel contains a dedication. Some of the inscriptions are today quite weathered and indistinct in places, but, fortunately for us, they were recorded in Edward Wedlake Brayley's *A Topographical History of Surrey* (Robert Best Ede and Tilt & Bogue, 1848, five volumes).

When we first began delving into the history of Esher Place and Pelham's memorial, we were unable to visit the UK together, so, keen to push on with our research, we contracted a local photographer to visit it for us. We asked him to shoot a series of photos of the estate and the monument because we had found that very few clear photographs of the memorial existed.

The results did not disappoint. As we scrolled through the images the photographer sent over, the memorial revealed itself to us in glorious HD. The sculpted stone panels were crystal clear and perfectly legible. We knew that, up until this point, very few people were aware that there was a *second* sculpted monument in the UK featuring Poussin's *The Shepherds of Arcadia II*. Most have only heard of the enigmatic monument at Shugborough Hall, so it was thrilling to see the photos from Esher Place.

The first thing the images confirmed was that, just as at Shugborough Hall, Poussin's famous scene was shown as a mirror image of the original painting. Looking more closely at the photos, we then studied the main dedication:

Henrico Pelham patrono svo optimo semperqve eonorato Beneficiorvm; grata vt decvit recordatione posvit. I. R.

As is often the case with engraved Latin phrases, the letter "V" has been substituted for the letter "U," so in English this is:

Henry Pelham, most excellent patron, ever honoured for his kindness.
Grateful for a suitable remembrance place. John Roberts.

John Roberts was a politician and a close friend of Henry Pelham's, becoming his personal secretary when Pelham was prime minister. At first glance this dedication seemed nothing more than a touching statement written by a friend and colleague. However, that name, John Roberts, would not leave us in peace and it niggled away at us.

The reason for this was that we had encountered John Roberts before: and he has his own memorial in Westminster Abbey. This seems an incredible honor for an individual who was merely a secretary, especially one employed by someone who is considered to have been a rather dull prime minister. What is more striking is that Roberts' memorial is situated in a prominent, central location of the famous Poets' Corner. In fact, part of Geoffrey Chaucer's tomb—his arms—had to be removed to make way for Roberts' monument. Chaucer is considered to be the father of English literature. Additionally, medieval arcading in the abbey was cut through to make room for the sculpted white marble panel dedicated to Roberts.[1]

Clearly, something of great significance must have occurred for such sacrifices to have been made to install a memorial dedicated to this seemingly insignificant secretary. So, we looked again at the memorial in Westminster Abbey, eager to unravel the mystery behind this event.

At the top of Roberts' memorial, depicted in bas-relief, is a seated woman holding a scroll. She is staring at a monument that looked very familiar to us: a large urn set on a square pedestal, exactly like Pelham's monument at Esher Place. To the right of the woman there is a nautical telescope, a mask, and a map, while on the left is what appears to be the stump of a sawn-down tree. The scene left us with more questions than answers.

We discovered that, while working for Henry Pelham, Roberts was often charged with paying the then Prime Minister's secret agents. Roberts had clearly been much more than a simple clerk and administrator. That there is a monument to him in such a prestigious location in Westminster Abbey no less, surrounded by some of the UK's greatest and most well-known individuals, was clear evidence that there was more to Roberts' story than had registered in the history books. To add to the intrigue, we had traced a copy of Pelham's will and noticed that it had first been drawn up in September 1748, not long before the Treaty of Aix-la-Chapelle was signed. John Roberts and Richard Arundell were the designated executors. Once again, we began to question just what secrets Pelham, Anson, and Roberts had been privy to.

To try to solve this riddle, we returned to Pelham's own memorial at Esher Place. On the back panel of the pedestal, a woman is depicted in mourning, with her head resting on her hand. She is leaning on a memorial that we suspected was meant to represent the very memorial we were looking at, with the exact same pedestal supporting an urn. We suddenly noticed that the scene was composed around a triangle of 60, 30, and 90 degrees, the SLMN, or Solomon triangle, we had already encountered several times on our journey (see Chapter 7).

Such a find made us wonder if this monument contained clues that might point to the location of Solomon's treasure and the menorah. Just as on Roberts' memorial in Westminster Abbey, the woman depicted at Esher Place is holding a scroll. The pedestal bears an inscription but unfortunately we were unable to decipher it.

Now it was time to turn to the star witness: the Poussin panel on Pelham's memorial. The scene is configured so it is exactly the same as *The Shepherds of Arcadia II* painting, except for the obvious difference, which is that Scheemakers mirrored the entire scene. Incidentally, this alteration means that Venus now moves from right to left or, more accurately, from east to west, matching how she moves through the sky at night. This seemed a rather poetic change.

The shepherds are pointing at the center of the tomb, just as in the original painting, but the famous "*Et in Arcadia ego*" inscription is missing, presumably because the letters would have been too small to carve properly. Instead, there is a Latin inscription around the scene, which we recognized as a famous line written by Roman lyric poet, Quintus Horatius Flaccus (commonly known as Horace), taken from *Ode* 1.24 (again with the letter "v" rather than "u" in a couple of places):

desiderio nèc pvdor aut modvs

This means "grief has no shame nor limit," which, clearly, is a suitably moving text for a memorial. However, both of us had been Classics students, so we spotted a glaring error or, perhaps more likely, an alteration that had been made to the text.

We had been taught to recite this work by Horace worded as, "*desiderio SIT pudor aut modus.*" We double checked and, sure enough, every version of the poem that we could find clearly contained the word "*sit*" in place of the word "*nec*" that is on the memorial. These words, in fact, mean the same thing, which is "nor" in English. That being the case, why had the wording been changed for this memorial, especially when it is such a famous phrase and considered by scholars to be a perfect classical text?

We were puzzled by this strange and seemingly unnecessary substitution, but decided to come back to this conundrum later. We turned our attention instead to the next panel of the monument.

The next side of the square pedestal depicts a man standing in a boat, clutching what at first glance appears to be an oar. To his left there is a figure we recognized as Hermes—his identity revealed by the staff that he holds, as it is encircled by two snakes. This staff, known as a caduceus, is the symbol for Hermes, the eternal guide of the dead, called a "psychopomp," and he is possibly the most famous one in ancient mythology.

Both of us agreed that the man in the boat was Charon, the mythological boatman who ferries the deceased across the water to the underworld. To his right, there are two more figures. One looked to be a man, presumably supposed to represent the deceased, and he is saying goodbye to a female figure, who we recognized as the same woman we had seen on the other side of the monument, mourning by the urn.

We were now certain that this woman was none other than Henry Pelham's wife, Catherine Manners. This panel also contained an inscription from Horace (*Ode* 2.14), but this time the original text was unchanged:

linquenda tellus et domus et placens uxor

It means, "leaving earth, house, and pleasing wife," a statement that marries up perfectly with the scene on the panel.

However, on closer inspection, we did spot one oddity in the scene. Charon's oar looked very curious and the more we stared at it, the less it looked like a paddle. To our eyes, it more closely resembled a shovel. Was this a hint that something had been buried, something other than the deceased? Just as on the Poussin panel, we felt that there was also some underlying geometry hidden in the structure of the composition. Hermes' staff, or caduceus, appeared to be placed at a perfect 60-degree angle. Something about the way it was depicted also reminded us of the menorah.

We noticed that the inscriptions around the panel were not evenly distributed. They had been added to separate rectangular stone slabs that had then been fitted around the main scene, looking as though they could be repositioned. We cast our minds back to Poussin and recalled how he had laid out his painting—the original image on which this scene, sculpted on Pelham's memorial, was based. Poussin had first constructed a pentagram to give the structure for his composition—the pentagram extending partially beyond the frame—and then the figures in the scene within the frame were carefully aligned with the lines of that geometric construct. The question we had to ask ourselves was: did Scheemakers use a similar technique before sculpting this relief?

We therefore drew a pentagram over our photo of the relief, centering it on the caduceus. We suddenly noticed how the lines of the pentagram rested on and highlighted certain letters of the inscription around the outside of the central panel.

Then the magic happened and the mystery hidden in the relief for all those years revealed itself. As we rotated and adjusted the size of the pentagram, we happened on a placement that meant Charon, Hermes, and Pelham were all present within an inner pentagon, while the lines of the pentagram outside the panel crossed six letters, which spelled out the word "menora." The letters were also in the right order, beginning with the "m" in *"domus"* (house). We were stunned. Could this have been intentional? It was an unconventional spelling of menorah—the Latin for it, without the "h"—but that seemed fitting because all the text on the memorial is in Latin.

It would be accurate to say that this discovery of the word in the inscription rocked us.

We circled back to the Poussin panel, overlaying our pentagram once again, and we almost couldn't believe what happened next. If we positioned the pentagram in an almost identical, but mirrored position to the one on the panel with Charon, Hermes, and Pelham, it again hit the letters that spell "menora" (see Figure 15). Furthermore, they occurred in exactly the right order, just as they had on the preceding panel.

This explained why Horace's text had been altered, why the original word *"sit"* had been replaced with *"nec."* The letter "n" was needed for the word "menora."

We were shell-shocked. This could not be a coincidence, we realized. The chances of finding a Latin inscription that concealed the word "menora" on not one but two panels of the same monument were incredibly small. When you took into account that the letters are in exactly the right order, and found by using an underlying pentagram, there was only one conclusion we could make: this had been done deliberately and was designed to conceal a great secret.

Having stumbled on this revelation and seeing the word "menora" appear before us, we knew we were now very close to fully decoding the puzzle and discovering the secret that had remained hidden in the gardens all these years. We thought, the solution had to be somewhere on these four panels of Pelham's memorial.

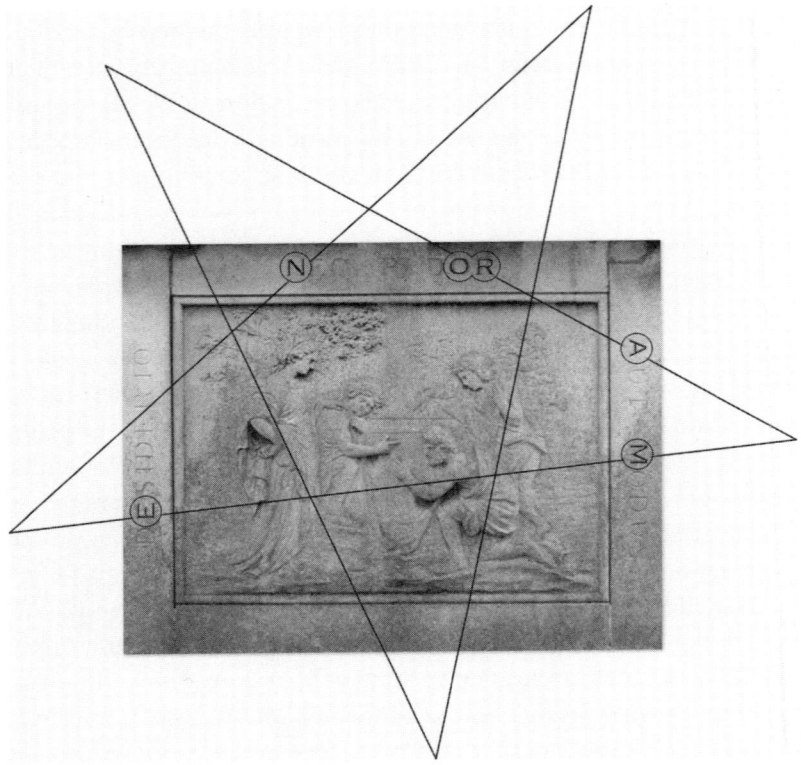

Figure 15 The pentagram indicating the letters to spell "menora" from the inscription on the Poussin panel on Henry Pelham's memorial (Corjan Mol and Christopher Morford)

We knew that in Poussin's original *The Shepherds of Arcadia II* painting, there had been further messages hidden in it, layers of meaning that only became apparent after subsequent investigation. Could that also be the case with Scheemakers' Pelham memorial?

Because the word "*nec*" had been deliberately introduced into the inscription, we began to wonder if it also contained an anagram. Had they needed an "n" to form part of the word "menorah," then perhaps thought to make it part of a longer hidden anagram.

We started with what we already knew, that "*desiderio nec pvdor aut modvs*" contained the word "menora." We experimented with the rest of the sentence until we finally struck gold. The letters could be rearranged into "*vos deduco id menora perditus.*" When we translated this into English, the full meaning was revealed:

I lead you to the lost menora.

There it was; confirmation that we were on the right path. The memorial itself was telling us that our search had not been in vain. The clues were all there: the hidden word "menora," spelled out twice, along with the pentagrams we had found. The memorial held the answers and pointed the way.

We were beyond excited and convinced that we were the first people since 1754 to decipher Pelham's memorial. We were one step closer to rediscovering the lost menorah of Jerusalem.

We quickly looked at the other inscriptions on the monument, eager to find more anagrams. We had no luck on the Charon panel, unable to arrive at any Latin phrases that made much sense, so we moved on to the panel with the mourning Lady Pelham. This was the panel where we had already spotted the Solomon triangle, so we had high hopes that we might find something there.

The inscription was too weathered to fully make out, but Edward Brayley's book saved the day. In it, the inscription had been meticulously transcribed as "*debita spargens lacryma favillam*," which means "shed a tear on the still warm ashes." That meant, once again, we were looking at a passage from Horace's *Odes*—2.6 on this occasion. What was even more encouraging was the discovery that, yet again, the text had been altered.

In the original text the phrase "*sparges lacrima*" was used, but on the memorial an "n" has been added to "*sparges*" and a "y" used in the place of the "i" in "*lacrima*" (which means "tears"), resulting in "*spargens lacryma*." There are very few words in Latin that contain the letter "y," so this addition was intriguing. We instantly thought of one that did, and that word is "crypt," so we took a guess that this might be the first hidden word and used it as our starting point. Ah hour later, we discovered the true message concealed in the anagram and were astonished to find that it revealed a location we knew only too well. The newly assembled sentence read:

ab cryptam fana Migdal Versailles

which means:

In the crypt of the Migdal Temple at Versailles.

This was more than we could have hoped for and it justified our long search for the menorah, which had included several visits to Versailles. Now Pelham's memorial gave us two messages that, when put together, declared:

I lead you to the lost menora. In the crypt of the Migdal Temple at Versailles.

At first we thought that maybe this was a reference to the giant menorah that we had already discovered woven into the landscape of Versailles, the palace where the Sun King Louis XIV of France had built the largest royal estate on the planet. That grand menorah pointed to Nova Scotia and Oak Island, and Pelham seemed to have played a significant role in protecting the menorah and handing Louisbourg back to the French. However, reading the message on Pelham's memorial once again, we realized that this was not what the decoded inscription was referring to. Instead, we were being directed to somewhere very specific at Versailles: in the crypt of the Migdal Temple.

Back to Versailles

To check this and solve the riddle, we knew that we needed to return to Versailles, so a hastily arranged trip was organized. We met at the entrance to Versailles and made our way in. Sitting in the grounds, we focused on decoding the message we had revealed, turning our attention first to the word "crypt" in the anagram. We remembered that there had once been a "crypta" at Versailles, forming part of the fabled Grotto of Thetis, but it had been demolished not long after it was constructed, to be replaced by Louis XIV's new royal chapel, the building that aligns precisely with the spine of Nolan's Cross on Oak Island. Could the message from Pelham's memorial have been pointing to this location?

To answer that question satisfactorily we knew we had to solve the other clue—the word "Migdal." We had encountered this term before and knew that it was a Hebrew word meaning "tower." There are still several Migdals in Israel, one of which, Migdal Eder, is mentioned in the book of Genesis (35.21). There is also a modern town called Migdal on the Sea of Galilee in northern Israel, which is said to have been constructed on the ancient site of Magdala, a settlement founded between the 2nd and 1st centuries BC that, it is claimed, was the birthplace of Mary Magdalene. It is also the site of the oldest synagogue in Galilee, which was home to what is called the "Magdala Stone" —a carved stone featuring a relief of the menorah from the time of Jesus.[2] Was there a Migdal Temple at Versailles, or something that resembled one, or was the use of this word a reference to Mary Magdalene herself?

There are very few references to Mary Magdalene to be found at Versailles. There is a small painting of her in a medallion over Louis XIV's bed, but very little else. Reluctantly, we ruled out a connection with Mary Magdalene.

Instead, we turned to the literal meaning of the word "Migdal," which is "tower." However, here, too, we drew a blank. Despite Versailles being known as a château— French for "castle"—there is not a single tower. Louis XIV simply did not like them and decided not to use this architectural feature anywhere at Versailles.

The first tower we found was on a sculpted panel in the palace that was commissioned by Louis XV in 1733 to commemorate his famous predecessor. Nicolas and Guillaume Coustou created the panel, which featured Louis XIV crossing the Rhine, and you may recall that it was something we had investigated on a previous visit to Versailles (see Chapter 17). This is the artwork that contains a life-size image of the mythical River God, Alpheus, exactly like that present in Poussin's *The Shepherds of Arcadia I* and *Midas Washing at the Source of the Pactolus*. On the panel at Versailles, Louis XIV himself is shown dressed as a Roman emperor and the King is pointing across the water at a burning tower or Migdal. This is significant because a burning tower is sometimes used as an allegory for the demise of the Templars.[3]

This symbolic image is all the more significant because today the panel can be found at the entrance to the royal chapel at Versailles, placed there by King Louis-Philippe I in 1840. Louis XIV, the subject of the scene, was the king who had embedded the pattern of the giant menorah in the landscape of Versailles and, because this very chapel where the panel is displayed is itself perfectly aligned with Oak Island, the King, therefore, is pointing directly to Acadia in the East, or, more specifically, to the spine of Nolan's Cross on the island. We asked ourselves, had there had been a tower on Oak Island once, and was this the Migdal that was being shown across the water, that water being the Atlantic Ocean? As intriguing as this question was, it didn't help us in our quest to locate the Migdal Temple at Versailles.

We continued our search at Versailles and found another tower in a painting of Louis XIV's immediate successor, the king regent Philippe II of Orléans, who had ruled France during Louis XV's childhood. In fact, we found an identical small tower in the background of two of his portraits. We remembered that Louis XV had personally searched for paintings to adorn the new Cathedral of Versailles that he was building, so, perhaps he had been looking for this exact symbolism?

It is not widely known that, in fact, Louis built two cathedrals, not one. The Cathedral of Saint-Louis of Versailles has an identically named sister cathedral, designed and built at exactly the same time, by the same group of people, utilizing a shared budget.[4] Initially, both buildings were to be built by a single architect, but at the last moment Louis decided instead to employ two separate architects, deeming the projects too important to fall under the responsibility of one man. The foundations for both cathedrals were begun in May 1742 and the sister cathedral stands in a location that has a very familiar name: La Rochelle, at a spot indicated by the sacro pentagram itself, aligned with the very heart of Chartres.

The first three chapels of the cathedral at La Rochelle are adorned with the tombstones for Knights Templar, excavated from the site of the former Templars church there. The cathedral also features a stained-glass window with an image of a ship and Christ being carried across the water in a boat. In one of the many dizzying connections we kept encountering, we learned that the entrance to each of these new cathedrals had been modeled on the facade of the Church of Saint-Roch.

In 1749, at the time Louisbourg was returned to the French and secured once again, Louis XV purchased a painting by Rubens from 1619 and it was the King's intention to place this image in pride of place above the altar of his new cathedral. This painting features Christ on the cross, the Virgin Mary, Mary Magdalene, and John.[5]

Louis' interest in the painting encouraged us to take a closer look at it. Much to our surprise, at the left edge of the painting is a tower like the one in the painting of Philippe II of Orléans, as well as the sculpted panel of Louis XIV. Intriguingly, in the end, the painting by Rubens was never installed in the chapel at the cathedral and Louis instead commissioned a new artwork by Collin de Vermont entitled *La Presentation de la Vierge au Temple*, and it was this painting that was finally hung over the altar of the Virgin.[6]

Was Louis making a statement with this last-minute change of heart? By using this painting was he declaring that his cathedral at Versailles was a *temple*? If so, was *this* the temple mentioned in the message from Pelham's memorial? It was possible, but we still had to identify and locate the Migdal.

We decided that we needed to investigate further and walk over to the cathedral, but first we had to visit one more feature: a statue in the gardens, positioned close by the giant menorah so carefully hidden in the landscape at Versailles. We made our way down the axis, walking in the direction of Oak Island, until we finally arrived at the sculpture. It is of a sleeping Ariadne, the mistress of the labyrinth whose twisting, weaving thread we had been following throughout our adventure. This sculpture was commissioned by Louis XIV himself and is a copy of the famous 2nd-century BC Roman statue *Sleeping Ariadne* that today can be found in the Vatican Museum. This was also the exact same image that Poussin recreated in wax and carried on his person for years (see Chapter 17).

When you stand in front of this version of Ariadne, you have the Cathedral of Saint-Louis directly in the background. Lifting our gaze from the sleeping goddess for a moment, it was then that we spotted the final clue that had been eluding us. Towards the rear of the cathedral stands a steep spire, and on top of this there is a small tower. Could this be our Migdal at last?

In answer to that question, we suddenly saw something: the tower was topped by a five-pointed star, a pentagram. Here was the final confirmation. It felt as though Ariadne had pointed the way for us. We had been following her lead for so long and, in the same way that her presence was a constant thread in our journey, so, too, was the pentagram—the ancient symbol of Jerusalem. We also could not forget the huge sacro pentagram that we had found hidden in plain sight in France, the sacred sanctuary, protector of the menorah. We knew instantly what the symbol atop the tower of the cathedral signified. The Pelham memorial told the story: "I lead you to the lost menora. In the crypt of the Migdal Temple at Versailles." The cathedral itself was that temple, identified by the Migdal above it.

We immediately hurried towards the cathedral, rushing through the gardens. It took us some 15 minutes to reach our destination and, when we entered the sacred space of the church, we found that there was not another soul inside.

We walked across the nave, past a modern altar that is set near the rear of the church. Finally, we stood in a round chapel under the very dome that supports the spire with the small tower: the Migdal and its accompanying pentagram. We stood at the center of this room, staring at the much older original altar that had been installed against the back wall. Beautifully inlaid in the marble floor before us was a five-pointed pentagram star. As above, so below.

We had been to this chapel before, when we had explored every tiny bit of Versailles for clues on our earlier visits. Back then we had not known the full significance of this place, but it meant we were aware that on the right-hand side of the chapel there is a large stone slab that seals the entrance to a subterranean vault, a gentle spiral slope leading down to an arched crypt supported by one central pillar. This crypt is part of a much larger underground space, accessible via a large rectangular slab in front of the main altar. There is an inscription on the stone that seals that section of the crypt shut, a quote from Hebrews 13.7 (NIV): "*Mementote Praepositorum Vestorum*" in Latin, which means "remember your leaders."

Here it was again, a hint that someone had been secretly directing affairs, steering the menorah safely through the squalls of history. It reminded us suddenly of the star Alkaid, hidden by Samuel de Champlain in the shape of Ursa Major on his map of 1612 and marked with the letter "R" (see Chapter 14). The meaning of the name Alkaid is "the leader." Exactly who was this hidden leader and, more importantly, had they ultimately brought us here, leading us through the maze and guiding our every step?

The presence of the quote resonated with us for another reason to. Chapter 13, verse 7 forms the number 137. We knew that 1-3-7 can be a numerological reference to the menorah—1 central stem, 3 legs, 7 arms holding oil lamps, 137.

As if to underline that we were in exactly the right spot, we noticed that there were two intertwined letters beside the inlaid pentagram star: an "A" and an "M." "*Auspice Maria*," "under the protection of Mary"—the very same phrase that was used in the logo of the Sulpicians, whose trail we had followed to Nova Scotia. If you unravel the anagram that is *auspice Maria*, you arrive at "*Apius America*." When we had first encountered this phrase, we had concluded that, via the symbolism of the serpent and the pole, it signified that knowledge of the menorah, the light, had traveled from

France to America and back again, but now the full implication of this phrase struck us. It was more literal than that.

We now knew exactly what had happened to the menorah after the ship *Le Grand Esprit*, the great universal spiritual force, had docked in the harbor of Louisbourg on the evening of October 17th, 1750. Up until this point, we had assumed that Louis XV had ordered the menorah to be moved from Louisbourg to Oak Island and the Money Pit, but we now knew that was wrong.

On August 24, 1754, almost four years after *Le Grand Esprit* left Louisbourg with a great treasure aboard, and exactly 500 years after Louis IX's arrival back in Paris after the Seventh Crusade, a new cathedral was consecrated in Versailles, a short walk away from the entrance to the palace. Building had been in full swing when Thomas Anson visited Versailles in 1748 and now it was finally finished. It was surely the most auspicious occasion for King Louis XV. Only the previous day, on August 23, a new dauphin had been born, the future Louis XVI of France. It was also the day before France commemorated the death of Louis IX, on August 25, 1270.

The King must have been anticipating this day for years. He was approaching the end of his life and had ruled France for almost 55 years, so this must have felt like his crowning achievement.

What made this moment even sweeter for Louis XV was the realization that he had almost lost the menorah when Louisbourg had been taken from the French, but it had somehow remained hidden beneath the fortress, unbeknown to the British. Despite how unlikely such a story might look to the outside world, this precious artefact had been saved for posterity—and for France—by the intervention of Thomas Anson and Henry Pelham. Now the menorah sat safely in the crypt below Louis' new cathedral, hidden once again, this time at the heart of France where it would surely be safe forever.

A month later, in September, in the Church of Saint-Roch in Paris, which featured that secret tunnel for royal visitors, a communion chapel was inaugurated at the back of the church under a giant square Templar Cross. A life-size copy of the Ark of the Covenant was unveiled to the world, with two menorahs flanking it, crafted from gilded bronze by Paul-Ambroise Sold.[7] The placement of these replicas matched the direction of the frozen stares of the busts of the royal gardener André Le Nôtre and First Painter Pierre Mignard. This was clearly an event designed to celebrate and commemorate the safe return of the treasures of Jerusalem to France.

Bringing the menorah to Versailles also neatly closed this chapter of the sacred lampstand's history. It had now resided at three points on the prime alignment that swept from Versailles to Oak Island: first Jerusalem, then Oak Island, and now Versailles. It was apparent that this had always been at the heart of the layout of Versailles, this had always been the intention. The menorah was meant to be here, this moment had been planned for centuries, and now that the menorah was in the crypt, the design was finally complete.

Standing directly above the very spot where we believed the menorah had been safely stored, we wondered if anyone would ever believe us. Would a search be initiated? Would this great treasure ever see the light of day again or would it remain deep beneath the marble flagstones of this chapel in Versailles, locked in its crypt forever?

As it turned out, we never had the chance to properly frame these questions because there was one final, unexpected twist in our quest. Even as we stood in the Cathedral of Saint-Louis , the Temple of the Migdal, location of the lost menorah, we were blissfully unaware that the menorah had made *another* journey from this spot, years before we took up our quest. We returned home from Versailles believing that it was locked in that crypt. It would be several weeks before the full truth revealed itself.

CHAPTER 21
A RETURN TO AMERICA

When we returned home from Versailles, the first thing we did was double check our Oak Island Money Pit conclusions. If we were going to present our evidence to the world and declare that the menorah was hiding in the crypt of the Cathedral of Saint-Louis of Versailles, then we needed to tie up a few loose ends. Where there was doubt there would be questions, and the Money Pit had always generated way more questions than answers.

After more than ten years of research, with armies of experts poring over the site, the consensus among the *Curse of Oak Island* team is that the original Money Pit, as found by McGinnis and his friends, had a diameter of around 12 to 13 feet (3.5 m). A reasonable question might be, why was it necessary to make it so big?

If only a person with a shovel and a few chests full of gold needed to fit inside, a hole that size sounds excessive, and it would have taken a long time to excavate. In comparison, the access tunnel to the tomb of Tutankhamen in the Valley of the Kings was only some 6½ feet high and 5½ feet wide (2 m by 1.7 m).[1] The dimensions of the tunnel were dictated by the sizes of the items that needed to be stored in the burial chambers beyond. Using that logic, the Money Pit is definitely oversized if it only accommodated the menorah, as it is said to be roughly 3 feet (1 m) wide, and still would be if it was the intended home of the rest of the Temple treasure. Therefore, the sheer size of the Money Pit would indicate that perhaps a large vault was constructed, formed of stones of a considerable size to make it secure. If so, then building it would have needed a significant construction team, which would have incurred the risk that the work might have been spotted by someone. At the very least, rumor of such a construction site might have caused ripples across Nova Scotia.

Officially, the peninsula of Acadia had been ceded to the British by the 1713 Treaty of Utrecht. However, a map from the 1700s by Captain Cyprian Southack indicates that the Mahone Bay area was inhabited by numerous French families.[2] There are no official British government documents mentioning Mahone Bay until at least 1749, a year after the Treaty of Aix-la-Chapelle was signed. It appears that, in reality, the area including Oak Island remained in French hands and there is clear evidence that the French still owned these lands.

In the end, the lengths the French went to to conceal this project were not required. As we outlined in Chapter 20, the French seem to have created the Money Pit as a safe hiding place for the menorah after Louisbourg lost its air of invulnerability, but instead of depositing the Jewish treasure on Oak Island at this time, they decided instead to return it to France and hide it beneath the Cathedral of Saint-Louis of Versailles. It would remain there for several years until events swiftly overturned even the best-laid plans of Louis XV.

This was the thread we picked up a couple of weeks after our return from Versailles. We had started to realize that a seismic shift had occurred not long after the menorah was installed in Versailles, one that meant it could not possibly have stayed in France, despite everything we had believed up to this point. It was the same pattern repeating itself again: whenever there was approaching danger, it appears that the menorah has been moved. It meant that our work was not over just yet and there was one last journey to document. So, what exactly had upended the plans of the house of Bourbon?

Despite warning signs growing throughout the late 1700s, a sudden uprising swept through France, and a violent conflagration ensured. This cataclysm reached its first peak in 1789, and the political landscape of France was radically overhauled, altering the course of French history forever. The French Revolution had arrived and nothing would ever be the same again in France.

Revolution!

Louis XV's son, Louis XVI, was King of France when the Revolution kicked off. Having been born at Versailles, he would have been acutely aware of his father's plans for the menorah. Residing at the Palace of Versailles, he regularly visited the Cathedral of Saint-Louis where the treasure was safely hidden. As he grew up and assumed power, the menorah became his responsibility.

Louis XVI may have had a deep understanding of this esoteric secret at the heart of France, but he seems to have been far less suited to managing matters of state and domestic affairs. He missed all the warning signs of the growing unrest in his kingdom and wildly underestimated the people he ruled over.

The Revolution began quietly, as dissatisfaction grew in France, but it quickly reached a flashpoint and, after the famous storming of the Bastille prison in Paris, it became unstoppable and irreversible.

The "*ancien régime*," the feudal system that had been in place in France since the Middle Ages, was suddenly no more, replaced by a new constitution based on a document known as the Declaration of the Rights of Man and of the Citizen that was drawn up by the Marquis de Lafayette with the aid of Thomas Jefferson, who later became the third president of the USA. The document shared tenets of the American Declaration of Independence of 1776 and echoed the Magna Carta, but did not rely wholly on ancient charters. Prior to this collaboration with an American, de Lafayette had himself fought in the American Revolution (also called the American War of Independence or American Revolutionary War).

Two years later, despite desperate efforts by Louis to retain approval and control, and even after initiating the disastrous French Revolutionary Wars—with French forces attacking the borders of Austria and Prussia in an effort to distract France from its own internal battles—the monarchy was suspended and Louis was taken into custody. His trial followed soon after and ended with him being sentenced to death for treason.[3] So it was that the long, uninterrupted line of the house of Bourbon as kings of France finally came to an abrupt and violent end on January 21, 1793, when Louis XVI was executed by guillotine at what is now the Place de la Concorde. Afterwards, his head was held up to the crowd as a sign of change. France would become a republic soon after and, despite a brief resurgence a few years later, the monarchy would never regain the power it had once enjoyed.

In October 1792 the Cathedral of Saint-Louis of Versailles was closed and an inventory was conducted by the new French revolutionary authorities. We know that there were still treasures housed in the building, because a relic of St Louis and a piece of the true cross are listed as being present at the time, but the menorah was not on the inventory and no trace of it was ever found.[4] The great secret seems to have been preserved at all costs and the sacred artefact appears to have been moved before the final tide swept over Versailles.

Oak Island was a British territory during this period, including the years prior to the French Revolution, and a contingent of the British navy was stationed at Lunenburg at this point, close to Oak Island. However, if our conclusion is correct and the menorah had been under the protection of a supranational order, then it was likely taken from France at the first stirrings of the French Revolution and returned in secret to its original hiding place in North America, that island where the Portuguese had first stored it after transporting it from Tomar: Oak Island.

Was this perhaps when the Money Pit was finally used for its original purpose? It had been designed to store the menorah when Louisbourg became unsafe, before that decision was then overruled, but perhaps the Money Pit's construction had not been in vain and it was finally put to use. If this is true, then it was not used for long, because there is evidence that the new American government, with its links to de Lafayette, who, as we saw earlier in this chapter, was a key player in both Louis XVI's court and the American Revolution, began immediately to plan a new, more permanent home for the menorah. The Money Pit would only ever be a temporary solution.

Washington, DC

On April 28, 1909, a mile-long funeral procession slowly worked its way from the US Capitol building in Washington, crossed the Potomac River, and headed up the hill to a grassy terrace at the top in Arlington National Cemetery. It is a site that enjoys most dramatic views of the city of Washington across the river. Originally named Mount Washington, this plot of land had been purchased by the father of George Washington Parke Custis—the adopted stepson of George Washington—in 1778. In 1803, George Washington Parke Custis began construction of a grand Greek Revival-style house on the estate, a mansion that would become known as Arlington House, the name taken from a village in Gloucestershire, UK, where the Custis family originally hailed from. Today, the house and estate form part of the Arlington National Cemetery.

The procession in question had one purpose: to move the remains of Pierre-Charles L'Enfant to a new burial plot in Arlington National Cemetery. L'Enfant, who was born in Paris but spent his adult life in America, had been the architect and city planner who designed the street plan for Washington, DC, from 1791 onward. However, despite his reputation and many successful years as an engineer and architect, he died in poverty in 1825 and ended up being buried on a rural farm in Maryland.

When L'Enfant's remains had completed their final journey in 1909, they arrived at the burial site in Arlington National Cemetery: the middle of a lawn, overlooking the city. All the gathered dignitaries stood in silence and the Reverend James Russell made a speech, highlighting the great debt that the American nation owed to the French:

> France—Catholic France—was our only ally, when we most needed friends. But for the ready financial aid with which Catholic France replenished our exhausted treasury, whereby our patriots were persuaded to keep the field, and but for the timely aid of Rochambeau and Grasse—it may well be questioned how long our independence would have been deferred.[5]

The speech was profound and those present were acutely aware of the significance of Russell's words.

In 1776, not long after the beginning of the American Revolution, France secretly began shipping supplies to the Continental Army, the national army of the first Thirteen Colonies. These colonies were attempting a separation from Great Britain, and as there was obviously no love lost between the French and the British, France sought to aid the Thirteen Colonies. In 1778 a Treaty of Alliance was signed between France and the Continental Army, formalizing this support, and troops, equipment, and, most importantly, money, flowed from France to the USA. France's aid was a key factor in winning a victory for the USA, and France racked up 1 billion livres in debt. This huge sum, in turn, led to a dramatic rift in public finances in France, which was one of the factors that brought about the birth of the French Revolution. By financing one revolution overseas, Louis XVI had caused another one at home—a conflict that eventually cost him his head.

The Reverend Russell proceeded to praise L'Enfant himself, whose body had finally been reinterred in Arlington National Cemetery:

> The City Beautiful at his feet is the proudest and most endearing monument
> we can erect to his memory. May God grant to him who planned and
> dreamed the City Beautiful before us, an abode in the new Jerusalem, the
> Celestial City Beautiful.[6]

After a moment of absolute silence, the Corps of Engineers fired three volleys from the cannons. Some 84 years after his death, L'Enfant had finally received the honor he deserved.

By referencing the term "City Beautiful," Russell emphasized that L'Enfant's plans for Washington served a higher purpose. Architecture can not only be beautiful but also serve the greater purpose of providing monumental grandeur, harmony and moral virtue to its inhabitants.[7]

L'Enfant was born in August of 1754, 21 days before the birth of the final absolute king of France, Louis XVI. In a strange twist of fate, L'Enfant also spent his childhood, or part of it, at Versailles, as he was the son of one of Louis XV's court painters. L'Enfant followed in his father's footsteps initially and studied art at the Royal Academy of Painting and Sculpture, but he left in 1776 to fight in the American Continental Army, serving alongside the Marquis de Lafayette.

During the war, L'Enfant was called on to employ his artistic talents once again when he was commissioned by de Lafayette to paint a portrait of George Washington. L'Enfant was captured after being wounded at the Second Battle of Savannah, but was released in 1780 in a prisoner exchange, after which George Washington asked L'Enfant to serve on his staff for the remainder of the war. When the war was finally won, L'Enfant set up a successful civil engineering firm in New York and gained a reputation as a renowned architect. He also became a Freemason while there, and was initiated on April 17, 1789.[8]

That same year, the American press started to ask questions of George Washington regarding the establishment of a federal district and capital for the newborn nation, as outlined in the Constitution. L'Enfant was appointed as the planner of this new federal city, a city that would be named after George Washington himself. L'Enfant began work on March 9, 1791, and by June that year he presented his first map and detailed plan to George Washington and the three commissioners who were overseeing the development of the District of Columbia. The plans were then refined and went on to shape what we now know as the US capital on the Potomac River, Washington, DC.

L'Enfant was well aware of the work of André Le Nôtre, who had laid out the gardens of Versailles, as it was there that L'Enfant had spent a happy time as a young child, alongside another boy exactly the same age. That boy became Louis XVI. Le Nôtre's influence played a large part in the plans for Washington as L'Enfant copied significant parts of the layout of Versailles and used them in the new city:[9]

[Washington, DC's layout] is most directly derived from the seventeenth-century baroque landscape architecture of the seat of the court of France, and the rise of urbanism in the eighteenth century. L'Enfant, whose father was a painter at the court of Louis XIV, spent his youth at Versailles, where he would have seen the perspectives depicted in his father's views, as well as the physical manifestation of the visual device in the imposing landscape at Versailles.[10]

If you walk east from the US Capitol building today you are essentially walking through Versailles, as the layouts for the most part are identical. However, L'Enfant added several improvements to his Washington plan.

L'Enfant's final design is incredibly significant to our story because it means that the giant menorah which can be seen laid out in the gardens of Versailles is also present in the street plan of the city of Washington. This results in two giant menorahs, one either side of the Atlantic (see Figure 16). The US Capitol building itself corresponds with Louis XIV's palace, while the central lamp of the Versailles menorah corresponds with the circular Robert F. Kennedy Memorial Stadium. The two smallest arms closest to the central lamp of the landscape menorah at Versailles were replaced by two much longer arms in Washington, extending from the Capitol along Maryland Avenue NE and Pennsylvania Avenue SE.

Regardless of these small adjustments, L'Enfant had not only rebuilt Versailles on the Pontomac but he had also brought the menorah over to America.

The Fool

We were having lunch in the food court below the entrance to the US Capitol building, by the entrance to the tunnel that leads to the Library of Congress. We had plenty to wrestle with.

Had we become wiser or were we still fools? The Fool is the first card of the tarot, the deck of cards originally designed as a game but now better known as a tool for divination and the telling of fortunes. As such, the card that represents the Fool is numbered zero. No thing. An infinite circle. When you begin a journey, you are a fool:

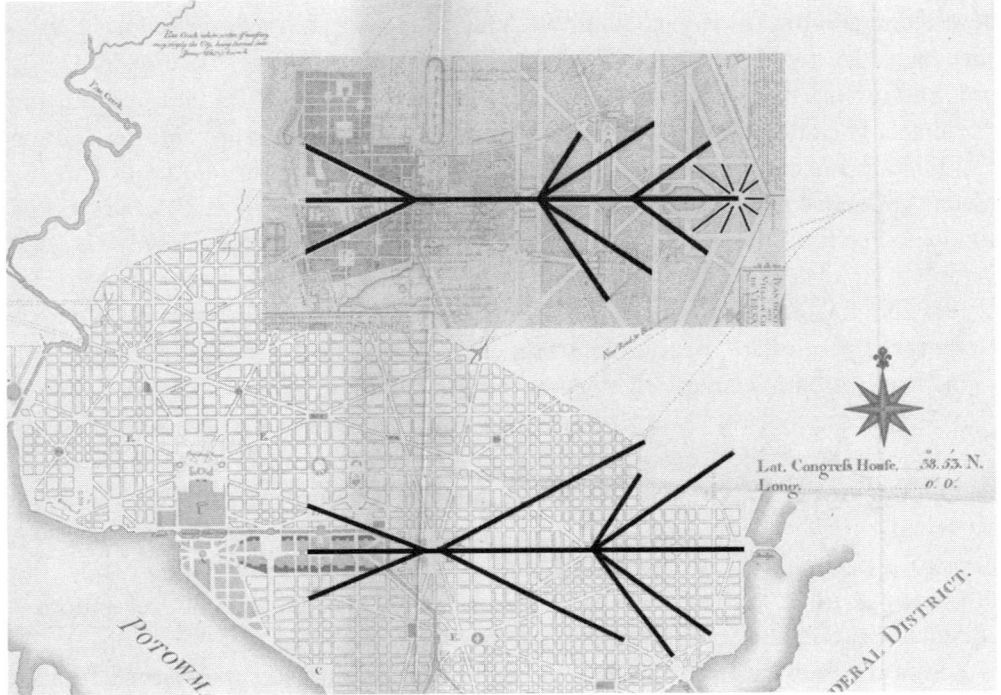

Figure 16 The Versailles menorah mirrored in the one at Washington, DC, image by Corjan Mol based on Boston Public Library Facsimile of the manuscript of Peter Charles L'Enfant's 1791 plan for the federal capital city (U.S. Coast and Geodetic Survey, 1887)

you know nothing, yet you imagine you know everything. The Fool is also the final card of the tarot, so, at the end of your journey, after all you have learned, you are still a fool, albeit a wiser one. What becomes clear is just how much you still do not know. This metaphor seemed to perfectly describe how we felt at this stage of our odyssey.

Exactly what had we uncovered? History, a conspiracy, or perhaps a chain of events that existed only in our imagination? A sequence of connected coincidences that, as we had discovered, is sometimes sarcastically labeled "pseudo-history" by people better educated than us. Despite that, we remained convinced that we had found something real—a sequence of events that lurked just below the surface of what is known as "accepted history." Furthermore, we seemed to have arrived at the crux of the whole endeavor.

While we finished our lunch, we pretended that we were instead at the Sun King's palace in France as we studied our tourist map of Washington. Clearly, the left leg of the tripod of—if we dared to name it as such—the Washington menorah began at the White House itself. There was more, however. Zooming out, we recognized a familiar shape: a giant cross of St John, the emblem of the Knights Hospitallers, heirs of the Knights Templar, extended from the White House in all four directions.

What had inspired George Washington and L'Enfant to embed these features in the final layout of the city?

The statements from L'Enfant's reinterment ceremony regarding a "new Jerusalem" seemed to give a clear message, and this was exactly what Louis XIV had endeavored to achieve with his grand plans at Versailles. Even though L'Enfant had served in the French and Continental Army, to be allocated a tomb at Arlington National Cemetery was a very rare honor for someone who, primarily, had been a civil engineer and town planner. Furthermore, prior to the reinterment and its accompanying ceremony, L'Enfant's body had lain in state in the rotunda of the US Capitol building. At the time, L'Enfant was only the eighth person to have been afforded this honor, and to this day he is the one and only foreign national to have received it. The link between George Washington, L'Enfant, the street plan of Washington, and Versailles was highlighted and underscored for all eternity by aligning L'Enfant's tomb with the central axis of the palace of Versailles.

We began to walk along L'Enfant's elegant layout, to see what other revelations it might have for us. As we walked, further avenues of research opened before us, literally. We came to New York Avenue NW, a defining diagonal alignment that formed part of the outline of the Washington cross of St John and pointed with uncanny precision to that other rotunda at the headquarters of the Knights Templar who had survived the purge of their order: the Convent of Christ in Tomar (see Figure 17).

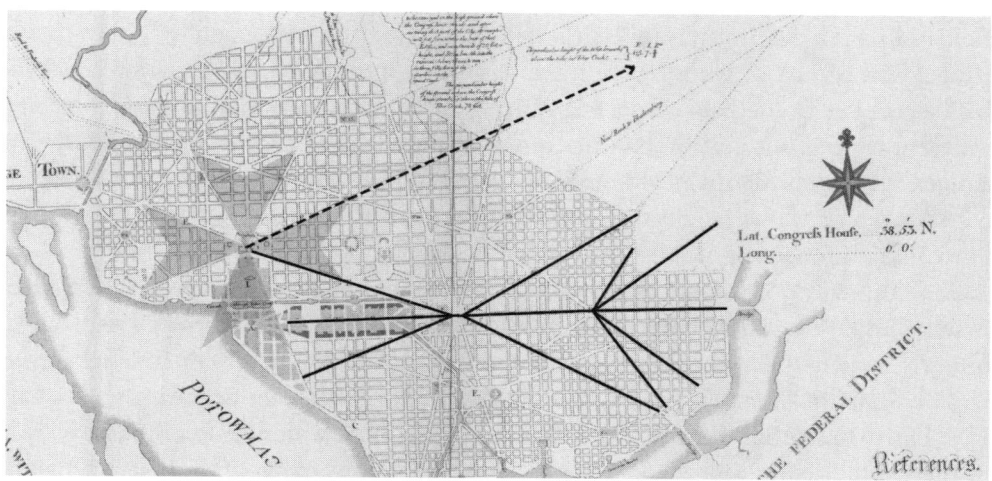

Figure 17 The Washington menorah, the cross of St John around the White House and the alignment to Tomar, image by Corjan Mol based on Boston Public Library Facsimile of the manuscript of Peter Charles L'Enfant's 1791 plan for the federal capital city (U.S. Coast andGeodetic Survey, 1887)

It was becoming clear that someone had wanted the history of the menorah etched into the landscape of the capital of the USA, as a permanent reminder of the sacrifices many had made to bring this sacred object to the New World.

A tale of two revolutions

On May 4, 1789, the Cathedral of Saint-Louis of Versailles witnessed the very start of the French Revolution and a dramatic chain of events when the Estates General was convened and met under its roof in the presence of King Louis XVI. Louis stood in front of the altar in the cathedral, right above the stone slab that concealed the entrance to the crypt below, safeguarding the menorah. The next day, the session proper took place, in a small temporary room a short distance away. Not satisfied with the speeches made by Louis and his ministers, the members of the Third Estate, which represented the people, decided to take matters into their own hands and so the Revolution began. This event was to lead to the members of the Third Estate declaring themselves the new National Assembly on June 17 and, on July 9 taking on the title National Constituent Assembly, the beginning of the new form of government for France and the end of its monarchy. Thus, that day, May 4, now seems highly symbolic because many of the people present in that vaunted space in the cathedral would send Louis to the guillotine less than four years later. It was also four days after George Washington had become the first president of the newly founded United States of America.

Two prominent Americans played a significant role on the eve of France's Revolution. Benjamin Franklin first visited Paris in 1767, where he met scientists, along with King Louis XV, all of whom were interested in his groundbreaking work, especially his discoveries in the field of electricity. In 1776, Franklin returned to Paris in a very different capacity, as a commissioner representing the newly formed United States of America. He would remain in France for some nine years, representing his fledgling country, which was still fighting for independence from the British, tirelessly working to maintain French support for the American Revolution across the ocean.

Franklin was well known to King Louis XVI when the American visited Versailles in March 1778. In 1783, Franklin witnessed the signing of his masterpiece, the Treaty of Paris, which ended the American Revolution and sealed the independence of the United States of America, finally ending the dominion of Great Britain.

It is worth noting that, in 1776, Franklin submitted a design for the Great Seal of the United States and the image he chose was Moses parting the Red Sea, while the Shekinah appeared in the sky above as a pillar of smoke and fire.[11] In the end, his design was not chosen, but this seems a clear indication to us that Franklin was aware of the larger game that was being played out behind the scenes.

Franklin was also an active Freemason during his time in France, presiding over the Lodge of the Nine Sisters in Paris, a lodge that was influential in organizing French support, established in 1776. When Franklin finally left Paris in 1785, his Masonic duties were taken over by Thomas Jefferson, who had arrived in August 1784 but primarily to take over from him as the American minister to France. Jefferson was still in Paris when the French masses stormed the Bastille on July 14, 1789, and he stayed until September of that year, witnessing the events of the French Revolution unfurl.[12] Both Franklin and Jefferson worked on the American Declaration of Independence and Jefferson became the third president of the United States in 1801.[13]

The question we had to ask ourselves was: did Franklin and Jefferson know of the menorah hidden in France?

One clue that points to them having such knowledge lies in an early design of the US dollar from 1776—a coin known as the Continental dollar, on which Franklin again included an image of the Shekinah. The second clue is a marble sculpture of *Sleeping Ariadne* obtained for Thomas Jefferson in Paris by his minister to Spain. It still resides at Jefferson's historic home, Monticello. It is a smaller version of the sculpture in the Vatican, copied for the palace at Versailles and once found in the gardens of the Villa Medici. The same mistress of the labyrinth modeled in miniature in wax and carried by Poussin. The third and much grander clue is to be found in the work of Pierre L'Enfant himself, with the embedding of the menorah in the street plan of Washington—clearly a message that the Americans were not only aware of this sacred object but also instrumental in knowing of its whereabouts and its safekeeping.

A key figure in what happened next was Louis-Philippe, of the house of Orléans, son of the Duke of Chartres. Thomas Jefferson himself witnessed a young, 16-year-old Louis-Philippe becoming a Freemason. This teenager, who had been born in the Palais Royal, which was connected to the Church of Saint-Roch by means of a secret tunnel, would grow up to become the very last king of France.

The future king traveled extensively throughout Europe before finally heading to the USA in 1796, where he showed up at several locations that readers of this book will find very familiar. After being George Washington's guest at his Mount Vernon House in April 1797, Louis-Philippe set off for New Orleans, where he attended mass at the Cathedral-Basilica of St Louis King of France, facing the large mural of King Louis IX announcing the Seventh Crusade. Louis-Philippe's next stop was Halifax in Nova Scotia, very close to Oak Island, where he befriended the Duke of Kent, son of King George III of Great Britain.[14]

After this series of adventures, it would take another 31 years for Louis-Philippe to become France's last monarch, in 1830, after the Bourbon Restoration.

In the first year of his reign, Louis-Philippe did two remarkable things. First, he changed the Order of the Holy Spirit into a dynastic order. This ensured that what had once been France's most prestigious royal chivalric order became a private order, one managed and controlled by his direct family, the house of Orléans. In doing so, he took the Order of the Holy Spirit out of the public eye, moving it into the shadows. Second, he created a new royal necropolis at Dreux. There, when the time came, he would rest for eternity, surrounded by the other members of the royal house of Orléans.[15]

Louis-Philippe also made some striking alterations to Versailles. In 1840 he moved the sculpted mural of Louis XIV crossing the Rhine to the entrance to Louis XIV's royal chapel. This was the very panel commissioned by Louis XV in 1733 that featured Louis XIV dressed in the uniform of a Roman emperor, pointing to a burning tower across the water. The sculpture also shows the River God, Alpheus, lying at Louis XIV's feet, just as in Poussin's *The Shepherds of Arcadia I* and *Midas Washing at the Source of the Pactolus*. As we outlined in Chapter 20, the burning tower or Migdal on this panel seems to replicate the small tower above the Cathedral of Saint-Louis of Versailles, and the symbolism is highly suggestive of Oak Island across the Atlantic Ocean. It is worth noting once more that a burning tower has sometimes also been used to represent the fall of the Knights Templar. Crucially, the chapel where Louis-Philippe moved this artwork to is aligned precisely with Oak Island. For us, Louis-Philippe was making grand gestures and reinforcing our belief that he knew exactly what had happened to the menorah.

Louis-Philippe's final gesture was perhaps the most telling. As with the bust of André Le Nôtre, Louis-Philippe's statue inside the Royal Chapel of Dreux is positioned with its back toward the viewer as you walk into the chapel. Louis-Philippe's eyes are fixed intently on three beautiful stained-glass windows depicting Louis IX of France, St Louis, during the Seventh Crusade, while the dove of the Holy Spirit hovers inside the dome over his head. Without saying a word, Louis-Philippe indicates with his gaze exactly what he spent his final years trying to achieve: ensuring that the legacy of the menorah lived on.

In the same way that Versailles is a grand estate that was created to represent France's ownership of the menorah, Washington, DC, was laid out to mark its transition to the safety of America, as the sacred treasure made one last journey. The caretakers of the menorah continued to use the familiar symbols that had always shrouded and protected it.

L'Enfant first wrote to George Washington to offer his services as the designer of the new capital less than two months after the storming of the Bastille in 1789—a day that still marks the official start of the French Revolution. As soon as that death knell rang out for the French monarchy, L'Enfant, and everyone else who was secretly working to secure the menorah's safety, knew that it would have to move to a new location. This is the very moment when the Money Pit was first used for its intended purpose, and the menorah was secretly moved to Nova Scotia and stored on Oak Island while preparations were being made in the District of Columbia, and the city of Washington rose from the ground.

Louis XVI must have played a key role in the transfer of the menorah from France. His family had been bound up with the story of the menorah for centuries and it is beyond comprehension that it moved without his knowledge. It would have been a hard decision but, judging that the sacred artefact would be safer in the new American Republic, a country he had himself financed and helped as it fought to gain independence, Louis would have sanctioned the move—in absolute secrecy. Louis did not live to see his plan come to fruition, but he died knowing that the menorah would be secure across the sea.

A final resting place

Theodore Roosevelt, often known as "Teddy," was the 26th president of the United States. He built a family home in Sagamore Hill in Oyster Bay, Long Island, and, in his study, two seven-branched menorahs once stood in the bookcase at the entrance.[16] The house is situated close to the alignment that extends from the Versailles menorah to America. Remarkably, the same is also true of the summer house of his equally famous fifth cousin, Franklin D. Roosevelt, the 32nd president. Built a thousand miles (1,600 km) from Sagamore Hill, this summer home, known as the Little White House, in Warm Springs, Georgia, is also found near this exact same line—an alignment that begins in Versailles, or in Jerusalem, depending on your viewpoint and where you believe the origins of the alignment began. The family crest of the Roosevelts includes three roses that are depicted like five-pointed pentagons and positioned around an upward-pointing triangle. These are symbols for the menorah for those who know the signs. It would be Franklin D. Roosevelt who would be responsible for the final journey of the menorah.

On September 11, 1941, the ground was broken to mark the beginning of construction on the biggest pentagon on Earth: the US Pentagon, the new headquarters for the Department of War of the USA. The site that was finally chosen was in Arlington County, Virginia, across the Potomac River from Washington, DC. It was Franklin D. Roosevelt himself who insisted on using this exact shape for the building, in that very location, going against every recommendation from his staff and military leaders.[17]

Days before work was about to begin on the new headquarters at the foot of the Arlington Memorial Bridge—a favourable site with good, solid foundations—

Roosevelt drove General Somervell to another location, known as "Hell's Bottom," positioned on the road known as Columbia Pike. He pointed to what was then a swampy shanty town and ordered the General to build the new headquarters there instead. To do this, 150 people were evicted and 680,000 tons of sand were dredged from the Potomac to make the concrete needed for the 150-acre (60-ha) project. In the end, more than 41,000 concrete piles had to be driven into the marsh, to prevent the Pentagon from sinking into the mud.[18]

The more you look, the more you realize just how unsuitable the site was, especially for a building that had to be constructed "immediately." The shape of the building was also vehemently opposed, the generals labeling it the "world's largest target." However, Roosevelt remained adamant and insisted on the pentagonal shape.

The design hides some quite interesting details. For example, the height of the Pentagon is 72 feet (22 m), and 72 is an angle found in pentagonal geometry. Looking at the building from the air, it is easy to spot the similarities with the labyrinths at Chartres and Amiens. Although the building is pentagonal instead of circular, the layout resembles the labyrinth menorahs with its concentric design. Officially, the Pentagon has five floors above ground and two below, making a total of seven. The building also sits at 77 degrees west. Finally, the Pentagon is aligned with both the Oval Office—the room that holds the desk of the US president—and the Naval Observatory in Washington. Both these locations are linked to the city's intricate sacred geometry, as designed by L'Enfant.

Returning for a moment to the Roosevelts' coat of arms, with those three pentagonal roses configured around a triangle, growing on a green hill of grass, by the time Franklin D. Roosevelt was elected president, 24 years after Theodore Roosevelt left office, the grass on the emblem had disappeared, the pentagonal roses had been picked, and they were now displayed as a triangular tripod with seven branches on top, a very familiar shape. The accompanying motto is "*Qui plantavit curabit*," meaning "Whoever planted it, takes care of it."[19]

Something extraordinary happened in 1909, four months after L'Enfant's reinterment in Washington. Franklin D. Roosevelt, who was then a young man, became a financier in a company called the Old Gold Salvage & Wrecking Co. This company landed on Oak Island in August 1909 and proceeded to dig in and around the Money Pit. While the company's public records show that it was unsuccessful in recovering gold or treasure, we have to wonder how accurate those documents are.

We believe this could have been the exact moment when the menorah was moved to Washington. While definitive proof of this recovery is impossible to find, and would be beyond our reach even if it does exist, we believe there is a fair chance that not only had the menorah made one last journey to America, resting again on Oak Island for one more time, it now sat at the beating heart of that new country, taken to Washington by a young Franklin D. Roosevelt. Here was a man who had great plans for the menorah and would realize his ambitions when he became president of the USA.

A return to America

Could it be that, in 1941, the menorah found its final resting place, hidden deep below the fortress that defends the world's most powerful democracy: the Pentagon. When the menorah was held safe in the heart of France all those centuries ago, it was protected in the sanctuary of a giant pentagon, a geometric shape that forms the circumference of a pentagram. Wouldn't it be a beautiful symmetry if in Washington, this same device continues to safeguard the menorah? This symbol that once represented Jerusalem itself and seems bound to the menorah for all eternity?

We considered a final presidential clue as we completed our journey in Washington, DC. At the age of 39, Franklin D. Roosevelt was struck down by a debilitating illness that is thought to have been polio, and he was left permanently paralyzed from the waist down. This meant that he was unable to walk unaided—he needed to use leg braces or a wheelchair. Roosevelt would often resort to using a wooden cane to keep himself upright, secretly, when he was out of the public's gaze. To our amazement, we discovered that some of his private walking sticks had a carved serpent encircling it, as on the staff of Asclepius, and the logo of the Sulpicians. They are now on display in his summer residence in Warm Springs, Georgia. One of these canes even has the head and skin of a real snake for a handle. The serpent and the pole had appeared once again and, this time, they neatly closed the chapter on not only our time in Washington but also our quest to rediscover the menorah. Wherever it lies hidden today, we knew for sure that it was not only sacred knowledge that had traveled across the ocean from Europe to the USA—the menorah itself had followed.

Our journey, like that of the menorah, seemed complete.

However, there was one last question to address before we could rest. We now had the when, the where, and the how, but what we were still missing was the *who*. It was finally time to answer that riddle once and for all.

CHAPTER 22
THE UNSEEN HAND

Throughout our months of travel and research, there had always been a nagging feeling that something or, more accurately, *someone*, had been directing things from behind the scenes, just beyond our peripheral vision. This invisible, yet familiar *someone* had always left their calling card at key moments of discovery along the road.

We had never been great believers in all-encompassing conspiracy theories, or in some grand, overarching scheme—there were simply too many moving parts, too many people involved. So, initially, we did not believe that we were looking for a central coordinating force—an individual or a group—who orchestrated everything and dictated a set of rules and symbols to such a large variety of artists, nobles, and scientists. However, there was clearly some unifying hand at work that shaped the themes. There were undeniable patterns, common elements, shared endeavors, all occurring with such frequency and predictability—and across a vast timeframe—that it became hard to dismiss all these synchronicities as nothing more than coincidence.

On our quest we had bumped into a number of organizations and societies, some well known, others a little more obscure: the Knights Templar, the Order of Christ, the Company of New France (otherwise known as the Hundred Associates), the Sulpicians, and the Company of the Blessed Sacrament, to name but a few. The relationship between these groups was not always immediately clear, but it was obvious that they were all navigating the same underground stream.

There is something important that we must consider when it comes to investigating all these groups and societies: in the era in which they operated, the amount of knowledge in the public domain was significantly different from how much we have access to now. Let us take the Company of the Blessed Sacrament as an example. Today, we can read about this organization on the Internet, at work, at home, wherever we like, but in the 17th century, it was truly a secret society. Almost no one outside the company knew that it existed. These days, it is claimed that the company existed as a charitable organization, and worked to spread the Christian faith, but that does not explain why it had to be kept *so* secret. However, because everything was conducted with such secrecy, we cannot be certain that we fully understand why it was set up and what its true aims were. Furthermore, you could argue that what remains to us today are the documents that they were happy to leave behind as their legacy, so we might only have one side of the story. There is a deeper question: for every highly secretive organization like this that we are now aware of, how many others remained completely hidden? What if there had been other organizations that had existed yet remained in complete obscurity, so they are almost or entirely absent from historical records? What if we had missed an important one? Perhaps *the* most important one?

Up until this point, we had assumed that if there was a single entity that had orchestrated all these events, then it must have been the Order of the Holy Spirit. This assumption led us to consider that people such as Henry Pelham and Thomas Anson might have been secret, invisible members, making it a supranational organization, the objectives of which were not restricted by national boundaries and interests. However, as our quest went on and the true history of the menorah unfurled before us, it seemed clear that this was not the whole story. The Order of the Holy Spirit was so public, so prominent, that there was fierce competition among members of the French nobility to be invited into it. The fame and reputation of this order meant that not everyone who was a member could have been privy to the secrets regarding the true location of the menorah. Also, it would not have been in the order's interests to reveal its true secrets to so many members. We had learned from the trials of the Templars that there had been an inner circle operating at the heart of the Knights Templar. What if the same had been true of the Order of the Holy Spirit?

We first came across a hint of such an inner circle in a work by Karl von Eckartshausen, an 18th-century Christian mystic, who wrote:

Therein are mysteries that our philosophy does not dream of, the key to which is not to be found in scholastic science. Meanwhile a more advanced school has always existed to whom this deposition of all science has been confided, and this school was the community illuminated interiorly by the Saviour, the society of the elect, which has continued from the first day of creation to the present time. Its members, it is true, are scattered all over the world, but they have always been united in the spirit and in one truth.[1]

He goes on to say:

a hidden assembly, a society of the Elect, of those who sought for and had capacity for light. This Interior Society [IS] was called the Interior Sanctuary [IS, again].[2]

He then expands on this idea:

> The inner truth has always been confided to him who in his day had the most
> capacity for illumination, and he became the sole guardian of the original
> Trust, as High Priest of the sanctuary.

> The priests had the external possession of the Ark, of the Shewbread, of the
> Candlesticks (Menorahs), of the manna, of Aaron's Rod, and the prophets
> were in possession of the inner spiritual truth which was represented
> exteriorly by the symbols just mentioned.[3]

We looked at this with some confusion. It was like reading our own research notes,
and suddenly here were those two letters again: "I" and "S." Was this the serpent
and the pole yet again? An image started to reveal itself, rising out of the mist and
murk of history. Had there been a hidden, inner church, a home throughout the
ages for a long line of unknown and invisible masters?

Perhaps others before us had found a tell-tale glimpse of this ancient order and
observed their machinations, their deeds? There had to be so much more to the sudden
reappearance of these two letters, "I" and "S," in this context—and so it proved.

In 1751, German Freemason Baron Karl Gotthelf von Hund introduced a new
Masonic rite, the mysteries of which had been communicated to him by an unknown
group of knight Masons in France, led by the mysterious Brother von der Rothen
Feder (Knight of the Red Feather), whose true identity has never been revealed.
By 1764 this order was known as the Rite of Strict Observance or the Order of
the Temple. The members used ciphers and aliases to communicate and the entire
operation was said to be overseen by a group of *"Supérieurs Inconnus"* (the SI),
which means "Unknown Superiors" (US).

In 1768, Frenchman Louis-Claude de Saint-Martin was initiated into the Masonic
fraternity of Élus Coëns (Elect Priests), a Rite founded by Freemason and mystic
Martinez de Pasqually.[4] The secrets of this rite, de Pasqually claimed, had been
passed to him by seven "Universal Sovereigns" (US), secret chiefs, each overseeing a
different continent, all working under the direction of a Supreme Chief, of whom de
Pasqually would only speak in riddles and allegory.

In 1744, de Pasqually died in the Caribbean and, after this, de Saint-Martin went
on to found an order of Christian mysticism now known as Martinism, which owes
much to de Pasqually's teachings. By this time, de Saint-Martin was using a pen name,
"The Unknown Philosopher," a nod to the French Order of Unknown Philosophers,
which, it is claimed, was descended from an initiatic fraternity known as "Les Frères
d'Orient," established in Constantinople in AD 1090. He also became involved with

an order known as the "Society of Initiates" (SI yet again). He then included in his degree system (of progress in the order) the grade of "Unknown Superior' (US), which in French is "*Supérieur Inconnu*" (SI).

Here we had tangible links between mystical, esoteric groups and individuals, stretching in a long line back in time, and the letters "S" and "I." Incredibly, the emblem by which the *Supérieurs Inconnus* were known consisted of three dots, configured in the form a triangle. By this point we probably shouldn't have been surprised by this revelation, but some discoveries still had the power to shock us. Here it was again, then—the *segol*, that ancient Hebrew symbol we knew to be intrinsically connected to the journey of the menorah and which we had been following almost from the start.

Had de Saint-Martin disclosed the missing piece we had been searching for? Being forced to consider the letters "S" and "I" once again, we recalled the "51" we had found on de Champlain's map—the clue that had first revealed to us the symbolism of the serpent and the pole. Had de Champlain himself been an Unknown Superior, a member of the *Supérieurs Inconnus* that operated below the veneer of known history? Furthermore, was there a deeper meaning to this number, rather than simply the fact that the letter "S" looks similar to a "5" and "I" like a "1"?

We decided that we needed to look further into the history of Freemasonry, because much of the esoteric symbolism which had evolved down the ages had become embedded in this tradition, a tradition that survives to this day. The degree system of modern Freemasonry, for example, leads up to the 33rd degree of the Scottish rite. While any Mason will tell you that there is no higher degree than the 3rd, which is that of Master Mason, the 33rd is the highest numerically, if not importance. We assumed that this meant there could be no 51st degree to investigate, but we soon discovered we were wrong.

It turned out that, once upon a time, there had, in fact, been a 51st Masonic degree (they went as high as 99 degrees in the past). What we discovered about this degree was astounding.

The 51st degree revolved around the Masonic Rite of Mizraim (an archaic name for "Egypt"), founded by an Italian alchemist and occultist known by his alias of Count Alessandro Cagliostro. His symbol, to our amazement, was a pierced serpent. The "S" and "I" once again. Even the arrow that pierces the serpent in his symbol rests at an angle of 51 degrees—eerily similar to the pierced serpentine glyph used by de Champlain, which features the very same angle. Cagliostro, who lived in the second half of the 18th century, was a charismatic figure, popular in the royal courts of Europe.[5] Had he also been an Unknown Superior?

We dug into the rituals involved for Cagliostro's 51st degree, hoping to find some clue that the number 51 held some special significance, and we were not disappointed. This now clandestine degree made a direct reference to the metallic element known as antimony. This substance has been known since antiquity, when it was used as a cosmetic by the Egyptians. It is also known by the Latin name of *stibium*, which provides the root for its symbol on the periodic table—Sb—and, more importantly, there it is element number 51.

Being an alchemist, Cagliostro would have been well acquainted with antimony (sometimes disguised by using the name "Saint Anthony" in alchemical texts). In illustrations, the symbol used for antimony was a wolf, as it was used in the quest for the philosopher's stone, to devour any impurities in matter that contained gold, leaving only the purest gold behind. Clearly, de Champlain had been aware of all these connections when he marked not only the number 51 but also the wolf on his map of Nova Scotia.

We began to realize that what we had before us was the signature of an invisible hand. We had unmasked de Champlain, but who else had been involved?

We circled back through our research to Louis XV. Had he been "LouIS I5," the mirror of the number 51? His new cathedral at Versailles was consecrated in 1754, 500 years after Louis IX's return from Acre. St Louis had brought back not only the menorah but also many other holy relic and objects.

We looked at the Bible. There are very few chapters in the Bible with 51 verses, but the book of Isaiah, in chapter 51 (v. 1, KJV), has the following words:

Hearken to me, ye that follow after righteousness, ye that seek the LORD:
look unto the rock whence ye are hewn, and to the hole of the pit whence
ye are digged.

This sounded remarkably like the Money Pit on Oak Island. We had to seek the Lord in a pit? We were also acutely aware that Isaiah's name starts with "IS"—again, the mirror of "SI."

During our research at Versailles, we had run into the number "17" several times, but what came to mind now was the Hall of Mirrors at the palace, which has 17 mirrors overlooking 17 windows, each looking out on to the menorah embedded in the landscape. We realized that if you add the 17 reflections the mirrors create, you end up with 51 (3 x 17). Mirrors or mirroring was also a significant thread that had kept cropping up in the course of our research.

Our minds wandered back to the mirrored *The Shepherds of Arcadia II* imagery on Henry Pelham's memorial (see Chapter 20). There, the shepherds point toward the letter "R." It began to dawn on us that "R" is the 17th letter of the Latin alphabet. There it was, the number 17 yet again. Was "R" significant somehow as well?

We suddenly remembered the star Alkaid, found in Ursa Major and marked on Samuel de Champlain's map with the letter "R" (see Chapter 14). The name for this star meant "the leader." Was that what "R" and the number 17 meant to the *Supérieurs Inconnus*? Was it used to symbolize their guiding hand as they steered the menorah through history?

We thought again of the three 17s equaling 51, and considered the symbol of the *Supérieurs Inconnus*, the three dots in the shape of a triangle, the *segol*. Could each dot represent 17? Another intriguing "coincidence" is the fact that there are 50 states in the USA. If you add Washington, DC, to that number—the final resting place of the menorah, unless we were very mistaken—you end up with 51.

We wondered what else we could find to test our growing theory that 17 and 51 are significant and shrouded in the symbolism of the serpent and the pole. We tried mirroring 17, but 71 did not occur anywhere in the research we had undertaken so far, and that line of questioning did not lead us to anything else. We decided to look instead inside the one book that seemed the most likely to contain the answer to a question regarding numbers: the book of Numbers in the Bible.

We turned curiously to the 17th verse and it was as though the missing capstone of our research dropped into place from the heavens. It (Numbers 17.1–13, NIV) reads:

> The LORD said to Moses, "Speak to the Israelites and get twelve staffs from them, one from the leader of each of their ancestral tribes. Write the name of each man on his staff. On the staff of Levi write Aaron's name, for there must be one staff for the head of each ancestral tribe. Place them in the tent of meeting in front of the ark of the covenant law, where I meet with you. The staff belonging to the man I choose will sprout, and I will rid myself of this constant grumbling against you by the Israelites."

> So Moses spoke to the Israelites, and their leaders gave him twelve staffs, one for the leader of each of their ancestral tribes, and Aaron's staff was among them. Moses placed the staffs before the LORD in the tent of the covenant law.

> The next day Moses entered the tent and saw that Aaron's staff, which represented the tribe of Levi, had not only sprouted but had budded, blossomed and produced almonds. Then Moses brought out all the staffs from the LORD's presence to all the Israelites. They looked at them, and each of the leaders took his own staff.

> The LORD said to Moses, "Put back Aaron's staff in front of the ark of the covenant law, to be kept as a sign to the rebellious. This will put an end to their grumbling against me, so that they will not die." Moses did just as the LORD commanded him.

The Israelites said to Moses, "We will die! We are lost, we are all lost! Anyone who even comes near the tabernacle of the LORD will die. Are we all going to die?"

At last we had found the staff that had been alluded to in the imagery of the serpent and the pole; it was nothing less than Aaron's rod, a relic that had been kept in the Ark of the Covenant itself. In the book of Exodus, Aaron's staff becomes a serpent. We knew that Poussin had painted this very scene and we also knew who had purchased it: Louis XIV, a year before acquiring the second version of *The Shepherds of Arcadia II*.

Of the kings of France, 29 were crowned at Reims Cathedral between 1027 and 1825, and the most important part was the "*Sacre*." This was a ritual anointing, as the king needed to be legitimized before God. We had looked at this rite before, but now, armed with our new insights, one phrase jumped out at us. In 1364 a new ritual was added and, from that date, at every coronation, the Archbishop undertaking the *Sacre* would recite the following prayer:[6]

O God, the Strength of the Elect, and the uplifter of the humble, who in the beginning didst punish the world with a flood of waters, and didst make known by the dove carrying the bough of olive, that peace was yet anew restored to the earth, and hast with the holy anointing oil consecrate as priest Aaron Thy servant, and by the infusion of this unction hast appointed the priests and kings and prophets to govern the people of Israel, and hast by the prophetic voice of Thy Servant David foretold that with oil should the face of the church be made to shine, so we pray Thee, all-powerful Father, that Thy good pleasure may be sanctified in the blessing of this Thy servant with the oil of this heavenly dove, so that he may bring as did the dove of old, peace to the people committed to his charge. May he follow with diligence the example of Aaron in the service of God, and may he ever attain in his judgments to all that is most excellent in wisdom and equity and with Thy aid, and by the oil of this unction, make him to bring joy to all his people through Jesus Christ our Lord.

We read one particular sentence in this passage three times, trying to wrap our heads round what was being revealed: "with the holy anointing oil consecrate as priest Aaron Thy servant." There was only one way to interpret this line: during the coronation ceremony, the anointing transformed the French king *into* the physical manifestation of the priest Aaron.

Aaron's brother, Moses, also carried a staff with very similar powers and attributes, and in the book of Exodus, the staff of Moses is transformed into a serpent and back again. There has been some debate between rabbinical scholars down the centuries concerning whether Aaron's rod and the staff of Moses were actually one and the same. According to the Midrash Yelammedenu:

> the staff with which Jacob crossed the Jordan is identical with that which Judah gave to his daughter-in-law, Tamar. It is likewise the holy rod with which Moses worked, with which Aaron performed wonders before Pharaoh and with which, finally, David slew the giant Goliath. David left it to his descendants, and the Davidic kings used it as a sceptre until the destruction of the Temple, when it miraculously disappeared. When the Messiah comes it will be given to him for a sceptre in token of his authority over the heathen.[7]

Whether there was originally one staff or two, the inference is clear, Aaron's rod was a hugely symbolic object, and the overriding imagery connected with it is that of the serpent and the pole.

After fully understanding the part Aaron played in the anointing of the French sovereigns, we were convinced that we had positively identified the inaugural Unknown Superiors: they had been the kings of France. The missing pieces of the puzzle we had been assembling revealed themselves at last.

The Aaron ritual had been added to the *Sacre* in 1364, meaning that it was introduced during the reign of John II, the Grand Master of the Order of the Star, great-great-grandson of Louis IX. This confirmed to us that the descendants of this great Bourbon king, St Louis, were the *Supérieurs Inconnus*. It was their unseen hands that had been directing events over the centuries and shepherding the menorah on its many journeys.

We were also aware of the enormous implications of this simple phrase in the anointment ritual. Aaron had been the high priest, the only person allowed to approach the Ark of the Covenant, a tradition that continued even after the Ark had been set up in the holy of holies in the Temple in Jerusalem.

Menorah Bay

With our new insights and knowledge, we turned back to de Champlain's map and the word "menorah" hidden as an anagram in the constellation of Ursa Major. We had already revealed that de Champlain himself was a member of the *Supérieurs Inconnus*, but were there other features on this map that would help us to identify more Unknown Superiors? The wolf, perhaps, or the bear—or maybe something else that we had not yet deciphered?

We zoomed out and looked at the figures representing the people of the First Nations in the bottom left corner of the map. The second individual in from the left has a beard and a distinctly European face. With the fourth figure along from the left, we noticed that his bearded face bore more than a passing resemblance to Henry IV of France, the king who had taken de Champlain under his wing and urged the cartographer to travel to the unchartered lands of Acadia. We now knew that Henry IV had been anointed as Aaron—and a senior member of the *Supérieurs Inconnus*—when de Champlain was first sent to New France. Henry IV died in 1610 and was succeeded by another man with a similar taste in beards, Louis XIII, who was 33 years old at the time. Was this likeness on his map a tribute to Henry IV?

However, there was another candidate for who this could be, and he was perhaps the best match of all: Cardinal Richelieu, founder of the Company of New France (otherwise known as the Hundred Associates), arch plotter, political schemer, and spymaster of 17th-century France. Looking closer, we now noticed that the bearded Richelieu figure was wearing an earring with three round dots in a triangle. There it was, the identifying badge, invisible to all except those who knew what to look for. We had yet another Unknown Superior who was unknown no longer. We also noticed that the figure is wearing feathers on his head. During his lifetime, Richelieu was known as the "Red Eminence." Was Richelieu the mysterious Knight of the Red Feather?

The reappearance of Richelieu in our story also shone a light on what might have motivated this shady character. The Cardinal had spent much of his life and fortune promoting the sciences and educating people. He was a patron of the Sorbonne, Paris, the famous university founded by Louis IX's chaplain and confessor Robert de Sorbon and endorsed by St Louis in 1257, after his return from Acre. Richelieu became responsible for the Sorbonne in 1622 and the institution benefited greatly when he ascended the ranks of the powerful.[8] This fusion of science and religion drove Richelieu and represented God and man living side by side in unity. God, as the creator, was the ultimate designer, and Richelieu believed that our role was to explore and enhance all creation. A sacred menorah, laid out at Versailles by using the latest scientific knowledge, and divine alignment, created using the most advanced mathematics of the age, this all seemed to fit Richelieu's modus operandi perfectly. Here was a movement focused on advancing the whole of the human race, without denying the supreme divine being who had created it.

Returning to the anointing of the kings of France, we are aware that Aaron is not the most prominent character in the Bible. If the *Sacre* specifically turned the monarch into Aaron, then there had to be a very special reason for that. The most likely reason, we concluded, was that Aaron's rod and its legendary receptacle, the Ark of the Covenant, had perhaps also been recovered by the Knights Templar when they unearthed the menorah. If that was the case, then it is probable that these sacred objects were also brought back to France and played a very significant role for the French monarchy. It now seemed clear that we had not only been on the trail of the menorah but we had also identified the final resting place of Aaron's rod. If only Aaron had been allowed to touch it, and Louis-Philippe had been the last member of the royal house of France to be in its presence, it could still be resting on Oak Island.

Returning to the now revealed designs of the *Supérieurs Inconnus*, finally knowing who had been behind the movement of the treasures of Solomon's Temple meant that we were in a strong position to reveal the final page of their story.

So, what did we have before us? During the life of Louis XV—Lou-IS, one of the *Supérieurs Inconnus*—a sizeable pit had been dug on Oak Island, a pit in which we had to seek the Lord, according to the Bible. The name "Arcadia," the home of Oak Island, had been coined in 1525 for another French Aaron, King Francis I, but it had since morphed into "Acadia." By adding the 17th letter of the Latin alphabet, the letter "R," Arcadia was restored.

Some time around 1750, when the Money Pit was beginning to be dug on Oak Island, the bay around the island was named Mahone Bay on maps for the very first time. If our research is correct, this was directly after the menorah had been rescued from Louisbourg. The French were clearly in two minds about where to house the menorah and, in the end, a decision was made not to store it in the Money Pit at this time. Instead, the menorah was brought back to France and safely deposited in Louis XV's new cathedral at Versailles. If our calculations were correct, Oak Island had been the home of the menorah for years, centuries even, after the Portuguese had brought it from Europe to Nova Scotia—long before the Money Pit had even been thought of. It looked to us as though Louis XV and the other Unknown Superiors had created a permanent memorial to this place that had once been the home of the menorah by naming the inlet Mahone Bay.

According to local sources, the name "Mahone" was given to the bay by the French and was a derivative of the word "*mahonne*," which means "barge," said to refer to the long, low boats used by pirates in the area. While this sounds plausible, there is another, more likely candidate for the origin of the name. It turns out that the word is also an old Celtic word and a family name. The definition of the Celtic "mahone" refers to that very same figure that de Champlain used to designate the location of the menorah: the Great Bear, Ursa Major, the Mother of Arcadia.

We remembered again that, on de Champlain's map, he had used the letter "R" to label the star Alkaid in his hidden Ursa Major constellation, a star the name of which means "the leader." With a jolt, we realized that if you take the word "mahone," a bay that is marked on de Champlain's map with the letters "V R S," which can be read as "urs," signifying a bear, and add the "R" that represents the star Alkaid, you have another anagram for "menorah":

mahone + R = menorah

By giving the bay this name, the French had thus marked their maps—maps made at exactly the time when the menorah was about to leave Nova Scotia—with a simple cipher that, once decoded, read "Menorah Bay."

Furthermore, in exactly the same way that the hidden *Supérieurs Inconnus*—the *leaders* we had been searching for all this time—had restored Arcadia by adding the 17th letter of the alphabet, "R," to "Acadia," so Mahone Bay was revealed to have been the home of the menorah by the addition of this same single, very significant letter.

A final hint

What is real and what is imagined? We are so used to seeing patterns as human beings that we sometimes recognize them when they aren't actually there. We see a face in the clouds or in the bark of a tree, buildings on Mars. Jesus on a piece of toast. There is even a word for this phenomenon: "pareidolia." It is "the tendency for perception to impose a meaningful interpretation on a nebulous stimulus, usually visual, so that one sees an object, pattern, or meaning where there is none."[9]

It is obvious that we have to take great care to ensure that we do not create arbitrary patterns and connections when they don't truly exist, but there is another, equally important consideration that is almost the opposite problem. What about patterns that are there but most people never spot, patterns so well hidden they remain almost entirely unnoticed. While we are good as a species at noticing patterns, sometimes something is so well hidden, or so plainly obvious, that no one ever notices it. Occasionally the truth can be right in front of us, concealed for years, centuries even, and we have no idea that we are staring right at it, simply because we often only look for the obvious and don't peer beneath the surface. Take Versailles as a case in point. The menorah hidden in the layout of the palace grounds went unnoticed for hundreds of years, until we recognized it for what it was (see the alignments in Figure 18).

Of course, another question this raises is: if Louis XIV had wanted to keep the location of the concealed menorah a secret, why did he create an outline of it the size of a city and that pointed directly to the spot where the menorah was hidden?

Like every king of France before him since Louis IX, the Sun King must have believed that he was the rightful guardian of the treasures from Solomon's Temple. It had been a French holy man, St Bernard of Clairvaux, who had been the catalyst for the founding of the Knights Templar, French knights who had become the first Templars, French Templars who had unearthed the menorah in Jerusalem, and a French king, Louis IX, who had brought the menorah back to France. In the eyes of the French, the menorah had been stolen from them, taken unlawfully by Gérard de Villiers when he fled to Portugal with the remnants of the Paris Temple.

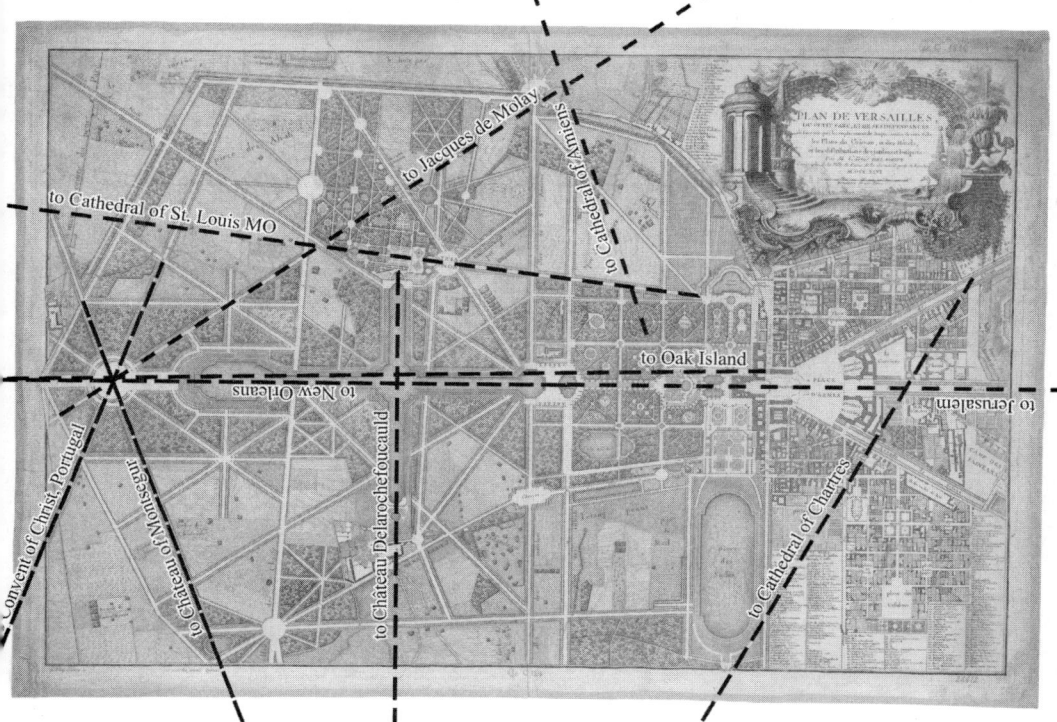

Figure 18 The alignments of the Versailles menorah on a map from 1746, image by Corjan Mol based on https://gallica.bnf.fr/ark:/12148/btv1b530278779

Perhaps the King felt the need to record this knowledge in some way or maybe he was driven by the notion that ownership of the menorah legitimized his divine kingship by directly connecting him to the house of David and Solomon, and so he wanted to advertise this affirmation of his status, even if no one else could see it. The King's ego is yet another motive, coupled with a mischievous sense of humour. Louis XIV would surely have been greatly amused watching his entire court live side by side with the giant menorah without ever seeing it for what it truly was or realizing what it concealed.

As a final litmus test, we wondered if there was any further evidence that the royal house of France—all of whom were members of the *Supérieurs Inconnus*—had harbored and nurtured a great secret, and it was not long before we uncovered one last clue that confirmed they had.

In 1701, French painter Hyacinthe Rigaud completed and signed what is arguably one of the best-known royal portraits in history (see Figure 19). It shows Louis XIV, 63 years old, at the height of his power, resplendent in his majesty and royal robes. In the painting, Louis, who was a skilled dancer in his youth, stands in a balletic pose, wreathed in his ermine coronation cloak while Charlemagne's own sword, Joyeuse, hangs at his side. It is a carefully composed portrait, designed to make an impression and leave the viewer in no doubt as to the absolute power and high-ranking position of its subject.

For us, the most interesting thing about this portrait isn't the imposing figure of the Sun King himself but what sits in the shadows behind. The King stands in front of a box that is concealed under a draped length of sumptuous royal blue fabric, with fleur-de-lis motifs embroidered on it in gold thread. It is the box, rather than the King himself, that is "wearing" the crown of France, as it is sitting on a cushion on the box. Louis XIV is holding a sceptre that had belonged to his grandfather, Henry IV, but it is upside down, so is suggestive of a head, as it is fashioned in the shape of a golden fleur-de-lis. It is resting on, and pointing directly to, the box.

The box that the sceptre highlights—a box invested with the crown of France—looks remarkably similar to another box that is shown hidden under a cloth, found high up on the ceiling of the royal chapel at Versailles. The box in that image is used as a prayer altar by a kneeling St Louis IX. We had previously questioned what exactly was stored in the box and now we asked the same question of the box in the portrait of Louis XIV—one that is clearly the star of the show once you look afresh at the painting with an enquiring eye. We now had another question: rather than asking what might be in such a box, we wondered whether the box might be the Ark of the Covenant itself, hidden beneath this shroud.

As if to confirm our suspicions, we noticed that the sceptre forms one side of a distinct triangle that appears in the image, aligning with the grand cross of the Order of the Holy Spirit that the King is wearing around his neck. This triangle has the angles of 30, 60 and 90 degrees. So, here it was, the final proof, the now very familiar Solomon triangle embedded in the composition of the painting. Louis XIV looks out at us with the faintest suggestion of a smile. Here was a man with a great secret, one of the *Supérieurs Inconnus*.

If our conclusions were correct, then he and the other Unknown Superiors had orchestrated the movement of the treasures of Solomon's Temple ever since they had been uncovered once again in Nova Scotia by the French. A long line of *Supérieurs Inconnus* were peering out at us from the pages of history, guardians of this great secret: Samuel de Champlain, Louis XIV—plus his son and grandson, Louis XV and Louis XVI—Jean-Baptiste Colbert (who chose the serpent for his armorial), Henry Pelham, Thomas Anson, Nicolas Poussin, John Roberts, Benjamin Franklin, Thomas Jefferson, George Washington, and Pierre-Charles L'Enfant, to name but a few.

We were convinced that, at the very least, the menorah had been a part of that treasure, but did the hoard also include Aaron's rod? Had that ancient relic also

Figure 19 Louis XIV by Hyacinthe Rigaud, 1701

passed between Europe and America, finally ending up beside the menorah beneath the Pentagon in Washington, DC? Or was it still on Oak Island? Finally, what of the Ark of the Covenant? Had that also traveled with these other treasures from the Temple, remaining intact as one complete cache and traversing the centuries together, or had the Ark, perhaps the most famous of the Temple treasures, made a separate journey? While the menorah has left clear footprints that we have been able to follow, there are only the faintest rumors concerning the Ark, and it has only ever been whispered about and discussed in hushed tones, its movements shrouded in mystery. Perhaps this indicates that the Ark was never recovered from Jerusalem and still remains lost? Or, maybe the trail *is* out there—we simply need to look harder or uncover that missing, so far unknown clue and finally pick up the scent.

One thing we can reveal is that we haven't stopped looking and, now that we have uncovered and documented the labyrinthine, secret journeys of the menorah, we can turn our attention to the Ark of the Covenant and search both the ancient world and the present day for signs and footprints of this missing piece of the treasure of Solomon.

Our results so far have given us hope. Just as we followed the thread of Ariadne as she led us across the globe, from Jerusalem to France and then over to America, guiding the way and illuminating the trail of the menorah as it glided beneath the surface of history, we now need to look for similar waymarkers and see what else has been obscured over the centuries.

Perhaps, like the giant sacro pentagram laid out across France, or the menorah in the gardens of Versailles, the next clue is hidden right in front of us, concealed where we would least expect to look.

APPENDIX

TIMELINE

1099	Jul	15	Conquest of Jerusalem during the First Crusade	Jerusalem	Holy Land
1104			Hugh de Payns first visits Jerusalem, accompanying Hugh, Count of Champagne	Jerusalem	Holy Land
1114			Second pilgrimage of Hugh de Payns	Jerusalem	Holy Land
1118			Creation of the Knights Templar by Warmund of Jerusalem	Jerusalem	Holy Land
1118	Mar	4	Gualdim Pais born	Amares	Portugal
1120			Council of Nablus	Nablus	Holy Land
1120			Knights Templar acknowledged by King Baldwin II of Jerusalem	Jerusalem	Holy Land
1124			Warmund of Jerusalem is appointed supreme commander of the crusader forces	Tyre	Holy Land
1125			Perceived discovery of the treasures of Jerusalem	Jerusalem	Holy Land
1125			Hugh of Champagne abdicates to become a Knight Templar	Jerusalem	Holy Land
1126			The Knights Templar are given lands in northern Portugal	Fonte Arcada	Portugal
1126			Ground broken for the extension of the crypt of the new cathedral at Chartres	Chartres	France

1128	Jun	2	Afonso Henriques defeats his mother's troops and becomes Count of Portugal	São Mamede	Portugal
1128			Hugh de Payns makes a tour around Europe to seek support for the Knights Templar		Rome, France, Flanders, UK
1129	Jan	13	Council of Troyes, publication of Bernard of Clairveaux's Templar Rule	Troyes	France
1134			Death of King Afonso I of Aragon, leaving a third of his country to the Knights Templar		Aragon
1136			Death of Hugh de Payns		Holy Land
1139			Gualdim Pais is made a knight and leaves for the Holy Land		Portugal
1139	Mar	29	Pope Innocent II issues the papal bull *Omne Datum Optimum*, granting unprecedented rights to the Knights Templar, while claiming anything they find at Temple Mount for the Church	Rome	Italy
1146	Jul		Afonso Henriques writes to Bernard of Clairvaux for support in rallying crusader forces to help him beat the Moors in Portugal	Porto	Portugal
1147	Jun	16	Some 164 ships, carrying crusaders from England, Germany, Flanders, Frisia and Scotland, arrive in Porto and meet Afonso Henriques	Porto	Portugal
1147	Jul	1	A crusader fleet assists Afonso Henriques in the conquest of Lisbon.	Lisbon	Portugal

1147	Oct 24	Fall of Lisbon to Afonso Henriques, expulsion of the Moors. Most of the crusaders settle in Lisbon	Lisbon	Portugal
1150		Letter of Everard of Les Barres to the Abbott of Cluny mentioning a "new light"	Jerusalem	Holy Land
1152		Afonso Henriques of Portugal issues a charter in which the village of Sintra and 13 of its properties are donated to Gualdim Pais	Braga	Portugal
1157		Gualdim Pais becomes Grand Master of the Knights Templar in Portugal	Tomar	Portugal
1159		Portugal becomes an independent kingdom	Lisbon	Portugal
1160		Construction of the Convent of Christ by Gualdim Pais, Grand Master of the Knights Templar in Portugal	Tomar	Portugal
1170		William of Tyre writes his chronicle, *A History of Deeds Done Beyond the Sea*	Tyre	Holy Land
1190		Chrétien de Troyes writes *Perceval, ou le conte du Graal*	Troyes	France
1195	Oct 13	Death of Gualdim Pais on Friday 13th. He is buried in Santa Maria do Olival	Tomar	Portugal
1218		Labyrinth installed in Chartres Cathedral	Chartres	France
1220		Labyrinth installed in Sens Cathedral	Sens	France
1223		Abbey du Trésor-Notre-Dame founded by Raoul de Bus	Bus-Saint-Remy	France

1226	Nov	8	Death of Louis VIII, so Louis IX becomes King of France and owner of the lands of Beaumont-sur-Oise, covering the heart of the sacro pentagram and the Templar fortress at Val Pendant	Montpensier	France
1226	Nov	29	Louis IX's coronation in Reims Cathedral	Reims	France
1228			Louis IX buys lands adjacent to the Forest of Carnelle and names them Mons Regalis or Royaumont	Royaumont	France
1232	Oct	31	Consecration of chapel of Abbey du Trésor-Notre-Dame	Bus-Saint-Remy	France
1234	May	9	Louis IX marries in Sens Cathedral	Sens	France
1235	Oct	19	Royaumont Abbey is finished and consecrated	Royaumont	France
1239	Aug	10	The crown of thorns is transferred to France, Louis IX carrying it barefoot into Paris	Villeneuve-l'Archeveque	France
1239	Aug	11	The crown of thorns is used during mass at Sens Cathedral	Sens	France
1241–1242			Louis IX receives more Passion relics, including pieces of the true cross, the holy lance, stone from the tomb, the Mandylion and relics of the Virgin Mary	Paris	France
1242	Oct		Raid of Mount Gerizim at Nablus by the Knights Templar	Nablus	Holy Land
1242			Renaud de Vichiers becomes Grand Master of the Knights Templar in France	Paris	France
1244	Mar	13	Fall of Montségur, ownership transferring to Louis IX	Montségur	France
1246			Renaud de Vichiers becomes Visiteur Cismarin of the Knights Templar (Treasurer)	Paris	France

1246		Renaud de Vichiers and Hospitaller Andrew Pollin travel to Marseille and Genoa to arrange ships for the Seventh Crusade	Genoa	Italy
1247	Oct 13	The Knights Templar transport a vial of holy blood to England as a present to King Henry III of England	London	UK
1248	Apr 26	Consecration of Sainte-Chapelle, giant reliquary for Louis IX's Passion relics	Paris	France
1248	Jun	Final donation to Abbey du Trésor-Notre-Dame made by Louis IX before leaving France	Bus-Saint-Remy	France
1248	Aug 12	Louis IX leaves Paris for Aigues-Mortes, start of the Seventh Crusade	Paris	France
1250	Apr 6	Louis IX captured by the Ayyubids at Fariskur	Fariskur	Egypt
1250	Jun 6	Louis IX decides to stay in the Holy Land, despite losing the Seventh Crusade	Acre	Holy Land
1250	Jul	Louis IX makes Renaud de Vichiers Grand Master of the Knights Templar	Acre	Holy Land
1252	Mar 1	Insubordination of Renaud de Vichiers	Acre	Holy Land
1254	Apr 25	Louis IX leaves Acre for France with holy relics	Acre	Holy Land
1254	Jul	Louis IX lands in France	Salines d'Hyères	France
1254	Oct	Louis IX installs a collection of documents in the Trésor de Chartes	Paris	France

1257			Robert de Sorbon, chaplain and confessor to Louis IX, founds the Collège de Sorbonne with support from the King	Paris	France
1260			Labyrinth installed in the Amiens Cathedral	Amiens	France
1260	Jan	24	Consecration of Chartres Cathedral in the presence of Louis IX	Chartres	France
1264	Jan	23	At the Mise of Amiens, Louis IX settles a dispute between King Henry III of England and his barons in Amiens Cathedral	Amiens	France
1270	Aug	25	Death of Louis IX in Tunis	Tunis	Tunisia
1280			Labyrinth installed in Reims Cathedral	Reims	France
1291	May	18	Fall of Acre, end of kingdom of Jerusalem	Acre	Holy Land
1295			Gérard de Villiers joins the Order of the Knights Templar		France
1306	Mar	25	Robert the Bruce becomes King of Scotland	Edinburgh	Scotland
1307	Oct	13	Arrest of the Knights Templar on the orders of King Philip IV of France		France
1307	Nov	22	Papal bull *Pastoralis Praeeminentiae* and arrest of remaining Knights Templar in all territories by Pope Clement V	Vienne	France
1308	Jun		Testimony of Templar Jean de Châlons, Preceptor of Nemours	Poitiers	France
1309	Nov	17	Testimony of Templars William of Middleton and Walter Clifton to the Inquisition	Holyrood	Scotland
1310	May	11	Testimony of jurist Ralph de Prelles	Sens	France

1312	Mar 22	Papal bull *Vox in Excelso* and dissolution of the Knights Templar by Pope Clement V	Vienne	France
1312	May 2	Papal bull *Ad Providam* and goods and lands of the Knights Templar are given to the Hospitallers by Pope Clement V	Vienne	France
1314	Mar 18	Jacques de Molay is burned at the stake	Paris	France
1319		Order of Christ founded in Portugal by King Dinis I	Tomar	Portugal
1344	Jun	Pope Clement VI sends a series of six letters to Jean, Duke of Normandy and son of King Philip VI of France, suggesting the reorganization of the Knights of France	Avignon	France
1351	Jan 16	Order of the Star founded by King Jean II of France. Pierre I de Villiers is among the first promotions	Rouen	France
1351	Jun	Order of the Holy Spirit and the Right Desire founded by Louis d'Anjou, son of Jean II of France and titular King of Jerusalem	Naples	Italy
1356	Sep	Jean II of France is taken captive by the English and Sir John Pelham takes his sword and buckle. Also present is Edward Despenser	Poitiers	France
1357		The Convent of Christ becomes the main seat of the Order of Christ in Portugal	Tomar	Portugal
1364		Pierre de Villiers buys the château and lands at L'Îsle-Adam adjacent to the Forest of Carnelle	L'Îsle-Adam	France

1375		Pierre de Villiers becomes bearer of the oriflamme	Paris	France
1390		Alleged voyage of Henry I Sinclair to North America		
1455	Mar 13	Santa Maria do Olival becomes the mother church for all churches in the overseas territories of Asia, Africa and America	Tomar	Portugal
1492	Oct 12	Columbus lands in the Bahamas		
1499		King Manuel I starts expanding the Convent of Christ and has the *charola* decorated with paintings	Tomar	Portugal
1521		Philippe de Villiers of L'Îsle-Adam becomes Grand Master of the Hospitallers		Rhodes
1525		Giovanni da Verrazzano explores the Atlantic coast of North America and names it "Arcadia" for King Francis I of France	Nova Scotia	Canada
1528		During renovations in the church of Santa Maria do Olival, most of the Templar tombs are destroyed	Tomar	Portugal
1530	Oct 26	The Hospitallers arrive on Malta and become known as the Knights of Malta	Rabat	Malta
1560		Bartolomeu Velho draws Mahone Bay as Gulf of Saint Bernard in his Atlas	Mahone Bay, Nova Scotia	Canada
1561		Martial de Loménie buys the lands and the ruined castle at Versailles after having become rich as Secretary of State for Finance to the King	Versailles	France
1571	Apr 6	Martial de Loménie is imprisoned for Protestantism	Châtelet	France

1572	Aug 23	Martial de Loménie is strangled in his cell during Massacre of St Bartholomew's Day	Châtelet	France
1574		During a visit to Venice, King Henry III of France is presented with the statutes of the Order of the Holy Spirit	Venice	Italy
1575		Albert de Gondi buys the Seigneury of Versailles	Versailles	France
1578	Dec 31	Order of the Holy Spirit is founded and Albert de Gondi is among the first inaugurated into it		France
1603		First voyage to North America by Samuel de Champlain	Nova Scotia	Canada
1604	Mar 7	Second Voyage of Samuel de Champlain, on ship *Don-de-Dieu*	Nova Scotia	Canada
1605		Abduction of Vincent de Paul	Tunis	Tunisia
1612		Samuel de Champlain publishes his map of New France	Paris	France
1618		Cosimo II de Medici commissions *Et in Arcadia ego* and *The Flaying of Marsyas by Apollo* from Guercino	Florence	Italy
1621		Anne of Austria founds the church of Val-de-Grâce	Paris	France
1624		Nicolas Poussin arrives in Rome	Rome	Italy
1624		King Louis XIII of France builds a hunting lodge at Versailles	Versailles	France
1626		Isaac de Razilly writes memo advising Cardinal Richelieu to focus on New France	Paris	France
1627		Order of the Blessed Sacrament founded	Paris	France
1628		Company of New France, or the Hundred Associates, founded by Cardinal Richelieu	Paris	France

1629		Nicolas Poussin paints *The Shepherds of Arcadia I* and *Midas Washing at the Source of the Pactolus* for Giulio Rospigliosi	Rome	Italy
1630	Nov	Day of the Dupes, when enemies of Louis XIII's chief minister, Cardinal Richelieu, aided by the King's mother, Marie de Medici, try to take over the government. The King defeats the plot and sends his mother into exile	Paris	France
1631		First château at Versailles built by Louis XIII	Versailles	France
1632		Isaac de Razilly, Lieutenant-General for New France, arrives in La Hève, sent there by Cardinal Richelieu	Nova Scotia	Canada
1632	Apr 8	Louis XIII buys the Seigneury de Versailles from Jean-François de Gondi, first Archbishop of Paris	Versailles	France
1632		The château at L'Îsle-Adam becomes property of the Grand Conti, François-Louis, Prince of Conti	L'Îsle-Adam	France
1638		Poussin paints *The Destruction and the Sack of the Temple of Jerusalem*, commissioned by Cardinal Francesco Barberini and offered as a gift to Cardinal Richelieu	Rome	Italy
1674	Aug 2	Philippe II of Orléans born, receiving the new hereditary title Duke of Chartres	Saint-Cloud	France
1640	Dec	Nicolas Poussin is summoned by Cardinal Richelieu to be First Painter for Louis XIII in France	Saint-Germain-en-Laye	France

1641		Society of Saint-Sulpice founded by Jean-Jacques Olier	Paris	France
1642		On his return to Rome, Nicolas Poussin has a ring engraved with a lady holding a ship and the text Confidentia	Rome	Italy
1642		Charles Le Brun starts working as an apprentice under Nicolas Poussin	Rome	France
1643	May 14	Death of Louis XIII, Louis XIV becomes King and Anne of Austria queen regent	Paris	France
1646		First stone laid for the Church of Saint-Sulpice by Anne of Austria	Paris	France
1649	Sep	Nicolas Poussin paints a self-portrait with Masonic influences and Venus from *The Shepherds of Arcadia II*. The painting is commissioned by his friend and patron Paul Fréart de Chantelou	Rome	Italy
1650		Portrait of Nicolas Fouquet by Charles Le Brun in which, behind a curtain, a shepherd appears to be standing on a boat with an oar	Saint-Mandé	France
1653	Mar 23	First stone laid for the Church of Saint-Roch by Louis XIV and Anne of Austria	Paris	France
1655		Nicolas Poussin paints *The Shepherds of Arcadia II,* which becomes property of Chevalier Henry d'Avice, an art collector and engraver of some of his works	Rome	Italy
1655		Louis Fouquet is in Rome for a year, to purchase art for his brother Nicolas, with the help of Nicolas Poussin	Rome	Italy

1656	Apr	17	Louis Fouquet writes a letter to his brother about Poussin's secret	Rome	Italy
1656	Aug	1	Nicolas Fouquet signs the contract for Château de Veaux-le-Vicomte, worth 600,000 livres	Saint-Mandé	France
1657			Four Sulpicians are sent to New France as missionaries to the colonists; they settle in Ville-Marie, Québec	Nova Scotia	Canada
1661	Mar		Following death of Cardinal Mazarin, Louis XIV reigns France in his own right	Saint-Germain-en-Laye	France
1661	Aug		Arrest of Nicolas Fouquet. His brother, Louis, wants to burn Saint-Mandé, where Nicolas' papers are. Louis, François and Basile Fouquet are exiled	Vaux-le-Vicomte	France
1663			Pierre Mignard starts painting the dome at Val-de-Grâce, creating what is still the largest fresco in Europe	Paris	France
1664			Louis XIV donates valuable golden treasures to the custodians of the Church of the Holy Sepulchre	Jerusalem	Holy Land
1664			Start of the construction of the Grotto of Thetis at Versailles	Versailles	France
1666			Company of the Blessed Sacrament abolished by Louis XIV	Versailles	France
1666			French Royal Academy of Sciences founded	Paris	France
1667	Mar	7	A pentagonal piece of land is bought by the King just outside Paris on which to build the Royal Observatory of the Royal Academy of Sciences	Paris	France
1668			Sulpician Mission to the Mi'kmaq of Acadia	Nova Scotia	Canada

1670	Jul	On orders of the King, Colbert sends a mission to Acadia to measure latitudes and longitudes. On board are Jean Richer and Jean Deshayes carrying Huygens' clocks	Nova Scotia	Canada
1674		Le Brun creates the painting on the ceiling for the cupola of the chapel at the Château de Sceaux	Sceaux	France
1674		Louis XIV raises Chartres from a duchy to a duchy peerage in favor of his nephew, Duke Philippe II of Orléans	Versailles	France
1679		Nicolas Fouquet is visited by his brother Louis Fouquet and André Le Nôtre in his prison at Pignerol	Pignerol	Italy
1682		Louis XIV officially announces that he will build a new chapel at Versailles with Jules Hardouin-Mansart as its architect	Versailles	France
1682	May 5	Château de Versailles becomes seat of French government	Versailles	France
1683		Louis XIV buys Nicolas Poussin's painting *Moses Changing Aaron's Rod into a Serpent*, a pendant for *The Infant Moses Tramples on Pharaoh's Crown*	Versailles	France
1684		Louis XIV commissions a copy of *Sleeping Ariadne*, in the Vatican, to be executed by Van Cleve	Versailles	France
1684		Louis XIV requests Jules Hardouin-Mansart to plan the space for a new parish church of Saint-Louis, and a cemetery, on the site of a former deer park, which will later become the Cathedral of Saint-Louis of Versailles	Versailles	France

1685	Mar	12	At Louis XIV's request, the Marquis of Louvois asks Henri de La Chapelle-Blessé to find a Poussin painting	Versailles	France
1685	Apr	3	The Marquis of Louvois acquires *The Shepherds of Arcadia II* (listed as *Pasteurs d'Arcadie*) for Louis XIV for 6,600 francs from art dealer Charles Antoine Hérault	Versailles	France
1687			The final location of the royal chapel at Versailles is defined by the King	Versailles	France
1701			Hyacinthe Rigaud finishes a portrait of Louis XIV at the height of his power and glory. Louis is pointing at a covered box with his sceptre	Versailles	France
1705	Sep		Testard de Montigny and Nescambiouit, Abenaki Indian Chief from Acadia visit Louis XIV at Versailles and return home "in gay attire, their necks hung with medals, and their minds filled with admiration, wonder, and bewilderment." Nescambiouit is knighted by the King in the Order of Saint Louis	Versailles	France
1705			The former house of Nicolas Fouquet at Saint-Mandé is sold to the Hospitallers	Saint-Mandé	France
1706	Nov	30	Anonymous memo received by French government, urging it to build a fortress at Louisbourg.	Versailles	France
1715	Jul		Louis XIV approves building of Fortress Louisbourg	Versailles	France
1715	Sep	1	Death of Louis XIV. French court moves to the Louvre	Versailles	France

1719		Building of Fortress Louisbourg starts. The cross-shaped tunnels are part of the early works	Louisbourg	Canada
1720		Cathedral-Basilica of St Louis King of France founded in New Orleans	New Orleans	USA
1720	May 29	First stone laid for the King's Bastion at Louisbourg, which includes its chapel and tunnels	Louisbourg	Canada
1722		The French court returns to Versailles from the Louvre	Paris	France
1727		Louis XV orders a painting of St Louis, Louis IX, for the new church of Saint-Louis of Versailles, where mass is said from April of that year	Versailles	France
1731	Dec	By royal edict, the parish of Saint-Louis of Versailles is established by Louis XV and the approval is given to start building the Cathedral of Saint-Louis of Versailles	Versailles	France
1732		The Colbert family sells its library to Louis XV	Paris	France
1733		Nicolas and Guillaume Coustou sculpt Louis XIV crossing the Rhine with a tower and the River God, Alpheus	Versailles	France
1741		Shakespeare memorial is placed in Westminster Abbey, sculpted by Peter Scheemakers the Younger. Shakespeare points at a line from *The Tempest*, "solemn temples"	London	UK
1742	May 8	Ground broken for building the new Cathedral of Saint-Louis of Versailles	Versailles	France

1742	Jun	12	Louis XV lays the first stone for the new Cathedral of Saint-Louis of Versailles	Versailles	France
1742	Jun	18	First stone is laid for the Cathedral of Saint-Louis of La Rochelle by Menou de Charnisay, the sister-project of the Cathedral of Saint-Louis of Versailles	La Rochelle	France
1745	Jan	28	First fall of Fortress Louisbourg to the British	Louisbourg	Canada
1746	Jun		The Duc d'Anville leaves France for Louisbourg, heading an armada of 64 ships with 11,000 men	Île d'Aix	France
1746	Jul		An auxiliary force arrives in Nova Scotia from Québec of 700 soldiers, 21 officers, meeting 300 Abenaki and 300 Mi'kmaq people who join them too	Isthmus of Chignecto	Canada
1746	Sep		The remaining 44 ships of the Duc d'Anville's fleet arrive at Chebucto (Halifax)	Halifax	Canada
1746	Sep	27	The Duc d'Anville dies of a stroke	Halifax	Canada
1746	Oct	15	Almost half the men from the Duc d'Anville's fleet who made it to Nova Scotia are dead or ill	Halifax	Canada
1746	Oct	24	Some 13 ships with 1,500 men are sent to lay siege to Louisbourg	Halifax	Canada
1746	Oct	26	The ships sent to lay siege to Louisbourg are recalled and ordered to return to France	Cape Negro	Canada
1747			Louis-François I de Bourbon, retires to the Château de L'Îsle-Adam	L'Îsle-Adam	France
1748			Château de la Reine Blanche in Asnières is abandoned by Louis XV	Asnières	France

1748	July	British MP Thomas Anson is dispatched on a secret mission and spends four days and nights at Versailles, where he negotiates with King Louis XV, the Duc de Choiseul, and Madame de Pompadour. The proceedings take place in the Cabinet de la Pendule (clock room), where the King has hung *The Shepherds of Arcadia II* by Poussin	Versailles	France
1748	Aug 1	Peter Scheemakers starts working for Thomas Anson	Shugborough	UK
1748	Oct 18	Signing of the Treaty of Aix-la-Chapelle, which means France has to retreat from Austria and the Netherlands, but regains Fortress Louisbourg	Aachen	Germany
1748		Thomas Anson commissions the *Shepherd's Monument* from Thomas Wright with a Poussin panel by Peter Scheemakers the Younger	Shugborough	UK
1749		Louis VX acquires painting *Christ en croix, la Vierge, saint Jean et sainte Madeleine* by Rubens for the altar of the Cathedral of Saint-Louis of Versailles, which has a tower at its left edge	Versailles	France
1749	Sep	The remains of Duc d'Anville are exhumed from George's Island and reinterred beneath the altar of the chapel in the King's Bastion at Fortress Louisbourg	Louisbourg	Canada
1750		Prime Minister William Cavendish, 4th Duke of Devonshire, acquires *Shepherds of Arcadia I* by Poussin	London	UK

1750		The *Shepherd's Monument* at Shugborough is completed	Shugborough	UK
1750	June 7	Elisabeth Anson is painted by Thomas Hudson holding an original sketch of Poussin's *Shepherds of Arcadia I*, bought from Jonathan Richardson's collection	Carshalton	UK
1750	July	The Reverend Sneyd Davies makes a visit to Shugborough and writes a poem about it, mentioning the Poussin panel on the *Shepherd's Monument*	Shugborough	UK
1750	Aug 9	Joseph-Bernard de Chabert arrives in Louisbourg to determine latitude and longitude of Fortress Louisbourg and to correct the maps of Newfoundland and Nova Scotia. He installs the first observatory in North America on the ramparts of the King's Bastion	Louisbourg	Canada
1750	Sep 20	Lady Elizabeth Anson writes to Thomas Anson, mentioning "a very material discovery" and later addressing him as "my shepherd"	Carshalton	UK
1751		Joseph François Parrocel paints *Adoration of the Magi* for the chapel of St Peter and St Paul in Amiens Cathedral, featuring a pentagram star	Amiens	France
1754		Jacques Prevost places the cornerstone at Fortress Louisbourg	Louisbourg	Canada
1754	Mar 6	Death of British prime minister Henry Pelham	Esher	UK
1754	Mar 30	Memorial to Henry Pelham commissioned by his private secretary, John Roberts	Esher	UK

1754	Aug 2	Charles-Pierre L'Enfant born	Paris	France
1754	Aug 23	Louis XVI born	Versailles	France
1754	Aug 24	Cathedral of Saint- Louis of Versailles consecrated, 500 years after St Louis returned to France from the Seventh Crusade	Versailles	France
1754	Sep 20	Communion chapel in the Church of Saint-Roch inaugurated, the ceiling featuring *Triumph of the Virgin* by Jean-Baptiste-Marie Pierre, and the altar decorated with a life-size gilded bronze copy of the Ark of the Covenant and two menorahs by Paul-Ambroise Sold	Paris	France
1755		Henry Pelham's memorial is placed in the gardens of Esher Place	Esher	UK
1758	Jul 26	Final fall of Fortress Louisbourg to the British	Louisbourg	Canada
1763	Sep	Gilbert-Antoine de Saint-Maxent picks the spot for what is today the city of St Louis, Missouri	St Louis	USA
1764	Apr	Pierre Laclède (Liguest) produces a street plan for St Louis, Missouri, based on that of New Orleans. The Cathedral-Basilica of St Louis King of France in New Orleans is aligned with the Grand Trianon building at the Palace of Versailles	St Louis	USA
1767	Dec 21	Benjamin Franklin visits Paris for the first time, where he is treated as a celebrity scientist, and meets King Louis XV	Paris	France

1776			Memorial for John Roberts is installed in Poets' Corner, Westminster Abbey, for which parts of Chaucher's tomb and a medieval arch have to be removed	London	UK
1776	Aug		Benjamin Franklin submits a design for the Great Seal of the USA that features the Shekinah	Washington, DC	USA
1776	Dec		Benjamin Franklin arrives in Paris	Paris	France
1778	Mar	19	Benjamin Franklin visits the young king Louis XVI (aged 24)	Versailles	France
1783	Sep	3	Treaty of Paris signed, ending the American Revolution and sealing independence of the USA	Paris	France
1784	Aug		Thomas Jefferson arrives in Paris	Paris	France
1785	Dec		Benjamin Franklin leaves Paris	Paris	France
1789	Apr	17	Pierre-Charles L'Enfant becomes a Freemason	New York	USA
1789	Apr	30	George Washington becomes the first President of the USA	Washington, DC	USA
1789	May	4	In the Cathedral of Saint-Louis of Versailles, the new general assembly of the people is inaugurated, in attendance of the King, preluding the Revolution	Versailles	France
1789	Jul	14	Storming of the Bastille, marking the start of the French Revolution	Paris	France
1789	Sep	11	Pierre l'Enfant writes to George Washington offering his services for the street plan of the new US capital	Washington, DC	USA
1789	Sep		Thomas Jefferson leaves Paris	Paris	France
1790	Mar	17	George Washington is given the key of the Bastille by Lafayette	Mount Vernon	USA
1791	Aug	19	Charles-Pierre L'Enfant submits the streetplan for Washington, DC, to George Washington	Washington, DC	USA

1792	Aug	10	Storming of the Tuileries Palace	Paris	France
1793	Jan	21	King Louis XVI executed by guillotine	Paris	France
1795			Daniel McGinnis discovers the Money Pit on Oak Island	Oak Island, Novia Scotia	Canada
1797	Apr		Louis-Philippe is the guest of George Washington at Mount Vernon	Mount Vernon	USA
1799	Jun		Louis-Philippe arrives in Halifax, where he is the guest of the Duke of Kent, son of King George III of Great Britain	Halifax	Canada
1802			George Washington Parke Custis, the adopted stepson of George Washington, buys the land that is now part of Arlington National Cemetery (formerly known as Mount Washington)	Washington, DC	USA
1883	Sep		Theodore Roosevelt is given two miniature menorahs, which he keeps in the bookcase at the entrance of his study at Sagamore Hill	Sagamore Hill	USA
1909	Apr	28	Charles-Pierre L'Enfant is reinterred at Arlington Cemetery	Washington, DC	USA
1909	Aug		The Old Gold Salvage & Wrecking Co. starts work, digging on Oak Island	Oak Island, Novia Scotia	Canada
1941	Sep	11	Ground broken for the the Pentagon, the biggest pentagon on Earth	Washington, DC	USA

NOTES

Chapter 1 The Light of God

1 Michael Brooks, "There's a Glitch at the Edge of the Universe that Could Remake Physics," *New Scientist*, October, 2018.

2 Arthur I. Miller, *137: Jung, Pauli and the Pursuit of a Scientific Obsession* (New York: W. W. Norton & Co., 2010).

3 J. Immanuel Scochet, *Tzava'at Harivash: The Testament of Rabbi Israel Baal Shem Tov* (New York: Kehot Publication Society, 1998), Harivash 137.

4 David MacDonald, "Is Oak Island Cursed," *Reader's Digest*, January, 1965.

5 Anthony Blunt, *The Paintings of Nicolas Poussin: A Critical Catalogue* (London: Phaidon, 1966), p. 80.

6 Gérard and Sophie de Sède, *Le Trésor maudit de Rennes-le-Château*, (Paris: J'ai Lu, 1968).

7 Henry Lincoln, *The Holy Place: The Mystery of Rennes-le-Château: Discovering the Eighth Wonder of the Ancient World* (London: Jonathan Cape, 1991).

Chapter 2 The Origins of the Menorah

1 Flavius Josephus, *The Wars of the Jews,* Book VII, in *The Works of Flavius Josephus*, tr. William Whiston (Auburn and Buffalo, NY: John E. Beardsley, 1895), p. 132.

2 Flavius Josephus, *The Antiquities of the Jews*, Book III, in *The Works of Flavius Josephus*, tr. William Whiston (Auburn and Buffalo, NY: John E. Beardsley, 1895) p. 144.

3 Shubert Spero, "The Menorah: A Study in Iconic Symbolism," *Tradition: A Journal of Orthodox Jewish Thought*, 14(3), Spring 1974, p. 89.

Chapter 3 The Symbolism of the Menorah

1 Philo, *On the Cherubim*, Part 2, XIV, 49.

2 Raphael Patai, *The Hebrew Goddess*, 3rd edn (Detroit, MI: Wayne State University Press, 1990), p. 130.

3 A. Marmorstein, *Studies in Jewish Theology: The Maromorstein Memorial Volume*, eds J. Rabbinowitz and M. S. Lew (Oxford: Oxford University Press, 1950), pp. 130–131, and Raphael Patai, *The Hebrew Goddess*, p. 139.
4 William G. Dever, *Did God Have a Wife?: Archaeology and Folk Religion in Ancient Israel* (Grand Rapids, MI: Wm. B. Eerdmans, 2005).
5 Sara A. Rich, "She Who Treads on Water: Religious Metaphor in Seafaring Phoenicia," *Journal of Ancient West and East*, 11, 2012, pp. 19–34.
6 Rabbi Shlomo Yitzchaki (Rashi), commentary on the Torah and Tanakh, on Exodus 25.32.
7 Mark Fairchild, "Turkey's Unexcavated Synagogues," *Biblical Archaeology Review*, 38(4), July/August 2012.
8 Jacques Dubourg, *Les Templiers dans le Sud-Ouest* (Bordeaux: Éditions Sud Ouest, 2001).
9 Vincenzo Pisciuneri, *Cappella templare di Montsaunès II: Gli affreschi sulle pareti laterali*, 2019.
10 Golden Calf symbolism once again?

Chapter 4 The Journeys of the Menorah

1 Flavius Josephus, *The Wars of the Jews*, Book I, in *The Works of Flavius Josephus*, tr. William Whiston (Auburn and Buffalo, NY: John E. Beardsley, 1895), p. 152.
2 Peter Schäfer, *The History of the Jews in Antiquity* (Abingdon: Routledge, [1995] 2013), pp. 191–192.
3 Josephus, *The Wars of the Jews*, Book VII, in *The Works of Flavius Josephus*, p. 149.
4 Gedaliah ibn Yahya ben Joseph, Shalshelet HaKabbalah (1587).
5 Steven Fine, *Art, History and the Historiography of Judaism in Roman Antiquity*, Volume 34, The Brill Reference Library of Judaism (Leiden, Netherlands: Brill, 2014), p. 63.
6 Theophanes the Confessor, *The Chronicle of Theophanes Confessor*, tr. Cyril A. Mango, Geoffrey Greatrex, and Roger Scott (Oxford: Clarendon Press, 1997), p. 167.
7 Procopius, *History of the Wars*, Volume IV, Loeb Classical Library, tr. H. B. Dewing (Cambridge, MA: Harvard University Press, 1914), p. 9.
8 Otot ha-Mashiah (The Portents of the Messiah). Translated from Adolph Jellinek (ed.), *Bet ha-Midrasch: Sammlung leiner Midraschim und vermischter Abhandlungen aus der jüdischen Literatur*, Volume 2 (of 6 volumes, Leipzig, 1853–1877; reproduced in Jerusalem: Bamberger & Wahrmann, 1938), pp. 58–63. (Taken in turn from R. Makhir, *Sefer 'avqat rokhel* (Amsterdam: Nehemiah b. Abraham, 1716), pp. 2b—5b.)

9 Ferdinand Gregorovius, *History of the City of Rome in the Middle Ages*, Volume II, tr. Annie Hamilton (Cambridge: Cambridge University Press, 2010), p. 211.

10 Flavius Josephus, *The Wars of the Jews*, Book VI, in *The Works of Flavius Josephus*, Chapter 8, section 3.

Chapter 5 The Rediscovery of the Temple Treasures

1 Karen Ralls, *The Templars and the Grail: Knights of the Quest* (Wheaton, IL: Quest Books, 2012), pp. 9–10.

2 Dan Jones, *The Templars: The Rise and Spectacular Fall of God's Holy Warriors* (London: Viking, 2017), Chapter 2.

3 Joachim Rother, "Embracing Death, Celebrating Life: Reflections on the Concept of Martyrdom in the Order of the Knights Templar," *Ordines Militares Colloquia Torunensia Hisorica: Yearbook for the Study of the Military Orders*, 19, July 13, 2015, pp. 169–122. DOI: 10.12775/OM.2014.010.

4 Malcolm Barber, *The New Knighthood: A History of the Order of the Temple* (Cambridge: Cambridge University Press, 2012), p. 45.

5 Jones, *The Templars*.

6 William of Tyre, *A History of Deeds Done Beyond the Sea*, tr. Emily A. Babcock and A. C. Krey (New York: Columbia University Press, 1943), p. 535.

7 Steven Runciman, *A History of the Crusades*, Volume II (Cambridge: Cambridge University Press, 1952), pp. 169 and 176.

8 J. M. Upton-Ward and Henri de Curzon, *The Rule of the Templars: The French Text of the Rule of the Order of Knights Templar* (Martlesham, Suffolk: Boydell Press, 1997), p. 20.

9 William of Tyre, *A History of Deeds Done Beyond the Sea*, p. 526.

10 Graham Hancock, *The Sign and the Seal: The Quest for the Lost Ark of the Covenant* (London: Arrow, 1992).

11 Runciman, *A History of the Crusades*.

12 Walter Map, *De Nugis Curialium (Courtier's Trifles)*, tr. Frederick Tupper and M. B. Ogle (London: Chatto & Windus, 1924), p. 33.

13 William of Tyre, *A History of Deeds Done Beyond the Sea*.

14 Jones, *The Templars*.

15 Guillaume de Tyre, *Historia rerum in partibus transmarinis gestarum*, Book 12, Paul Halsall, Internet Medieval Sourcebook, Fordham University, New York (August 1988), Chapter 7.

16 Jones, *The Templars*, Chapter 4.

17 Louis Charpentier, *Les mystères templiers* (Paris: Robert Laffont, 1967).

18 Sylvia Schein, "Between Mount Moriah and the Holy Sepulchre: The Changing Traditions of the Temple Mount in the Central Middle Ages," *Traditio*, 40, 1984, pp. 175–195.

Chapter 6 The Knights Templar: A Catholic Creation

1 Malcolm Barber and Keith Bate, *The Templars: Selected Sources* (Manchester and New York: Manchester University Press, 2002), p. 101.
2 Louis Charpentier, *Les mystères templiers* (Paris, Robert Laffont, 1967), p. 38. Translation by Corjan Mol.
3 Barber and Bate, *The Templars*, p. 218..
4 Edward Burman, *The Templars: Knights of God* (Wellingborough, Northamptonshire: Aquarian Press, 1986).
5 Burman, *The Templars*.
6 Graham Hancock, *The Sign and the Seal: The Quest for the Lost Ark of the Covenant* (London: Arrow, 1992).
7 Rabbi Moshe ben Maimon (known as Maimonides), Beit Habechirah, Misneh Torah, tr. Eliyahu Touger.
8 Papal bull *Omne Datum Optimum*, March 29, 1139, quoted in Barber and Bate, *The Templars*, p. 60.
9 Captain Charles W. Wilson, under the direction of Colonel Sir Henry James, *Ordnance Survey of Jerusalem*, Volume 1 (London: HM Treasury, 1865), p. 13.

Chapter 7 Excavations in Jerusalem

1 Captain Charles W. Wilson, under the direction of Colonel Sir Henry James, *Ordnance Survey of Jerusalem*, Volume 1 (London: HM Treasury, 1865), p. 34.
2 Daniel Foliard, *Dislocating the Orient: British Maps and the Making of the Middle East, 1854–1921* (Chicago, IL: University of Chicago Press, 2017), p. 42.
3 Captain C. W. Wilson and Captain W. Warren, *The Recovery of Jerusalem: A Narrative of Exploration and Discovery in the City and the Holy Land*, ed. Walter Morrison (New York: D. Appleton & Co., 1871), p. 128.
4 Wilson and Warren, *The Recovery of Jerusalem*, p. 128.
5 Wilson and Warren, *The Recovery of Jerusalem*, p. 128.
6 *Lost Cities with Albert Lin*, series for the National Geographic channel, Season 1, Episode 1, at: www.imdb.com/title/tt10366494
7 Dan Jones, *The Templars: The Rise and Spectacular Fall of God's Holy Warriors* (London: Viking, 2017), Chapter 4.
8 Louis Charpentier, *Les mystères templiers* (Paris, Robert Laffont, 1967).
9 Bernard of Clairvaux, Treatises, On Consideration, XIII.27, in *Selected Works*, tr. G. R. Evans (Mahwah, NJ: Paulist Press, 1987), p. 168.

10 Bernard of Clairvaux, Treatises, On Consideration XII.29, in *Selected Works*, p. 170.

11 Sergew Hable-Selassie, *Ancient and Medieval Ethiopian History to 1270* (Addis Ababa, Ethiopia: United Printers, 1972), pp. 255–261.

12 Malcolm Barber and Keith Bate, *The Templars: Selected Sources* (Manchester and New York: Manchester University Press, 2002), p. 228.

13 Paul de Saint-Hilaire, *Les Sceaux templiers et leurs symbols* (Paris: Pardès, 1996).

14 De Saint-Hilaire, *Les Sceaux templiers et leurs symbols*.

15 M. Dubuisson, *Armorial des principales maisons et familles du royaume, particulièrement de celles de Paris et de l'Îsle de France* (Paris: Jean de Bonnot, 1757).

16 Anne-François Arnaud, *Voyage archéologique et pittoresque dans le département de l'Aube et dans l'ancien diocèse de Troyes*, (Troyes: L.-C. Cardon, 1837).

Chapter 8 O Jerusalem, O Jerusalem

1 Michael Lower, *The Tunis Crusade of 1270: A Mediterranean History* (Oxford: Oxford University Press, 2018), p. 121.

2 Georgia Sommers Wright, "The Tomb of Saint Louis," *Journal of the Warburg and Courtauld Institutes*, 34, 1971.

3 J. Charles Wall, *Relics from the Crucifixion: Where They Went and How They Got There* (Nashua, NH: Sophia Institute Press, 2016).

4 Gualterus Cornutus, *Historia Susceptionis Coronae Spineae Jesu Christi: Quam Ludovicus rex a Balduino imperii Constantinopolitani herede obtinuit ac Parisiis reportauit* (1649).

5 Letter from Pope Gregory IX to Blanche of Castille, Queen of France, Raynaldo, *Annuales Ecclesiastici*, 21.16–17, 1229.

6 Royal Society of Canada, *Mémoires et comptes rendu de la Société Royale du Canada pour l'année 1884*, Volume II [*Proceedings and transactions of the Royal Society of Canada for the Year 1884*, Volume II] (Montreal, Québec: Dawson Frères, 1885).

7 Jean de Joinville, *Vie de Saint Louis* (1330–1340).

8 Jan Hosten, *De Tempeliers in de Lage Landen* (Amsterdam and Antwerp: Horizon, 2020).

Chapter 9 Louis IX Returns to France

1 Geoffrey of Beaulieu and William of Chartres, *The Sanctity of Louis IX: Early Lives of Saint Louis*, tr. Larry F. Field, eds M. Cecilia Gaposchkin and Sean L. Field (Ithaca, NY: Cornell University Press, 2013), section 29, On his return to France, and how he acted.

2 F. Gaufridum de Bello-loco confessorem and F. Guillelmum Carnotensern, *Sancti Ludovici Francorum regis: Vita, conversatio, et miracula* (Paris: Sumptibus Sebastiani Cramoisy, 1617).

3 Jean Joinville, *Histoire de Saint Louis: Les annales de son règne, par Guillaume de Nangis: Sa vie et ses miracles, par le Confesseur de la Reine Marguerite* (Paris: L'Imprimerie Royale, 1858), p. 195.

4 Jean de Joinville, *Memoirs of John Lord de Joinville, Grand Seneschal of Champagne*, tr. Thomas Johnes (Hafod, Ceredigion: Hafod Press, 1807).

5 Jean de Joinville, *Memoirs of John Lord de Joinville, Grand Seneschal of Champagne*, p. 203. Translation by Corjan Mol.

6 Geoffrey of Beaulieu and William of Chartres, *The Sanctity of Louis IX*, section 30, How he acted when in danger of shipwreck.

7 Christopher Lucken, "L'évangile du roi Joinville, témoin et auteur de la vie de Saint Louis," *Annales*, 56, 2001, pp. 445–467.

8 Simcha Jacobovici and Barrie Wilson, *The Lost Gospel: Decoding the Ancient Text that Reveals Jesus' Marriage to Mary the Magdalene* (New York: Pegasus, 2014).

9 Meredith Cohen, "The Doors of the Chapel and the Keys to the Palace of Louis IX," *Journal of the Society of Architectural Historians*, 76(2), June 2017, pp. 175–196.

10 Meredith Cohen, "The Doors of the Chapel and the Keys to the Palace of Louis IX," note 67.

11 John J. Robinson, *Dungeon, Fire and Sword: The Knights Templar in the Crusades* (Lanham, MD: M. Evans, 1991), p. 199.

12 John J. Robinson, *Dungeon, Fire and Sword*, p. 299.

Chapter 10 A Sacred Pentagram in France

1 John James, "The Mystery of the Great Labyrinth at Chartres," *Studies in Comparative Religion*, XI, 1977, pp. 92–115.

2 Georges Durand, *Monographie de l'église Notre-Dame, cathédrale d'Amiens* (Paris: A. Picard et Fis, 1901).

3 Olivier Richard, "Henri Sanglier fit bâtir la cathédrale," *L'Yonne Républicaine*, July 28, 2013.

4 Bernard Brousse, Claire Pernuit, and Lydwine Aulnier-Pernuit, *Sens: Première cathédrale gothique* (Paris: Éditions À Propos, 2014).

5 Nicétas Periaux, *Histoire sommaire et chronologique de la ville de Rouen: De ses monuments, de ses institutions, de ses personnages célèbres, etc., jusqu'à la fin du XVIIIe siècle* (Rouen: Lanctin et Métérie, 1874).

6 Jean-François Pommeraye, *Histoire de l'abbaye royale de S. Ouen de Rouen ... par un religieux bénédictin de la congrégation de Saint Maur* (Rouen: Richard Lallemant, 1662).

7 José Vasconcelos, *Pitágoras: Una teoría del ritmo* (Mexico City, Mexico: Trillas, 2012).

8 Fernando Coimbra, "The Symbolism of the Pentagram in West European Rock Art: A Semiotic Approach," Art and Communication in pre-literate societies, XXIV Valcamonica Symposium, Centro Camuno do Studi Preisotrici, Capo di Ponte, Italy, 2011, pp. 122–129.

9 Graham Hancock, *The Sign and the Seal: The Quest for the Lost Ark of the Covenant* (London: Arrow, 1992), Chapter 3.

10 Louis Charpentier, *Les Mystères de la cathedrale de Chartres* (Paris: Robert Laffont, 1966), Chapter IX and p. 96.

11 Hancock, *The Sign and the Seal*, Chapter 3.

12 "Cathédrale Notre-Dame d'Amiens (anciennes basiliques Saint-Firmin et Sainte-Marie)," POP: le plateforme ouvert du patrimonie, Région Hautes-de-France—Inventaire general, Conseil régional de Picardie, Minstère de la Culture website, 2002.

13 Jean-Luc Boulleret, Aurélien André, Xavier Boniface, *Amiens: La grâce d'une cathédrale* (Strasbourg: Editions La Nuée Bleue, 2012).

14 François Laborde, "L'église des Templiers de Montsaunès (Haute-Garonne)," *Revue de Comminges Saint-Gaudens*, 92, 1979, pp. 355–373.

15 Compare this to an image from the book of Scriptures of the Order of Christ from the 1560s in Tomar. Here the flanking lances are clearly arrows, which are symbols of the martyred apostle Judas Thomas Didymus, the apostle Jesus called his twin.

16 Emmanuel Bénézit, *Dictionnaire critique et documentaire des peintres, sculpteurs, dessinateurs et graveurs de tous les temps et de tous les pays* (Paris: Ernest Gründ, 1924).

17 M. Brézillon and J. Tarrête, "Deux sculptures inédites de l'allée couverte de la Pierre Turquaise à Saint-Martin-du-Tertre (Val-d'Oise)," *Gallia préhistoire*, 14(2), 1971, pp. 263–266.

18 Paul Bisson de Barthelemy, *Histoire de Beaumont-sur-Oise* (Persan: Imprimerie de Persan-Baumont, 1958), and Alain Erlande-Brandenburg, *Royaumont: Abbaye royale* (Paris: Les Éditions du Palais, 2011).

19 Simcha Jacobovici, "Last of the Minoans," *Times of Israel*, September 25, 2013.

Chapter 11 St Louis

1 The second antiphon of the First Vespers of the Nativity, taken from 1 Kings 10.23 (ESV), where it reads thus: "King Solomon excelled all the kings of the earth."

2 Martha Mel Stumberg Edmunds, *Piety and Politics: Imagining Divine Kingship in Louis XIV's Chapel at Versailles* (Newark, DE: University of Delaware Press, 2002).

3 Brice Bauderon, Seigneur de Sénecey, *L'Apollon François, ou Le Paralelle des Vertus Heroiques du Tres-Auguste Tres-Puissant & Tres-Invincible Roy de France & de Navarre Louis le Grand XIV* (Mâcon: Simon Bonard & Robert Piget, 1693), p. 180. Translation by Corjan Mol.

4 Thomas Andrew Archer and Charles Lethbridge Kingsford, *The Crusades: The Story of the Latin Kingdom of Jerusalem* (London: Fisher-Unwin) 1894, p. 393.

Chapter 12 The Downfall of the Knights Templar

1 Malcolm Barber and Keith Bate, *The Templars: Selected Sources* (Manchester: Manchester University Press, 2002), p. 290.

2 Barber and Bate, *The Templars*, p. 289.

3 Barber and Bate, *The Templars*, p. 257.

4 Helen J. Nicholson, *The Knights Templar on Trial: The Trials of the Templars in the British Isles 1308–1311* (Cheltenham, Gloucestershire: The History Press, 2009).

5 Julien Théry, "A Heresy of State: Philip the Fair, the Trial of the 'Perfidious Templars', and the Pontificalization of the French Monarchy," *Journal of Medieval Religious Cultures*, 39(2), 2013, pp. 117–148.

6 Dan Jones, *The Templars: The Rise and Spectacular Fall of God's Holy Warriors* (London: Viking, 2017), Chapter 19.

7 Edward Peters, *Torture* (Oxford: Blackwell, 1985), pp. 50 and 57–58.

8 Papal bull *Ad Providam* (1312). Translation by Corjan Mol.

9 Monseigneur Jager, *Histoire de l'Eglise Catholique en France d'après les documents les plus authentiques: tome dixième* (Paris: Adrien Le Clere et Co., 1865).

10 Malcolm Barber, *The Trial of the Templars* (Cambridge: Cambridge University Press, 1993), p. 165.

11 *Registre de Philippe le Bel, contenant des lettres et des mémoires sur l'affaire des Templiers et sur les rapports avec la cour de Rome*, July 1308, online BnF Archives et Manuscrits, Latin 10919, folio 236v. Translation by Corjan Mol.

12 Heinrich Finke, *Papsttum und untergang des Templerordens* (Munster: IW, 1907), p. 839. Translation by Corjan Mol.

13 Albert Ollivier, *Les Templiers: Collection "Le temps qui court" n°10* (Paris: Edition du Seuil, 1958), p. 181.

14 Susan Rose, *England's Medieval Navy 1066–1509: Ships, Men and Warfare* (Barnsley, South Yorkshire: Seaforth Publishing, 2013).

15 As attested to by Professor Helen Nicholson of Cardiff University.

16 Robert Aitken, "The Knights Templar in Scotland," *Scottish Review*, July, 1898.

17 Alan Denis Macquarrie, "The Impact of the Crusading Movement on Scotland 1095–1560," PhD thesis, University of Edinburgh, 1982, Part II, Chapter 5.

18 Thomas W. Parker, *The Knights Templars in England* (Eugene, OR: Wipf & Stock, 1963).

19 David Wilkins, *Concilia Magnae Brittanniae et Hiberniea a Syndo Verolamiensi ab anno MCCLXVIII ad annum MCCCXLIX*, Volume II (London, 1737), p. 381. Translation by Corjan Mol.

20 "Thurs. 27 November 1309: The Interrogation of Brother Ponzard de Gizy, Commander of Payns (Champagne)," in J. Michelet (ed.), *Le procès des Templiers*, Volume 1, pp. 36–39 (Translated into French in G. Lizerand, *Dossier de l'affaire des Templiers* (Paris, 1923), pp. 154–163).

21 Gérard de Sède, *Les Templiers sont parmi nous: L'énigme de Gisors et le secret du Temple* (Paris: René Julliard, 1962), pp. 180–181.

22 *Registre de Philippe le Bel, contenant des lettres et des mémoires sur l'affaire des Templiers et sur les rapports avec la cour de Rome*, folios 84–84v. Translation by Corjan Mol.

Chapter 13 Lifeline: The Knights Templar in Portugal

1 National record of the Torre del Tombo, in Paulo Alexandre Louçáo, *Os Templários na Formação de Portugal* (Lisbon: Ésquilo, 2009), p. 160.

2 Jonathan Wilson, "The Filthy Animal and Saint Bernard of Clairvaux: Re-assessing the Case for Letter 308 and the Conquest of Lisbon, 1147," *Al-Masāq*, 32(3), 2020, pp. 332–352.

3 Alan Forey, "The Siege of Lisbon and the Second Crusade," *Portuguese Studies*, 20, 2004, pp. 1–2.

4 Lucas Villegas-Aristizábal, "Norman and Anglo-Norman Participation in the Iberian Reconquista *c.*1018–*c.*1248," PhD thesis, Bader International Study Centre, Queen's University, Hailsham, East Sussex, January 2007.

5 Miguel Real, *Tracos fundamentais da cultura portuguesa* (Lisbon: Editorial Planeta, 2017), p. 90.

6 The marble slab is now at the entrance to the Convento de Cristo, transferred there from Almourol. Inscription translated by Corjan Mol.

7 Freddy Silva, *First Templar Nation: How Eleven Knights Created a New Country and a Refuge for the Grail* (Rochester, VT: Destiny Books, 2017).

8 Paulo Alexandre Louçã, "The Templars of Portugal: Historical Synchronicity Between the Founding of the Order del Temple and the Kingdom of Portugal," Instituto Hermes, 2016, p. 4.

9 Barbara Jursic, "Order of Christ and the Age of Discovery," *Viteska Cultura [Chivalrous Culture]*, V(III), 2021, pp. 202–234.

10 Jursic, "Order of Christ and the Age of Discovery," pp. 202–234.

11 Michel Lamy, *Os Templarios* 4th edn (Lisbon: Noticias, 2001), p. 262.

12 Captain Montrésor, "Map of Nova Scotia, or Acadia; with the Islands of Cape Breton and St. John's, from actual surveys" (London: A. Dury, 1768).

Chapter 14 The Menorah in Arcadia

1 Lawrence C. Wroth, *The Voyages of Giovanni da Verrazzano, 1524–1528* (New Haven, CT: Yale University Press, 1970), p. 137.

2 Edouard Richard, *Acadia: Missing Links of a Lost Chapter in American History* (New York: Home Book Company; Montreal: John Lovell & Son, 1879), p. 27.

3 David Hackett Fischer, *Champlain's Dream* (Toronto, Onario: Knopf Canada, 2009), Chapter 4.

4 Samuel de Champlain, *Voyages of Samuel de Champlain 1604–1618*, ed. W. L. Grant (New York: Charles Scribner's Sons, 1907).

5 De Champlain, *Voyages of Samuel de Champlain 1604–1618*, p. 114. Translation by Corjan Mol.

6 L.-A. Vigneras, "The Voyages of Diogo and Manoel de Barcelos to Canada in the Sixteenth Century," *Terrae Incognitae*, 5(1), July 19, 2013, pp. 61–64.

7 Robin Hard, *The Routledge Handbook of Greek Mythology* (7th edn, Abingdon: 2003).

8 The authors are still considering the option that Champlain intended the "R" spot to represent Mahone Bay on his 1612 map since on Poussin's *Shepherds of Arcadia II*, "R" is clearly the letter that is pointed at, while the area on the map does resemble Mahone Bay.

9 Heinrich Cornelius Agrippa, *De Occulta Philosophia*, Book 1 (Paris: Coloniae 1531).

10 Victoria Dickenson, *Drawn From Life: Science and Art in the Portrayal of the New World* (Toronto, Ontario: University of Toronto Press, 1998).

Chapter 15 The Versailles Alignments

1 Jacques-Bénigne Bossuet, and Jean Siffrein Maury, Sermon "Sur le devoir des rois," in *Sermons choisis de Bossuet* (Paris: Firmin Dido Frères 1845), p. 233. Translation by Corjan Mol.

2 Gilles Rousselet d'après Charles Le Brun, *Thèse de Charles d'Orléans, comte de Saint-Pol, dédiée à Louis XIV* (1664), burin, BnF, Estampes, AA-6 (Rousselet, Gilles). Providence here is the same woman shown in a self-portrait by Nicolas Poussin that we encounter in Chapter 17.

3 Charles Perrault, cited in Frédéric Tiberghien, *Versailles: Le chantier de Louis XIV, 1662–1717* (Paris: Perrin, 2002), p. 91. Translation by Corjan Mol.

4 Mathieu Da Vinha and Raphaël Masson, *Versailles: Histoire, dictionnaire et anthologie* (Paris: Robert Laffont, 2015).

5 (n.a.) *A New Guide to the Museum, Palace and Gardens of Versailles* (Versailles: Klefer, 1854) and "Les victimes de la Saint-Barthélemy, a Paris: Essai d'une topographie et d'une nomenclature des massacres: D'après les documents contemporains" (1572), *Bulletin de la Société de l'Histoire du Protestantisme Français* (1852–1865), 9(1/3), Janvier à Mars, 1860, pp. 34–44.

6 This did not go unnoticed by Nicolas Poussin, as he seems to have included the pentagram of Astaroth in his *The Shepherds of Arcadia II* painting. Astaroth, who appears in the Goetic grimoire, *The Lesser Key of Solomon the King*, has as his adversary St Bartholomew, who was skinned alive for converting followers of the demon. Both Guercino and Poussin painted their images of Marsyas, the satyr flayed alive by Apollo (a not-so-subtle reference to St Bartholomew), concurrently with their *Et in Arcadia ego* paintings. In the case of Guercino, the same two shepherds appear in both paintings. In Poussin's, we see the kneeling Hercules as the only uncrowned figure in the scene, just as Catherine's youngest son, Hercules Françoise, who sided with the Huguenots, never wore the royal crown. Hercules points to the star known as Astaroth in the painting, the central star of Corona Borealis, the crown of Ariadne, also called Gnosia.

7 Marie-Nicolas Bouillet, *Dictionnaire universel d'histoire et de geographie* (15th edn, Deuxième Partie, Paris: Librairie Hachette, 1867), Verbo "Retz," p. 1,599.

8 Madeleine Foisil, *Journal de Jean Héroard, médecin de Louis XIII*, Volume 2 (Paris: Fayard, 1989), p. 1,287 (August, 24 1607).

9 Joanna Milstein, *The Gondi: Family Strategy and Survival in Early Modern France* (Abingdon: Routledge, 2016).

10 Voir Jean Coural, "Documents inédits sur le premier château de Versailles (1623–1629)," *Bulletin de la Société de l'histoire de l'art français*, 1959, pp. 135–143.

11 Claude Mollet, *Théâtre des plans et jardinages: Contenant des secrets et des inventions* (Paris: Charles de Sercy, 1610–1613).

12 Jacques Boyceau, *Traité du jardinage, selon les raisons de la nature et de l'art, en 3 livres* (Paris: Michel Vanlochom, 1638).

13 Ludovicus de Compiègne de Veil, *De cultu divino, ex R. Mosis Majemonidae, Secunda lege, seu manu forti*, Volume VIII (Paris: Guidonem Caillou, 1678).

Chapter 16 The Alignment Discovery

1 It is worth noting here that $48 + 48 + 2 + 9 + 1 = 108$.

2 Edith Mora, "La Rochefoucauld, fils de Mélusine," *Revue des Deux Mondes*, November 1, 1964, pp. 35–48.

3 G. Goyau, "Compagnie du Saint-Sacrament," in *The Catholic Encyclopedia* (New York: Robert Appleton Company, 1908). Available online at New Advent: www.newadvent.org/cathen/04184a.htm (accessed July 2023).

4 René II de Voyer de Paulmy d'Argenson, *Annales de la Compagnie du Saint-Sacrement, publiées et annotées par le R. P. Dom H. Beauchet-Filleau* (Marseille: Saint-Léon, 1900), p. 17.

5 Alain Tallon, *La Compagnie du Saint-Sacrement, 1629–1667: Spiritualité et société* (Paris: Les éditions du Cerf, 1990), p. 189.

6 Vincent J. Pitts, *Embezzlement and High Treason in Louis XIV's France: The Trial of Nicolas Fouquet* (Baltimore, MD: Johns Hopkins University Press, 2015).

7 Charles Drazin, *The Man Who Outshone the King* (London: William Heinemann, 2008).

8 Michel Vergé-Franceschi, *Colbert: La politique du bon sens* (Paris: Payot, 2005).

9 E. Stewart Saunders, "Politics and Scholarship in Seventeenth-Century France: The Library of Nicolas Fouquet and the College Royal," *Journal of Library History*, January, 1985.

10 Anatole de Montaiglon, *Archives de l'art français* (Paris: J.-B. Dumoulin, 1851).

Chapter 17 Versailles: The Influence of Nicolas Poussin

1 Anthony Blunt, *Nicolas Poussin: The A. W. Mellon Lectures in the Fine Arts* (London: Phaidon, 1958).

2 Gilles Rousselet d'après Charles Le Brun, *Thèse de Charles d'Orléans, comte de Saint-Pol, dédiée à Louis XIV* (1664), burin, BnF, Estampes, AA-6 (Rousselet, Gilles).

3 A set of engravings of Le Brun's fresco for the cupola at Sceaux by Girard Audran (1640–1703) is kept in the graphic arts collection of Princeton University.

4 The dome of the church at Mondaye Abbey has a copy of Le Brun's fresco from Sceaux, executed by Eustache Restout (1655–1743), who was a prior of the abbey. His father, Marc-Antoine Restout (1616–1684), was a personal friend of Nicolas Poussin and visited him in Rome in 1642.

5 Le Département des Hauts-de-Seine and Ville de Sceaux, "L'influence de Colbert à Sceaux" (brochure, 2019).

6 Duchesne Aîné, *Musée de peinture et de sculpture, ou Recueil des principaux tableaux, statues et bas-reliefs des collections publiques et particulières de l'Europe*, Volume IV (Paris: Audot, 1829).

7 William F. Goodyear, "Lessing's Essay on Laocoön and its Influence on the Criticism of Art and Literature," *Brooklyn Museum Quarterly*, 4(4), October, 1917, pp. 221–239.

8 Irene Tayler, "Blake's Laocoön, Blake," *An Illustrated Quarterly*, 10(3), Winter 1976–1977, pp. 72–81.

9 Fulcanelli, *Le mystère des Cathédrales et l'interprétation ésotérique des symboles hermétiques du grand œuvre* (Paris: Jean-Jacques Pauvert, 1964), p. 49. Translation by Corjan Mol.

10 Walter Friedlaender, *Nicolas Poussin: A New Approach* (New York: Harry N. Abrams, 1964), p. 19.

11 Pierre Rosenberg, *Nicolas Poussin: Les tableaux du Louvre* (Paris: Somogy and Musée du Louvre, 2015), p. 151.

12 Thierry Sarmant and Raphaël Masson, *Architecture et Beaux-Arts à l'apogée du règne de Louis XIV,* Volume 2 (Paris: Comité des travaux historiques et scientifiques, [1685], 2007), p. 96.

13 Anthony Blunt, *The Paintings of Nicolas Poussin: A Critical Catalogue* (London: Phaidon, 1966).

14 It concerned the painting *La Circoncision* by Vindicor Tommaso di Andrea, from the early 16th century, which is now in the Louvre.

15 Michel Vergé-Franceschi, *Colbert: La politique du bon sens* (Paris: Payot, 2005), p. 170

16 Charles Drazin, *The Man Who Outshone the King* (London: William Heinemann, 2008).

17 A. Chéruel, *Mémoires sur la vie publique et privée de Fouquet, surintendant des finance* (Paris: Charpentier, 1862).

18 François Ravaisson, *Archives de la Bastille*, Volume III (Paris: A. Durand & Pédone-Lauriel, 1880), p. 123. Translation by Corjan Mol.

19 Thierry Mariage, *The World of André Le Nôtre*, tr. Graham Larkin (Philadelphia: University of Pennsylvania Press, 1999), p. 109.

20 Mariage, *The World of André Le Nôtre*, p. 99.

21 Francis Loring Payne, *The Story of Versailles* (New York: Moffat, Yard & Co., 1919).

Chapter 18 The Serpent and the Pole

1 *Mémoires de l'académie royale des sciences, depuis 1666, jusqu'a 1699* (Paris: La Compagnie des libraires, 1729), entry for May 4, 1669.

2 Christine Marie Petto, *When France was King of Cartography: The Patronage and Production of Maps in Early Modern France* (Plymouth: Lexingron Books, 2007, eBook).

3 Michael S. Mahoney, "Charting the Globe and Tracking the Heavens: Navigation and the Sciences in the Early Modern Era," prepared for the William Andrews

Clark Memorial Library Conference, "War and Science during the Old Regime," University of California, Los Angeles (UCLA), November, 20–21, 1998.

4 J. W. Olmsted, "The Voyage of Jean Richer to Acadia in 1670: A Study in the Relations of Science and Navigation under Colbert," *Proceedings of the American Philosophical Society*, 104(6), December 15,1960, pp. 612–634.

5 M. Richer, *Observations astronomiques et physiques faites en l'Île de Caïenne*, (Paris: Imprimerie Royale, 1679).

Chapter 19 Secrets of Louisbourg

1 J. S. McLennan, *Louisbourg: From its Foundation to its Fall 1713–1758* (London: Macmillan, 1918), p. 22.

2 James Pritchard, *Anatomy of a Naval Disaster: The 1746 French Naval Expedition to North America* (Montreal, Québec: McGill-Queen's University Press, 1995).

3 Andrew Baker, "Thomas Anson of Shugborough and the Greek Revival" (July 2020, revised February 2021). Available at: https://andrewbakercomposer.com (accessed July 2023).

4 Baker, "Thomas Anson of Shugborough and the Greek Revival," p. 88.

5 Baker, "Thomas Anson of Shugborough and the Greek Revival," p. 95.

6 Baker, "Thomas Anson of Shugborough and the Greek Revival," p. 99.

7 Edward McM. Larrabee, *Archaeological Research at the Fortress of Louisbourg, 1961–1965* (Ottawa, Ontario: National Historic Sites Service, 1971).

8 Baker, "Thomas Anson of Shugborough and the Greek Revival."

9 Stevens Curl, "The Tomb in the Garden: A Few Observations on 'The Shepherdess's Tomb' at Shugborough, Staffordshire," *Georgian Group Journal*, XXIV, 2016, p. 60.

10 Baker, "Thomas Anson of Shugborough and the Greek Revival."

11 Stevens Curl, "The Tomb in the Garden: A Few Observations on 'The Shepherdess's Tomb' at Shugborough, Staffordshire," p. 62.

12 Baker, "Thomas Anson of Shugborough and the Greek Revival," p. 3.

Chapter 20 Henry Pelham and the Lost Menorah

1 Peter Cunningham, *Westminster Abbey: Its Art, Architecture, and Associations: A Hand-Book for Visitors* (London: John Murray, 1842).

2 Mordecai Aviam, "The Decorated Stone from the Synagogue at Migdal: A Holistic Interpretation and a Glimpse into the Life of Galilean Jews at the Time of Jesus," *Novum Testamentum*, 55(3), January 1, 2013, pp. 205–220.

3 For example, it was used as such in the *Grandes Chroniques de France, section sur la vie de Philippe IV le Bel, de la condemnation des Templiers* (Bibliothèque nationale de France, Département des Manuscrits, Français 2813).

4 Philippe Cachau and Xavier Salmon, *La cathédrale Saint-Louis de Versailles: Un grand chantier royal du règne de Louis XV* (Paris: Somogy, 2009).

5 Louvre collection, *Christ en croix, la Vierge, saint Jean et sainte Madeleine* (painting, Paris: Louvre, *Département des Peintures*) *INV 1766; MR 988.*

6 Cachau and Salmon, *La cathédrale Saint-Louis de Versailles*, p. 209.

7 Jean-François Fortchantre and Père Jacques Fournier, *Saint-Roch* (Paris: Association des amis des oeuvres et des écoles de Saint-Roch).

Chapter 21 A Return to America

1 Nicholas Reeves, *The Complete Tutankhamun: The King, the Tomb, the Royal Treasure* (London: Thames & Hudson, 1990).

2 Cyprian Southack, "An actual survey of the sea coast from New York to the I. Cape Brition, with tables of the direct and thwart courses & distances from place to place" (London: J. Mount, T. Page and W. Mount, [1735]). Map on display at the Boston Public Library.

3 John Hardman, *The Life of Louis XVI* (New Haven, CT: Yale University Press, 2016).

4 Philippe Cachau and Xavier Salmon, *La cathédrale Saint-Louis de Versailles: Un grand chantier royal du règne de Louis XV* (Paris: Somogy, 2009).

5 James Dudley Morgan, "The Reinterment of Major Pierre Charles L'Enfant," *Records of the Columbia Historical Society, Washington, DC*, 13, 1910, pp. 119–125.

6 James Dudley Morgan, "The Reinterment of Major Pierre Charles l'Enfant," pp. 119–125.

7 William H. Wilson, *The City Beautiful Movement* (Baltimore, MD: Johns Hopkins University Press, 1994), Chapter 1.

8 Bernard Pailhès, *Pierre-Charles L'Enfant: L'architecte de Washington* (Paris: Maisonneuve & Larose, 2002).

9 Sue Kohler and Pamela Scott (eds), *Designing the Nation's Capital: The 1901 Plan for Washington, DC* (Washington, DC: US Commission of Fine Arts, 2006).

10 US Department of the Interior National Park Service's National Register of Historic Places Registration Form, certifying the L'Enfant Plan of the the City of Washington, DC, or Federal City's entry on the register. Quote is from Section 8, page 3 (April 24, 1997), available at: https://npgallery.nps.gov/pdfhost/docs/NRHP/Text/97000332.pdf

11 Benjamin Franklin and Thomas Jefferson, "Proposal for the Great Seal of the United States," July 4, 1776, in William B. Willcox (ed.), *The Papers of Benjamin Franklin: Volume: 22 March 23, 1775, through October 27, 1776* (New Haven, CT: Yale University Press, 1982), pp. 562–563.

12 Conor Cruise O'Brien, *The Long Affair: Thomas Jefferson and the French Revolution, 1785–1800* (Chicago, IL: University of Chicago Press, 1998).

13 In one of those fascinating historical coincidences, Jefferson and friend and fellow US president John Adams both died on July 4, 1826, which was the 50th anniversary of the Declaration of Independence.

14 André Castelot, *Louis-Philippe: Le méconnu* (Paris: Librairie Académique Perrin, 1994).

15 M. le Chanoine Martin, *Dreux: La chapelle royale Saint-Louis: Sepulture de la famille d'Orleans* (Paris: Durand, 1918).

16 The Forward and Seth Rogovoy, "The Secret Jewish History of Teddy Roosevelt," *Haaretz*, January 7, 2019.

17 Steve Vogel, "The Battle of Arlington: How the Pentagon Got Built," *Washington Post*, April 26, 1999.

18 Vogel, "The Battle of Arlington."

19 John Matthews (ed.), *Matthews' American Armoury and Blue Book* (Champaign, IL: Crest Publishing, [1907], 1962).

Chapter 22 The Unseen Hand

1 Karl von Eckartshausen, *The Cloud Upon the Sanctuary* (Santa Cruz, CA: Evinity Publishing Inc, [1795], 2009), p. 13.

2 Von Eckartshausen, *The Cloud Upon the Sanctuary*, p. 14.

3 Von Eckartshausen, *The Cloud Upon the Sanctuary*, p. 21.

4 Jean-Louis de Biasi, *Le Martinisme: Les Serviteurs Inconnus du Christianisme* (Las Vegas, NV: Éditions Theurgia, 2018).

5 Philippa Faulks and Robert Cooper, *The Masonic Magician: The Life and Death of Count Cagliostro and His Egyptian Rite* (London: Watkins Publishing, 2016).

6 Nicolas Menin, *An historical and chronological treatise of the anointing and coronation of the Kings and Queens of France ... To which is added an exact relation of the ceremony of the coronation of Louis XV* (London: W. Mears, S. Chapman, and J. Woodman, 1727).

7 Isidore Singer (ed.) *The Jewish Encyclopedia: A Descriptive Record of the History, Religion, Literature, and Customs of the Jewis People from the Earliest Times to the Present Day* (New York, Funk & Wagnalls Co., 1901).

8 Jean-Vincent Blanchard, *Richelieu: La pourpre et le pouvoir* (Paris: Éditions Belin, 2012).

9 Dictionary.com online dictionary.

LIST OF ILLUSTRATIONS

INDEX OF NAMES